46.50

HQ
536
.M412
2006

D0759819

*The Place of Families*

# The Place of Families

FOSTERING CAPACITY, EQUALITY, AND RESPONSIBILITY

Linda C. McClain

HARVARD UNIVERSITY PRESS

*Cambridge, Massachusetts*
*London, England   2006*

**Library of Congress Cataloging-in-Publication Data**

McClain, Linda C.
  The place of families : fostering capacity, equality, and responsibility /
Linda C. McClain.
      p.   cm.
  Includes bibliographical references and index.
  ISBN 0-674-01910-5 (alk. paper)
    1. Family—Political aspects—United States   2. Marriage—Political
aspects—United States.   3. Family policy—United States.   4. Equality—
United States.   5. Sex role—United States.   6 Civics.   7. Feminist
theory.   I. Title.
  HQ536.M412   2005
  306.8'0973—dc22        2005050230

*For Jim, Sarah, and Katherine*

# Contents

# Acknowledgments

In writing this book, I have benefited from the valuable contributions of many friends and colleagues as well as from institutional support. The basic ideas for this book formed during my year as a faculty fellow at Harvard University Center for Ethics and the Professions, 1999–2000. I am grateful to Dennis Thompson, Arthur Apfelbaum, and Martha Minow for their valuable input about the book during that time, as well as to the other fellows, Victoria Beach, Paula Casal, Sharon Dolovich, James Fleming, Robert Gordon, Ashish Nanda, Jim Sabin, and Noam Zohar, for helpful discussion of a draft chapter. Conversations with Anita Allen, Lisa Dodson, Abner Greene, Mona Harrington, Jane Mansbridge, Frank Michelman, John Rawls, Katherine Silbaugh, Avi Soifer, Robin West, and Lucie White also aided my thinking about the contours of the project.

I am especially indebted for the opportunity to present early drafts of several chapters of the book in workshops sponsored by Martha Albertson Fineman's Feminism and Legal Theory Project, in its former venues at Columbia University and at Cornell Law School and at the 20th Summer Workshop, held at University of Wisconsin-Madison. I am grateful to the many participants in those events for constructive exchanges. In October 2001, I was a visiting scholar in the Baldy Center for Law and Policy at SUNY Buffalo and had a chance to develop my analysis of marriage policies. Presenting my chapter on marriage promotion in the New York University School of Law Colloquium on Law, Philosophy, and Political Theory, along with the generous input of Ronald Dworkin and Thomas Nagel, greatly benefited my analysis.

I am also grateful for the opportunity to present aspects of this work in a variety of forums: the Harvard Women's Law Journal 25th Anniversary Conference; panels at the 2002 and 2003 annual meetings of the Association for the Study of Law, Culture and the Humanities; workshops with the law faculties at Boston University, Brooklyn Law School, Fordham University, Rutgers University (Newark), and Hofstra University; a colloquium of the Feminist Sexual Ethics Project at Brandeis University; student seminars at Columbia University and St. John's University; a lecture in the Urban Dialogues Series at Metropolitan College; and a presentation to the New York Society for Women in Philosophy. Brian Bix, June Carbone, Maxine Eichner, and Joanna Grossman commented on the manuscript in a panel at the 12th World Conference of the International Society of Family Law. In addition, it was helpful to discuss this project, in its earliest stages, in a reading group with Michele Adams, Mary Anne Case, Sherry Colb, Julie Goldscheid, Katherine Franke, Sally Goldfarb, Tracy Higgins, and Denise Morgan. To Mary Anne Case and Tracy Higgins, I am also grateful for ongoing conversations about liberal feminism.

Planning and participating in the conference "Marriage, Democracy, and Families" held at Hofstra on March 14 and 15, 2003, stimulated my work on the book. I thank my former dean, David Yellen, and Vice Dean Marshall Tracht for their generous support of that conference and Dawn Marzella for indispensable help with it. Generous research leave as well as summer research grants from Hofstra University greatly facilitated this book, and I am thankful for the support of my present dean, Alan Resnick, and to my former dean, David Yellen, as well as to Stuart Rabinowitz both during his tenure as dean and now as president.

At every step of the way, I was aided by outstanding research help from law librarians Connie Lenz and Cindie Leigh, who tirelessly followed the issues discussed in this book. Their enthusiasm and friendship also provided appreciated support. Thanks to my secretary, Michelle Tunsuden, for her help; to Krista Smokowski and Jennifer Callinan for cite checking; and to Bella Blat, Suzanne Mikos, and Christina Paquette for research assistance.

As I thought through how best to present the book, Sotirios Barber, James Fleming, my colleagues John DeWitt Gregory and Joanna Grossman, Mary Lyndon (Molly) Shanley, and Ben Zipursky provided much appreciated help. Thanks also to Amy Baehr, Lisa Brush, John Gregory, Joanna Grossman, Milton Regan, and Ruth O'Brien for constructive comments on drafts of chapters. I thank Molly Shanley not only for her comments on several chapters, but also for her constructive engagement with the project. I am especially grateful to my editor, Elizabeth Knoll, for her support of this book and her incisive comments.

Friends and family provided valuable support along the way. Thanks to Tania Taubes, Béla Schwartz, Stephen Greenwald, Jill Levine, Suzanne Rostock, and Katina Zachmanoglou, and to my parents and siblings for encouragement. Finally, my greatest debt is to my husband, Jim Fleming, whose love and companionship and generous and tireless support of this project were indispensable. He carefully read and constructively commented on numerous drafts of every chapter. In addition, I thank our daughters, Sarah and Katherine. Not only were they patient when this book took me away from them, but they also lovingly encouraged my work. Because they illustrate for me the place of family in my own life, it is appropriate, then, that I dedicate this book to my family.

Some of the arguments in this book were developed in earlier writing and are incorporated here in substantially revised form: Chapters 1 and 7 draw on "Toleration, Autonomy, and Governmental Promotion of Good Lives: Beyond 'Empty' Toleration to Toleration as Respect," 59 *Ohio State Law Journal* 19 (1998). Chapter 2 grew out of "The Domain of Civic Virtue in a Good Society: Families, Schools, and Sex Equality," 69 *Fordham Law Review* 1617 (2001) and "Some Questions for Civil Society-Revivalists," 75 *Chicago-Kent Law Review* 301 (2000) (with James E. Fleming). Chapter 3 adapts "Care as a Public Value: Linking Responsibility, Resources, and Republicanism," 76 *Chicago-Kent Law Review* 1673 (2001). Chapter 7 includes a brief excerpt from " 'Irresponsible' Reproduction," 47 *Hastings Law Journal* 339 (1996). Permission to use this material is gratefully acknowledged. Finally, I discuss some of the points in Chapter 4 in a chapter in the anthology *Marriage Proposals: Questioning a Legal Status* (Anita L. Bernstein, ed., New York University Press, 2005).

*The Place of Families*

# Introduction

ℱ AMILIES ARE AT THE CENTER of a number of important, contentious public debates in the United States. The ideas that a significant link exists between the state of families and the state of the nation, and that strong, healthy families undergird a strong nation, are animating a number of social movements as well as governmental efforts to strengthen families. A common premise of all these efforts is that the weakening of families both reflects and leads to moral and civic decline and imposes significant costs on society. Diagnoses of America's moral and civic health warn that, although families historically have played a prominent role as "seedbeds of civic virtue" and generators of "social capital," their current condition hampers them in doing so.[1]

Marriage is at the heart of contemporary public discussion of family values. The social movement known as the "marriage movement" argues that shoring up the institution of marriage is vital to the nation's social health and urges a return to a "marriage culture" to stem the tide of divorce, cohabitation, and nonmarital childbearing.[2] So, too, many politicians argue that the best way for government to support strong families is to promote "healthy marriages." Politicians have proposed making the promotion of marriage a central goal of welfare reform because of acute concern over low-income unmarried parents.[3] But the aims of marriage promotion are more wide ranging than that.

1

Many states have launched marriage initiatives aimed at imparting to their citizens the skills and knowledge they need to have happy, long-lasting marriages. Propelling such efforts is the premise that strong marriages are the foundation of society. As Texas's attorney general put it, "Your commitment to your marriage is the backbone of our society."[4]

Even as the marriage movement and marriage initiatives seek to strengthen the institution of marriage by expanding its reach, efforts are being made to "defend" or "protect" it by limiting its reach. Thus, in 2003 when Massachusetts's highest court, in Goodridge v. Department of Public Health,[5] held that the state constitution required that same-sex couples be permitted to marry, federal lawmakers and President George W. Bush pledged support for a federal constitutional amendment to "protect marriage in America" and to prevent change to "the most fundamental institution of civilization."[6] Such an amendment would define marriage throughout the United States as a male-female union and bar any state or federal court from extending marriage-like rights and responsibilities to same-sex couples. Moreover, marriage defenders warned that recognizing same-sex marriage was a first step down a slippery slope leading to the destruction of marriage itself.

The political rhetoric that commonly rages during presidential election campaigns vividly illustrates a common impulse to link strong families to a strong nation as well as conflicting views on how best to strengthen families. In the 2004 presidential campaign, both Democratic and Republican party platforms proclaimed the importance of strong families. "Family is the center of every day American life," declared the Democratic platform, for "strong families" are "the heart of a strong America."[7] A plank in the Republican party platform spoke of "protecting our families": as "the building blocks of a strong society"—"unseen pillars of civilization"—families "must remain strong" because they are among the "fundamental institutions" in America that instill values.[8] Even though Congress thus far has fallen short of the two-thirds vote necessary to propose the federal marriage amendment, Bush's avowed support for it resonated with those voters in the 2004 election who viewed same-sex marriage as a threat to family values. Moreover, in many states voters helped pass state constitutional amendments that defined marriage to exclude same-sex unions, and some states prohibited bestowing on a domestic union, whether of a same-sex or an opposite-sex couple, any legal status substantially equivalent to marriage.[9] These election results seem to reflect the conviction that fostering strong families requires defending traditional marriage. Complicating the picture, however, is evidence of near-majority support for according legal recognition—along with the benefits, protections, and obligations of marriage—to same-sex couples, through "civil unions" akin to those permitted in Vermont and Connecticut; and a sizeable minority supports same-sex marriage itself.[10]

Despite sustained concern over the state of families, the question of the place of families in our constitutional and political order has received insufficient attention. In this book I argue that underlying the common impulse to link the state of families to the state of the nation is an important idea: families have a place in the project of forming persons into capable, responsible, self-governing citizens. Society depends upon such a formative process, but sharp points of disagreement have arisen about its contours.

What, for example, is the appropriate division of responsibility among families, other institutions of civil society, and government for shaping persons into good people and good citizens? If institutions within civil society, such as families, have the primary responsibility, what role should government have in regulating and supporting such institutions? What place do such public values as liberty and equality, and such virtues as mutual respect and tolerance, have in shaping families, and what roles do families have in inculcating such values and virtues? Is the family a private place, such that persons' intimate decisions of whether to form or not form families are none of government's business? Or does government have a proper interest in regulating families, by defining the rights and duties of their members? May it educate and persuade persons about how to order their intimate, sexual, and reproductive lives? Should government, for example, promote a national standard of sexual abstinence until marriage?

What is the relationship between the place of families and the place of marriage? Does marriage warrant special governmental support? Is it, as some contend, the only institution that ensures the healthy development of children and promises the realization by adults of goods such as intimacy and commitment? Or should sound family policy move beyond marriage to recognize and support other forms of family? What do constitutional principles imply about whether marriage must assume one particular form to perform its civic and social roles or whether a plurality of family forms (including same-sex marriage) deserves public support and recognition?

In this book I view the task of producing persons capable of responsible personal and democratic self-government as a *formative project*. I argue that government has an important responsibility to carry out such a formative project but that families and other institutions of civil society are also significant sites in which this development occurs. I propose a framework based on three salient ideas for thinking about the place of families: *fostering capacity*, *fostering equality*, and *fostering responsibility*. I apply this framework—informed by key liberal and feminist principles—to a cluster of hotly contested issues of family law and policy: how best to support the civic role of families; welfare policy and the proper balance between personal and public responsibility for the care and support of children; governmental promotion of marriage; the recognition of same-sex marriage; the extension of family rights and responsibilities to nonmarital families; the protection of constitutional rights to reproductive freedom; and sex education.

*Fostering capacity* refers to developing citizens capable of democratic and personal self-government. The aim is to facilitate persons' use of their moral powers, or capacities, so that they can take part in public life (democratic self-government), and conceive and live out a good life, including forming relationships and associations (personal self-government).[11] Government, families, and other institutions of civil society all play vital roles in this formative project, or the process of social reproduction. Government's formative responsibilities have two dimensions: (1) a responsibility actively to foster the capacities for self-government and (2) an obligation to refrain from coercive action with respect to a range of decisions and behaviors (or what I call toleration as respect).[12] Through governmental action and restraint, government fosters individuals' capacities for self-government and regulates families in ways that help them to develop the capacities of their members. As I will explain in Chapter 1, many passionate debates about governmental regulation of families implicate the tension between governmental action and restraint.

How do families foster capacity? As Chapters 2 and 3 elaborate, two vital tasks relate to social reproduction: promoting civic virtue and providing the care that enables persons to become responsible, self-governing citizens. Families also foster capacity by allowing adults who form intimate associations to enjoy intimacy and family life. But even though society depends upon families to engage in social reproduction and has a stake in families successfully doing so, there is insufficient recognition of a public responsibility to support families' efforts. Feminist theorists (for example, Martha Fineman and Eva Kittay) explain the indispensable, but underappreciated, role of care in meeting the needs of human dependency and the disproportionate role of women (both as paid and unpaid caregivers) in meeting those needs.[13] Both welfare reform—with its imperative to move mothers "from welfare to work"—and the ongoing problem of work/life, or work/family, conflict illustrate the problems that flow from a lack of support for care as a public value and from notions of personal responsibility that define such responsibility primarily in terms of market work, to the neglect of family care work. Politicians claim that government should support "working families" because parents make a vital contribution to society, but at the same time politicians champion the goal of families being "independent" of any governmental support. I urge an understanding of the social contract pursuant to which families' contributions to social reproduction warrant public support.

By proposing a focus upon *fostering equality*, I invite attention to two dimensions of equality—*equality within families* and *equality among families*. Is sex equality within families, for example, a vital component of—or in tension with—supporting strong families? A frequent refrain heard in calls to promote marriage and to renew civil society is that "no one wants to turn back the clock" on gains in women's equality or return to a marital regime premised on male domination. Yet an ambivalent "but" often follows this refrain. Moreover, current calls to promote marriage and responsible fatherhood accept the premise of a natural male (paternal) irresponsibility, contrasted with female (maternal) responsibility. Marriage, in this view, is the tool that society uses to civilize men. These positions, I argue in Chapter 4, undermine sex equality; they fail to look beyond conventional gender ideology and to reflect, constructively, upon what marriage is *for* in a polity committed to women's equal citizenship.[14]

What of equality among families? Should government equate fostering strong families only with shoring up marital families, as traditionally defined? Perhaps the most sharply contested battle is over same-sex marriage. Although some states have taken steps toward granting gay men and lesbians equality by recognizing and supporting their intimate relationships and families (not only through Massachusetts's recognition of same-sex marriage, but also Vermont's—and now Connecticut's—creation of civil unions with all the benefits and obligations of marriage),[15] proponents of strengthening families oppose these developments as threatening marriage. Federal and state lawmakers enact "defense of marriage" laws that define marriage as the union of one man and one woman.

The same-sex marriage question yields vexing puzzles: one might imagine that opponents of same-sex marriage would reject any legal recognition of same-sex domestic unions. Yet some would support official recognition of same-sex relationships—and extension of the legal incidents of marriage—through a civil union or an expansive domestic partnership law (for example, as in California).[16] An impulse toward equality among families and toward supporting intimate commitment vies with a conviction that altering the definition of marriage so undermines it that, even if all of marriage's legal incidents extend to same-sex couples, its name must not follow.

At the core of the struggle over same-sex marriage is a basic question: does society best support the institution of marriage, and the important public values underlying it, by freezing its definition and guarding against any departure from "tradition," or by viewing marriage, as did *Goodridge*, as an "evolving paradigm"?[17] This book argues for the evolving paradigm approach. Challenges to state marriage laws, I contend in Chapter 5, bring to the fore important questions about government's interest in civil marriage and invite critical reflection upon the functions and purposes that society associates with civil marriage and the individual needs and goods that it promotes (for example, love and friendship, security for adults and their children, economic protection, and public affirmation of commitment). Critical reflection upon the evolution of marriage from a legal relationship of gender hierarchy and fixed roles to one of gender equality also calls into question the insistence that marriage simply must be the union of one man and one woman. Support for recognizing same-sex marriage, I argue, flows from respect for constitutional principles of liberty and equality as well as concern for capacity, equality, and responsibility. For if a purpose of marriage law is to foster intimate commitment and stable families, why not allow same-sex couples and their children to benefit from this facilitative governmental role?

The issue of equality among families raises even more fundamental questions, taken up in Chapter 6: Why should government recognize and support marriage? and why *only* marriage? Does marriage deserve to continue to be the unique source of a protective umbrella of rights, benefits, and obligations, or does this, as some argue, amount to un-equal—and unfair—treatment not only of unmarried couples but also of single persons? And given that family law has already moved some-what beyond marriage—by recognizing, even in the absence of mar-riage, parental rights and responsibilities and some rights and obli-gations between unmarried adult partners—why not move wholly beyond marriage to an entirely different basis for family law and policy? For example, Martha Fineman argues that, for all relevant societal purposes, we do not need marriage and should abolish it as a legal category. Reorienting family law around the caretaker-dependent relationship would focus more properly on the most significant func-tion of families. Sexual relationships between adults would move to the realm of private contract.[18]

In this book I reject the proposal to abolish marriage and resist the move to identify caring for dependents as the only family function that government should support. Instead, I argue that government may properly support marriage, but should extend its facilitative role by recognizing and supporting a broader range of family forms and committed adult relationships capable of carrying out some or all of the functions that society assigns to families. Government has an in-terest in supporting emotional and economic interdependency be-tween adults, and a system of private contract cannot substitute for this official support. Moreover, as the American Law Institute *Princi-ples of the Law of Family Dissolution* recognized in 2002, bargaining in the context of intimate relationships raises public policy concerns about protecting persons from economic vulnerability that arises in such relationships and about promoting the well-being of children.[19]

One form of support that this book explores is establishing a kinship registration system. Such a development would be consistent with con-cerns for respect for persons' equal moral capacities and with govern-

ment's interest in encouraging committed, caring, and responsible relationships, whether or not they are conjugal. Such ideas underlie
recent proposals made in Canada to establish a registration scheme
and are already at work in Europe and (if incompletely realized) in
domestic partnership laws in the United States.[20] By linking relational
rights to relational responsibilities, such a kinship registration system
need not erode the value of commitment by allowing people, as Milton
Regan puts it, to "calibrate" their commitment.[21]

A common sentiment is that families—and marriage—are wholly
private and thus are not the proper "business" of government. This
sentiment is one reason for public skepticism about governmental promotion of marriage. But in this book I contend that government properly takes an interest in families in light of the goods associated with
families, the functions that families serve, and the political values at
stake in the institution of the family. For example, government may
foster family formation through educational measures and economic
programs aimed at securing the preconditions for stable family life.
But government's formative responsibilities with respect to families
should be guided by respect for relevant public values, such as sex
equality and orderly social reproduction, and by principles of toleration and respect for individual intimate association.

By *fostering responsibility*, I refer to the allocation of responsibility to
individuals, rather than to government, to make personal decisions
about sexual intimacy, marriage, reproduction, and parenting. The
U.S. Constitution recognizes the rights of individuals to exercise moral
responsibility and self-determination in these areas, free from unwarranted governmental interference.[22] But a common culprit in diagnoses of families as weakened is an alleged imbalance between rights
and responsibilities. It has been widely contended that the 1960s
opened a Pandora's Box of dangerous ideas of individual rights to
privacy, liberty, and equality, threatening the possibility of ordered
liberty and stable families.

I favor a different moral accounting: that personal responsibility
with respect to forming families and parenting is an important value
that government may properly foster, and that gains in rights and in
women's equal citizenship have been vital steps toward redressing inequality and injustice within the family and fostering responsible self-
government by women and men. By the same token, ambivalence

about sex equality and women's right to personal self-government remains, hindering the development of responsible public policies to encourage responsible self-government in matters of sexual intimacy and reproduction. Lofty rhetoric about constitutional protection of women's reproductive liberty and their right to control their own "destiny" goes hand in hand with support for restrictions that hinder, rather than foster, women's responsible self-government.[23] As Chapter 7 explains, rather than encouraging responsibility in the sense of reflective self-government, or *autonomy*, these restrictive policies insist upon responsibility in the sense of *conformity* to a state-approved vision of appropriate sexuality and reproductive choices.[24] Yet society's views of what constitutes "responsible" and "irresponsible" reproduction are often contradictory, and public opinion manifests ambivalence about women's decisions both to bear and not to bear children.

To promote the responsible exercise of reproductive rights, it is necessary to embrace more firmly a public responsibility to promote reproductive health and to facilitate the preconditions for responsible decision making. One way that government can do so, Chapter 8 argues, is through sex education that prepares youths for sexual and reproductive responsibility. According to one view, the best form would teach "abstinence-only" (that is, abstinence until marriage). This approach—adopted in the mid-1990s welfare reform law, the Personal Responsibility and Work Opportunity Reconciliation Act (PRWORA)[25]—reflects the triumph of a conservative sexual economy in which women have the vital role of serving as gatekeepers by controlling men's sexuality and steering them into marriage. Such gatekeeping is a similar feature in calls to educate young people about courtship as the proper pathway to marriage. This vision conflicts with principles of sex equality, denies basic information essential to developing responsibility, and insults the moral capacity of boys and men. An alternative approach, rooted in respect for women's and men's equal moral capacities and attentive to the place of gender-role stereotypes and expectations in shaping adolescents' sense of sexual agency and responsibility, would better foster responsible self-government.

᠍᠍   WHAT CAN THE liberal feminist account offered in this book add to debate about families? Beneath the impulse to link the state of families to the state of the nation is an important intuition:

families play a vital role in the formative process of shaping their members to be capable, responsible people and good citizens. As illustrated in recent work by historians Nancy Cott and Hendrik Hartog, the idea that there is an important link between family self-government and democratic self-government has a long history.[26] Yet this idea has existed within a broader history of state-sanctioned gender inequality.

In the last few decades, important works in political theory have developed the idea of government's responsibility to carry out a formative project of shaping self-governing citizens. But these works, growing out of the traditions of civic republicanism (for example, Michael Sandel's *Democracy's Discontent*)[27] and liberalism (for example, works by William Galston, Stephen Macedo, and Joseph Raz)[28] do not offer a feminist perspective. Nor do they provide a sustained treatment of the place of families in a formative project.

This book aims to provide such a sustained account. Over fifteen years ago, liberal feminist scholar Susan Moller Okin observed that families and gender are neglected topics in political theory.[29] Today, her observation remains surprisingly apt. How, Okin asked, could families serve as schools for citizenship or, to use the current rhetoric, "seedbeds of civic virtue," if they frequently were sites of male domination and an unjust division of labor? Okin's book, *Justice, Gender, and the Family*, continues to inspire feminist critiques of liberalism for its apparent inattention to injustice within families. But it has also led some liberals (notably, John Rawls)[30] to address these problems more explicitly. Similarly, feminist legal scholarship highlights the idea that law insufficiently supports the role of families in providing care, nurture, and intimacy and insufficiently attends to the problems of inequality and violence within families.[31]

In offering a liberal feminist approach to the place of families, I recognize that some feminists are skeptical about whether liberalism can support an adequate formative project. In part, this is due to the gap they perceive between the liberal ideals of free and equal citizens and autonomous selves and the reality of women's lives.[32] A liberal feminist account of government's formative responsibilities can meet this challenge, for feminism shares with liberalism a commitment to develop meaningful personal self-government. Moreover, a commitment to toleration does not bar government from addressing obstacles to such self-government, including those arising within the "privacy" of the family. By focusing on capacity, equality, and responsibility, I provide an account of the place of families that embraces equality, defends rights as facilitating responsibility, and supports families while respecting women's—and men's—capacities for self-government.

# I

## Fostering Capacity

# ⤳ 1

## The Place of Families and Government in a Formative Project

$\mathcal{T}$HE FOCUS ON THE FAMILY in recent public discourse brings to the fore the important question: How does a liberal constitutional democracy produce citizens with the capacities for responsible democratic and personal self-government? Through what institutions does society carry out this vital task? There is common ground, across the ideological spectrum, on the general idea that society depends on a formative process to shape persons to become members and citizens. A common intuition is that families are an important site in which this process takes place. But there is sharp contention about the proper scope of such a project and how society best carries it out. What is the division of labor, for example, between government and the institutions of civil society, such as the family? Do families best carry out this formative task if government leaves them alone or if government actively regulates them?

In this chapter, I explore the connection between the place of families and of government in this formative process. Government, I contend, has an important responsibility to carry out a formative project of fostering persons' capacities for democratic and personal self-government. Families and other institutions of civil society are also significant sites in which this development should occur. I sketch a formative project with two dimensions: (1) a principle of governmental responsibility to take affirmative steps to foster the capacities for dem-

ocratic and personal self-government, and (2) a principle of governmental responsibility to refrain from coercive action with respect to a
range of decisions and behaviors, which I call *toleration as respect*. Toleration as respect draws on three rationales for toleration: (1) the anticompulsion rationale—that is, that compulsion or coercion corrupts
belief or choice and violates autonomy; (2) the jurisdictional (or personal sovereignty) rationale—that is, that there is a realm of personal
belief, choice, and conduct that is not the proper "business" of government to regulate; and (3) the diversity rationale—that is, that it is
inevitable that people freely exercising their moral powers will choose
and pursue different ways of life and that imposing orthodoxy would
require an objectionable level of governmental coercion.

Through governmental action and restraint, government fosters individuals' capacities for self-government and regulates families in ways
that enables them to develop those capacities. By insisting on both
governmental action and restraint as two necessary components of a
formative project, my approach rejects the view that a commitment to
one bars a commitment to the other. A common criticism of liberal
toleration is that, because it protects a realm of freedom from governmental intrusion, it bars government from promoting any vision
of the good life. For example, political philosopher Michael Sandel
contends that liberalism, in contrast to civic republicanism, lacks the
resources to carry out a "formative politics" of shaping persons into
self-governing citizens.[1] The idea that government should actively
help citizens to live good and valuable lives is sometimes called perfectionism.[2] Perfectionists claim that too thick a model of governmental restraint leads to too thin a conception of the proper business
of government. Conversely, critics of the argument that government
should promote good lives counter that such a robust governmental
role intrudes too deeply into human freedom.[3]

Some of the most passionate public debates over the place of families concern the proper interplay of governmental action and restraint.
For example: is it government's business to promote a particular conception of family values or family structure, or should government
be neutral about such matters? Is it appropriate for government to
promote marriage and a national standard of sexual abstinence until
marriage? Has recognizing a constitutional principle of personal self-
government, or privacy, in family matters unduly constrained govern-

ment from promoting strong families? Or has government's commitment to this principle been too weak in the case of nontraditional families? May government attempt to promote personal responsibility in the exercise of constitutional rights to reproductive autonomy? In this chapter, I preview a framework for thinking about such challenging questions. My framework melds liberal and feminist principles, while finding a place for civic republican concerns for fostering civic virtue.

## Fostering Self-Government

A formative project aims at fostering persons' capacities for democratic and personal self-government. Democratic (or political) self-government and personal self-government capture two significant dimensions of self-government protected in the American constitutional order.[4] My schematic draws on political liberalism, which (as elaborated by John Rawls) posits that free and equal citizens have two moral powers pertaining to self-government: the capacity for a conception of justice and the capacity for a conception of the good.[5] Democratic self-government connotes what democratic theorists refer to as "deliberative democracy" and implicates a person's capacity to deliberate about his or her conception of justice, including engaging in various forms of political activity and discussion.[6] Sandel observes that "deliberating with fellow citizens about the common good and helping to shape the destiny of the political community" is a central value within the civic republican strand of the American constitutional and political tradition.[7]

Personal self-government connotes what some liberal theorists refer to as autonomy, or "deliberative autonomy," and implicates a person's capacity to deliberate about his or her conception of the good, including self-determination and personal decision making with respect to forming, acting on, and revising a conception of a good life. Generally, "autonomy is said to consist of a capacity, or the exercise of certain competencies, that enables one to reflect on one's aims, aspirations, and motivations and choose one's ends and purposes through such a reflective process."[8] Personal self-government, or "deliberative autonomy," has a firm anchor in the federal constitutional scheme, and yet, as James E. Fleming explains, it remains controversial.[9] Indeed, debate over the proper scope of this principle is heated with respect to the place of families, especially rights to sexual intimacy, reproduction, and parenting. Nonetheless, cultivating capacities for personal autonomy has a vital place in a formative project.

Autonomy does not imply atomism. The atomism critique charges that the liberal focus on rights, autonomy, and individuals ignores responsibility, connection, and community. Some feminist critics contend that liberal autonomy is inherently tied to an unrealistic picture of the rugged, self-interested, and self-sufficient individual.[10] This critique inaccurately caricatures important liberal accounts of autonomy and overlooks elements within liberal theory attentive to issues of care, connection, and responsibility.[11] Autonomy, in the sense of personal self-government, is not inherently atomistic.

In this book I adopt a notion of autonomy that recognizes that the self is socially situated and develops in the context of, rather than independent of, society and relationships. My approach is in harmony with feminist models of relational autonomy, which recognize that relationships in families and other parts of civil society—as well as the broader social structure—play a formative role in shaping a person's identity and cultivating and enabling self-government.[12] It is by virtue of a person's participation in relationships of nurture and care, initially within families and eventually in other forms of association, that he or she is able to develop the capacity for autonomy. Bringing such a relational approach to family law, as Martha Minow and Mary Lyndon Shanley observe, highlights a "paradoxical feature" of family life: family members are individuals, but also persons "deeply involved in relationships of interdependency and mutual responsibility."[13]

The two dimensions of government's role in a formative project—action and restraint—are logically related. Both are necessary to secure self-government. When government refrains from coercive action out of respect for personal self-government, one justification for doing so is that persons possess the capacity for such self-government and are entitled to exercise it. But how do persons develop such capacity? As liberal philosopher Joseph Raz explains, government should not only "stand back and let people have the choice as to how to conduct their own lives," but it "must take active steps, where needed, to ensure that people enjoy the basic capacities (physical and mental) and have the resources to avail themselves of an adequate range of options available in their society."[14]

A helpful example is freedom of intimate association. As constitutional precedents establish, persons are entitled to be free from "unwarranted governmental intrusion" in certain matters of fundamental importance to their intimate lives.[15] One rationale for this liberty is that criminal prosecution and punishment, for example, for using contraception or engaging in consensual sexual practices, would hinder persons' exercise of their moral capacities. Yet this freedom from intrusion is a necessary, but not sufficient, condition to secure certain goods of intimate association. To take an important contemporary example, a same-sex couple, no longer threatened by criminal prosecution for engaging in sexual intimacy, may want public affirmation and support of their relationship. Affirmative governmental acts—issuing a marriage license and recognizing a marriage—are prerequisites to extending to such couples and their children all the tangible and intangible benefits, protections, and obligations that flow from the status of being married.[16] Similarly, a principle of governmental restraint underlies the allocation—in the federal constitutional order—to parents of the right and responsibility to nurture, educate, and rear their children. However, families also need affirmative governmental support through having access to good schools, safe neighborhoods, and a framework of strong public and private institutions that help children to flourish. And government acts affirmatively when it imposes parental duties to ensure the healthy development of children.

How does society carry out a formative project? Government has a responsibility to take steps to help develop persons' moral powers, or moral capacities, for self-governing citizenship. One helpful starting point is political liberalism's list of "primary goods"—as formulated by Rawls—based on "what citizens need and require when they are regarded as [free and equal] persons and as normal and fully cooperating members of society over a complete life." Such goods include basic rights and liberties, freedoms, institutional opportunities, income and wealth, and the social bases of self-respect.[17] Beyond that, as feminist critics of Rawls urge, an account of primary goods should include such goods as care and should recognize issues of interdependency.[18]

A similar recognition of an affirmative governmental responsibility to foster persons' development arises from the human capabilities approach, identified with Amartya Sen's and Martha Nussbaum's work on international development. This approach identifies important human capabilities that enable persons to perform various important "functionings" they have "reason to value."[19] A good society would foster such human capabilities.[20]

My schematic of promoting capacities linked to democratic and personal self-government does not utilize Nussbaum's detailed list of central human functional capabilities.[21] Nonetheless, my approach has important affinities to the capabilities approach. First, it embraces a principle of affirmative governmental responsibility. Second, it focuses on the capacities, or capabilities, of each person, and thus targets inequalities in capabilities, particularly in the family. Sen has documented how women's unequal roles and opportunities within the family and in the broader culture, in developing and poor countries, impair women's agency and well-being.[22] Nussbaum argues that "women in much of the world lack support for fundamental functions of a human life," and highlights how women suffer damage within families because they are not treated as ends in themselves.[23] On both of these accounts, government has a general responsibility to foster each person's capabilities and to redress such inequalities.

## How Do Families Foster Capacity?

What place do families have in fostering capacity? A focus on primary goods, human needs, or capacities suggests at least three tasks for families. The first two relate to the process of social reproduction, or how society reproduces itself by preparing persons to take their place as capable, responsible, self-governing members of society. A third concerns the family's role in allowing the realization of the goods of intimate association by their adult members.

The first traditional task assigned to families is to be "seedbeds of civic virtue"—that is, to support the political order by cultivating important virtues in children and adults. On this view, families, along with other institutions of civil society, foster democratic self-government by forming good citizens. But another venerable idea is that children are not "mere creature[s] of the state" and that families inculcate in them particular conceptions of the good life, thus molding them as good persons and good members of communities.[24] This family role also serves a political function: "the preservation of social diversity" as a check on governmental power.[25] This dual role of families leads to hard questions about governmental regulation, as I will take up in Chapter 2.

A second task for families involves providing care. A just society must ensure that its members are able to meet their basic needs for nurture, care, food, shelter, and other material goods. Children offer the most dramatic example of these needs, or what Martha Fineman calls "inevitable dependency," but they are not the only members of society with such needs.[26] Families are assigned primary—if not sole—responsibility for providing this kind of care. However, Fineman contends, clinging to the "myth" of autonomy as self-sufficiency keeps our social institutions, laws, and policies from valuing such care and recognizing a collective responsibility to provide for dependency.[27] A model of relational autonomy helps to support an argument for public responsibility to ensure care for all members of society and to support the work of families in providing such care. In Chapter 3, I argue that society should recognize and support care as a public value.

Caregiving also fosters families' civic role. Families have the important task of ensuring the "nurturing and development" of children, who, as citizens, must "have a sense of justice and the political virtues that support political and social institutions."[28] As one of society's basic institutions, Rawls argues, families play a "prior and fundamental role" in "establishing a social world within which alone we can develop with care, nurture, and education, and no little good fortune, into free and equal citizens."[29] Thus, families play a vital role in the task of social reproduction.

A third role played by families is to afford adults the chance to realize the goods of intimate association. What are these goods? The long history of the institution of marriage offers an evolving, rather than a static, answer to the question "What is marriage *for?*"[30] Current controversies over whether government should promote marriage, whether marriage should extend to same-sex couples, and whether family law and policy should move beyond marriage entirely implicate such questions. Is the core purpose of marriage, for example, procreation or to support intimate commitments?

As a federal constitutional matter, "the freedom to marry has long been recognized as one of the vital personal rights essential to the orderly pursuit of happiness by free men."[31] Why? In Griswold v. Connecticut, the U.S. Supreme Court loftily described marriage as a "coming together for better or worse, hopefully enduring, and intimate to the degree of being sacred."[32] In Turner v. Safley, while striking down restrictions on the freedom of prison inmates to marry, the Court noted these goods, or "important attributes," of marriage: an expression of "emotional support and public commitment," an "exercise of religious faith," an expression of sexual intimacy, and "a precondition to the receipt of government benefits."[33] Notably, this list of attributes includes not only emotional, spiritual, and intimate goods, but also tangible governmental benefits premised on marital status.

In the political order, families are simultaneously a site of private life and an institution of public importance because of the goods they foster and the functions they serve. As family law scholars observe, there are two sometimes conflicting vantage points from which to regard families: one looks at the individual's interest in family life, the other at society's interest in the family (and in marriage) as social institutions.[34] Similarly, viewing families solely as a realm of "private" life, free from governmental intrusion, misses the active role of government in regulating families by defining "family" and the roles, rights, and obligations of family life.[35] Even though a consistent theme in American jurisprudence is that regulation of the family falls to state governments, the federal government also has actively engaged in such regulation.[36]

My approach to the place of families and how government should regulate them focuses not only on the goods associated with families and the functions they serve (for example, fostering relational responsibility and interdependence), but also on the relevant political values at stake. What political values are relevant to the institution of the family? Rawls identifies several, including "the freedom and equality of women, the equality of children as future citizens, the freedom of religion, and finally, the value of the family in securing the orderly production and reproduction of society and of its culture from one generation to the next."[37] Two additional political values are autonomy in intimate matters and equality among families. A number of these values are manifested in federal constitutional principles.

Like the idea of the goods of marriage, the notion of political values undergirding families is an evolving one. Embracing the freedom and equality of women as a contemporary political value, for example, departs radically from an earlier regime of family law that linked marriage's capacity to create good citizens to maintaining a gender hierarchy of husband as head of household and breadwinner and of wife as obedient and economically dependent. Defenses of "traditional marriage," for example, fail to reckon with how the contemporary value of sex equality calls for critical reflection on whether government justifiably adheres to the traditional definition of marriage as being between one man and one woman.

To take another example: the recognition of a realm of constitutionally protected liberty in intimate decision making (for married and unmarried persons) departs sharply from a tradition of using the criminal law to advance what family law scholar Carl Schneider describes as family law's "channeling function": channeling men and women into marriage as the only lawful and socially acceptable place to express sexuality, reproduce, and become parents.[38] Also dislodging marriage's place has been an emerging constitutional principle that, as a matter of equal protection, children should not be penalized for the circumstances of their birth, and thus, societal disapproval of "irresponsible" nonmarital procreation and parenting does not justify excluding nonmarital children from a range of benefits and protections available to marital children.[39] A parallel development in many state courts and legislatures has been a more functional approach to families, so that concerns for equality, fairness, and child well-being lead to facilitating procreating and parenting outside of marriage and even outside of heterosexual unions.[40] In addition, demographic changes of the last century, as the Supreme Court recently observed, have led to such variation in family composition, from household to household, that it is "difficult to speak of an average American family."[41]

The contemporary debate over the place of marriage in society and how to "strengthen families" occurs against the backdrop of such demographic changes and these evolving political values and constitutional principles of liberty, equality within and among families, and fairness to children. As I elaborate in Part II, a focus on political values and on the functions families serve bolsters my argument that government may support marriage, but it must do so in a manner supportive of sex equality. It should also recognize same-sex marriage and support other forms of family and intimate association in light of the goods they foster and the functions they fulfill.[42]

## Situating Families in the Political Order

Public institutions play a vital role in fostering the capacities of children and in supporting the work of families. The constitutional order does not assign to families exclusive responsibility to promote children's healthy development and to prepare them for democratic self-government. It also affirms governmental authority to carry out such tasks, for example, through compulsory education. Through common public schools, government aims at fostering the capacities for good citizenship and for successful participation in the economic and cultural realms.[43] Individuals as well as families benefit from governmental support of education and the arts, and affirmative measures to ensure fair or equal opportunity (including through affirmative action) and to foster political participation.[44]

Economic inequality among families warrants concern. A lack of economic resources may critically affect the capacity of adults to form and maintain a stable family life. When children from families with fewer resources lack access to good education, child care, and safe neighborhoods, they are at unequal starting points. This contributes to subsequent economic and social disadvantage. This inequality offends an important national value of equal opportunity and the conviction that all children, whatever the circumstances of their birth, deserve a good start in life.[45] A public responsibility to help members of society secure the basic resources necessary to participate successfully in society and in public life is an important dimension of the sort of governmental action necessary to foster personal, family, and democratic self-government.[46] Some constitutional scholars offer persuasive arguments that the federal constitution requires such governmental action.[47]

Institutions of civil society besides families—for example, workplaces, the myriad civic and cultural voluntary organizations long a feature of American life, and religious institutions—are also important places that may foster the capacities for personal and democratic self-government and the development of attitudes and virtues important for civic life.[48] As with families, one important role of other institutions of civil society is to foster and support diversity and to serve as important buffer zones between the individual and the state.[49] These institutions of civil society may also play a vital role in shaping and supporting families (for example, when neighborhood organizations provide after-school and athletic programs for children).

But what if families and other institutions of civil society hinder, rather than nurture, the capacities of their members? What if tension arises between personal and associational self-government? A voluntary association's rules and norms may limit the liberty and equality of some of their members (for example, religiously based restrictions on women's roles), yet if government does not tolerate such rules, does it wrongfully infringe upon associational and religious freedom?

Under what conditions, for example, may families carry out their tasks of social reproduction? Susan Moller Okin's influential book, *Justice, Gender, and the Family*, criticized Rawls's *A Theory of Justice* for assuming that families were just and thus could form children into self-governing members of a well-ordered society.[50] The forms of injustice that Okin identified—problems of domination and family violence and an unequal division of household labor—still persist. Women, for example, are disproportionately the victims of intimate partner violence, which hinders their well-being and personal self-government and negatively affects children in the home.[51] And despite growing agreement by men and women that family labor should be shared, truly equal sharing of child care and housework is rare, even when both parents hold jobs.[52]

These dilemmas identify the need for an account of governmental regulation that supports family and associational life but also ensures protection of individuals within families and associations. My account engages feminist concerns over obstacles to women's autonomy in families and other parts of civil society. It also responds to communitarian concerns that personal autonomy within families weakens families.

## Personal versus Family Self-Government

### Feminist Concerns about Autonomy

A frequent subject of feminist critique is the unequal power between men and women within families. In contrast to communitarian extolling of the bonds of family, or to the image of families as seedbeds of civic virtue, some feminists identify family life and intimate relationships as sites of injustice, inequality, and danger for women. Catharine MacKinnon famously contends that, too often, the private sphere has been a "hellhole" rather than a haven for women and children and that, owing to domestic violence and sexual abuse within families, the constitutional right of privacy "is a right of men 'to be let alone' to oppress women one at a time."[53] Robin West claims that women's fear of male violence and their internalizing of norms of female responsibility for domestic labor lead women, within families, to turn themselves into "giving selves." She conceives such compromises to autonomy as gender-based injuries.[54]

This critique of autonomy, which I call the illusion critique, highlights the gap between the ideal of an autonomous liberal self and the reality of women's lives. The argument is that, under conditions of sex inequality, personal self-government by women is an illusion. Liberals assume that a right to freedom from governmental intrusion into private life protects the capacity for personal self-government. But when women and men do not have equal power in the "private" sphere— for example, in families—such governmental restraint leaves women subject to the private power or sovereignty of men. Far from fostering freedom, when government stays out of "private" life, it fails to give women the affirmative help they need to be free, equal, and self-governing.[55]

Feminists also caution that women's preferences and choices concerning family or associational life may reflect not their exercise of autonomy, but the effects of sex inequality, gender socialization, and constraint.[56] This critique highlights the role of social construction in such choices: living in a patriarchal society, women's very desires, preferences, and choices may reflect patriarchal definitions of what a woman is and what she can be, as expressed through laws, customs, and social rules.[57] For example, the presence of sex-based discrimination in the workplace and cultural norms about proper gender roles call into question the idea that women who are mothers make a voluntary "choice" to devote more time to household labor and child care than to market labor.[58] Women may adapt their preferences in light of unjust circumstances and make the rational choice given their limited options.[59] As Nancy Hirschmann argues, the process of social construction "happens to and is participated in by everyone," but women and other disadvantaged groups "systematically and structurally" may have less power to do such shaping than do others.[60]

Such feminist work on obstacles to autonomy highlights the "tangle of love and domination" within families.[61] In other words, relationships within families and other institutions of civil society may sometimes hinder, rather than nurture, a person's capacity for self-government.[62] Both justice and care are relevant to the institution of the family.[63] Hence, on my approach, government has the responsibility to foster the capacity of each individual and to protect the capacity of individual members within families.[64] As Rawls puts it, "the equal rights of women and the basic rights of their children as future citizens are inalienable and protect them wherever they are."[65] Civil society is not a realm free of governmental regulation.[66]

My invocation of relational autonomy accepts the notion that a person is shaped by (as well as shapes) her environment and that "inner" constraints rooted in socialization may pose obstacles to the exercise of freedom. This approach is consistent with both historical and contemporary accounts of liberal feminism, which condemn gender hierarchy and inequality in families and in public life as barriers to women's development and exercise of the capacity for autonomy. Similarly, liberal feminism recognizes the force of gender socialization in perpetuating gender role assumptions about women's—and men's—place within families and society.[67]

A formative project that entails governmental action and restraint can meet feminist concerns about obstacles to autonomy. Notably, a number of feminist scholars seek to reconstruct, rather than abandon, autonomy.[68] Using the benchmark of a self-governing life provides a basis for indicting the lack of autonomy in women's lives and thus affirms "a regulative ideal of enhancing the agency, autonomy, and selfhood of women."[69] Governmental action, for example, should address discrimination and other lingering obstacles to women's self-government and the self-government of other historically disadvantaged groups.[70]

Governmental restraint, in the form of toleration as respect, also enables personal and family self-government. A principle of freedom from governmental coercion and a corresponding right of autonomy (or privacy), at least some feminists acknowledge, is vital.[71] This commitment to governmental restraint does not prevent government from addressing private sources of injustice threatening personal self-government, whether within families or other parts of civil society. Nor does it preclude government from promoting important political values, such as the freedom and equality of women. Indeed, government's efforts to strengthen families should be guided by these political—and constitutional—values.

*Communitarian Critiques of Autonomy in Family Life*

Communitarian scholars argue that the embrace of a principle of personal autonomy (or privacy), particularly in the domain of family life, erodes the bonds of family and community.[72] Morever, they worry that a "transformation" in family law has shrunk its role of embodying communal moral judgments about proper family life, and family roles and responsibilities, and has shifted responsibility for moral decision making to individuals.[73] For example, Bruce Hafen charges that American law's "extreme preoccupation with individual liberties virtually has captured the field of family law," as well as constitutional law, and heralds a "waning of belonging."[74]

Such scholars point to the U.S. Supreme Court's transition from the defense of the privacy rights of a family entity, the married couple (in *Griswold*), to the defense of privacy rights of individuals, married or unmarried (in Eisenstadt v. Baird).[75] This transition to the protection of the "freely choosing, autonomous self," Sandel contends, exalts the value of individual choice instead of the substantive goods of association. Similarly, he critiques the ascent of a "voluntarist" conception of family and marriage, evident in the rise of "no-fault" divorce law and the evolution of marriage away from a fixed set of duties based on one's status as husband or wife. Such changes, he contends, erode the idea of family as a place in which persons identify themselves by reference to their duties and in which they may realize important human goods, such as loyalty and interdependency.[76]

To the contrary, I contend that a principle of personal self-government facilitates rather than erodes a person's capacity to realize the goods associated with family life. It corrects historical injustices: an earlier regime of family law imposed sex-linked duties, denied married women the capacity for self-government, and reinforced their economic dependency upon and submission to their husbands. An important transformation in family law is the recognition of husbands' and wives' equal capacities for self-government and their mutual rights and responsibilities within marriage.[77] Such developments need not erode the value of belonging. Responding to Sandel, Shanley aptly observes: "Recognition of the individual rights of those wishing to form families can coexist with an appreciation of the value of intimate association and group life; they are vital to the project of revisioning the human interdependence fostered and sustained in diverse families."[78] Indeed, counterintuitive though it may seem, enhancing a right to exit from marriage (through no-fault divorce law) appears to be linked to better quality marriages, for example, by enhancing wives' mental health and limiting domestic violence.[79]

## Governmental Restraint, or Toleration as Respect

Government fosters the capacities of individuals and families both through taking affirmative measures and through exercising restraint. Governmental restraint facilitates capacities for personal self-government because it affords freedom to individuals to decide for themselves about their idea of a good life. It accords the freedom to form families, friendships, and other relationships, in which individuals may realize goods such as love, intimacy, mutuality, interdependence, and friendship. A right to privacy allows a space for the pursuit of such goods.[80]

My argument for such governmental restraint invokes a conception of toleration as respect (as distinguished from "empty" toleration). This idea has deep roots in political theory and practice, as well as in our nation's constitutional jurisprudence. It draws on three rationales for toleration: the anticompulsion rationale, the jurisdictional rationale, and the diversity rationale.

Despite its deep roots, toleration engenders strong criticism. Moreover, how it should limit government's formative responsibilities—particularly with respect to families—poses challenging questions. To set the stage for considering such questions, I explain the idea of toleration as respect, its rationales, and how it features in constitutional law about personal and family self-government.

What is toleration? The philosophical literature indicates that a common definition includes two elements: first, an impulse to use force because of disapproval of certain beliefs, choices, or conduct; and second, the decision, for reasons, to refrain from acting on that disapproval.[81] Thus, toleration simultaneously involves both "an impulse to intervene and regulate the lives of others" because of moral disapproval and "an imperative—either logical or moral—to restrain that impulse."[82]

These two elements of toleration prefigure two basic criticisms of it. The impulse to suppress because of moral disapproval draws the criticism that toleration is empty or grudging and fails to secure respect or appreciation among citizens. The second element—the decision to refrain from governmental regulation—elicits the criticism that toleration unduly limits government's authority to engage in a formative project.

Why should government be tolerant? My answer to this question draws upon several familiar rationales for toleration. One prominent rationale, which I call the *anticompulsion rationale*, is that toleration protects against the evil of forced beliefs and conduct. In this view, set out in John Locke's oft-discussed account, forcing or dictating what persons shall think, believe, or do distorts and corrupts belief formation.[83] Compulsion is irrational and also fails to accord respect to persons' moral capacities, or moral powers. For example, Ronald Dworkin opposes using the criminal law to bar certain forms of consensual sexual intimacy because no one's life can be improved against the grain of one's "most profound ethical conviction" that it has not been.[84]

In *On Liberty*, John Stuart Mill famously argued against the use of force in matters not implicating society's need for self-protection (that is, not causing harm to others). A person, free from coercive interference, grows and flourishes like a tree, pursuant to his or her best judgment about the best way of life. Moreover, Mill contended, "[m]ankind are greater gainers by suffering each other to live as seems good to themselves, than by compelling each to live as seems good to the rest."[85]

A second justification for toleration, which I call the *jurisdictional rationale*, is that government should refrain from acting or regulating in certain spheres of conscience and conduct because securing uniformity or orthodoxy in those spheres is not the proper business of government. I use the idea of jurisdiction to capture the intuitions that there should be a realm of personal sovereignty or moral independence from the state with respect to certain matters and that such freedom is necessary to foster the development and exercise of persons' moral powers.[86]

Antecedents for the jurisdictional rationale can be found in the work of Locke on toleration and Mill on liberty. Locke sharply distinguished the sphere of religious belief and salvation from the proper "business of civil government." He condemned members of one religion who would use the state to persecute others because this matter "does not at all belong to the jurisdiction of the magistrate, but entirely to the conscience of every particular man."[87]

Contemporary arguments for toleration translate the jurisdictional rationale from the sphere of religious belief to a broader realm of personal self-government. A famous precursor is Mill's defense of liberty, in which he proposed a jurisdictional principle to govern the proper limits of societal control over the individual. In contrast to conduct that concerns others, as Mill put it, "over himself, over his own body and mind, the individual is sovereign."[88] Hard questions arise about the proper application of the jurisdictional rationale to the regulation of families.

The model of toleration as respect draws upon a third justification, the *diversity rationale:* persons exercising their moral powers will inevitably have different, and diverse, beliefs and ways of life. Therefore, using government to secure uniformity is inappropriate and unduly oppressive. Locke and Mill also offer important historical precedents for this rationale. Defending religious toleration, Locke contended: "It is not the diversity of opinions (which cannot be avoided), but the refusal of toleration to those that are of different opinions (which might have been granted), that has provoked all the bustles and wars that have been in the Christian world upon account of religion."[89] Mill's defense of liberty rested on the assumption that human beings were diverse in their nature and needed diverse circumstances within which to develop and flourish. He also appealed to the value to society of being able to observe different "experiments of living" and learn from them.[90]

In contemporary arguments for toleration, the diversity rationale translates from religion, narrowly conceived, to the broader context of different comprehensive moral doctrines or ways of life. Rawls's political liberalism is a helpful illustration. "Diversity of reasonable comprehensive religious, philosophical, and moral doctrines," Rawls contends, is a permanent feature of a democratic public culture in which persons freely exercise their moral powers (the "fact of reasonable pluralism"). Achieving uniformity is not possible without "intolerable" oppressive state power ("the fact of oppression").[91] Given these facts, toleration is appropriate. Government should not attempt to secure agreement upon an orthodoxy concerning the best way to live, or to discover and impose the "whole truth" in politics. It is left to citizens themselves to settle the questions of religion, philosophy, and morality in accord with views that they freely affirm.[92]

Political liberalism posits that a stable polity is possible without an orthodoxy about the good life, or a unified comprehensive moral doctrine. Citizens who have different views about the good life, Rawls argues, can still agree on principles of justice and constitutional government. How? Persons can draw on the diverse comprehensive moral doctrines that they affirm and find in them a basis for an overlapping consensus on a political conception of justice in order to establish fair terms of social cooperation among citizens on the basis of mutual respect and trust.[93]

This argument may seem to be a prudential or pragmatic one. The impetus for toleration is peaceful coexistence in the face of diversity (as contrasted with civil war). But the diversity argument aims at more than a grudging modus vivendi, akin to a "treaty between two states whose national aims and interests put them at odds."[94] The idea of an overlapping consensus is a moral one and flows from respect for persons as possessing moral powers. As Rawls puts it, the fact of diversity is "not an unfortunate condition of human life,"[95] but a positive good for society. Political liberalism aims to go beyond a modus vivendi through honoring such duties as civility and mutual respect. In this sense, toleration is not "empty."

Respect for reasonable moral pluralism has implications for the proper aims of governmental regulation (including family regulation) as well as the way in which citizens argue for particular laws and policies. Citizens show mutual respect by not using the political process to impose their comprehensive moral views on other citizens. Pursuant to the duty of civility, citizens engage in reason-giving and attempt to understand each other's perspectives.[96] They abide by an ideal of reciprocity and desire "for its own sake a social world in which they, as free and equal, can cooperate with others on terms all can accept."[97] As democratic theorists Amy Gutmann and Dennis Thompson state: "In a pluralist society, comprehensive moral conceptions neither can nor should win the assent of reasonable citizens. A deliberative perspective for such societies must reject the unqualified quest for agreement because it must renounce the claim to comprehensiveness."[98] Even Sandel, one of political liberalism's most persistent critics, seems to share its recognition of diversity and moral pluralism as inevitable features of contemporary American society and to renounce the quest for a unitary common good.[99]

## Toleration as Respect in Constitutional Law

Constitutional law reveals a commitment to toleration as respect. The anticompulsion, jurisdictional, and diversity rationales all feature in articulations of why the U.S. constitutional order recognizes a principle of governmental restraint. The strongest affirmation of toleration concerns religious freedom. More controversial is the proper scope of toleration, and of permissible governmental regulation, in matters of intimate association and family life.

All three rationales for toleration serve as important underpinnings of the principle of religious toleration reflected in the First Amendment. Constitutional protection includes both barring government from establishing either an official religion or any other religion (the Establishment Clause) and from denying persons civil rights based on their religious beliefs (the Free Exercise Clause).[100] Both the anticompulsion and jurisdictional rationales are evident in Lee v. Weisman, in which the Supreme Court found a high school graduation prayer unconstitutional. It explained: "[a] state-created orthodoxy puts at grave risk that freedom of belief and conscience which are the sole assurance that religious faith is real, not imposed." By constitutional design, the preservation and transmission of religious beliefs and worship is "a responsibility and a choice committed to the private sphere"; government has a duty to respect the "sphere of inviolable conscience."[101]

The Court also drew on the diversity rationale for protecting freedom of conscience when, in striking down a compulsory flag salute that would infringe on the religious beliefs of certain students and their parents, it stated: "we apply the limitations of the Constitution with no fear that freedom to be intellectually and spiritually diverse or even contrary will disintegrate the social organization." Furthermore, the Court warned that compelling uniformity of belief could lead to "the unanimity of the graveyard."[102]

A principle of toleration as respect similarly figures in justifications for constitutional rights to liberty in matters of personal self-government other than religion. The anticompulsion, jurisdictional,

and diversity rationales all appear in the Supreme Court's early precedents concerning parental rights to direct their children's education
and upbringing. As the Court stated in Pierce v. Society of Sisters, in
striking down a law compelling parents to send their children to public
school:

> The fundamental theory of liberty upon which all governments
> in this Union repose excludes any general power of the state to
> standardize its children by forcing them to accept instruction
> from public teachers only. The child is not the mere creature of
> the state; those who nurture him and direct his destiny have the
> right, coupled with the high duty, to recognize and prepare him
> for additional obligations.[103]

This passage well illustrates the function of families in preserving diversity as against a standardizing state.[104]

Seventy-five years later, in Troxel v. Granville, the Court favorably
quoted *Pierce* and other early cases for pointing to "the fundamental
right of parents to make decisions concerning the care, custody, and
control of their children." The jurisdictional rationale—the idea of a
protected sphere of self-government—is evident in the Court's statement: "So long as a parent adequately cares for his or her children
(i.e., is fit), there will normally be no reason for the State to inject
itself into the private realm of the family to further question the ability
of that parent to make the best decisions concerning the rearing of
that parent's children."[105]

Constitutional cases recognizing rights of intimate association and
procreative autonomy also appeal to these three rationales for toleration. In Planned Parenthood v. Casey, in which the Court reaffirmed
Roe v. Wade's recognition of a woman's right to decide whether to
continue or terminate her pregnancy, the joint opinion appeals to an
anticompulsion rationale: "At the heart of liberty is the right to define
one's own concept of existence, of meaning, of the universe, and of
the mystery of human life. Beliefs about these matters could not define
the attributes of personhood were they formed under compulsion of
the State."[106]

This idea that governmental coercion hinders the development of
personhood features in the Court's recent decision, Lawrence v. Texas,

overruling Bowers v. Hardwick.[107] In *Bowers*, the Court rejected a constitutional challenge to Georgia's sodomy law based on a right to autonomy in matters of intimate association. It upheld governmental intolerance toward "homosexual sodomy" and the enforcement of a sexual orthodoxy (namely, a "presumed" belief by the majority that homosexuality was immoral) through the criminal law. Over vigorous dissents, the majority found it "evident that none of the rights announced" in its cases affirming protected decisions concerning family, contraception, and abortion "bears any resemblance" to a "claimed constitutional right of homosexuals to engage in acts of sodomy."[108]

By contrast, *Lawrence* rejects intolerance toward intimate association between same-sex couples and articulates a form of toleration as respect. The Court stated that the intimate sexual decisions of persons in same-sex relationships deserved "respect" and that "the state cannot demean their existence or control their destiny by making their private sexual conduct a crime." Constitutional liberty presumes an "autonomy of self that includes freedom of thought, belief, expression and certain intimate conduct."[109] The Court relies on *Casey*'s language, quoted above, about the impact of governmental compulsion upon a person's formation of belief and exercise of autonomy regarding such personal, intimate matters. Unlike the *Bowers* Court, *Lawrence* found a salient family resemblance between the intimate decisions of same-sex couples and those of opposite-sex couples.

The jurisdictional rationale for toleration features clearly in the Court's identification of a "sphere" or "realm" of constitutionally protected liberty "which the government may not enter," within which persons may make important "intimate" or personal decisions free from "unwarranted" governmental intrusion.[110] In *Lawrence*, the Court appealed both to a spatial notion of liberty—that "liberty protects the person from unwarranted government intrusions into a dwelling or other private places"—and to a "transcendent" dimension of liberty that "extends beyond spatial bounds"—"there are other spheres of our lives and existence, outside the home, where the State should not be a dominant presence."[111] It found these two dimensions in *Griswold*, which spoke both of the protected space of the marital bedroom and of the protection of the marital relationship itself. However, it reiterated the principle that protection of intimate decision making is not confined to the marital relationship. A striking feature of *Lawrence* is its emphasis on autonomy as relational, or what constitutional law scholar Laurence Tribe calls a "relationally situated theory" of substantive liberty.[112] Thus, the Court invalidated Texas's law for wrongly seeking to "control" and "define the meaning" of a personal relationship that "is within the liberty of persons to choose without being punished as criminals."[113]

The diversity rationale also undergirds a constitutional principle of governmental restraint. For example, in *Casey*, the joint opinion spoke of "reasonable people" having "different opinions" concerning contraception and abortion. It declared that its responsibility was not to impose the "moral code" of the members of the Court upon society, but to uphold the liberty of all.[114] In *Lawrence*, the Court repeated this declaration in concluding that a commitment to constitutional liberty precludes the use of criminal law to impose one view about homosexuality, no matter how conscientiously held, upon the whole of society.[115]

## Puzzles about Toleration and Families

This overview of prominent rationales for toleration, and of the embodiment in constitutional law of toleration as respect, sets the stage for considering some challenging puzzles about the scope of toleration with respect to intimate association and family life. These puzzles stem from the dual aspects of the place of the family in the political order, both as a site of private life and as a basic social institution. On the one hand, the constitutional order recognizes fundamental liberties in matters of intimate association, family life, and reproduction because of the significance of such matters to personal self-government. On the other hand, precisely because of the family's fundamental importance to society, it recognizes that the social and political interests at stake will justify some governmental regulation.[116] I will take up four challenging questions: (1) What is the boundary between individual liberty in intimate matters and governmental authority? (2) Is toleration "empty" because it does not require respect for the tolerated? (3) Does toleration's commitment to governmental restraint bar it from addressing problems of domination and private coercion within the home? and (4) If toleration requires that government refrain from coercion, may government nonetheless use other measures (for example, persuasion) to steer intimate choices and behavior?

## Evolving Understandings of Liberty

What intimate conduct falls within the realm of protected liberty? Delineating the proper business of government and the boundary between governmental authority and personal sovereignty is at the core of constitutional theory and adjudication. This boundary line shifts as interpretations of constitutional purposes and traditions themselves evolve. Justice John Marshall Harlan's often-quoted dissent in Poe v. Ullman described the scope of traditional liberty protected by the Due Process Clause: "That tradition is a living thing" and recognizes not only "the traditions from which [this country] developed" but also "the traditions from which it broke."[117]

Illustrating this evolution is the dramatic shift from *Bowers* to *Lawrence* on the constitutional limits to using the criminal law to punish same-sex sexual behavior. There is a powerful argument (drawing on Mill) that private, nonconforming consensual sexual conduct (for example, homosexual sodomy) does not harm the rights of others and does not (as H. L. A. Hart put it) threaten to unravel society's moral fabric.[118] Indeed, although contemporary American constitutional law does not fully embrace the proposition (inspired by Mill) of the Wolfenden Report (which recommended decriminalizing, in Britain, private consensual homosexual behavior) that "[t]here must remain a realm of private morality and immorality which in brief and crude terms is not the law's business,"[119] the notion of a "right to be let alone" reflects acceptance of such a jurisdictional argument to a point.[120] On this view, society's discomfort with or disapproval of same-sex sexual conduct is not a sound basis for criminal prohibition.

And yet, constitutional jurisprudence has retained a moralizing strand, resisting this limiting principle. In dissent in *Poe*, Justice Harlan acknowledged the "right to be let alone" and indicated that the use of criminal law to punish contraceptive use by married couples intruded too deeply into the "private realm of family life." However, he also contended that government had a proper concern for the "moral soundness" of its people and included forbidden sexual practices in the home, such as homosexual sexual conduct, adultery, and fornication, as proper subjects of "criminal enquiry."[121] And again, the majority in *Bowers* upheld Georgia's sodomy law on the basis of moral condemnation of homosexuality, notwithstanding Justice Harry Blackmun's poignant invocation (in dissent) of Hart's argument.[122]

*Bowers*'s much-criticized opinion seemed out of line both with the Court's prior precedents concerning the scope of a right of privacy and with the trend among states to decriminalize sodomy. Focusing on this historical shift, as well as on similar developments in Europe, *Lawrence* described an "emerging awareness that liberty gives substantial protection to adult persons in deciding how to conduct their private lives in matters pertaining to sex." Akin to a "no harm" principle, it affirmed that this liberty warrants protection "absent injury to a person or abuse of an institution the law protects."[123] *Lawrence*'s articulation of such evolving understandings of liberty no doubt will give rise to fresh questions about the scope of liberty in the areas of intimate and family life.[124]

## Empty Toleration or Toleration as Respect?

The *Lawrence* Court pointedly did not address the same-sex marriage issue, stating that the case before it "does not involve whether the government must give formal recognition to any relationship that homosexual persons seek to enter."[125] But what implications does the Court's language about "respect" for intimate life have for that issue? In part, the answer turns on a choice between two readings of toleration: empty toleration or toleration as respect.

One criticism of liberal toleration is that it is, in effect, empty. For example, Sandel claims that defending toleration by appealing to the private nature of the choice to engage in homosexual intimate association, rather than to the moral worth of such conduct, results in very tenuous protection. It suggests that homosexual intimate association is base and degrading, permissible only as long as it is hidden.[126] Another criticism is that supporting the decriminalizing of nonconforming, consensual sexual conduct (such as homosexual sodomy) on the rationale that it takes place in the private realm, and thus does no real harm, leaves persons who engage in such conduct in a status of second-class citizenship. They are permitted to practice "private" sexual acts, but they face legal sanction for any spillover or manifestation of their nonconformist (for example, gay or lesbian) identity into the public sphere, thus constraining their ability to shape the public culture.[127]

A model of "empty" toleration appears in Justice Antonin Scalia's angry dissent in Romer v. Evans. He interpreted Colorado's Amendment 2, which barred gay men, lesbians, and bisexuals from the protection of antidiscrimination law, as a "modest attempt by seemingly tolerant Coloradans," who were "entitled to be hostile toward homosexual conduct," to "preserve traditional sexual mores" against the law reform efforts of a "political powerful minority." Indeed, in Scalia's view, that minority, gay men and lesbians, sought to devote its political power "to achieving not merely a grudging social toleration, but full social acceptance of homosexuality."[128] Similarly, some contemporary arguments in favor of discrimination against gay men and lesbians and against same-sex marriage argue for this form of "tolerance": there may be prudential arguments against using the criminal law to condemn same-sex sexual conduct, but society must not let its laws go beyond tolerance to signal acceptance and condonation of such conduct.[129] Otherwise, decriminalization of formerly proscribed conduct may send a message that immoral behavior is now condoned because it is no longer punished.[130] Similarly, opponents of same-sex marriage maintain that the denial of the right to marry satisfies the requirements of tolerance, as distinguished from "acceptance."[131]

I vigorously dispute Scalia's suggestion that decriminalizing sodomy exhausts the requirements of toleration, and that governmental discrimination against gay men and lesbians is consistent with toleration. A model of toleration as respect does not lead to these consequences. It calls for the extension to gay men and lesbians of the same basic liberties accorded to other citizens. Thus, writing for the majority in *Romer* (1996), Justice Anthony Kennedy stated that the Constitution does not permit a state to make a class of citizens a "stranger to its laws" and that Amendment 2 violated the requirement that government be impartial. Kennedy concluded that a defense of discrimination on the basis of sexual orientation—as governmental moralizing to reflect public disapproval of homosexuality—was not a legitimate governmental interest, but instead constituted unjustified animus and a bare desire to harm a politically unpopular group.[132]

*Lawrence* reflects a vision of toleration as respect rather than empty, or grudging, toleration. Drawing on *Romer,* it noted a close relationship between the Equal Protection Clause's insistence upon equal treatment and the Due Process Clause's right to respect for conduct protected under the umbrella of constitutional liberty. Also evidencing its rejection of empty toleration is its attention to the harmful consequences of criminal prohibition—that it may invite or license individuals and institutions to discriminate in other areas of civic and public life.[133] In Chapter 5, I will argue that to deny gay men and lesbians the basic civil right of marriage denies them the autonomy and respect concerning their intimate lives and family arrangements afforded to other citizens by the Constitution. As state courts grapple with challenges to their marriage laws, they may, as Massachusetts's highest court did, find *Lawrence* and *Romer* evocative of the respect due to gay men's and lesbian's intimate relationships under their own state constitutional guarantees.[134]

## Toleration as Respect and the Problem of Private Coercive Power

Does a commitment to toleration—and to a right to privacy—bar government from addressing harms that persons experience in the private sphere? Feminist scholars argue that the idea that government has "no business" interfering in families and with what goes on in the privacy of men's "castles" and bedrooms leads to government failing to take responsibility for protecting women and children, within the home, from abusive exercises of "private" power.[135] Such power, they contend, often poses a greater threat to women's agency and liberty than state power, but constitutional rights to privacy, or negative liberty, leave women vulnerable to it.[136] This critique usefully highlights a risk of an overly literal reading of the notion of a protected sphere, or realm, of personal self-government. This image may imply a sharp public/private distinction, as though we could divide the world into distinct spheres: (1) the private—the home, family, marriage, civil society, and (on some accounts) the market—and (2) the public—politics and (on other accounts) the market. This literal, spatial notion of privacy and of toleration wrongly implies that entire spheres of life—such as the family—are immune from governmental regulation because they are "private."

Can toleration as respect meet this feminist critique? Feminist critiques of privacy correctly attack the misuse of the rhetoric and reach of privacy. Undeniably, historical doctrines of family privacy, marital unity, and the sanctuary of the marital bedroom have contributed to the unequal protection of married women in their homes and have sanctioned injustice against women and children within the family, leaving them unprotected against rape, incest, and physical assault.[137] The protection of family self-government, and of a husband's sovereignty, came at the expense of women's personal self-government.

To the extent feminists indict contemporary understandings of constitutional rights of privacy as sanctioning such violence, however, they are mistaken. To the contrary, in striking down such doctrines as the exemption in criminal law against prosecuting husbands for rape within marriage, state courts have rejected the notion of the home as a fortress impervious to the law's reach and have drawn support from constitutional privacy precedents such as *Griswold, Eisenstadt,* and *Roe.*[138] In *Casey,* the joint opinion invalidated a spousal notification requirement in Pennsylvania's abortion law, observing that while giving a husband this degree of "dominion" over his wife and her personal decision making may have been compatible with common law understandings of marriage and a husband's prerogatives, it was incompatible with current understandings of "the family, the individual, or the Constitution." The joint opinion observed that upholding a pregnant woman's individual right to privacy, rooted in her right to bodily integrity, was all the more important because of the societal problem of violence against women.[139] As feminist scholar Elizabeth Schneider observes, as a result of feminist efforts to bring about public recognition of problems arising from the "private" sphere, *Casey* and many lower-court cases "have recognized the harms of intimate violence in a way that did not seem possible thirty years ago."[140]

*Lawrence* offers further evidence that respect for a protected sphere of private decision making does not entail abdicating governmental responsibility to protect persons within that sphere. The Court carefully explained that the constitutional liberty it recognized protected fully consensual, intimate sexual activity between adults in the home. Its ruling did not bar the state from regulating relationships, no matter how private, that involved minors or persons who might be easily "injured or coerced" or situations in which consent "might not easily be refused."[141]

A commitment to toleration does not support an unqualified jurisdictional principle of governmental noninterference with "private" life. The better feminist argument is that the negative liberty secured by

toleration is a necessary but not a sufficient condition of women's well-
being. It is necessary because the unrestricted exercise of governmental
power may pose a significant threat to women's pursuit of self-
governing lives (for example, laws restricting women's reproductive
choices). As privacy theorist Anita Allen concludes, women "have won
important gains under the banner of constitutional privacy," and privacy, as clarified by vigorous feminist critiques, deserves a place as a
"core" political value.[142] One may acknowledge that private power may
impinge upon and constrain women's capacity to direct their own lives
without dismissing the specter of coercive state power as a liberal
bogeyman.

Government properly uses its powers to secure women's equal citizenship and basic liberties within and outside of families. Thus, in
adopting the Violence Against Women Act in 1994 to protect women
against "private" violence, Congress properly exercised its authority—
and constitutional responsibility[143]—to remedy the lingering problems
of gender discrimination, including official resistance to enforcing domestic violence laws. The Supreme Court, in striking down the civil
rights remedy component of the Act, erroneously failed or refused to
see the connection between such violence and women's national citizenship.[144] Cogent feminist criticism points out that the Court fell
back on a model of federalism and states rights that ignored both the
active role of the federal government in regulating families and a cooperative model of state and federal governments working together to
enforce individual rights.[145]

A word about constitutional limits to parents' authority over children may be in order. In contrast to the revocation of husbands' authority over wives, constitutional law and family law still protect the
exercise of parental authority over children. Does this, as some family
law scholars contend, treat children as the property of their parents?[146]
In cases where families are divided, does the rhetoric of family privacy,
and deference to parental authority, "serve to mask conflict and coercion behind an ideal of family harmony and love"?[147]

The status of children within families raises challenging questions.
Just as a child is not the "mere creature of the state," so a child is not
the mere creature of his or her parents. In my view, government's
formative responsibilities to children include not only preventing harm
but also fostering their capacities to live their own lives. This justifies

some limits on parents' rights to exercise authority over their children. Thus, the federal constitutional scheme justifies parental liberty, or a realm of protected decision making, on the premise that fit parents act in their children's best interest. But it also recognizes that children, even though minors, have constitutional rights, although these are limited in some respects to reflect their lack of full capacity. Moreover, government has the authority to foster the healthy development of children and may act to protect the best interests of children in ways that limit parental liberty.[148] For example, in *Troxel*, some members of the Court filed opinions cautioning that too much deference to parents' wishes could hinder a child's own liberty interest in preserving intimate relationships that "serve her welfare and protection."[149]

## Does Toleration as Respect Bar Governmental Persuasion?

A difficult question about the interplay of governmental action and restraint arises with respect to governmental persuasion, as distinguished from compulsion. Even if respect for the rights of the person requires that government may not prohibit certain sexual conduct (as *Lawrence* concludes), may government use its persuasive power to try to steer how people exercise constitutionally protected liberties in "matters pertaining to sex"? For example, may it preach the comparative benefits of heterosexuality? May it steer the exercise of persons' constitutionally protected liberty in the areas of family life and reproduction?

A paradigm case concerning when governmental persuasion is inappropriate is freedom of religion. As the Court explained in *Lee*, governmental action short of outright coercion may also threaten freedom of conscience. The historical lesson behind the Establishment Clause was recognition that "in the hands of government what might begin as a tolerant expression of religious views may end in a policy to indoctrinate and coerce."[150]

The prophylactic rule that the Supreme Court has raised against governmental persuasion concerning religion has not translated into a general prohibition on persuasion in matters of democratic and personal self-government.[151] Rather, constitutional jurisprudence distinguishes between compulsion and persuasion. In West Virginia State Board of Education v. Barnette, the Court rejected the notion of governmental officials dictating an orthodoxy through a compulsory flag salute. However, it did not question the state's authority to foster the ends of "national unity" and patriotism "by persuasion and example" (for example, the curriculum), a voluntary flag salute, or other "patriotic ceremonies."[152] As *Barnette* and cases involving conflicts between parental rights and the state's authority to educate children imply, fundamental constitutional rights of self-determination protect against governmental use of coercion or criminal sanction, but not necessarily against government taking sides through noncoercive means.[153] For example, forbidding parents to send their children to private schools violates a fundamental right of parents to direct the upbringing of their children; preferring public over private education does not.

A similar distinction between compulsion and persuasion features in case law about rights of intimate association, marriage, and procreative autonomy. As a threshold matter, defining the scope of individual liberty as a right to be free from "unwarranted" governmental interference implies that certain forms of governmental action may be warranted. Even when constitutional rights concerning intimate association, family, and reproduction are in play, persons have protection only against "unwarranted" governmental interference, or "unduly burdensome" regulation; promoting a compelling or important governmental interest may justify restrictions on liberty.[154]

In some instances, the Court has struck restrictions on intimate association both because of the means they employ and the ends they advance. For example, in Loving v. Virginia, the Court struck down a ban on interracial marriage not only because an outright bar to marriage burdened the fundamental right to marry, but also because the State of Virginia had no legitimate purpose for its law: restricting the right to marry by a racial classification "designed to maintain White Supremacy" violated the Equal Protection Clause.[155]

By contrast, in Zablocki v. Redhail, the Court accepted the contention that Wisconsin had "legitimate and substantial interests" in counseling a parent who sought to marry about the need to fulfill prior child support obligations and in protecting the welfare of children not in that parent's custody. However, the Court struck down a law premising permission to marry upon such a person paying all prior child support and showing that his children would not be public charges. It did so because the law "interfere[d] directly and substantially" with the constitutional right to marry, and yet was not likely to advance the state's interests as effectively as less restrictive measures would.[156]

The *Zablocki* Court's contemplation of the precise scope of the regulation of marriage is unclear, but it seems to leave room for facilitative and persuasive measures (for example, counseling a person about support responsibilities but still issuing a marriage license). Thus, a law that "significantly interferes" with the exercise of the right to marry "cannot be upheld unless it is supported by sufficiently important state interests and is closely tailored to effectuate only those interests." But not every state regulation relating to marriage warrants rigorous scrutiny: "reasonable regulations that do not significantly interfere with decisions to enter into the marital relationships may legitimately be imposed."[157]

The problem of government pursuing a permissible end but using an impermissible means is also evident in Carey v. Population Services, in which the Court struck down state bans on distribution of contraceptives. Government, it noted, could seek to deter nonmarital sex by teens, but it was irrational to presume a "scheme of values" whereby the state sought to do so by prescribing pregnancy, the risks of abortion, and unwanted childbirth as punishment for fornication.[158] In this case, criminal prohibition was not an appropriate means to promote a permissible message. As Justice John Paul Stevens, concurring, memorably stated, it would be "as though a State decided to dramatize its disapproval of motorcycles by forbidding the use of safety helmets. One need not posit a constitutional right to ride a motorcycle to characterize such a restriction as irrational and perverse."[159]

The most extensive discussion of governmental persuasion appears in the Court's cases about abortion. The Supreme Court has upheld state and federal laws funding poor women's childbirth, but not abortion, on the rationale that such selective funding promotes government's interest in childbirth and does not unduly burden a pregnant woman's right to choose abortion.[160] In *Casey*, the joint opinion ruled that the state, to further its respect for unborn life, could use an informed consent scheme to try to persuade pregnant women in favor of childbirth as long as it did not constitute an "undue burden" on (or "substantial obstacle" to) their right to make the "ultimate decision." It asserted: "What is at stake is the woman's right to make the ultimate decision, not a right to be insulated from all others in doing so."[161]

Under my approach, a commitment to toleration does not impose a categorical bar on governmental persuasion. In a modern regulatory state, which routinely undertakes to educate, inform, and persuade citizens, government properly acts for many reasons and may use a range of measures to do so.[162] Rather than trying to delineate the scope of governmental persuasion in the abstract, I will address it in the context of specific issues of family law and policy. Here, I mention certain guidelines to preview the approach taken to those issues in later chapters.

The first guideline is to ask: is government's purpose for such persuasive measures to foster the capacity for self-government? Is this the likely effect of such measures? This focus on self-government is one helpful way to distinguish between when it is proper for government to seek to steer persons in their exercise of protected liberties and when it is not.[163] For government's formative responsibilities, I argue, include fostering the skills and capacities needed for both democratic and personal self-government.

This distinction is consistent with the anticompulsion rationale. If the evil of intolerance is the corruption of belief or choice due to compulsion, then noncoercive measures, such as persuasion, may avoid that evil because they seek to shape or inform, rather than compel, belief or choice. Influential historical accounts, such as those of Locke and Mill, as well as some contemporary liberal accounts of toleration, admit this distinction.[164] This defense of persuasion assumes that it fosters, rather than undermines, the exercise of the capacity for personal self-government. Persuasion is compatible with respect for moral powers and the requirements of personhood only if it does so. Thus, as Ronald Dworkin argues, government may legitimately encourage *responsibility* in the sense of reflective and thoughtful exercise of rights because persons remain the proper locus of decision making; but it may not insist on *conformity*, that is, force persons to decide in accordance with government's view of what is best.[165]

Government, I will argue, may seek to encourage responsible and informed decision making in matters of intimate association and family life. For example, governmental efforts to encourage reflective decision making in reproductive matters is consistent with respect for a right to personal self-government, or autonomy. However, in Chapter 7, I will argue that the regulation of women's reproductive decisions, under the "undue burden" approach adopted in *Casey* and other precedents, too often has hindered, rather than fostered, their exercise of responsible reproductive choice.

Attending to the impact on self-government also highlights the problem of drawing the line between persuasion and coercion. One liberal concern about persuasion is that, because the state has a monopoly on the legitimate use of coercive power, and its "ability to undertake any activity at all rests on its coercive power," the coercive power of the state "stands in the background even when it is not overtly deployed."[166] It is difficult to find a formal line, or categorical distinction, between governmental coercion and persuasion, or between governmental speech that denies citizens' autonomy and that which enhances it.[167] Between the most obvious cases of compulsion (direct physical force) and persuasion (changing one's mind in response to a good argument) lie many examples that raise concerns about subtle or indirect coercion. As I will argue in Chapter 7, this problem is especially acute in the context of governmental measures adopted to deter abortion and steer women toward childbirth.

A second guideline I will propose is whether persuasive measures seek to advance important political values and virtues, such as the ones I have argued are relevant to the institution of the family, as distinguished from general moral values and virtues. Critics of liberal toleration contend that it commits government to a neutrality that bars it from cultivating virtues necessary for responsible citizenship,[168] but the idea that citizens should have political virtues and be willing to take part in public life—and that government may promote such virtues—unites rather than divides liberalism and its republican critics.[169] Thus, I accept political liberalism's tenet that government may persuade to promote the virtues (or values) characterizing the ideal of the good citizen, such as tolerance, civility, reciprocity, and cooperation. I also accept its caveat that government should not promote personal virtues characterizing ways of life belonging to particular comprehensive moral doctrines (or ideals of the good person).[170]

But is this distinction tenable when it comes to regulation of the family? The institution of the family has both private and public dimensions. As Rawls himself notes, important political values are at stake, and society depends on families to cultivate both personal and political virtues. If, as liberal perfectionist Joseph Raz argues, governmental persuasion in favor of morally worthy ways of life fosters persons' autonomy, should government promote certain family forms over others?[171] Or, by contrast, as liberal philosopher Jeremy Waldron argues, does Raz give inadequate attention to the "insult" involved when "government actually takes it upon itself to think about such matters in the first place."[172]

Government does need "to think about such matters" as orderly social reproduction, intergenerational dependency, equality within and among families, and the like.[173] But is there a limiting principle concerning the scope of governmental persuasion in such matters? A helpful guide is political liberalism's contention that, given the "fact of reasonable pluralism" and "the fact of oppression," it is inappropriate for government to promote an orthodoxy concerning what views citizens should hold about a good life. For example, citizens and lawmakers should not argue for family policies that would enact—or persuade in favor of—religious conceptions of marriage, sexuality, and reproduction.[174] Instead, debate over whether government should favor marriage or take a more inclusive approach to family would attend to relevant public values and family functions.[175]

Government properly concerns itself with facilitating individuals being able to form and sustain families. Doing so helps persons realize the valuable goods linked to family life and also helps families to carry out the significant functions assigned to them in the political order. At the same time, respect for diversity cautions against government promoting a national standard for the expression of sexuality or seeking to persuade citizens that there is only one good, or true, way to order their intimate and family lives.[176] In Parts II and III, I will apply these guidelines to governmental campaigns to strengthen families and foster sexual and reproductive responsibility.

## Conclusion

In this chapter, I have offered an account of the place of families and government in nurturing persons' capacities for democratic and personal self-government. Both governmental action and restraint, I have contended, help individuals to develop into capable and responsible citizens and members of society and enable families to nurture such development.

In the next two chapters, I will explain how government might help families carry out two important functions: fostering the civic virtue and providing the care and nurture that enable persons to become capable and responsible citizens and members of society.

# ⪼ 2

# Families as "Seedbeds of Civic Virtue"?

> [D]iscussing family life is not simply an appeal to sentiment.
> Throughout the ages, political philosophers, social historians, and
> civic and religious leaders have praised the family as the foundation
> of the social order, the bedrock of nations, and the bastion of
> civilization. Cicero, for example, spoke of the family as
> "the first society" and "the seedbed of the state."
> ⪼ *Wade F. Horn, Assistant Secretary for Children and Families,*
> *U.S. Department of Health and Human Services*

$O$NE RECURRING ANSWER to the question, "What is the place of families?" is that families are, or should be, "seedbeds of civic virtue": families support the political order by cultivating in their members those virtues necessary for participation in democratic self-government. This task is part of the process of social reproduction, or how society prepares persons to be capable, responsible members of communities and good citizens.

The idea that families are—or should be—seedbeds of civic virtue has a long history, but that does not mean that it is clear. It raises a number of challenging puzzles. What is civic virtue? Is it related only to democratic self-government and public life, or also to personal self-government and private life? How do families foster civic virtue? By shaping children, or also by shaping adults? Do families, as systems of personal self-government, model and prepare members for democratic self-government? If so, for families to be seedbeds of civic virtue, should they be governed by strict democracy? Must the values and virtues taught in families be in harmony with, or congruent with, democratic values and virtues? Can families serve as schools of citizenship—or seedbeds of civic virtue—if there is injustice within families?

50

In this chapter, I examine calls to renew or revive families in order better to carry out their civic role. The idea of families as seedbeds of civic virtue suggests that families serve as places to nurture the growth and development of capacities, skills, and virtues important to democratic self-government. This image of cultivation also implies that families have the potential to cultivate virtues linked to becoming good people, which in turn may grow into virtues linked to becoming good citizens. But, as with gardening itself, such seeds may not take root and such growth may not occur.

I shall explain the basic claims of proponents of shoring up families, or "civil society-revivalists." Their appeals to fortify families usefully draw attention to the civic role assigned to families, but they have some serious limitations. One is their ambivalence about, or even hostility toward, autonomy and the related skill of reflecting critically upon tradition. Another is the link they seem to find between the assertion of rights to liberty and equality and the decline in civic virtue and the weakened condition of families. Another limitation is ambivalence about the place of sex equality in conceptions of civic virtue and the virtuous family. I argue that contemporary discussions of the civic role of families should attend to the history of sex inequality within the family and more firmly embrace a commitment to sex equality both as a basic civic virtue and as a principle relevant to the regulation of families.

To call for critical reflection on injustice and inequality within the family is not to be globally "antifamily," but instead to try to hold fast at once to the important idea of the civic role of families and to contemporary commitments to equality. How should a commitment to sex equality shape family life and governmental regulation of families? I offer an approach that recognizes government's interest in shaping the capacity of individuals and in promoting political values such as sex equality, but also counsels governmental restraint in light of commitments to toleration, freedom of intimate association, and parental liberty. It insists that sex equality is a political value that bears on family life, but it also refrains from insisting that government seek to bring about complete congruence between democratic values and those of family life.

## The Civil Society Proposition

The erosion or disappearance of civil society is a common diagnosis of what underlies all manner of discontent, disorder, and divisiveness in America. In the widely discussed article and subsequent book, *Bowling Alone*, Robert Putnam found evidence of the disappearance of civil society and loss of social capital in such phenomena as the decline of bowling leagues and of families eating dinner together.[1] Task forces on civil society warn that America faces serious problems of civic and moral decline: growing distrust of government, decreasing civic and political engagement, increasingly coarse and uncivil popular culture and politics, and growing economic inequality.[2]

Family "breakdown" is a key indicator of crisis.[3] For example, two task forces organized in the 1990s, the National Commission on Civic Renewal and the Council on Civil Society, both point to rates of divorce and nonmarital childbearing as evidence of a decline in America's civic health.[4] What is more, other institutions of civil society on which the family depends to support shared values—for example, neighborhoods—are also declining, so America faces a fraying "moral fabric" and a weakened "social ecology."[5]

Why does the supposed decline of civil society signal a crisis? What does it mean to call the institutions of civil society seedbeds of civic virtue? The Council on Civil Society explains: "the essential social task of civil society—families, neighborhood life, and the web of religious, economic, educational, and civic associations—is to foster competence and character in individuals, build social trust, and help children become good people and good citizens."[6] America's version of the democratic experiment, Mary Ann Glendon argues, "leaves it primarily up to families, local governments, schools, religious and workplace associations, and a host of other voluntary groups to teach and transmit republican virtues and skills from one generation to the next."[7] Glendon, like other civil society-revivalists, invokes *The Federalist*, No. 55, in which James Madison observes: "As there is a degree of depravity in mankind which requires a certain degree of circumspection and distrust, so there are other qualities in human nature which justify a certain portion of esteem and confidence. Republican government presupposes the existence of these qualities in a higher degree than any other form."[8]

Politicians also call for the revival of civil society. In the 1990s, First Lady Hillary Clinton called for building up civil society ("our churches, our families, our civic associations") in order to inculcate values in children.[9] President Bill Clinton proposed a strengthened civil society to address problems that government alone cannot solve.[10] Subsequently, President George W. Bush invoked the institutions of civil society—particularly, faith-based groups—as "armies of compassion" that government should enlist to solve difficult social problems, and tapped figures active in the civil society movement to launch his "faith-based" initiative.[11] The Bush Administration, as evidenced by the above-quoted address by Wade Horn, appeals to the family's civic role as one reason that government should support strong families by promoting "healthy marriages."[12]

The appeal to strengthen families is therefore part of a broader effort to renew, or revive, civil society.[13] But the family, civil society-revivalists stress, is the "first and most basic" seedbed, the "cradle of citizenship."[14] The Council on Civil Society declares that it is in the family that a child first learns, or fails to learn, the essential qualities necessary for governing the self: "honesty, trust, loyalty, cooperation, self-restraint, civility, compassion, personal responsibility, and respect for others."[15] Self-government, in other words, begins with governing the self.

To stop the erosion of civil society, civil society-revivalists argue, individuals, the myriad institutions of civil society, and all levels of government must commit themselves to renewing civil society.[16] Such renewal depends especially on strong families. The National Commission on Civic Renewal warns: "Our civic condition cannot be strong if our families remain weak." Thus, it recommends: "As a nation, we must commit ourselves to the proposition that every child should be raised in an intact two-parent family, whenever possible, and by one caring and competent adult at the least."[17] The Council on Civil Society urges that public policy at all levels "seek explicitly to recognize and protect marriage as a social institution," and exhorts nongovernmental organizations, especially "communities of faith," to create a "culture of marriage."[18] Civil society-revivalists urge legislators to consider reforming no-fault divorce laws through such measures as waiting periods, marital counseling, and covenant marriage, both to lower the divorce rate and to improve the quality of marriage.[19]

Reversing "family fragmentation" is civil society-revivalists' primary prescription for strengthening families, but not their only one. They also criticize parents' preoccupation with careers and with acquiring "more and more material things," and they admonish them to spend more time with their children and provide them with greater moral guidance.[20] Civil society-revivalists acknowledge that economic pressures require some parents to spend more time on the job. Thus, they exhort businesses and economic institutions to devise arrangements "to permit parents to spend more time with their children," and they call for governmental policies to support this goal.[21]

## What Caused the Erosion of Civil Society?

If the institutions of civil society—especially, families—are endangered, what are the causes of this decline? Civil society-revivalists often point to an imbalance between rights and responsibilities. Because the Founders took the seedbeds of virtue for granted, Glendon contends, they did not see a need for a Constitution that exacted virtue (for example, through a Bill of Duties or Responsibilities to complement the Bill of Rights). However, the ascent of "rights talk," with its focus on the individual, drives out attention to responsibility and to ensuring the vitality of the institutions of civil society.[22]

Liberal political philosophy is another supposed root of the crisis. Civil society-revivalists pose the question of whether "by some cruel paradox, liberalism is intrinsically inimical to some or all of the very qualities and institutions that it needs in order to survive."[23] For example, the virtue of liberal tolerance, taken too far, could be "lethal" to the seedbeds because it "slides all too easily into the sort of mandatory value neutrality that rules all talk of character and virtue out of bounds."[24] Moreover, civil society-revivalists attribute to liberal political philosophy (such as that of John Rawls) a conception of the "sovereignty of the self" and an "ethic of expressive individualism" that denies that persons are "intrinsically social beings, not autonomous creatures who are the source of their own meaning and perfection."[25]

How does an ethic of expressive individualism harm families? Whereas an earlier generation of parents, guided by an ethic of self-sacrifice, responsibility, and mutual obligation, would have stayed in unhappy marriages "for the sake of the children," today far fewer parents are willing to do so. Instead, civil society-revivalists contend, parents today treat marriage as a contract for personal fulfillment.[26] As one report, *A Nation of Spectators*, asks ominously: "Dare we continue to place adult self-gratification above the well-being of our children?"[27] Greater constitutional liberty with respect to intimate matters also reduces the area of collective moral judgment, thus encouraging "neutrality" about marriage and more protection for different forms of families.[28]

Another root of this ethic of expressive individualism is the civil rights movement of the 1960s and the cultural changes associated with that decade. For example, William Galston argues that, well into the 1950s, there was a dominant and effective traditional morality in which such virtues as self-restraint, self-reliance, and fidelity shaped family life. This cultural consensus rested on the dominance of white Anglo-Saxon Protestant men. The 1960s, he grants, properly brought challenges to some unjust aspects of this traditional morality, such as racial inequality and segregation, gender inequality within the household and workplace, and the marginal status of certain ethnic and religious groups. But alongside these legitimate challenges, he contends, the civil rights movement was "an inspirational metaphor" for "other aggrieved groups," opening a veritable Pandora's Box of challenges, in the name of "freedom, equality, and the recognition of legitimate differences," to all hierarchies and authority that formed part of traditional morality and cultural consensus.[29]

Some civil society-revivalists trace this impulse to question authority and assert rights to even earlier roots. James Q. Wilson views the 1960s as a radical expression of a "modernism" linked to the Enlightenment. This transformation entailed a shift away from traditional morality and "the fundamental virtues of daily life" to "extreme understandings of liberty and quality."[30] The Enlightenment redefinition of marriage from a sacramental and patriarchal relationship to an agreement between freely choosing, equal, rights-bearing adults, he contends, evolved into the idea of marriage as a negotiable contract, a relationship defined by the preferences of its members.[31]

These analyses trace the decline of civic virtue to the ascent of rights talk and, in particular, the introduction of notions of rights and entitlement into the family. They imply that treating husbands and wives as equal, rights-bearing individuals undermines the family stability that generates civic virtue. I will challenge such diagnoses after examining the history of the idea of the civic role of families.

## Marriage as a Model of Democratic Self-Government

For the Founders, the marital family was a metaphor for and model of democratic self-government. In her book *Public Vows*, historian Nancy Cott reveals that, from the Founding onward, American political theory and practice have harbored the assumption that the health of the nation depended upon the successful establishment of marriage in a particular form: monogamous, Christian, heterosexual marriage. Paradoxically, the Founders viewed this hierarchical, asymmetrical relationship—in which the wife properly submitted to her husband's authority—as one of consent, not bondage, and as a model for a new nation based on consent.

Marriage was a "school of affection" and a foundation for national morality. Reflecting eighteenth-century assumptions about differences between the sexes, the Founders assumed that associating with women would "gentle" men, subdue their selfishness and egotism, and develop the qualities of the "heart" and good manners that undergird the social virtues.[32]

Marriage constituted men and women as responsible, gendered citizens and had dramatically different impacts on their capacities for citizenship and self-government. It expanded men's capacity for citizenship by imbuing husbands with the role of head of household and (until the Nineteenth Amendment recognized women's right to vote) the political representative of the family. Historian Hendrik Hartog observes: "Being a householder . . . was a foundation for republican political virtue. As the caretaker of a wife, children, and servants, a man became the sovereign of a domain, able to meet with other rulers and to participate with them in government." A man's failure to establish himself as a successful husband was "a disaster, a source of overwhelming shame."[33]

In the political theory of the Founders, married women fulfilled their civic obligations—and fostered civic virtue—by serving their husbands and children, even as they were denied personal self-government within marriage and equal citizenship in the polity. Historian Linda Kerber refers to this civic role as "republican mother-hood."[34] The colonies, and later the states, adopted common law rules of coverture: a system of family governance under which wives were under various legal disabilities excluding them from participation in the economic, civic, and political spheres and in which men had au-thority over wives' bodies, property, and freedom of movement. These disabilities rendered married women less free than single women, for example, to make contracts, own and manage property, or earn a living. The colonists' rejection of hierarchy and insistence upon equality in politics did not extend to rejection of these rules of family governance. All free women, married or unmarried, lacked the right to participate formally in democratic self-government.[35] Furthermore, among the deprivations of liberty forced on African Americans held in slavery was the denial of legal access to marriage and of protection of family life.[36]

An important root of the link between marriage and the state was the "commonwealth model of marriage," found in the Anglican the-ological tradition. In this tradition, John Witte explains, marriage had a formative dimension: its "definition and discharge of duties was es-sential for civic order, liberty, and rule of law."[37] In the marital com-monwealth, the husband was the "head" (the defender, protector, and teacher of the family), and the wife owed the husband obedience and service. Certain British accounts of marriage as a commonwealth ar-gued that the hierarchy of the family (under the rule of the "paterfa-milias") was replicated in the political hierarchy of the state (under the king). But American political thought sided more with John Locke's vision of the model, which denied any natural or necessary link between the domestic and political commonwealths, and also re-interpreted the "conjugal society" between husband and wife in terms of a contract, or voluntary agreement. Although Locke's vison stressed the freedom of the marital contract and greater equality of husband and wife than did other models of marriage, he also appealed to a biblical norm of marriage as a hierarchy with the wife subject to the husband's authority.

By the nineteenth century, the ideal of the "republican family" no longer made explicit appeal to patriarchal authority, but preserved the husband's authority through elaborating a model of separate spheres, and roles and responsibilities, for husbands and wives. Popular legal treatises defined marriage as furthering civil and social purposes premised on distinct sex roles. Historian Michael Grossberg observes: "by charging homes with the vital responsibility of molding the private virtue necessary for republicanism to flourish, the new nation greatly enhanced the importance of women's family duties."[38]

Early feminists protested this system of domestic relations, which assigned women the role of generating virtue but denied them personal self-government and full citizenship. Feminists sought a right to "co-sovereignty" within the marriage relation and a woman's right to her own person, as well as a right to political representation through the right to vote.[39] An early plea to repudiate patriarchy in the home, and not just in politics, was Abigail Adams's letters to her husband, statesman John Adams, urging: "Do not put such unlimited power into the hands of Husbands."[40] Feminists from Mary Wollstonecraft to those who drafted the Seneca Falls Declaration condemned the legally-enforced subjection of women within families to male governance and sought greater equality within marriage.[41] Such feminists questioned how families could generate virtue and model democratic self-government if they denied women full citizenship. John Stuart Mill and Harriet Taylor Mill famously criticized marriage as a "school of despotism" because of the unjust power that marriage laws accorded husbands over wives; they contended that "the family, justly constituted," would be "the real school of the virtues of freedom."[42]

Feminists found important parallels between the denials of self-government in slavery and those in marriage, and the abolition movement spurred feminist arguments for civil and human rights. Both opponents and defenders of slavery linked the institution of slavery with the institution of marriage as systems of domestic relations.[43] The "Enlightenment tradition," Witte argues, sought to retain the goods and goals of marriage, but to "purge the traditional household and community of its excessive paternalism, patriarchy, and prudishness, and thus to render the ideal structure and purpose of marriage a greater reality for all."[44]

One significant reform was a move away from the idea of marital unity—and of the family as "an organic part of the body politic"—to the legal concept of the family as "a collection of separate legal individuals."[45] And yet, Grossberg argues, "partial capacity" continued to be the central reality of women's place in nineteenth-century family law. Husbands' patriarchal authority yielded to the authority of judges, who awarded wives and children legal powers based on judicial discretion. Furthermore, even as Married Women's Property Acts eliminated aspects of a husband's legal right of control over his wife's property, they did not eliminate the other elements of the marital contract, such as the wife's duty to obey and provide domestic service.

Some family reformers warned that women's rights threatened both the family and the republic. As one opponent of women's suffrage argued, "the greatest danger to American society is, that we are rapidly becoming a nation of isolated individuals, without family ties or affections. The family has already been much weakened, and is fast disappearing;" when the "family goes, the nation goes too."[46] Opponents of expanding women's rights appealed both to nature and to divine mandate.

Emancipation of the slaves and the Reconstruction Amendments left in place male "headship" within marriage. Indeed, Cott explains that, as the Freedmen's Bureau worked to establish marriage among former slaves, "policing and reforming freed*men*, not freedwomen, was the bureau men's concern." Deeply rooted in American political thinking was "the presumed conjunction of marriage, property-owning, household headship, and male citizenship."[47] Thus, as with freed slaves, when immigrants became citizens, federal law and policy sought to bring them within the embrace of this preferred model of marriage, on the rationale that marriage would civilize and properly constitute male citizens as productive, responsible heads of households. As the national campaigns against Mormonism (because of polygamy) and the "civilization" programs aimed at Native Americans illustrate, an additional impulse was to free women from the despotism and degradation assumed to flow from alternative forms of family life.[48]

In 1920, women gained the right to vote (upon passage of the Nineteenth Amendment), and husbands were no longer the political representatives of households. Still, public policy and the culture often manifested a marked ambivalence about women's citizenship and held to the conviction that marriage and motherhood were women's destiny. For example, in 1961, the U.S. Supreme Court upheld Florida's inclusion of men but exemption of women on the jury list (unless they volunteered) as a reasonable classification in light of the fact that "woman is still regarded as the center of home and family life."[49] In this twentieth-century version of domesticity, despite women's increasing participation in the labor force, the prevalent model of marriage retained the husband's role as primary provider and the wife's as his dependent.[50] Moreover, the family law of many states still allocated to husbands, as head of household, the right to govern the family and its resources in ways that denied wives the personal self-government that feminists had long sought.[51]

## Sex Equality as a Political and Constitutional Value

Since the 1960s, public understandings of both marriage and women's citizenship have undergone a significant transformation. This transformation establishes sex equality as an important public value and constitutional principle, and signals a shift from marriage as a hierarchical relationship, premised on gender complementarity, to one of mutual self-government, premised on gender equality. It should inform contemporary appeals to families as seedbeds of civic virtue.

Beginning in the 1970s, federal constitutional equality norms, emerging out of a series of Equal Protection challenges to state and federal laws brought by feminist litigators (led by now Supreme Court Justice Ruth Bader Ginsburg), have put limits on government's authority to perpetuate traditional gender roles in family life. The U.S. Supreme Court struck down sex-based classifications in family law— concerning such things as employee benefits, alimony, and child support—that would perpetuate the gendered dyad of male breadwinner/ female dependent and caregiver. For example, in Orr v. Orr, in striking down a statute requiring only men to pay alimony, the Court observed that the requirement was part of a larger statutory scheme (reflecting wives' common law disabilities) "which invidiously discriminated against women, removing them from the world of work and property and 'compensating' them by making their designated place 'secure.' "[52] In Stanton v. Stanton, in striking down a state law requiring parental support obligations of sons until age 21, but of daughters only until age 18, the Court stated: "[n]o longer is the female destined solely for the home and the rearing of the family, and only the male for the marketplace and the world of ideas."[53]

As Laurence Tribe has observed of the laws invalidated in such cases: "All either prevented, or economically discouraged, departures from 'traditional' sex roles, freezing biology into social destiny. And government's almost uniform argument in justification of these laws emphasized the economy achieved by the accurate and therefore 'rational' assumption of traditional male and female inclinations and capacities."[54] The Supreme Court came to take a more skeptical view toward claims that men's and women's different capacities justified different roles in such domains as family life, employment, and civic life. Under this heightened scrutiny, when government regulates, it may not simply reinforce "archaic stereotypes" about the sexes, and may not use sex-based classifications without an "exceedingly persuasive justification."[55]

In the wake of these constitutional changes, states to a significant degree have repudiated the patriarchal model of family governance and revised their laws about rights and responsibilities within marriage to apply equally to husbands and wives.[56] Moreover, beginning with the enactment of Title VII and other civil rights acts of the 1960s, Congress has affirmatively legislated to prohibit public and private discrimination on the basis of sex in many spheres of life—such as education, employment, and housing—in which assumptions about women's capacities and family responsibilities have hindered their opportunities.

The emergence of sex equality as a public value and constitutional principle shapes family roles and responsibilities. It precludes states from requiring or supporting a patriarchal form of family governance. As noted in Chapter 1, in Planned Parenthood v. Casey, the Supreme Court made clear that our constitutional order no longer permits states to grant husbands the type of authority over their wives' bodies and decisions that an earlier regime of family law permitted them.[57]

## What Room for Sex Equality in Families and Civic Virtue?

Contemporary discussions of the civic role of families should reflect critically upon this history of inequality and upon the emergence of sex equality as a principle of family law and constitutional law. In identifying sex equality as among the "core" set of principles, virtues, and values that exemplify and undergird our constitutional democracy, I follow the method of proponents of civic education who look to fundamental texts such as the Declaration of Independence and the

Constitution, and to historical understandings, to identify the content of political values.[58] "Equality" is among that core set of principles, virtues, and values.[59] Sex equality, however, often receives insufficient attention or, at best, an ambivalent embrace.[60]

The better approach would be to state explicitly that a commitment to antisubordination and to women's equal citizenship is a core public value and civic virtue, as reflected in federal constitutional and statutory norms, transformations in family law, and state antidiscrimination laws. Central to the story of the emergence of sex equality as a public value and constitutional principle was "dissident citizenship"[61]— women on the margins challenging structures of power in the polity and claiming rights and equal status based on a core set of national commitments. Such "dissident citizenship," evident in both the abolitionist and suffrage movements, brought about a critical transformation of women's subordinate legal and social status in light of critical reflection on the demands of those national commitments.[62] Women's unequal status and men's unjust power within the family were also targets of feminist reform.[63]

Questioning authority and hierarchy, critically reflecting on tradition, and demanding rights played vital parts in repudiating women's unequal citizenship. Many calls to revive civil society seem to long for a time when virtue was more abundant and claims of rights were less strident. Some civil society-revivalists contend that they do not want to "roll back the clock" or "reverse the gains made by women and minorities."[64] Nonetheless, when they favorably compare strong and stable families of earlier generations to families today, this history of inequality receives scant attention. For example, civil society-revivalists often point out the special role women have played in the moral education of children and in preparing them for citizenship, as well as through volunteer work in their communities.[65] But they fail to reckon with the puzzle about how women served as generators of civic virtue even as they were denied "co-sovereignty" within the home, and to ponder whether their lack of formal political rights encouraged such volunteer work.

Civil society-revivalists' diagnoses of why contemporary families are in crisis similarly fail to consider the problems posed by inequality in such families. Indeed, David Blankenhorn explains that those who seek to shore up families "assume that the family is a good thing," and he practically equates raising such issues as whether family structure "promotes inequality" or "oppresses women" as making a case that "the family is a bad thing."[66] Moreover, the agendas that various civil society task forces formulate to strengthen families do not include such items as family violence and women's disproportionate responsibility for household labor and caregiving—the very targets of feminist critique.[67]

So, too, linking the decline of families—as well as of civil society more broadly—to a proliferation of rights claims and challenges to authority may overlook the fact that assertion of rights is a necessary correction to forms of family governance that have hindered individual capacity. As Michael Schudson argues in *The Good Citizen,* "there can be too much trust as well as too little": the levels of trust in the 1950s and the early 1960s "surely reflected a moment of unusual consensus in American life held together by Cold War paranoia, middle-class complacency, postwar affluence, and the continuing denial of a voice in public life to women and minorities." The "rights-regarding citizen" often appealed to "common American traditions of liberty and equality, in many cases from the point of view of the people who had been left out of the founders' compact." The civil rights efforts of Rosa Parks, for example, redefined rather than rejected community and demonstrated "that community's premise was one of inequality and inhumanity."[68]

I have focused on just one aspect of this inequality: the coexistence of sex inequality with the idea that families generate civic virtue and model democratic self-government. However, as Rogers Smith argues in *Civic Ideals,* the history of U.S. citizenship laws is "shot through with forms of second-class citizenship, denying personal liberties and opportunities for political participation to most of the adult population on the basis of race, ethnicity, gender, and even religion."[69] Well into the twentieth century, the laws of some states banned interracial marriage, and state courts upheld such laws as means "to preserve the racial integrity" of their citizens and prevent "a mongrel breed of citizens."[70] Given the link between marriage and good citizenship, bans on intermarriage also served to mark certain immigrant groups as "unassimilable and unfit for citizenship."[71] These problems of racism, sexism, and nativism were not marginal, unfortunate elements of history that can be easily removed (like a weed among the seedbeds).

They challenge the very notion of a more virtuous past, to which the present compares unfavorably.[72] The story of "We the People" is both one of exclusion and gradual inclusion of the excluded, along with the gradual extension of the obligations and privileges of citizenship.[73] This unfolding story makes the virtue of critical reflection all the more important. It is to that I now turn.

## A Fresh Start: Families and Civic Virtue

With this history of the family as a model for self-government and the emergence of sex equality as a public value in mind, let us make a fresh start in examining the claims of civil society-revivalists that the family is the "cradle of citizenship." What does this claim mean? How and under what conditions do families create good citizens?

To begin with, what is civic virtue? Does it relate only to democratic self-government, or also to personal self-government? Are civic virtues distinct from or closely related to personal virtues? If virtue (etymologically) connotes excellence, then *civic* virtue implies excellence in carrying out the role of citizen.[74] Civic virtue encompasses the set of qualities of character, skills, and dispositions that are necessary for democratic self-government. Civic education, then, should focus on cultivating this set so that persons can be competent and responsible citizens in our constitutional democracy.[75] Some accounts of the "preconditions of active citizenship" focus more broadly on fostering important dimensions of personal as well as democratic self-government. For example, Stephen Macedo argues that liberal political institutions should promote "the capacities and dispositions conducive to thoughtful participation in the activities of modern politics and civil society."[76]

These narrower and broader definitions raise the question of whether there is a set of virtues identifiable as *civic* virtues, which characterize the ideal of a good citizen, distinct from the set of virtues characterizing the ideal of the good person. Some declare that "civic virtue is distinct from those virtues that are relevant to private or personal lives."[77] In this view, although personal and civic virtues may overlap, the distinct domain of "civic" virtue includes those dispositions and commitments that "enable the political process to work effectively to promote the common good" and "contribute to the realization of the fundamental ideals of the American political system including protection of the rights of the individual."[78] A political leader might possess civic virtue, so defined, but lack personal virtue because of marital infidelity. Similarly, political liberalism distinguishes between, on the one hand, civic or political virtues and, on the other hand, personal virtues or virtues that characterize "ways of life" and relate to forms of associational life such as families.[79]

By contrast, civil society-revivalists typically view the virtues of the good person as being closely linked to the virtues of the good citizen. Thus, virtues important for personal self-government, or governing the self, form the foundation for democratic self-government. This continuity is suggested by the characterization of families as "foundational sources of competence, character, and citizenship," as well as the claim that among civil society's "essential" tasks is the duty to "help children become good people and good citizens."[80] Moreover, such continuity is evident in the slippage from talk of families as "seedbeds of civic virtue" to talk of them simply as "seedbeds of virtue."[81] *A Nation of Spectators* contends that the defense of liberty requires "the modest but vital virtues of loving parents, faithful spouses, good neighbors, law-abiding citizens, and sober patriots."[82] In this view, just as a president who was a good father and grandfather presumably would possess the civic virtue needed to be a good president, a president who failed to honor his marital vows would not.

These different approaches to the content of civic virtue may mask underlying points of convergence. The literal meaning of "seedbed" suggests that families may be a place or source of the growth and development of a wide range of human capacities, including skills, attitudes, and virtues.[83] These capacities by no means relate exclusively or even primarily to democratic self-government as distinguished from personal self-government. Rather than viewing these two forms of self-government as requiring two wholly distinct set of capacities, it is more plausible to imagine that there is spillover between the domains in which such capacities are useful and significant overlap in the skills, attitudes, and virtues helpful to each.

This approach to families as "seedbeds" does not insist that the good person and the good citizen are one and the same. Rather, there is no sharp discontinuity between the capacities and virtues required for personal self-government and those required for democratic self-government.[84] For example, political liberalism, which seems to assume discontinuity between virtues of personal self-government and those of democratic self-government, expects some degree of continuity, or congruence, between the domain of civil society and that of the political. Experiences in families and other institutions of civil society, Rawls posits, will generate support for political principles, public values, and civic virtues such as reciprocity. Principles of justice shape the domain of civil society. In turn, the institutions of civil society are a "fund of implicitly shared ideas and principles" that make possible an overlapping consensus on a shared political conception of justice.[85]

Thus, both civil society-revivalists and political liberals expect that formative experiences within the family help generate attitudes and dispositions—such as trust and empathy—that may bear fruit in civic and political participation.[86] However, the idea of seedbeds also implies that there are no guarantees either that seeds will be planted or that, once planted, they will take root and grow.

A practical illustration will elaborate my interpretation of the image of families as "seedbeds." During the Clinton Administration, the White House convened a conference to consider "strategies for raising responsible and resourceful youth."[87] A report by the Council of Economic Advisers found that "parental involvement" was a "major influence" in helping teenagers avoid risky, harmful behavior—such as smoking, alcohol and drug use, early sexual involvement, violence, and suicide attempts—and in "increasing educational achievement and expected attainment." The report stressed two aspects of parental involvement: (1) the practice of eating dinner together as a family, and (2) teenagers' "feeling 'close' to their mother and/or father."[88]

How do these two forms of parental involvement foster a teenager's capacity for self-government? Do they promote civic virtue? The family meal may be an important time when family relationships are nourished. Notably, in cataloging the loss of social capital, Putnam reports that the evening meal, a "traditionally important form of family connectedness," is in dramatic decline among married Americans.[89] Does eating dinner together strengthen good citizenship? Some civil society-revivalists argue that "table talk," or conversation at the family meal, is a resource for countering America's individualist public rhetoric and renewing civil society. How so? Such talk, Glendon argues, includes "recollection and retelling of the family's concrete experiences, and . . . the household's fund of stories about relationships, obligations, and the long-term consequences of present acts and decisions," as well as "dialogues about freedom and responsibility, individual and community, present and future."[90] So conceived, table talk seems to pertain at least as much to nurturing qualities relevant to personal self-government and to building family solidarity as to fostering civic virtue and a broader sense of social solidarity and citizenship.

How does a close parent-teen relationship foster civic virtue? The benefits to teenagers from "feeling 'close'" to a parent, mentioned in the report, like those from the family dinner, relate to important areas of personal self-government, such as negotiating sexual relationships, not harming one's body or mental development, developing one's intellectual capacities, and finding one's own path in life.[91] Social science research bears out the importance of a secure attachment to parents to children's learning to "govern the self," exploring and choosing life directions, and achieving success in life.[92] Indeed, "close and satisfying relationships" between adolescents and parents appear to be significant for positive outcomes at school and at home, regardless of family form.[93]

But a close parent-teen relationship does not, in and of itself, vouchsafe good citizenship. A role of families is to provide children, and other dependents, with the care and nurture that are indispensable to survival and human development. Such caregiving may not directly foster children's civic virtue. But in laying the foundation for children's development of their capacities for democratic and personal self-government, it indirectly fosters civic life.

The best interpretation of the idea that families are seedbeds of civic virtue is that families are places of moral learning that may create the good person and may contribute to creating the good citizen. Families may nurture capacities, or virtues, vital to personal self-government that may also grow into virtues important to democratic self-government. Or they may not. I shall offer two examples of important moral learning that may take place in families: (1) fostering the capacity for autonomy, which may contribute to such civic skills as critical reflection and the civic virtue of respect for diversity, and (2) fostering the capacity for empathy, which may lay a foundation for the civic virtue of reciprocity. The first example illustrates that those who agree that families have a civic role may differ on precisely what capacities families should promote. The second raises the practical problem that personal virtue may not always spill over into civic virtue, and introduces the feminist argument that certain systems of family governance may hinder the development of civic virtue.

## From Autonomy to Critical Reflection

Developing the capacity for autonomy is a core part of becoming a responsible, self-governing person. Like many liberal theorists, I contend that this capacity—and the related skill of critical reflection—are important for both personal and democratic self-government.[94] In linking civic and moral decline and family breakdown to extreme understandings of liberal autonomy and the "sovereignty of the self," some civil society-revivalists pose a sharp tension between autonomy and respect for authority. They stress that teaching respect for authority and tradition helps persons learn to "govern the self" and become good citizens. Thus, schools should reinforce the moral lessons taught at home, and teach respect for teachers' authority, as well as for ideals and history.[95] Implicitly, civil society-revivalists seem skeptical of the value of the skill of critical reflection; or, as Galston's critique of the 1960s suggests, they fear that an impulse to reflect critically upon tradition may lead to an indiscriminate attack on all forms of authority and hierarchy.

But need this tension between cultivating respect for authority and cultivating the capacity for autonomy be so sharp? Families play a vital role in cultivating both of these capacities, or dispositions, albeit at different stages of a child's life. William Damon's *The Moral Child* synthesizes available research and offers a model of how children's morality develops in their early years. He claims:

> The child's respect for [parents'] authority is the single most important moral legacy that comes out of the child's relations with the parent. . . . [It] sets the direction for civilized participation in the social order when the child later begins assuming the rights and responsibilities of full citizenship.[96]

Thus far, Damon's claim echoes accounts of civic virtue that stress the place of families in teaching respect for authority. However, there is a "natural developmental progression in the way that children think about adult authority": as they get older, children have a growing sense of equality in relationships, and they reflect on such matters as the legitimacy of authority and the rationale for obedience to it; they finally come to see authority as a "consensual" relation that serves the interest of all who participate in it.[97] This developmental idea resonates with political philosopher Amy Gutmann's argument that democratic education should foster "critical deliberation" because "[c]hildren will eventually need the capacity for rational deliberation to make hard choices in situations where . . . authorities do not supply clear or consistent guidance."[98]

Families and schools would best foster children's growing capacity and development of virtues and values, Damon argues, through affording contexts in which moral learning takes place through "respectful engagement," between the child and others, in a "web of participation, observation, and interpretation."[99] In effect, autonomy develops in the context of relationships. Damon cautions that it is a myth that "moral education means telling children about the values held by our society and the virtues expected of them."[100] Focusing on the work of William Bennett, a prominent civil society-revivalist as well as former secretary of the Department of Education, Damon worries that Bennett's emphasis on moral habit rather than on moral reflection and conscious decision making may be "so misguided as to present a threat to the very democratic traditions that he professes to cherish."[101] Accounts of civic education similarly distinguish between "indoctrination" and education that "enables citizens to make wise choices" among alternatives and to make a "reasoned commitment" to the values and principles undergirding a "free society."[102]

Fostering children's capacities for self-government should cultivate not only respect for authority but also autonomy and critical reflection. There is both a place for respect for tradition (for example, America's civic ideals) and legitimate political authority, and a place for critical reflection (for example, upon historical and contemporary failures to live up to such ideals).[103] Critical reflection is especially apt in considering the history of the idea of the family as a site for generating civic virtue.

But what if some parents believe that cultivating autonomy and critical reflection in their children will impede inculcating their belief systems in their children? In his "parentalist manifesto," legal scholar

Stephen Gilles asserts: "Many people think a child gradually achieves true autonomy by making choices and acting well within a belief system that the child's parents adhere to and instruct the child to accept as true."[104] In response to the argument that "uncritical" education stunts children's capacity for critical deliberation, Gilles counters that "religious and traditionalist parents can with equal reason reply that critical education deprives them of the capacity for faithful allegiance to a tradition."[105]

This "parentalist manifesto" highlights a difficult dilemma: should parents have unfettered authority to shape children in their own image, or may government through such means as public schools treat children as "independent persons-in-the-making with their own basic interests and their own lives to lead"?[106] My approach rejects such unfettered parental authority, focusing on the capacity of each individual member of a family, and accepts the dual authority of parents and schools to nurture children's capacities. Parents educate children about what it means to be part of a particular way of life; schools, through cultivating skills of critical reflection and perspective-taking, help children learn that there are other ways of life deserving of respect, laying a foundation for civic virtues like toleration.[107] In this view, family and schools are complementary, or compensatory, domains of moral learning: thus, even if families do not cultivate some qualities that enable good citizenship, schools may do so.[108]

"Parentalist" approaches like that of Gilles reject this dual scheme, questioning government's authority, through schools, to cultivate critical reflection as a component of civic virtue. They resemble Galston's argument that, to protect "the right to live unexamined as well as examined lives," parents may require "bulwarks" against "the corrosive influence of modernist skepticism" in the public education system.[109] However, Galston accepts a governmental educational mission to cultivate a core set of civic commitments and competencies, particularly because there is no guarantee that families will "reinforce liberal democratic virtues and beliefs."[110] By contrast, Gilles is skeptical that agreement on such a core is possible, and he contends that parents alone should decide the content of the civic virtue to be instilled in children, as long as they do not have "unreasonable" views.[111]

In what sense are such "parentalist" families "seedbeds of civic virtue"? To be sure, a commitment to individual rights entails that citizens may use their rights "to protect or advance the different ways of life they cherish," which may be in tension with important "liberal democratic ideals of character."[112] For example, many parents, Gilles contends, hold a view that "a private life that places little emphasis on citizenship" (but honors the legal obligations of citizens) is a good life and wish to teach these values to their children.[113] However, to argue further that government does not have authority to attempt to foster in children a different conception of civic virtue and good citizenship seems to encourage a form of radical pluralism that ill equips children for thoughtful and informed democratic participation.

## From Empathy to Reciprocity

Described as among the "core" moral emotions, empathy means "reacting to another's feelings with an emotional response that is similar to the other's feelings."[114] Damon notes that, as children develop their capacity for empathy, they learn that "every person's perspective is unique and that someone else may have a different reaction to a situation than onself." This cognitive skill is "perspective-taking." In late childhood, children's feelings of empathy expand from attention to the feelings of particular persons to include "the general conditions in which unfortunate people sometimes must live," which may lead children to engage in charitable and altruistic behavior and eventually shape their political views.[115]

Perspective-taking may make a crucial contribution to the capacity for personal self-government. Being able to imagine and understand other persons' ways of life, beliefs, and values may help people better appreciate their own as well as decide among different available ways of life.[116] It is also a skill linked to good citizenship: being able to take the perspective of others helps a person to acquire civic virtues such as toleration and mutual respect and to exercise the civic duties of civility and cooperation.

How do families foster empathy? Mutual respect between parents and children may nurture a "generalized respect for all other people."[117] Also, secure and stable ties of affection within a family may promote sociability as well as reciprocity, that is, a sense of engagement in a common enterprise and a willingness to bear one's fair share of burdens and to help each other.[118]

Empathy and reciprocity among family members may spill over into a more generalized reciprocity, shaping how persons deal with each other in the broader polity. "Generalized reciprocity," according to Putnam, is the "touchstone of social capital" and a norm so "fundamental to civilized life that all prominent moral codes have some equivalent of the Golden Rule."[119] Reciprocity is also an important civic virtue.[120] For example, Susan Moller Okin notes that Rawls's account of moral development in *A Theory of Justice* suggests the importance of a child's experience of loving parents as laying the foundation for the development of a person's "capacity for fellow feeling" and for "ties of friendship and mutual trust." Eventually, these experiences of association provide the groundwork for developing the virtue of reciprocity and for forming an attachment to the principles of justice themselves.[121]

This beneficial spillover from family life to political life, however, is not inevitable. The specific reciprocity cultivated by close family relationships may not grow into a general form that encompasses persons outside the family. In some close families, parents may teach children prejudicial and intolerant attitudes toward outsiders who differ. Parents may be distrustful of the outside world and may inculcate attitudes in children that leave them, as adults, unable to "establish enough trust outside the family" to form friendships.[122] It would seem, to use Putnam's terms, that such families may foster "bonding" (or exclusive) social capital, but not the sort of "bridging" (inclusive) social capital that can generate broader identities and reciprocity.[123] Parents who teach the superiority of their own ethnic, religious, or racial group, for example, may fail to inculcate in their children a broader sense of empathy and reciprocity. Remember the throngs of angry white parents, held back by federal marshals, shouting at Ruby Bridges when she, as a young black girl, attended a formerly all-white elementary school ordered to be integrated by a federal court.[124]

Another possible obstacle to cultivating reciprocity is that systems of family self-governance may model inequality rather than reciprocity and fairness. For example, even though the majority of men and women agree that responsibility for household labor should be shared, women continue to bear a disproportionate responsibility for caregiving and household work within families, whether or not women participate in the paid labor force.[125] This inequality has costs for both men and women (as I elaborate in Chapter 3). Moreover, the stronger association of men with the provider role often fosters inequality by yielding them more power and respect within the household.[126] Okin asks: if families are "not environments in which justice is normally practiced, work equally shared, and people treated with equal dignity and respect," then how will children be able to develop a sense of justice and of virtues such as empathy and reciprocity?[127] The continuing problem of domestic violence warrants the analogous question. Unjust family environments that model male entitlement and female subservience may hinder the development of empathy that Damon argues is vital to moral learning. Why? For children reared by a father and mother, the household may be their first model of how two people with a socially salient difference interact with each other. By contrast, if sex equality is a "fundamental norm" in the household, children are "surely less likely to grow into the habit of understanding differences such as those of race or ethnicity as reasons for unequal or disrespectful treatment."[128]

Damon's account of moral development suggests another feminist argument. As children mature, they learn to assess issues of legitimate authority and of "the social rationale for systems of leadership and followership."[129] If a family's internal governance features the male as head of the household, children within such families may come to believe that sex inequality is both prevalent and acceptable within society. This model of hierarchy may appear to legitimate other forms of hierarchy based on difference rather than mutual respect.

For these reasons, it is plausible that an egalitarian family in which roles and responsibilities are divided more equally would be an environment more favorable to developing civic virtue. For one thing, by rejecting gender hierarchy, it would better model equal opportunity for girls and boys. For another, it would better foster women's equal opportunity and be fairer and more just.[130] Thus, sex equality, as an organizing principle of family life, would benefit both adults and children and would enhance their capacities for personal self-government as well as for citizenship.

## "Bad Seeds" and the "Logic of Congruence"

Families may foster personal virtues important to being a good family member but may not nurture civic virtues essential to being a good citizen. What if families, rather than serving as seedbeds of virtue, plant "bad seeds" or are seedbeds of vices such as inequality, parochialism, prejudice, and intolerance? They might produce neither good persons nor good citizens. Just as the idea that families are seedbeds of virtue has a long history, so does the fear that the private orientation of families will encourage private rather than public good.[131]

The practical problem that families may sow "bad seeds" arises with respect to other institutions of civil society as well. This problem raises the question of "congruence": should (indeed, must) the internal structures and norms of families and other forms of associations be democratic in order to support political democracy?[132] In contemporary political appeals to families as a place of civic education, Nancy Rosenblum argues, the "logic of congruence" assumes a particular psychological dynamic: "just families create citizens with specific democratic capacities and dispositions that spill over from private to social and public spheres."[133] But if families must take a specific form, or inculcate a particular set of civic virtues and values, in order to fulfill this civic role, should government seek to achieve congruence by regulating families? Should it support only those families that instill and sustain democratic values, and should it weed out those that do not?

These are difficult questions. Indeed, commentators on civil society are in sharp conflict over "congruence."[134] This conflict stems in part from the tension between two distinct political roles served by families: (1) fostering civic virtue and (2) preserving diversity against a standardizing state. Commitment to both roles may require some hard choices about the proper scope of governmental regulation. The conflict also derives from different answers to challenging empirical questions: Are early experiences decisive for adult life? Do attitudes and dispositions developed in families spill over into other domains of life, such as political life? Is any one formative context—whether the family, the school, or other institutions of civil society—the only place to cultivate certain dispositions, capacities, and values?[135]

Civil society-revivalists recognize that not all families foster civic virtue. They warn that many parents fall short in the moral education of their children. However, they use the (heterosexual) marital family as the best proxy for the form of family most likely to teach "governing the self" and to foster virtues. They argue that divorce thwarts families' capacity to serve this role because it impairs the sense of per-

manence and trust children need in order to develop such personal virtues as trust and reciprocity.[136] By contrast, Okin's feminist argument is that it is not a marital family as such—but a just one—that is most likely to serve as a seedbed.

## Ambivalence about Sex Equality in "Private" Life

Why do civil society-revivalists hold back from a robust and clear affirmation of the principle of sex equality as important to families' roles as seedbeds of civic virtue? Their ambivalence about sex equality finds echoes in the broader culture as well as in discussions of civic virtue. One reason for this ambivalence appears to be wariness about the domain of sex equality. People may accept the idea that sex equality is an appropriate public value, but believe that its domain does not extend to "private" life (the family).

A leading work on civic education, *CIVITAS: A Framework for Civic Education*, illustrates this public/private distinction. To its credit, in discussing "Gender Issues," this work includes a history of women's exclusion from formal political life, women's activism, how beliefs about different male and female natures were thought to justify different roles, and social and legal changes in women's status. Although *CIVITAS* identifies "equality" as a "fundamental value," and among those civic commitments that comprise civic virtue, it does not refer to sex equality. Instead, it lists as "controversies for the 1990s" a series of "gender issues," such as wage inequality, job segregation, women's disproportionate role in child care, and their low number of leadership positions in government and the military.[137] These issues raise "open political questions," owing to "underlying disagreements about deeply held values, especially views about the proper roles for women and men in society." *CIVITAS* reports: "most Americans recognize questions of fairness in the treatment of both women and men as an important part of their values," but "[m]any Americans are wary of the fundamental changes in institutions that are demanded by advocates who wish to provide men and women with complete equality in every sphere of life."[138] This reported wariness informs other works on civic education, which distinguish between aspects of sex equality as to which there is national consensus (for example, a principle of antidiscrimination "in the sense of equal treatment, at least in the public sphere") and those as to which there is more cultural ambivalence (for example, challenging traditional gender-specific roles for men and women in the family and the market).[139]

Is this ambivalence about the domain of sex equality justified? Just as there is no easy recourse to a public/private schematic to render "private" life immune from governmental regulation, such a schematic is inadequate to delineate the domain of sex equality. Sex equality already reaches into families, or "private" life: contemporary family law repudiates coverture and replaces sex-linked duties with equal rights and responsibilities held by men and women in marriages. Constitutional norms prohibit governments from establishing or promoting families premised on gender hierarchy. Laws prohibiting domestic violence and marital rape repudiate husbands' historical authority over wives and signal a public interest in eliminating "private" abuse. In regulating and supporting families, government should do so in a way that rejects fixed gender roles within marriage and honors sex equality. As feminist scholar Mary Anne Case observes, it would pose serious constitutional problems for public officials, eager to champion "traditional family structures," to declare, "Welcome to Cobb County, Where a Woman's Place is in the Home."[140]

## Promoting Sex Equality within Families

Because sex equality is a public value and a component of civic virtue, government may and should promote it. But what are the limits to promoting sex equality in family life? Constitutional norms prohibit government from promoting an unequal division of labor and authority in the home and in the broader society. But what if men and women nonetheless choose to adopt such a family form? "However equalized men and women may be in the public sphere," argues Kathleen Sullivan, "at home women may still choose to be ladies."[141] More precisely, Martha Nussbaum argues that "it is wrong for the state to mandate the equal division of domestic labor or equal decision making in the household." In this view, "it just seems an intolerable infringement of liberty for the state to get involved in dictating how people do their dishes."[142]

Does government have an interest in how husbands and wives divide responsibility for decision making and for market and domestic labor, and in how they teach their children about gender? What if parents socialize children concerning appropriate gender roles in ways that may reinforce sexism and stereotypes of masculinity and femininity, thereby shaping children's development of their capacities? Do these matters of family life bear upon personal self-government and, ultimately, democratic self-government in ways that would warrant governmental action?

If there is merit to the feminist argument that just families are more conducive to fostering civic virtue, does it follow that government should mandate that families be egalitarian or, at least, encourage them to be so? Government, for example, does not mandate that families be antiracist, even though a commitment to racial equality is a core civic virtue. One critical response to Okin's call for egalitarian families, as well as to my assertion that sex equality is a public value relevant to family life, is to pose, as a reductio ad absurdum, the challenge: Surely you are not suggesting that government should dictate who does the dishes? The prospect of police searching the "sacred precincts" of the kitchen for "telltale signs" of an unequal division of labor calls to mind Griswold v. Connecticut's image of police searching "the sacred precincts of marital bedrooms for telltale signs of the use of contraceptives."[143]

Responding to this challenge requires considering the interplay of governmental action and restraint and determining whether there need be congruence between democratic and family forms. First, government does indeed have an interest in who does the dishes, given that patterns of inequality and inequity in the home may shape both adults' and children's capacities for and opportunities for self-government. Although there is reason to be cautious about the "logic of congruence"—the assumption that just families produce just citizens—it seems a plausible inference that families in which systematic sex inequality persists are less likely to foster important civic virtues like reciprocity and mutual respect than are more egalitarian families. Because families nurture capacities important to personal self-government—whether or not these ripen into civic virtues—gender inequality and injustice within families may hinder them from fostering those capacities, such as autonomy and empathy. Thus, there is reason for concern about such inequality and injustice, quite apart from the family's civic role.

I am not proposing, however, that government mandate an equal division of labor within the home—or dictate who does the dishes—in order to compel congruence between democratic and family norms. One of the historical wrongs of marriage regulation was that the laws structuring marriage did, in effect, mandate an unequal division of household labor and authority that severely constrained women's capacities for democratic and personal self-government and reinforced men's prominence in the political, economic, and social spheres. This division reflected an orthodoxy about women's and men's proper roles. A legal framework of equal rights and responsibilities rectifies this imbalance by according respect to individual moral capacity, but also leaving room for individuals to make choices about how to structure their own family life.

Second, toleration in such matters as intimate association, freedom of religion, and parental autonomy requires some limit on government mandating how to structure the daily details of family life. Such a governmental role would intrude too deeply into both spatial privacy and decisional liberty. Even as ardent a supporter of egalitarian families as Okin concluded that toleration, and a pluralism of beliefs about gender roles within families, should restrain government from compelling families to adopt an egalitarian division of labor.[144] Moreover, inegalitarian families may not cultivate the civic virtue of sex equality, but may still foster other goods and virtues and have value for their members.

This commitment to toleration does not preclude government from adopting an array of affirmative governmental measures other than coercion to foster equality within families and, within the broader society, to support women's and men's equal moral capacity and responsibility. For example, public education campaigns against domestic violence may help to repudiate ideas that a man is entitled to use such violence to control other family members or that violence in the home is a "private" matter immune from prosecution.[145]

Government could adopt laws and policies that create incentives for and remove obstacles to both fathers and mothers investing in caregiving and market labor. Such governmental measures are appropriate, as Nussbaum observes, because "rethinking the division of labor in the family is a crucial aspect of guaranteeing women's full equality as citizens."[146] For example, public policies aimed at systemic change could help with the dilemma faced by individual women who "value their intimate . . . associations with men, but wish they could take place on a more level field," yet avoid open conflict over equality because of the costs of such conflict.[147] The Family and Medical Leave Act is a good start, but it has not sufficiently addressed the structural problems that prolong gender inequity in the home and the market. New legislation that provided wage replacement, not merely unpaid leave, might address the problem that far fewer men than women take leave in part because the economically rational decision is to have the lower earning parent (usually, the mother) do so.[148]

Government should address other workplace practices as well as the many laws and policies (such as social security and tax laws) that continue to make it more "rational" for women—and not men—to invest in uncompensated homemaking rather than wage earning.[149] This sort of governmental initiative is in line with Rawls's proposal, in response to Okin's critique, that government should aim at a "social condition" in which the "involuntary division of labor" in the family is "reduced to zero," but should tolerate any remaining "voluntary" divisions of labor. Rawls also argued: "If a basic . . . cause of women's inequality is their greater share in the bearing, nurturing, and caring for children in the traditional division of labor within the family," political liberalism would support taking steps "to equalize their share, or to compensate them for it."[150] Beyond persuasive measures, government may also adopt ameliorative measures to value the contributions of the caregiver/homemaker and protect against economic vulnerability.[151] One example, used in many states' divorce laws, is to treat marriage as an economic partnership when courts decide support and property distribution issues in a divorce.

But there are limits to toleration, as argued in Chapter 1. Thus, if a religiously motivated family practice seriously impaired a child's development of her or his capacities, this would overcome the normal deference to parental authority and trigger a strong governmental interest in prevention, intervention, or amelioration.[152] Government could prevent certain parental family practices, motivated by convictions about women's proper role in society, that seriously hindered children from developing their capacities (for example, forbidding girls to attend school or arranging marriages for very young girls).[153] Government has a well-established *parens patriae* interest in children's well-being and healthy development,[154] enforceable through such means as abuse and neglect laws. Just as toleration should not extend to "unreasonable" world views that "assert the right to a mode of life involving serfdom or slavery" or require "the repression or degradation of certain persons on, say, racial, or ethnic, or perfectionistic grounds," it should not extend to systems of family governance that would replicate coverture and deny women and girls their basic rights and liberties as citizens.[155] For example, if religious groups seek enforcement, in civil courts, of their own religious laws concerning family, marriage, and divorce, this action may conflict with family law's commitments to gender equality.[156] For less drastic family practices, government could rely on ameliorative measures, such as civic education and vigorous enforcement of equal opportunity and antidiscrimination laws.

Third, government should not attempt to enforce complete congruence between democratic and family norms because families are not the sole incubators of civic virtue. Government itself may promote, in other domains, important civic virtues and public values, including sex equality. Governmental institutions have an important complementary, or compensatory, role in fostering civic virtues and promoting public values that families and other institutions of civil society may neglect or even reject.[157]

Citizens within civil society need to be civilized by the state: civil society, in an important sense, is "society 'civilized' by state action."[158] Government properly inculcates civic virtue, in the sense of inculcating the disposition to care about, and the capacity to deliberate about, the common good of the polity, not just about the good of forms of associations within civil society. Thus, it is reasonable to view civil rights laws concerning prohibiting discrimination on the basis of sex, race, and other grounds in spheres of civil society, like the workplace, as a way not only to shape conduct but also to promote a disposition not to discriminate and to teach that good citizens do not discriminate in certain dealings with others. Nancy Rosenblum observes: "these policies produce and enforce congruence—public norms of fairness and equality and due process—throughout society."[159]

Another way that government carries out its formative process is through education of children in common public schools, and, if parents choose private schools, ensuring that such schools teach "certain studies plainly essential to good citizenship."[160] Civil society-revivalists consider schools another seedbed of virtue, one that should foster "the knowledge, skills, and virtues our young people need to become good democratic citizens."[161] Schools may, as they suggest, reinforce lessons learned at home. However, when lessons at home are "incongruent with public principles of justice," schools may be a "preferred supplement and corrective."[162] Schools may offer a distinct domain conducive to certain forms of moral learning that will help nurture personal and civic virtues.[163]

Schools (including private schools) should foster sex equality and impart literacy about sex equality as a component of civic education.[164] Promoting sex equality should include cultivating certain skills and dispositions as well as norms, such as equal opportunity and the idea that one's sex is irrelevant to one's ability to contribute to society. Curricula with these messages might help to counter forms of gender role socialization in the home and the broader culture, and thus "eliminate differences" in boys' and girls' basic liberties and opportunities.[165] One might argue (as parentalist Gilles does) that a required curriculum fostering gender equality would violate a commitment to liberal pluralism, since many traditions teach that women and men have different roles and stations in life.[166] But a commitment to sex equality—and the political principle that equal respect for women's and men's moral capacities repudiates governmental regulation that would assign women and men different roles and stations in life—is not merely one sectarian norm battling others, but a public value and constitutional principle.

Undeniably, contemporary conflicts have arisen over the meaning and scope of commitments to sex equality. Thus, "constitutional literacy" should include teaching not only about the history of the exclusion of people on the basis of race, religion, ethnicity, and gender, but also about contemporary conflicts over what abstract constitutional principles such as equality mean in practice.[167] The very fact that understandings of sex equality evolve over time cautions against a hard governmental line that there is only one way to embody sex equality in families. This seems especially appropriate in light of ongoing cultural exploration of appropriate family roles, and the persistence of some form of division of labor along gender lines.

Fourth, an important reason to encourage, but not compel, congruence stems from the vital role played by institutions of civil society—

including families—as buffers against state power. Some scholars praise such institutions as protecting pluralism and "multiple sites of sovereignty."[168] Whatever zeal one might have in enlisting government to bring about egalitarian families, it is prudent to be wary of using governmental power to enforce orthodoxies about family life. Governmental campaigns on behalf of marriage have excluded many families from equal respect and subjected many families to intrusive governmental control.[169] In an imperfect democracy, the institutions of civil society can serve as "enclaves of protected discourse and action," where "counterpublics" can work out and nurture alternative conceptions of self, community, and justice.[170] Families may function as such enclaves. For example, African American families feel the need to socialize their children both to fit into the surrounding majority culture and to develop an oppositional consciousness that will protect them against discrimination and prejudice.[171] Also, lacking social and (in most states) legal validation of their intimate lives, gay men and lesbians must actively construct their family models and family values.[172]

A final reason for caution about government mandating that families be egalitarian stems from difficult empirical questions concerning the formative effects of family life on children and adults and their spillover into other parts of life. Just as Rosenblum finds that the formative effects of associational life are more "indeterminate" than proponents of reviving civil society have acknowledged, a similar caution may be appropriate in the case of families.[173] In thinking about the civic role of families, she helpfully poses the questions: "What can individuals get *only* in childhood and *only* at home?" She contends, for example, that "incongruent families" are not "fatal to democratic education if we credit the formative effects of other institutions in civil society."[174]

Furthermore, humility about the ability of parents to shape their children is in order. Public discourse tends to "go to extremes" about families, assuming either that family structure alone wholly determines a child's fate, or that parents have almost no impact on their children's development, with peers exerting a far more important influence.[175] The truth surely lies somewhere in the middle.

On the one hand, even parents in an egalitarian marriage who consciously seek to inculcate in their children a belief in gender equality cannot ensure that their children will accept this belief. For peers' beliefs about gender differences and gender-differentiated roles powerfully influence children.[176] On the other hand, even parents who fear and reject such values as autonomy may nonetheless provide the emotional support and nurture that lay the groundwork for children's future autonomy. As Meira Levinson contends, as long as children "are able to acquire from elsewhere the further capacities and habits of thought required for autonomy," such family nurture will advance their development.[177]

Will exposure to gender injustice lead girls (and women) to adapt their preferences, internalizing and accepting such injustice as the normal or natural course of affairs? Or might children, recognizing this injustice, seek equality and justice if and when they form their own families?[178] An important variable is the formative role of other institutions of civil society and the public culture. The impact of family hierarchy may be quite different in a society that reinforces such hierarchy than in one that counters messages of inequality by a commitment to the basic rights, liberties, and equal opportunities of women and men. For example, women raised in a household with a traditional division of labor may come, through participation in associations and public institutions, to a revised self-understanding. They may seek to reconstruct or exit from unjust family relationships.[179] These examples suggest that "for at least some dispositions, capacities, and values no single formative context is determinative and that one social experience can compensate for the deprivations and depredations of another."[180]

## Conclusion

The idea that families are seedbeds of civic virtue has a useful kernel of truth: families are a vital site for nurture and moral learning that foster the capacities for personal self-government and lay a foundation for democratic self-government. But calls to revive civil society do not adequately grapple with the history of sex inequality within families and in the broader society as well. Moreover, they take too dim a view of the place of autonomy and the skill of critical reflection in forming good people and good citizens. The idea of families as seedbeds of civic virtue should reflect contemporary principles of justice and equality. Government should promote equality but should not insist on complete congruence between democratic and family life. For families are not the sole incubators of civic virtue, and government has a proper role in civilizing civil society. The challenge is not only to hold onto the important idea that families play a generative role in nurturing children and in supporting the political order, but also to embrace more equality within and among families.

# ℘ 3

## *Care, Families, and Self-Government*

> More than any message [on welfare reform], . . . we hear that paid work
> is the only activity . . . that positions one as a "responsible" person. But
> many . . . [f]athers and mothers, middle-class and less privileged people
> argue that the work of caring for children and other kin is valuable work.
> Poor parents, however, face this unpaid, unrecognized work without some
> basic resources. . . . The kind of responsibility of tending to people who
> need your care is without mention or value in the policy debate, but it is
> the glue that keeps low-income families from falling apart. Who will take
> over this work when those who have been doing it leave for minimum-
> wage jobs that do not support the children left behind?
> ℘ *Lisa Dodson,* Don't Call Us Out of Name

> It's time to honor and reward people who work hard and play by the
> rules. . . . No one who works full time and has children at home should be
> poor anymore. No one who can work should be able to stay on welfare
> forever. We can provide opportunity, demand responsibility, and
> end welfare as we know it.
> ℘ *Bill Clinton and Al Gore,* Putting People First

𝒲HOSE RESPONSIBILITY IS IT to provide care for chil-
dren and other dependents? Is it solely the personal responsibility of
families, or is there also a public responsibility? If it is primarily the
responsibility of families, does society have any obligations to provide
the resources to help them do so? In this chapter, I explore the place
of families in performing a vital part of social reproduction: caring for
family members and preparing them to take their place as capable,
responsible, self-governing members of society. That society counts
on families to perform this task is evident in the connection made, in

rhetoric about families, between "strong, healthy families" and a "strong America."[1] But what is the underlying understanding—indeed, social contract—regarding the respective responsibilities of families and the public?

The quoted statements that begin this chapter offer different perspectives on this question. Both focus on the relationship between responsibility and resources. The first statement resists a conception of personal responsibility linking it exclusively to engaging in paid work and leaving out the work of social reproduction. It calls for public responsibility to help families provide care.

A different understanding of the social contract informs the second statement. In the 1992 presidential campaign, candidates Bill Clinton and Al Gore promised to reward people who "played by the rules." In this contract, the fundamental responsibility to be exercised by parents is to engage in market labor that will enable them to provide care for their children. That market labor does not by itself ensure the actual care of children (and almost by definition requires that someone else engage in such care) is beside the point. Here, responsibility for caring for children—or paying for the care of children—resides in the individual family. What government promises is that working families should not be poor families.

The welfare reform of 1996, the Personal Responsibility and Work Opportunity Reconciliation Act (PRWORA), proposed by Republican lawmakers and signed by President Clinton, was primarily concerned with moving poor people from welfare as a "way of life" to work and independence. The goal of this legislation was freedom from dependency on government. Indeed, in the legislative debates and public discourse surrounding the enactment of PRWORA, which replaced the Aid to Families with Dependent Children program with the Temporary Assistance for Needy Families program (TANF), politicians stressed the need to free the poor from a "web of dependency" and bring them into line with mainstream American values of personal responsibility: like working families, welfare families should not expect others to help them provide for their children.

As Congress debated the reauthorization of PRWORA during the Bush Administration, once again the rhetoric of "working toward independence" (as the Bush Administration expressed it) through participation in market labor rendered invisible the vital role of unpaid care work within families and any public responsibility to support it.[2] But there was also a subtle, yet significant, shift in rhetoric about the social contract. Lawmakers espoused a model of "supporting work" to help move families to "independence" from government.

My approach to the place of families in our political order questions the near-exclusive focus on "supporting work," that is, wage work, as exhausting public responsibility to families and on equating personal responsibility with market participation, without attending to the other responsibilities adults must discharge. That focus obscures the important work that families do in social reproduction and the vital role of care in fostering human capacities and social capital. I argue for recognizing care as a public value and for public responsibility to support care. This chapter will focus on two contexts where concern for this public value should inform public policy: welfare policy and the so-called work/family or work/life conflict.

By work/family conflict, I mean the dilemma that many workers experience: a tension between the demands of paid work and the responsibilities of family life. There is a gap between their aspirations for a balance between family life and work and their actual circumstances.[3] One consequence is the "care crisis": many families cannot fully provide for the care needs of their members, either by personally giving such care or by obtaining appropriate substitute care, and they lack adequate public supports for care.[4] The plight of low-income parents, including those making the transition from "welfare to work," is the most acute manifestation of the crisis.

Resolving this care crisis requires moving beyond a framework that conceives public responsibility to families primarily in terms of helping parents obtain access to child care as a "work support." The idea of "supporting work," in the sense of contributing to families' economic security, is important. Such governmental efforts could facilitate adults' needs for satisfying employment and help parents acquire economic resources to provide for their families. But a further necessary move is to recognize that care is not merely a work support to improve market participation, but is a public value because of its place in social reproduction. In other words, another component of the social contract should be supporting this dimension of family work.

Glimmers of a richer notion of personal responsibility appear in another theme in public discourse about families: being a parent is an important job and makes a vital contribution to society, and government should therefore support parents' efforts to balance the demands of paid work and family. Ironically, calls to move mothers "from welfare to work" have accompanied bipartisan calls to strengthen families by supporting "responsible fatherhood"—that is, fathering that entails not only financial support but also active involvement in children's lives.

In this chapter, I first explain the fundamental role of care in fostering individuals' capacities for self-government and healthy development. I argue for public responsibility to support care as a public value. Grounding my argument in liberal and feminist ideals, I also draw on, but reconstruct, civic republican ideals of independence and social citizenship in order to enable care as well as employment. I explain the "care crisis," focusing on its disproportionate effect on low-income families. I situate the care crisis in the context of women's historical responsibility for caregiving, which I call the "gendered care economy." I highlight women's continuing disproportionate responsibility (both as unpaid and paid caregivers) for caregiving and the costs of this system for children, parents, employers, and society as a whole. I call for an approach to care that moves from the gendered division of labor for care to a redistribution of responsibility between women and men, and among families, employers, and government. Studying the needs of families as they move from "welfare to work" as well as the broader problem of work/family conflict suggests convergence on some helpful orienting ideas about a new approach to family and public responsibility for care.

## Care as a Public Value

What is care? Why is it important? Care is fundamental to forming the capacities, or capabilities, of children and adults.[5] In *Care and Equality*, Mona Harrington proposes that "to assure good care to all members of the society should become a primary principle of our common life, along with the assurance of liberty, equality, and justice."[6] Conceived in this way, care not only is necessary for human survival but also is a precondition for civic and democratic life. Calling for a "care movement," Deborah Stone states: "Caring for each other is the most basic form of civic participation. We learn to care in families, and we enlarge our communities of concern as we mature. Caring is the essential democratic act, the prerequisite to voting, joining associations, attending meetings, holding office and all the other ways we sustain democracy."[7]

The idea of recognizing and supporting care as a public value clearly casts a wide net. As Berenice Fisher and Joan Tronto explain, caring includes not only attitudes, such as caring about, but also practices, such as taking care of and caregiving.[8] This chapter focuses on the place of families in caring for children, or what I refer to as social reproduction—the task of nurturing children and ensuring their moral development and education in order to prepare them to be responsible, self-governing persons. Such "reproductive labor," as John Rawls puts it, is "socially necessary labor," because it helps society to continue over time. Thus, "a central role of the family is to arrange in a reasonable and effective way the raising of and caring for children, ensuring their moral development and education into the wider culture." Society depends on families to nurture "a sense of justice and the political virtues that support political and social institutions."[9] This latter role was the subject of Chapter 2.

Society also depends on families to provide care to meet basic human needs and dependencies. Within families, it has assigned that task primarily to women, who disproportionately perform this work. All human societies face what Martha Fineman calls "inevitable dependencies"—that is, dependency that "flows from the status and situation of being a child and often accompanies aging, illness, or disability." Our legal system, she contends, assigns responsibility for this work to the "private" institution of the family, and, within the family, women are expected to be the caretakers and they are in fact. Caretakers themselves experience "derivative dependency"; that is, they need "some social structure to provide the means to care for others," and they may become economically vulnerable by devoting time to care work instead of paid work.[10]

A dilemma arises: even though society depends on caregiving work to produce persons capable of taking their place in society as employees, taxpayers, spouses, parents, friends, and citizens, it does not highly value care itself, and government does not adequately support caregiving work. Moreover, paid caregiving work (also performed disproportionately by women) is among the lowest paid forms of work.

Feminist scholars Paula England and Nancy Folbre argue that "the time, money, and care that parents devote to the development of children's capabilities creates an important public good." A "public good," a concept in economic theory, is a good that is difficult to put a price on because "someone can enjoy it without paying for it." This gives rise to the problem that individuals can "free ride" on the efforts of parents, and mothers in particular, who bear the costs of this socially necessary labor.[11] So, too, society receives an "unacknowledged subsidy" when it relies on the social contribution made by paid caregivers, but does not pay them commensurate with their skills or the value of their work.[12] To remedy this problem, Fineman argues, a more just social contract would recognize these forms of subsidy provided by caregivers and support caregiving labor.[13]

What is the best framework to ensure that families (and other institutions of civil society) carry out the vital task of social reproduction and that families (and, within them, women) do not unjustly bear the burdens of this task? Just as governmental action and restraint are complementary dimensions of how government helps develop the capacity of individuals, so both governmental action and restraint are necessary to help families engage in nurturing the capacities of family members. Families have a special—though not exclusive—role to play in fostering the capacities of children. Thus, an important dimension of governmental restraint is evident in constitutional law's allocating to parents a fundamental right—and responsibility—for the care, education, and upbringing of their children.[14] But my approach to government's formative project also posits an affirmative governmental responsibility to support care as a component of social reproduction. I draw on political liberalism's premise that cooperating members of a well-ordered society possess certain basic capacities for democratic and personal self-government and a just society has a responsibility to provide the basic, or primary, goods necessary to develop those capacities.[15] Cogent feminist analysis by Eva Kittay and others helpfully reveals that primary goods should include the needs of citizens for caregiving as well as the needs of citizens with significant obligations for caring for dependents.[16] Embracing care as a public value that should inform public policy, as well as public conversations about the place of families, is an important step toward promoting governmental responsibility.[17]

It is inaccurate to think of the family as "independent" of the state, since law sets the boundaries of what constitutes a family, of what are parental rights and responsibilities, and of what state interests justify intervening in family life.[18] Nor is it helpful to regard the family as "independent" in the sense of being a self-sufficient unit of caregiving meriting no support by government or other institutions of civil society. Indeed, such a notion of "independence" represents a serious stumbling block to formulating a sound family policy, as the ongoing debates over welfare reform illustrate. Nonetheless, precisely because "independence" is among what Fineman refers to as our "foundational myths,"[19] it is important to consider whether it can be recast in a way that will be more supportive of care as a public value.

## Care, Republicanism, and "Social Citizenship"

To understand the contemporary appeal to "independence" as a goal of welfare policy, it is helpful to situate it in the broader tradition of civic republicanism. I argued in Chapter 1 that this tradition is a resource for the important idea that government has formative responsibilities to foster self-government. Another idea is that government should promote the political economy of citizenship—that is, the institutional and economic arrangements conducive to democratic self-government.[20] Civic republicanism is also an important root of the idea of "social citizenship"—that is, that individuals have rights to the economic preconditions for democratic citizenship.[21]

The republican tradition might appear to be singularly unhelpful for grounding a public value of care. This tradition vividly linked citizenship to independence, to political participation, to manhood, and to certain forms of "productive" work (for example, the yeoman farmer, the independent producer). The work of social reproduction— the role of families in caregiving, rearing children, and fostering capacities—is invisible in the republican glorification of work that fosters independence. For example, the focus of Michael Sandel's history of republicanism's approach to the political economy of citizenship is almost exclusively on the impact of market labor on democratic citizenship. The concern is for developing and protecting "manhood," and for producing independent businessmen rather than serfs, slaves, or cogs in a machine.[22]

This republican vision of independence and citizenship was exclu-
sionary on the basis of gender, as well as class and race.[23] The Founders linked work and citizenship, but "not all kinds of labor qualified
one for citizenship—certainly not slave labor nor the uncompensated
toil of women in their husbands' households."[24] As explained in
Chapter 2, even as this tradition viewed the work of social reproduction done in families by wives and mothers as necessary to generate
civic virtue and independent citizenship, it viewed women as lacking
the capacity for such citizenship.[25] Feminist critiques of the meanings
of dependency and independence show, for example, that certain forms
of dependency (that of wives on the financial support of husbands)
posed obstacles to citizenship, whereas others (the dependence of a
worker on an employer for wages) promoted "independent" citizenship.[26]

Nonetheless, I believe that the republican ideas of independence
and of the political economy of citizenship would be helpful if recon-
structed in light of feminist criticisms. The continuing allure of the
ideal of "independence," manifested so vividly in debates over welfare
policy, offers a good reason to work to reconstruct that ideal rather
than to abandon it. I will argue for two reconstructions. First, the
important link between work and citizenship warrants governmental
responsibility to play a facilitative role in helping women and men
achieve their aspirations for satisfying, decent work. Second, concern
for the political economy of citizenship should expand to include such
questions as what institutional arrangements are conducive to fostering
social reproduction and the caregiving necessary to that task.

## The Political Economy of Citizenship, Work, and the Care Crisis

Attention to the political economy of citizenship is relevant to analysis
of the new social contract of government supporting working families
in two important ways. The first way is republicanism's emphasis on
work as an avenue to independence and citizenship. This aspect of
republicanism, as legal historian William Forbath argues, is part of
America's forgotten "social citizenship" tradition—a tradition that
makes a powerful case against class inequality and argues for a right
to decent work.[27] This tradition indicts workplace conditions that rob
persons of a sense of self-determination and that treat them as fungible

and leave them at the mercy of decision-making structures in which they have no voice.[28] (One can readily apply the nineteenth century's rhetoric about the dangers of concentrated corporate power and its human cost to contemporary concerns over a lack of corporate accountability for the human cost of downsizing, taking jobs overseas, "outsourcing," and the like.)

How does the movement of former welfare recipients from "welfare to work" measure up against the ideals of work as fostering economic independence and good citizenship—ideals many of these workers espouse? Many low-income workers are still in poverty and are not working at "good jobs," that is, jobs that provide them health insurance or pension benefits or that enable them to earn enough to support themselves and their families.[29] Even in some of the much-heralded state programs that have moved mothers from welfare to work, a substantial proportion of former participants remain in poverty.[30]

The republican notion of work as promoting self-government and conferring dignity is belied by the practical realities of the daily struggles of women who have moved from the ranks of the welfare poor to join the millions of Americans among the working poor.[31] Detailing those struggles, Sharon Hays contends that even though politicians claimed that paid work would lead to independence, mothers have instead achieved merely the "*appearance* of independence": the realities of low-wage work leave this ideal out of reach. Furthermore, the rhetoric of "personal responsibility" seems to imply no public responsibility to remedy this problem or to create conditions for family stability.[32]

The appeal to "social citizenship" would accept the premise of the important link between work and citizenship, and would argue for a right to decent, satisfying work as a component of responsible self-government.[33] For example, the 2004 Democratic Party Platform linked opportunity to a "good job" ("good jobs that support families") and the "rewards" and "dignity" of work, and affirmed a governmental responsibility to create an environment conducive to producing such jobs.[34] Government could facilitate such work by redressing continuing forms of sex-based discrimination in the workplace (including sex segregation of jobs and unequal pay for equal work) that contribute to the disproportionate poverty of women in the workforce.

The work/family conflict experienced by many workers, but most acutely by low-income workers, highlights a second way in which the idea of the political economy of citizenship is relevant to formulating a new social contract: the notion of political economy should incorporate a concern for fostering social reproduction. Defining citizenship primarily in terms of paid employment and independence misses the importance of caregiving as a form of social contribution.[35] If the republican tradition puts a high value on citizens' possession of certain competencies and capacities, it should likewise put a high value on caring for children to enable them to develop such competencies and capacities. If the current structure of the workplace and institutional arrangements for care are not conducive to fostering the "independence" of adults, or the successful nurture of children, this should warrant concern. Such a redirected focus invites attention not only to the relationship between resources and persons' capacity for personal responsibility, but also to public responsibility to develop capacity.

Revising the idea of the political economy of citizenship along these lines would remedy an important limitation in the social citizenship tradition: its inattention to the gendered economy of care, that is, women's disproportionate responsibility for caregiving, and how this responsibility limited their full participation in the labor market and their access to forms of economic security tied to employment.[36] A feminist conception of social citizenship would posit governmental responsibility to facilitate women's and men's participation in paid employment and in family work.[37]

## The Care Crisis

This revised view of the political economy of citizenship could help to address the care crisis. One root of the crisis is the transformation of women's roles in the gendered care economy. In the industrial era, the care arrangement in the United States was a male breadwinner/female caregiver model (more norm than fact for some families). Today, that traditional family no longer reflects the actual practice of the majority of American families. Women's increased participation in the labor force has markedly changed the structure of family life, particularly the need for child-care providers. The majority of married households have two parents in the paid workforce (at least part time), and the custodial parent in the majority of single-parent families is in the paid workforce.[38] And yet, as Harrington argues, "we have not devised any equality-respecting system to replace the full-time care-taking labor force of women at home."[39]

Work/family conflict ensues because this transformation in women's roles has not spurred a comparable transformation in men's roles, in the workplace, and in governmental policies. In their recent book, *The Time Divide*, Jerry Jacobs and Kathleen Gerson report that most workers seek a balance between paid work and family life, a balance that eludes them. The authors identify a mismatch between workers' aspirations and their workplace options. At one end of the spectrum are well-paid jobs demanding excessive time commitments that leave little time for family life; at the other end are low-paying jobs that fail to offer enough hours or income to meet workers' needs. Although workplaces offer "family-friendly" policies, and women and men would prefer a more flexible balance between home and the workplace, workers intuit that "any time they take for family pursuits will under-mine their credibility as committed workers and exact a heavy price in the long run." And women, who feel more pressure than men to attend to family, are more likely to make those sacrifices (what Ann Crittenden calls "the price of motherhood").[40]

Intensifying work/family conflict is the lack of adequate substitute child care. For parents to be successful workers in the market, safe, affordable, and high-quality child care is a critical resource, but the need for such child care exceeds the supply. An alarming percentage of child-care facilities are inadequate when measured against this benchmark. And those facilities that offer high-quality, developmen-tally appropriate care are too expensive for many families without em-ployer or governmental subsidies.[41]

The care crisis stems in part from the fact that society devalues paid caregiving. Research indicates that providing high-quality child care depends on a skilled and stable child-care workforce. However, even the most skilled child-care workers receive low wages, and the child-care workforce is characterized by low earnings, poor benefits, unequal opportunity, and high turnover. Child-care workers are a large sub-group among the working poor. Moreover, such workers, many of them mothers, often cannot afford quality child care for their own children. Ironically, as a component of "welfare to work" programs, more than half the states have initiatives to move welfare recipients into jobs as paid child-care workers. However, because these programs do not emphasize the skills training and education needed to prepare workers for better paying child-care jobs, such work is unlikely to be a path to self-sufficiency. One legacy of the gendered division of labor is the assumption that any woman can engage in care work. This, along with a lack of adequate regulation or licensing of much care work, contributes both to quality problems and to the devaluation of caregiving as a skilled profession.[42]

The care crisis disproportionately burdens parents who work in low-income jobs, a fact that is of considerable relevance to the "welfare to work" mandate of PRWORA. Child-care problems have been a major reason that poor mothers are not in the paid labor force in the first place, and they often are a serious obstacle for former welfare recipients who must find and hold onto paid work. Many low-income jobs fail to afford workers the financial resources to make safe and developmentally appropriate arrangements for the care of their children. Many families who are eligible for governmental assistance with child care do not receive it or cannot use it because of a lack of adequate facilities. And the terms and conditions of many low-income jobs (for example, unusual hours) make the task of finding such child care especially difficult, if not impossible. Finally, workers' child-care problems impose costs on employers, such as absenteeism, turnover, and billions of dollars of lost productivity.[43]

Pursuing a career and sustaining a healthy family life pose challenges to all working parents, but "[f]or families in the bottom third of the economy, . . . the challenge of maintaining a job and raising a family rises to the level of a daily crisis."[44] Indeed, in one study, the parents in low-wage jobs, employers, and teacher and child-care providers surveyed all agreed that "It's just not working": they identified "an entrenched mismatch between the imperatives of raising families and keeping jobs in low-income America" and described "intractable conflicts at the most basic level between the safety, survival, and education of children and their parents' ability to keep any kind of employment."[45]

These intractable conflicts impose costs on parents' capacities to direct their own lives, to provide for their children through market work, and to fulfill their responsibility to nurture, care for, and support their children. Failure to address this tension constructively also imposes costs on children. First, there is the cost of parents being un-available, because of work schedules, to care for their children, attend parent-teacher conferences, help with homework, and keep children safe and on the right path. Many a former welfare recipient has been torn between feeling positive about her employment setting a good example for her children and her concerns about not being there for her children.[46] When mothers have to leave their children in inade-quate child care or risk sanctions, children's cognitive and social de-velopment, safety, and overall well-being suffer.[47] Assessing the poor quality of child care available in their impoverished neighborhoods, some mothers "decide that the best way to protect their children is to keep them home, teach them how to make grilled cheese sandwiches, dial 911, and operate the dead bolt locks on the door."[48]

The care crisis therefore imposes costs on family life. Mothers' paid employment often benefits women and their children, but certain kinds of low-income jobs that former welfare recipients take may be detrimental to the quality of children's home life and to the quality of the parent-child relationship.[49] Adolescents, in particular, experience negative consequences when their mothers move from welfare to work. One possible reason for this negative effect is that, in a parent's absence, some of them assume the burden of care for siblings; another reason may be the lack of parental supervision or quality substitute care during critical after-school hours when adolescents most com-monly get into trouble.[50] Some children are simply left to care for themselves, putting them at risk for injuries and developmental prob-lems.[51]

If the republican ideal of fostering responsible self-government has any continuing hold, these costs for families warrant concern. Indeed, they should be a rallying point for insisting on a public commitment to address this tension between care and employment. How might such a commitment inform ongoing debates about how best to pro-mote family and child well-being?

## Child Well-Being and "Supporting Work"

To what extent does the new social contract of "supporting work" embody a commitment to social citizenship of the sort I urge? A prominent theme in debates over reauthorizing the Temporary Assistance for Needy Families program (the component of PRWORA that replaced Aid to Families with Dependent Children) is that mere reduction in the rolls of welfare recipients is not the sole measure of success. Instead, the focus should be on poverty reduction and on the well-being of children. But how should government pursue these goals?

The idea behind supporting "working families," rather than supporting "welfare," is that government gives such families various forms of assistance (ranging from job training and education to subsidies for child care, health care, transportation, the Earned Income Tax Credit, and the like) to help them out of poverty.[52] This conception of government's role is a significant shift from the one permeating debate over PRWORA itself: that welfare recipients were irresponsible and out of line with working families because working families did not expect any outside support for their families. By contrast, the idea of "supporting work" is that parents who manifest their personal responsibility by working deserve public support of their efforts. The rhetoric of "working toward independence" implies that this assistance should be temporary, since the ultimate goal remains independence from public subsidy. More progressive versions of this new social contract speak of reorienting social policy around a principle of support for low-wage workers: "No American family with a full-time worker should live in poverty," explains the Progressive Policy Institute (echoing a familiar trope from the Clinton era), and, as the 2004 Democratic Party Platform declared, "the dream of the middle class should belong to all Americans willing to work for it."[53] Why? When society requires people to work (as does PRWORA), and thus honor an important moral principle of contributing to society, it incurs a responsibility to help people work and to make work pay.

Both the conservative and progressive versions of the social contract have similar flaws: paid work is the only form of social contribution, of dignified labor, that merits support. Moreover, child well-being features primarily in discussing the provision of child care as a "work support." For example, the Bush Administration's own proposal for reauthorizing TANF would make improving the "well-being" of children its "overarching purpose." Child care, the proposal explains, furthers this goal and also is an "important work support" for low-income parents.[54] The Bush Administration notes the role of "quality child care" in promoting early childhood development and literacy skills.[55]

Yet nowhere does parental caregiving feature as a vital component in promoting child well-being. Nor does the plan for "working toward independence" include any policy initiatives to help low-income parents work toward independence and care for their own children. The Progressive Policy Institute's "blueprint" for TANF similarly omits such matters.[56]

Failure to recognize the importance of care as a form of family work leads to proposals that are likely to hinder, rather than foster, this component of child well-being. Thus, to address lingering poverty, the Bush Administration urged an increase from a 30-hour (for single-parent families) and 35-hour (for two-parent families) to a 40-hour weekly work requirement. Why? Because "these families should be engaged in a full workweek of activities," that is, engaged in "work and other constructive activities leading to self-sufficiency."[57] Invisible in this approach is the idea of nurturing one's own children as a "constructive" or time-consuming activity leading to their healthy development. Because family work involves time away from market work, it does not directly foster the caregivers' economic self-sufficiency.

Thus, the new social contract of "supporting work" omits care from the discussion of how to foster family and child well-being. Government's formative responsibilities should include both supporting "working" families, in the sense of facilitating market labor, and supporting the "work" of families, in the sense of creating persons capable of self-government. Government should provide the resources and facilitate the institutional restructuring necessary for both of these forms of work. Public policy should recognize and promote care as a public value, but should do so in ways that do not replicate the inequality and injustice of the gendered care economy that has characterized much of this nation's history. As a useful preface to my proposed alternative approach, I present a brief history of the gendered economy of care and of shifting notions of the social contract underlying welfare. I then turn to the costs of the contemporary forms of the gendered care economy and offer an approach that seeks to reduce these costs.

## The Gendered Care Economy

Throughout American history women have had a close association with caregiving. Under the law of coverture, the marriage contract delineated wives' duty to provide domestic services in exchange for their husbands' protection and economic support.[58] As discussed in Chapter 2, ideals of republican motherhood held that women fulfilled their civic obligations by serving their husbands and children; this role excluded them from certain obligations and privileges of citizenship. The ideology of separate spheres (and the "cult of True Womanhood") reinforced women's association with this role responsibility and legitimated women's exclusion from the market, politics, and public life.[59] Even late into the twentieth century, laws and policies invoked women's maternal role and caregiving responsibilities as justification for their exclusion from employment and certain aspects of civic life.[60] As the U.S. Supreme Court recently observed: "the history of the many state laws limiting women's employment opportunities is chronicled in—and, until relatively recently, was sanctioned by—this Court's own opinions."[61]

In its challenge to women's inequality within the family, the early feminist movement demanded that household labor be deemed "work" warranting compensation and that wives (rather than husbands) have a right to their own earnings from market work.[62] However, even into the present day, an array of policies and entitlement programs has reinforced and encouraged the breadwinner/caregiver division of labor and penalized married women for participating in the paid workforce. By regarding women's unpaid household work not as value-producing labor, but as an expression of affection, or a "labor of love," legal rules including the federal tax code exclude it from the benefits and protections linked to other value-producing labor.[63]

Women creatively expanded the separate sphere and the ideal of True Womanhood. Women's organizations claimed the mantle of motherhood as justification for attempting to improve society, influence policy, and gain suffrage. Their philanthropic work was a veritable "shadow government," engaging in the nurturing, life-sustaining work that "government" might otherwise neglect.[64] Even as women were formally excluded from politics, their organized efforts, or "municipal housekeeping," bore fruit in legislative enactment of such "maternalist" measures as mothers' pensions and protective labor legislation.[65]

But the ideology of separate spheres and the romanticizing of women's maternal role inaptly describe the historical experience of some women, most acutely, African American women and poor women. Enslaved African American women suffered harm to their family integrity from forced separations and lack of legal protection for their families, as well as from contributing "care" to white children (as well as to children born to them as a result of their being raped by slave masters). After emancipation, many African American women continued to engage in "caregiving" as domestics. Thus, both during and after the slavery era, the domestic labor of black women contributed to the social reproduction of white families, at a cost to their own families.[66] As Dorothy Roberts points out, far from valuing the domestic labor such women could contribute—as housewives—to caring for their own families and to maintaining their own homes, politicians warned against allowing such "idleness" and adopted policies aimed to secure their labor in the fields and in the homes of others.[67] Contemporary attempts to secure a place for care in the social contract should bear in mind these problems of devaluing the care work of some women and of exploiting care workers to foster social reproduction.

The separate spheres ideal of male breadwinner/female homemaker remained more an ideal than a reality for many families, particularly for African American, working-class, and poor families who had insufficient resources for the mother to stay out of the paid labor force. Different sorts of family arrangements, including sharing care for children with "other mothers," or "conscripting" kin, were prevalent among African American families.[68] Black women welfare activists were more supportive of married women's employment than their white counterparts, but also espoused maternalistic reform, believing that "slavery had undermined the bases of maternalism—home and family ties, the sanctity of marriage, and the instincts of motherhood."[69]

One fruit of the Progressive-era reform efforts launched by white and African American women's groups was legislation authorizing mothers' pensions, or governmental subsidies to allow women (usually widows) deprived of a male breadwinner to care for their children.[70] A central tenet of the "mothers' pensions" movement in the late nineteenth and early twentieth centuries was that mothers engage in the vital work of caring for children, and that they perform a valuable service by raising future citizens. This acceptance of maternal citizenship, or the idea of mothers' vital social—and political—contributions, is evident, for example, in President Theodore Roosevelt's remarks: "when all is said and done it is the mother . . . who is a better citizen even than the soldier who fights for his country. . . . [T]he mother is the one supreme asset of national life."[71]

This idea of social contribution was an important foundation for the Aid to Dependent Children program (the precursor of Aid to Families with Dependent Children (AFDC), whereby government assumed responsibility to provide a financial subsidy to allow (in theory) mothers without a breadwinner to stay out of the market to care for their children. This ideal was inclusive: it held that all women, whatever their ethnic or class background, could be educated toward and supported in this mothering role. However, it also afforded latitude for social control and intervention when mothers did not seem deserving or worthy (evident in "suitable home" requirements and restrictions on mothers' sexual behavior).[72] Another limitation of these efforts was that the white feminist activists who advocated such pensions (in contrast to black women's organizations) uncritically accepted the male breadwinner/female caregiver ideal and did not focus on fostering the economic self-sufficiency of women in the labor market. As Linda Gordon concludes in *Pitied but Not Entitled*: "Above all the welfare reformers' feminism was characterized by a class double standard. . . . For women of education and high status, they supported careers, public-sphere activism, and economic independence. For poor women, they recommended domesticity and economic dependence on men."[73] A legacy of the mothers' pensions movement was a two-tier public benefits system that treated ADC (and subsequently AFDC) as mere "welfare," while it viewed social security as an earned entitlement, subjecting recipients of ADC, but not social security, to moral scrutiny and supervision.[74]

Notwithstanding the normative ideal behind mothers' pensions—allowing mothers to engage in the important social task of rearing children—political compromises and discriminatory administration largely excluded African American women from its reach, just as the social security program exempted from its reach occupations disproportionately filled by African American men and women. It was not until the welfare rights efforts of the 1960s that African American women gained significant inclusion. This very inclusion fueled public resentment against welfare and the increasing association of AFDC with black mothers, viewed as manipulative, lazy, and irresponsibly bearing children at public expense.[75]

The social contract underlying AFDC—that society benefited by providing financial assistance to help mothers without financial resources to rear children in their own homes—began to erode with various reform efforts (in the 1960s, 1970s, and 1980s) to move such mothers from "welfare to work."[76] By the 1990s, the Republican Party's Contract with America and its proposed Personal Responsibility Act (which formed the basic framework of PRWORA, the 1996 welfare reform law) wholly repudiated that earlier social contract and made it emphatically clear that the state no longer wished to afford subsidies to mothers to enable them to care for children without husbands or without jobs.[77] This was *not* a valuable social contribution. Similarly, President Clinton, representing a "new Democratic" approach, promised to "end welfare as we know it" and to bring welfare recipients back into compliance with mainstream American values of family, work, and responsibility.[78] In other words, poor mothers should "play by the rules" and move "from welfare to work" and/or to marriage as a means of providing for their children. Notably, the Bush Administration's welfare proposal, "Working Toward Independence" condemns AFDC for its failure to further the proper aim of welfare: helping young people establish economic independence.[79]

One reason for this twin focus on work and marriage was that welfare reformers targeted the illegitimacy of children as a leading (if not the leading) social problem at the root of many other social problems, and viewed welfare as its "life support" system.[80] Feminist scholars critiquing this attack on single mothers reveal the rhetorical power of the notion of the "deviant mother" and how stereotypical construction of "welfare mothers" as women of color gave special intensity to the drive to "end welfare as we know it."[81] Nonetheless, this attack was aimed not only at poor single mothers who require public subsidy through welfare; it more broadly condemned a culture that facilitated single parenthood. As Fineman argues, from this perspective all single mothers are immoral and deviant because of the absence of the father from the household and because of the threat to marriage posed by such deviation.[82]

The new social contract reflected in PRWORA repudiates a "maternalist" view of state responsibility to support mothers' caregiving in favor of an unreflective adoption of a requirement that mothers be breadwinners (as it were, the "male" side of the old separate spheres model). Caring for children is visible only when the lack of paid child care is an "obstacle" to successful market participation. When Congress passed—and President Clinton signed—PRWORA, many welfare experts warned that moving women "from welfare to work" would require addressing the significant practical difficulties of combining caregiving for children with paid employment. One reason that women cycle on and off welfare is the difficulty of finding adequate child care for children and of paying for children's care and health insurance on minimum wage jobs without adequate benefits.[83] Historically, the states' problems in funding and finding child care was a reason that they exempted many mothers with small children from work requirements.[84]

Reflecting the view that mothers not in the paid workforce offended American values by their chronic "idleness," PRWORA greatly reduced the scope of exemptions from work requirements owing to a mother's child-care obligations. As the ongoing care crisis indicates, however, there has not been a parallel expansion of governmental assistance with paid child care adequate to address the practical difficulties of combining family care and paid work faced by such mothers as well as other low-income working parents. Notably, continuing points of disagreement in Congress over reauthorizing TANF have been how much to increase work requirements, whether proposed bills adequately fund child care at a level necessary to facilitate such requirements, and whether the minimum wage should be raised to ensure that work does pay and to alleviate poverty.[85] Such issues have divided not only Democrats and Republicans, but also Republicans: moderate Republicans defend—as a "critical" and "common sense work support for single moms"—a higher level of child-care funding than that supported by conservatives and the Bush Administration.[86]

Ironically, the importance of both nurture and paid work as dimensions of parental work is glimpsed in politicians' calls for "responsible fatherhood" as a component of welfare reform.[87] The idea of promoting "responsible fatherhood" is that because father involvement furthers child well-being, government should help fathers provide both financial and emotional support for their children. During the mid-1990s, around the time of the debate over PRWORA, a new "social movement" was emerging, calling for "responsible fatherhood." Proponents of responsible fatherhood often criticized welfare policy because it focused too much on women, subsidized fatherless families, and failed to recognize the important role of men in the family.[88]

During the Clinton presidency, the federal government invited research on fatherhood and evaluated how federal programs might strengthen the role of fathers in families.[89] Soon, nearly every state formed a task force or undertook initiatives to promote responsible fatherhood, and successive sessions of Congress considered "responsible fatherhood" legislation.[90] As President Clinton expressed it in a Father's Day statement: "For the health of our families, it is important that fathers have the time, the support, and the parenting skills necessary to fulfill their children's moral and emotional needs as well as provide for their physical well-being."[91] The Clinton-Gore Administration urged more "father-friendly workplaces" that would better allow fathers to play a role in their children's lives and championed responsible fatherhood as an important next step in welfare reform.[92] In the 2000 presidential campaign, Governor George W. Bush declared support for responsible fatherhood, stating: "[t]here is no more important mission in life than to love and care for a child. . . . Every man needs to know that no matter how lofty his job or position, he will never have a greater duty or more important title than dad."[93]

"Responsible fatherhood" initiatives are a component of the Bush Administration's programs to strengthen families and of TANF reauthorization proposals. I defer to Chapter 4 an evaluation of responsible fatherhood as a component of governmental promotion of "healthy marriage." Here, the relevant point is that, in the context of supporting fathers, politicians acknowledge the emotional and nurturing component of parenting as a task worthy of governmental encouragement. Administrative and legislative proposals to promote "responsible fatherhood" stress the benefits to children of having their fathers actively involved in their lives and—in contrast to the punitive and condemning rhetoric that accompanied the passage of PRWORA (focused especially on welfare mothers, but also on "deadbeat" dads)—aim to provide resources to help fathers be better providers and more capable parents.

## Beyond Care as Women's Responsibility Only?

Stereotypes about women's domestic roles are reinforced by parallel stereotypes presuming a lack of domestic responsibilities for men. Because employers continued to regard the family as the woman's domain, they often denied men similar accommodations or discouraged them from taking leave. These mutually reinforcing stereotypes created a self-fulfilling cycle of discrimination that forced women to continue to assume the role of primary family caregiver, and fostered employers' stereotypical views about women's commitment to work and their value as employees.

—*Nevada Department of Human Resources v. Hibbs*

I have proposed that care be recognized as a public value. Doing so in a way that embraces both care and equality helps keep in view both that present institutional arrangements insufficiently value and support care, and that historically care has been disproportionately the responsibility of women. This history should caution against attributing women's and men's preferences about and practices concerning caregiving to their fixed natures or unvarying choices. As indicated in the above language from a 2003 Supreme Court opinion, in which the Court explained why Congress passed the Family and Medical Leave Act, stereotypes about women's and men's responsibilities have shaped employment policies in ways that have treated caregiving in the home as exclusively a female domain and discouraged men from engaging in such care. Thus, fashioning a new approach to care requires bearing in mind both current practices and stereotypes that have shaped those practices.

Within contemporary families, traditional gender roles of provider/caregiver continue to be a major organizing feature of household labor. The majority of men and women hold the view that such labor is a shared responsibility, but women, on average, perform two or three times as much housework as do men. Women—both as mothers and as paid caregivers—also spend more time than do men providing care to children and other dependents. Wives, more than husbands, also engage in the emotional work that sustains families.[94] This division of labor results in employed wives enjoying less leisure and experiencing more stress than their husbands. Although many men and women evaluate these unequal arrangements as fair (a puzzle I take up in Chapter 4), at least some women who shoulder more than their share of responsibility for housework experience a sense of unfairness and marital dissatisfaction.[95]

The idea that care is more appropriately women's responsibility is deeply entrenched. Important studies in moral development amply illustrate that girls are socialized to be mothers, to accept responsibility for "caregiving" work, and to engage in the work of social reproduction.[96] Studies of household labor indicate that women feel responsible for family members' well-being and, more than men, alter their work and home schedules to accommodate family obligations.[97] In doing so, women, more than men, suffer the costs in terms of blocked career mobility and not being considered serious employees.

This gender ideology also is costly for men: many men—like women—aspire to a more flexible balance between family life and work, but fear the economic marginalization that may result if they do not appear to be committed employees.[98] When this balance eludes such men, they suffer the costs of a loss of participation in family life and of the rewards of emotional intimacy with spouses and children.[99] Conversely, as one study of married fathers found, when fathers actively care for children, they report not only a greater sense of parental competence (for example, being better attuned to their children's needs) but also a better sense of understanding and solidarity with their wives.[100]

Gender ideology thus exerts a powerful role in shaping patterns of caregiving. A related structural obstacle to transforming these patterns is the persistence of what legal scholar Joan Williams calls the norm of the "ideal worker": market work continues to be organized around "the ideal of a worker who works full time and overtime and takes little or no time off for childbearing or child rearing." When this norm combines with the persistent norm that caregiving is more naturally women's responsibility, it is misleading to speak of women's "choices" to invest more in caregiving than in market labor or, for that matter, of men's "choices" to invest more in employment.[101] Consider frequent media reports of mothers "opting out" of the paid workforce to stay home with their children. These reports reinforce the assumption that it is women's—rather than men's—responsibility to resolve work/family conflict in this manner.[102]

A better resolution is to support and recognize care as a public value in a way that facilitates both women and men integrating family and employment. This approach would rectify the injustice of women's disproportionate responsibility for care. In addition to the considerable costs of this injustice, it may also hinder the family from carrying out its civic role of fostering virtues important to self-government.

One concern about arguing for care as a public value is that doing so may reinforce the association of women with care rather than employment and reinforce notions of women's essential differences from men.[103] Should supporting care be viewed as instantiating a feminine—not simply feminist—perspective? Some research, for example, suggests that women's patterns of moral reasoning, more than men's, place a primary emphasis on care, connection, and taking responsibility for the needs of others.[104] I urge support for care on a more humanist basis: because care has a fundamental role in fostering all persons' capacities, it is unjust that women disproportionately bear responsibility for it.[105] Accepting my argument does not require any conclusion about the essential natures of men and women; such conclusions might insufficiently heed the influence of sex inequality and gender socialization.[106] Notably, Carol Gilligan, who famously associated women with an "ethic of care" in *In a Different Voice*, warned that "care" too readily becomes female self-sacrifice. Moral maturity for women, she argued, requires that they learn to think of their own needs, as well as the needs of others, in defining what "responsibility" requires of them (just as men should learn to think more of others).[107] Attending to both care and equality is akin to calling for an integration of care and justice.[108]

A fairer distribution of responsibility for giving care should also entail treating paid caregivers in a just manner and recognizing that quality caregiving fosters child well-being and makes a valuable social contribution. By facilitating better working conditions and higher wages for caregivers, society also facilitates the conditions under which children receive developmentally appropriate, quality child care.[109] Because most paid caregivers are women, this reform would also promote women's equal opportunity in the workplace.

The current structure of work/family conflict and the care crisis lead to a dynamic that seems to pit women against women. Women regard it as an important part of their responsibility as mothers to find appropriate "substitute" caregivers. Absent institutional reforms and greater support for care work, individual women juggling maternal and market labor are left to solve "their" care problems in ways that do not address, and may even perpetuate, these inequalities. A dynamic ensues in which more affluent women (predominantly white and middle-class) employ caregivers who are immigrant, ethnic minority, and working-class women.[110]

Some caution about this picture is in order, since most child-care workers are employed in child-care centers—rather than in private homes—and are not immigrants.[111] Nonetheless, the place of immigrants in providing care and household services does raise important questions of justice and equality. Focusing on the transnational dimension of the care crisis, Arlie Hochschild has urged attention to the human costs (especially for children) of the "global care chain," or "invisible human ecology of care," linking rich and poor countries. Some First World mothers depend on nannies from Third World countries, who in turn depend on other caregivers to care for their own children left behind.[112] This phenomenon invites the charge that "some women's access to the high-paying, high-status professions is being facilitated through the revival of semi-indentured servitude."[113] Indeed, as is evident from the recent (March 2004) *Atlantic* magazine cover story, "How Serfdom Saved the Women's Movement," the very conceptualization of this problem as one pitting women against women arises from the continuing assignment to women—rather than men or the broader society—of responsibility for meeting the dependency needs of children.[114]

The problem has implications for social reproduction. Caregivers in private homes may be more vulnerable to abuse and exploitation than workers in public settings, particularly if they are not proficient in English, do not have a support network, and, in some cases, are not in the United States legally.[115] Just as Okin asked how families can serve as schools for citizenship and develop a sense of justice if gender injustice permeates them, we should ask how families can create democratic citizens "if children witness the arbitrary and capricious interaction of parents and servants or if they are permitted to treat domestic servants in a similar manner."[116] Such arrangements may foster the social reproduction of privilege, even as they shift the burden of sex inequality to low-wage women workers.[117]

Finally, a more just care order could address the costs that the current gendered economy of care imposes on daughters. In low-income families, mothers often rely heavily on their daughters as "family workers," enlisted to provide housework, child care, and other work to help keep their families together. In the absence of economic resources for nannies, child-care centers, or house cleaners, the labor of these daughters is viewed as a necessary substitute. Such conscription of daughters comes with great costs to girls' identity: loss of sense of childhood, poorer school performance, and higher risk of dropping out, greater tendency to view gaining a boyfriend as the way to a different role, and readiness to become mothers at an early age.[118] Troubling findings that "welfare to work" policies have negative consequences for some adolescent children are attributable in part to the impact of adolescents' increased home responsibilities (particularly caring for younger siblings) on their school performance.[119]

Thus, the gendered care economy imposes costs that are often hidden and that hinder responsible self-government. Focus on the political economy of citizenship should attend to developing institutional arrangements that better support the work of social reproduction. What form might these arrangements take?

## A New Social Contract

Recognizing and supporting care as a public value should build upon and reinforce a definition of personal responsibility that does not define it solely in terms of market labor but affirms the value of care work as a component of social reproduction. Thus, supporting "working families" should mean facilitating both of these forms of work. Moreover, since most parents are in the paid labor market at least some of the time and must leave their children in someone else's care, we need to develop policies to secure high-quality substitute care and improve the status of paid care workers.[120]

What should the contours of a new social contract be? I shall not lay out a blueprint for reconstruction. Making concrete proposals and testing them should result from public conversations and deliberations in which different affected groups—families of different incomes and backgrounds, employers, paid caregivers, and community organizations—have a voice.[121] Perhaps the outcome of such deliberations would be an array of models suitable for different contexts.

Certain orienting ideas should guide this process. First, valuing care for its role in social reproduction should lead to an approach that facilitates caregiving within families without treating it as women's special responsibility. As Lucie White helpfully poses the challenge: "How could public policy encourage and enable parents of both genders, at all income levels[,] to play a major role in caring for their own children, without reinforcing either the gendered distribution of care work or the marginalization of caretakers from waged work and public life?"[122]

A promising answer to this question is to break down the breadwinner/caregiver dichotomy in favor of a new model that facilitates both women and men engaging in caregiving and in paid employment. This basic reconstruction is a central tenet of many feminist proposals for resolving work/family conflict.[123] If taken seriously, it could lead to restructuring the workplace in a way that would better reflect women's and men's aspirations about work and family as well as the changing dynamic of women's and men's roles within society. It would advance the important goal of *equality within families*, that is, treating care work as a responsibility for both men and women. It would also affirm and support women's aspirations for satisfying paid work and thus further their equal opportunity in the workplace. This feminist reconstruction of social citizenship finds a place for caregiving and for paid employment as forms of valuable social contribution worthy of governmental support. It seeks to foster child well-being without sacrificing gender equality.[124]

Another important guideline should be a concern for *equality among families*—that is, governmental responsibility to ensure that all children, whatever their family form, receive the care that will help them become responsible, capable members of society. This should include governmental policies that facilitate parental care as well as high-quality paid child care. An important component of such a policy should be to ensure fair and just treatment of paid child-care workers.

I have discussed the struggles of low-income families as the most acute manifestation of a broader problem often labeled work/family conflict. What policies are likely to help these low-income families and also reduce the broader conflict? Strikingly, studies of the challenges low-income families face in meeting the demands of care and employment make a number of findings similar to those studying work/family conflict in general.

One basic point of agreement is that families need "time to care." As the report, *Keeping Jobs and Raising Families in Low-Income America: It Just Doesn't Work*, concludes: "[l]ike families everywhere," low-income families need "time, not just to care for family emergencies but time to be a family, to enjoy and nurture each other, to be involved in their children's educations and in their communities."[125] In their recent comparative study, *Families That Work*, Janet Gornick and Marcia Meyers conclude that "one of the most important weaknesses of the family leave system in the United States is the lack of any paid leave for a substantial share of the workforce."[126] To foster parent-child bonding and continuity of care important to child well-being, for example, more generous leave and governmental allowances could facilitate parental care, particularly during infancy and early childhood.[127] Some states have successfully adopted programs that provide low-income mothers a child-care allowance—in lieu of a subsidy for purchasing child care—if they decide to stay home with their infant child. Another strategy some states have adopted is letting the time parents spend with children count toward the TANF work requirements—an important step away from defining "work" solely as paid employment.[128]

A second "basic" point of agreement is a reduced hourly work week. In the case of low-income families, this entails having sufficient income to support their families and to afford time off from work. Some of the most innovative approaches to welfare reform have found that an overall package of "supports for work," such as child-care subsidies and the Earned Income Tax Credit (EITC) (which may allow parents to reduce their hours in the labor market), can enhance families' economic and emotional well-being. Such supports may reduce parental stress and improve parent-child relations and child well-being.[129] Recent studies of work/family conflict propose setting the standard work week at below 40 hours, freeing up time for caregiving by full-time employees and improving the compensation and quality of part-time work.[130] The rationale for this reform is that the 40-hour work week was premised on a now-outdated model of the male-breadwinner family for which one income was sufficient. As Jacobs and Gerson conclude: "Since employers no longer routinely subsidize an unpaid (female) partner at home, it is time to reexamine a standard that emerged at a different time to fill different social and personal needs."[131] This reform, which might garner support from a range of groups concerned with strengthening families, moves in the opposite direction from welfare reauthorization proposals to increase the work requirements to a 40-hour work week to encourage "independence."

Reforms that help workers to balance family and employment by reducing work time could also aim to provide all workers with time away from work. Providing time for "self-care" would be beneficial because Americans work more hours than workers in many industrialized countries.[132] Time away from work, as Deborah Rhode observes, would also afford persons more time to participate in community and civic activities that promote a healthy civil society.[133] Such policies might blunt the criticism that family-friendly policies come at the expense of childless workers.[134]

A third "basic" is access to quality child care for times when parents cannot provide such care themselves. This "substitute" care should include not only child care (in the usual sense of day-care centers or in-home care) but also preschool programs and after-school programs.[135] Public support for such care would alleviate a troubling form of inequality among families: if low-income children receive poor quality child care and lack good after-school programs, while more affluent children have enriching programs, this exacerbates social inequality. Providing high-quality, publicly supported care furthers the important national commitments to equality of opportunity and to the idea that children, whatever their starting points, deserve an equal chance in life.[136] Public support would also resolve the dilemma that, without generous subsidies to low-income workers, the cost of quality care might well exceed their incomes or require such a substantial percentage of their incomes as to be out of reach.[137] Public subsidy could also help to address the problem that treating child care more like a profession might raise wages to the point where it would be out of reach for many parents.

## Conclusion

The problem of work/family conflict and the next phase of welfare reform offer important opportunities to think constructively about institutional arrangements that would recognize and support care as a public value and move the United States closer to a more just care-giving order. Contemporary political rhetoric about government "supporting working families" and "strengthening families" reflects a notable rhetorical shift from the welfare debates of the 1990s, when responsible parents were conceived as those who provided for their children with no expectation of outside assistance. This is a promising beginning, but family policy and welfare policy should focus in a more sustained way on the role of care in developing human and social capital, and recognize and support the important "work" parents and other caregivers perform in nurturing and rearing children. Such a focus would aid in conceiving a social contract that better reflects the roles of family and government in fostering capacity.

# II

## Fostering Equality

# 4

## *Marriage Promotion, Marriage (E)quality, and Welfare Reform*

I don't want to play Cupid. This isn't about telling anybody who should marry who. But when you have a couple who say, we're interested in getting married, or who are already married, it's about helping them develop the skills and knowledge necessary to form and sustain healthy marriages.

*⌖ Dr. Wade Horn, Assistant Secretary, Department of Health and Human Services*

"[M]en think that piece of paper says they own you. You are their personal slave. Cook their meals, clean their house, do their laundry. . . . A man gets married to have somebody take care of them 'cause their mommy can't do it any more." Most mothers don't want to be owned or slave for their husband. They want a partnerships of equals.

*⌖ Kathryn Edin (testifying before Congress in hearing on welfare and marriage)*

𝒜 PROMINENT FEATURE IN THE DEBATES over families is concern about the place of marriage. The social movement known as the "marriage movement," as well as many politicians, argue that shoring up the institution of marriage is vital to social health.[1] The best way for government to support families, it is said, is to promote "healthy marriages" by stemming the tide of cohabitation, non-marital childbearing, and divorce. Politicians propose to promote "healthy marriages" through welfare reform because of the acute concern over low-income unmarried parents. But the rhetoric sweeps more broadly. Various state and federal initiatives purport to give their

117

citizens the skills and knowledge they will need to have happy, long-lasting marriages.

The civil society movement and the marriage movement share personnel and have come to a common diagnosis: the decline of the two-parent, intact marital family is America's most urgent problem today. But the civil society argument calls for a return to personal and civic virtue and warns that spouses' and parents' untempered pursuit of personal happiness is undermining one's sense of sober duty. The social health argument posits that most people seek, but fail to achieve, a happy, long-lasting marriage and promises to help adults achieve marital happiness.

Calls to promote marriage raise significant questions about government's proper role in adults' intimate, committed relationships. Does the public have a stake in marriage as a social institution that justifies a governmental program that promotes marriage over alternative family forms? Will such a program include or exclude same-sex marriage? What concerns arise from using welfare reform as a vehicle to promote marriage among low-income (disproportionately minority) members of society? Is marriage promotion likely to help people achieve stable family lives? If government proposes to promote the "skills and knowledge" necessary to have "healthy" marriages, will it impart a tool box of communication skills that are readily applicable to any form of marriage? Will government's agenda include a normative commitment to certain public values? If so, what will they be?

With regard to the place of families, I support facilitative governmental measures to help people form and sustain committed, intimate relationships through education of both children and adults. Thus, I part company with those who argue that marriage is a wholly private choice and none of government's business. At the same time, I argue that the program of marriage promotion advanced by the marriage movement and by governmental actors championing marriage as an antipoverty strategy has serious flaws. Marriage promotion efforts have not adequately promoted equality within families and equality among families. Similarly, discussions of "healthy marriage" have insufficiently recognized the relationship between marriage *quality* and sex *equality*.

In this chapter, I evaluate the rationales that have been offered for marriage promotion. I also explore the place of sex equality—or equality within families—in a governmental program of fostering healthy marriage. Diagnoses of why marriage culture has weakened often emphasize feminism, women's increasing economic independence, and their higher expectations of sex equality, gender equity, and intimacy within marriage. On the one hand, marriage promoters make disclaimers about "not wanting to turn back the clock" to a prior marital regime based on male dominance and female subordination; some even assert that today healthy marriage must be premised on "equal regard."[2] On the other hand, proposals to promote marriage and renew a "marriage culture" fail to reckon adequately with whether a commitment to supporting sex equality is in tension with these purposes or, to the contrary, is a vital component of pursuing them. Marriage promoters frequently appeal to men's and women's different roles and natures to justify society using marriage as a tool to domesticate men.

For most marriage promoters, renewing a marriage culture does not include support of same-sex marriage. Gender role assumptions play a part in this exclusion. Key tenets of the marriage movement—that the purpose of marriage is to link men to women and children, and that children need both biological parents—collide with the proposition that same-sex couples can be capable and nurturing parents.[3]

In this chapter, I criticize the absence in marriage promotion efforts of a firm commitment to equality within families. I argue that governmental programs to support "healthy marriage" should honor the public value of sex equality that is reflected in constitutional law and family law norms of equal rights and responsibilities within marriage. A focus on equality and its link to marriage quality is also more likely to achieve a healthy marriage culture. In Chapters 5 and 6, I contend that respect for equality among families should also inform governmental efforts to strengthen families.

## The Social Health Argument for Marriage

Based on the premise that most Americans desire a happy, long-lasting marriage, the marriage movement seeks to restore a marriage culture.[4] Key texts in the movement offer several justifications for government promoting marriage and society restoring a marriage culture:

1. *"Married adults, women as well as men, are happier, healthier, and wealthier than their unmarried counterparts."*[5] Put in the currency

of social capital: "Marriage is a unique generator of social and human capital, as important as education in building the wealth of individuals and communities."[6]

2. *"Children do better, on average, when they are raised by their own two married parents."*[7] Marriage promoters contend that an abundance of social science evidence supports marriage's link to the child's well-being. Their more nuanced claim is not about marriage as such but "healthy marriage": children fare better in "healthy" marriages than in "unhealthy marriages," and the policy goal should be to foster child well-being through promoting "loving," "healthy," or "low-conflict" marriages.[8]

3. *"Divorce and unwed parenting generate large taxpayer costs."* This argument stresses the negative effects linked to particular family forms: "higher rates of crime, drug abuse, education failure, chronic illness, child abuse, domestic violence, and poverty among both adults and children." Such problems bring "higher taxpayer costs in diverse forms," for example, increased expenditure for welfare and "a range of increased direct court administration costs incurred in regulating post-divorce or unwed families."[9]

4. *"Marriage is society's way of engaging the basic problem of fatherhood—how to hold the father to the stronger mother-child bond."*[10] Why is marriage necessary? "Being a father is universally problematic for men in a way [motherhood] is not for women. Put simply, as marriage weakens, fathers stray."[11] The gender-neutral version of this argument claims that married couples stay together more often and longer than cohabiting couples: "only marriage creates a reasonable hope of permanence."[12]

In articulating the benefits of marriage, the social health argument—like the civil society argument—contends that the marital family—not a family as such—is the "seedbed from which healthy children and, ultimately, a healthy society spring."[13] Because of its formative effects on adults and children, marriage is more than a private relationship. It is a social institution and a social good and therefore a legitimate concern of the state. Thus, the marriage movement urges that local, state, and federal governments should "make supporting and promoting marriage an explicit goal of domestic policy."[14]

By promoting marriage, government could help people close the gap between their aspirations about marriage and their actual experience. Evidence of the gap includes the high divorce rate, the prevalence of cohabitation and nonmarital childrearing, the declining percentage of people who say they are in "very happy" first marriages, and increasing pessimism among young people (especially young women) about the chances for a happy and long-lasting marriage.[15] As "The Marriage Movement: A Statement of Principle" concludes: "We seek nothing less than to rebuild the shattered dream of lasting love and to pass on a healthier, happier, and more successful marriage culture to the next generation."[16]

Even though the marriage movement appeals to adult health and happiness as one rationale for promoting marriage, it places greater emphasis on the supposed link between marriage and child well-being. Marriage promoters also appeal to marriage's role in generating social goods, but these benefits, in and of themselves, do not make marriage a matter of urgent public concern. For example, David Popenoe, co-director of the National Marriage Project, argues: "[T]he need of every society for successful childrearing is why marriage has been a public institution and a focus of religious concern. . . . Without children, it is much more difficult to envision the institution of marriage as something that requires public attention and regulation."[17] Many of the taxpayer costs that the marriage movement links to divorce and nonmarital parenting relate to children. Even the argument that society requires marriage to domesticate men ultimately appeals to child well-being, since the claim is that marriage binds fathers to children.

## Marriage Promotion as the Next Step in Welfare Reform

Within the last decade, promoting marriage and "responsible fatherhood" have moved from being social movements to being governmental imperatives. Since the mid-1990s, every state has undertaken at least one policy initiative aimed at promoting marriage, strengthening two-parent families, or reducing divorce.[18] The lines between social movement and governmental program are quite porous. Indeed, Dr. Wade Horn, who is prominent in both the responsible fatherhood and marriage movements, became the Bush Administration's assistant director of the Administration for Children and Families (ACF) at the

Department of Health and Human Services (DHHS). ACF established a Healthy Marriage Initiative and a Fatherhood Initiative, and regularly funds marriage education programs and marriage-related research.[19]

Government, Horn argues, should not be "neutral" about marriage, but should instead support it because it produces child well-being and is a social good. Government should help couples who choose marriage (or are considering marriage) to develop the skills and knowledge needed to achieve healthy marriages.[20] Testifying before the Senate in support of Bush's welfare plan in 2002, Horn stated: "What we seek to do in our proposal is increase the number of children who grow up in healthy marriages, and decrease the number of children who grow up in unhealthy marriages."[21] He proposes to integrate a message about marriage into everything government does, where appropriate.[22] But federal marriage promotion efforts, consistent with the federal Defense of Marriage Act, will not extend to same-sex couples.[23]

The most visible vehicle for promoting a federal governmental message about marriage has been welfare policy, as is evident in the protracted debates over reauthorizing the Temporary Assistance for Needy Families (TANF) component of the Personal Responsibility and Work Opportunity Reconciliation Act of 1996 (PRWORA). In that Act, Congress found that "marriage is the foundation of a successful society." One purpose of TANF was to encourage the formation and maintenance of two-parent families.[24] Congress put a five-year limit on the funding of PRWORA, requiring it to enact new legislation to reauthorize or revise TANF by October 1, 2002.

As the reauthorization deadline approached, Congress held hearings on welfare and marriage. One impetus was the conviction that, despite the "pro-marriage" purposes of PRWORA, states had done far less to promote marriage than to move women on welfare into the paid workforce.[25] Yet, as some policy analysts argued, "if the single most potent antidote to poverty is work, marriage is not far behind." For "if marital rates could be increased, especially among poor and minority Americans, many of the social problems that are the target of social programs"—such as welfare—"under the jurisdiction" of Congress "would be reduced."[26] One conviction aired in these hearings was that marriage is the only way to secure responsible fatherhood.[27]

To counter charges that promoting marriage among low-income, unmarried parents is coercive or paternalistic, lawmakers have argued that doing so simply helps such parents do what they say they want to do. Some have invoked findings from the Fragile Families and Child Well Being Study (Fragile Families Study), a longitudinal survey of low-income, unmarried parents and their children. The study reports that 80 percent of unmarried parents are romantically involved at the time of their child's birth; the majority say there is a good or almost certain chance that they will marry (although few in fact do go on to marry).[28] Legislators proposed a more intensified effort to use welfare law to encourage people who otherwise would become parents outside of marriage to form stable marriages. Some dissenting voices in Congress challenged this focus on marriage, instead of poverty reduction,[29] just as some expressed skepticism over whether government has any business trying to shape "personal and private" choices like marriage."[30] But proposals to promote marriage and responsible fatherhood have enjoyed bipartisan support and indeed have engendered less disagreement than the battles over levels of work requirements and child-care funding.[31]

The Bush Administration's proposed welfare plan, "Working Toward Independence," identified "child well-being" as the overarching purpose of TANF and proposed "strengthening families" by "promoting healthy marriages" as a central pillar.[32] Invoking research concerning outcomes for children, it claimed: "it is simply wise and prudent to reorient our policies to encourage marriage, especially when children are involved." It identified the federal government's role as providing financial incentives to states to "find new and effective ways to encourage healthy marriages in appropriate circumstances." States must indicate what efforts they will make to achieve TANF's family formation goals. Reflecting a tenet of Bush's "compassionate conservatism," the plan envisioned state governments working with private and faith-based organizations to develop successful programs, which the federal government will evaluate and disseminate to other states.

The events of September 11, 2001, and the invasion of Iraq diverted the Bush Administration's and Congress's focus away from welfare policy to homeland security and foreign policy. Nonetheless, in 2002 and again in 2003, the House of Representatives approved Republican-authored bills embodying Bush's proposals. However, the Senate, in disagreement over the proper level of work requirements, child-care funding, and raising the minimum wage, delayed approving a bill, requiring Congress to extend the reauthorization deadline.[33]

Upon reelection in 2004, President Bush signaled continuing support for marriage promotion by nominating, as the new secretary of the DHHS, Michael Leavitt, who, as governor of Utah, actively championed marriage promotion.[34] In addition, the Republicans in the House promptly introduced an updated bill, the Personal Responsibility, Work, and Family Promotion Act of 2005 (H.R. 240). The Senate Finance Committee approved a "compromise" bill, the Personal Responsibility and Individual Development for Everyone (PRIDE) Act (S. 667). It mirrored H.R. 240's marriage promotion provisions, but—reflecting some lawmakers' skepticism about such untried programs—added provisions clarifying that participation in such programs must be voluntary and ensuring that such programs address domestic violence.[35] Thus, when Congress does pass welfare reauthorization legislation, it will likely resemble the Bush plan and these bills in making marriage promotion a more explicit goal. H.R. 240 amends TANF's purpose of encouraging "two-parent families" to encouraging "healthy, 2-parent married families, and encourag[ing] responsible fatherhood."[36] The bill allocates annual funding for "healthy marriage promotion grants," by which states, territories, and tribal organizations can develop programs to "promote and support healthy, married, 2-parent families." Fundable activities include public advertising campaigns "on the value of marriage and the skills needed to increase marital stability and health"; education about marriage and relationship skills for high school students, nonmarried expectant parents, and couples interested in marriage; marriage mentoring and enhancement programs; divorce reduction programs teaching relationship skills; and "programs to reduce the disincentives to marriage in means-tested aid programs." H.R. 240 includes a "Fatherhood Program," the aims of which are (1) "promoting responsible, caring, and effective parenting"; (2) enhancing unemployed or low-income fathers' "abilities and commitment" to provide material support for their families; (3) educating fathers about managing "family business affairs"; and (4) "encouraging and supporting healthy marriage and married fatherhood." The program authorizes competitive grants to public entities and nonprofit community entities (including religious organizations) to pursue these objectives. DHHS, along with a "national nonprofit fatherhood promotion organization," may carry out relevant projects.[37]

State governments also express keen interest in promoting healthy marriage and responsible fatherhood, as well as in using partnerships with nongovernmental actors (especially faith-based groups) to do so. A small number of states have "dedicated significant TANF dollars specifically to strengthen and promote marriage and couple relationships," and other states have undertaken a "diversity of initiatives" to "strengthen marriage and/or two parent families and reduce divorce."[38] Some initiatives focus on TANF recipients and others on the broader population. For example, in 1999, in Oklahoma, a Bible Belt state with one of the highest divorce rates in the nation, then-Governor Frank Keating created the Oklahoma Marriage Initiative and allocated $10 million of TANF funds to meet his pledge to reduce the divorce rate by one-third. One method was to enlist clergy of various denominations to sign a statement that, before performing marriages, they would require premarital counseling or training.[39] Several governors have signed marriage proclamations, proclaiming the importance of marriage to the public.[40] Florida passed the Florida Marriage Preparation and Preservation Act of 1998, becoming the first state to require teaching marriage skills as part of the high school curriculum. The Act, like those subsequently adopted in several other states, gives a discount on marriage licenses to couples who take a premarital education course; in Florida, couples who do not take such a course face a three-day waiting period.[41] And some states create premarital education materials to be distributed to all marrying couples.[42] Other state efforts aim more directly at legal reform to "reinstitutionalize" marriage and foster marital permanence: Arkansas, Arizona, and Louisiana, for example, have "covenant marriage" statutes, which permit couples to opt for a form of marriage in which divorce is more difficult to obtain; similar legislation is under consideration in other states.[43]

State marriage initiatives assert a public interest in the success of the marital family. Florida's legislation includes the following statement: "Just as the family is the foundation of society, the marital relationship is the foundation of the family."[44] It found that an inability to cope with marital stress threatens child well-being and leads to higher incidents of domestic violence and divorce. Invoking Cicero's assertion that "[T]he first bond of society is marriage," a video provided by Utah's Governor's Commission on Marriage declares: "The duty of government is to protect and foster the common good. Strong marriages are key to improving both personal and social well-being."[45] A handbook prepared by the Texas attorney general for marrying couples admonishes: "Your commitment to your marriage is the backbone of our society."[46]

Governmental officials share the marriage movement's basic optimism that the skills necessary for a successful marriage can be taught. Oklahoma's secretary of Health and Human Services testified before Congress in support of marriage education: "It is remarkable how much is known, but unused, in understanding how to make better marriage choices, to strengthen existing marriages, to cope with stress and reduce conflict, and to avoid divorce."[47] The Utah video is assuring: "Commitment, communication, and conflict resolution skills can be learned and used to enhance and fortify your marriage."[48]

## Should Government Promote Marriage?

One objection to governmental promotion of marriage is that marriage and family life are private matters and simply none of government's business. This conviction may underlie public opinion polls showing strong opposition to marriage promotion.[49] I do not voice this objection. In the political order, families are simultaneously a site of private life and an institution of public importance because of the goods they foster and the functions they serve. Society has an interest in both the healthy development of children and the intimate bonds of adults in family relationships. Historically, marriage has been the primary institutional medium for uniting these two dimensions. The marriage movement overstates the case for marriage.[50] There are, however, contemporary justifications for government to support marriage, provided that it does so in ways that foster equality within and among families.

My critique of the marriage movement has three parts. First, I agree that child well-being justifies governmental interest in fostering strong, nurturing families. However, using marital families as the sole proxy for family forms that secure child well-being offers too narrow a picture of what kind of families can be strong and nurturing and deserve governmental support. Second, supporting education to develop relationship skills is a governmental role that is compatible with my argument that government should foster persons' capacities for personal self-government. However, a governmental program of promoting "healthy marriage" may not truly facilitate responsible choice. Especially when marriage promotion is used as an antipoverty strategy, the risk arises that promoting "healthy marriage" will equate to promoting marriage as such. This may run counter to fostering adult and child well-being. Third, marriage promotion efforts insufficiently attend to the fact that marriage still benefits men more than women and to the connection between sex equality and marriage quality. These efforts—especially when combined with arguments about marriage's role in taming men—risk perpetuating historic and contemporary forms of inequality within marriage, which themselves have contributed to the supposed contemporary "marriage crisis." I argue for a firm commitment to sex equality in any governmental program of supporting marriage.

## The Appeal to Child Well-Being

The social health argument treats an intact heterosexual marriage between two biological parents as the best proxy for child well-being. Marriage promoters, including a number of social scientists, claim that an overwhelming body of data supports their agenda.[51] Other social scientists caution against an overstatement of consensus. For example, although social scientists across the spectrum agree that "on average" children fare better in an intact, two-parent family, some also caution that this "on average" may be misleading as a prediction about particular children and may encourage a false determinism.[52] Studies of children successfully reared by lesbian and gay parents challenge the premise that child well-being requires two *biological* parents, as discussed in Chapter 5. Overemphasis on family form as such obscures the importance of variables such as the emotional tenor of families and the quality of both the parent-child and the parent-parent relationships.[53] For example, a number of unmarried low-income parents have children from previous relationships; if such parents marry, they form a blended family, which may have worse outcomes for children than a stable, single-parent family.[54]

Single-parent families, on the whole, have fewer economic and social resources than two-parent families. Thus, although children in such families are at higher risk for certain unfavorable schooling and behavioral outcomes, much of this disadvantage appears to stem from poverty rather than from single parenting as such.[55] Considerable variation in social and economic resources also exists among single-parent families. For example, one recent longitudinal study, observing white, black, and Hispanic children at age 6 and again at age 13, found "little or no systematic evidence of adverse effects of single parenting" on children and that such factors as positive maternal attitudes and parenting resources and competencies can mitigate the likelihood of such effects. The study concluded that "single parenthood, in and of itself, need not be viewed as representing an inevitable development hazard to children." The study endorsed public policies focused on ways to "increase single parents' access to adequate economic, social, educational, and parenting supports."[56]

A narrow focus on marriage may overlook how different communities effectively use family forms other than that of two married, biological parents—such as kinship care—to foster child well-being.[57] Finally, because family research on racial and ethnic minorities is scarce, few studies adequately sort out how race, social class, and culture influence family functioning.[58]

The marriage movement's repeated references to a "consensus" on the benefits of marriage and the harms of nonmarital family forms may illustrate a "feedback loop": a group of social scientists cite repeatedly to each other's work so that a certain set of claims is presented as an "uncontested" consensus, even if there is credible social science to the contrary.[59] The response accorded distinguished psychologist E. Mavis Hetherington and John Kelly's recent book, *For Better or for Worse: Divorce Reconsidered*, suggests the high stakes surrounding establishing a "consensus" about the impact of marriage and divorce. Based on Hetherington's 30-year study of families, the authors argue that "much current writing on divorce—both popular and academic— has exaggerated its negative effects and ignored its sometimes considerable positive effects."[60] In particular, the marriage movement frequently relies on the more negative assessment found in Judith Wallerstein's studies of the impact of divorce on children, which some social scientists contend exaggerates the harm that divorce typically causes.[61] Voices in the marriage movement were quick to criticize Hetherington's book and to caution of a "backlash" against taking divorce seriously, even as other social scientists praised her rigorous research.[62]

The marriage movement's reliance an analogies between the marriage crisis and public health crises and epidemics implies a basic divide between marital and nonmarital families, with the marital fostering health and the nonmarital not doing so. To be sure, family problems can generate not only personal but also public costs. And states have the police power to promote health, safety, welfare, and morals. In this view, promoting marriage would be akin to governmental campaigns against smoking and, more recently, against obesity.[63] But quality of family life is important: just as healthy marriage may promote adult and child well-being, unhealthy marriage (for example, high-conflict marriage) may hinder it.[64] Indeed, marital stress negatively affects adults' health.[65] When marriage promoters claim that government should promote "healthy," "loving," or "low-conflict" marriages, they admit this.[66] Rather than focusing on the marital family as the one family form worthy of a special governmental campaign, why not propose governmental programs to develop the capacity of all families—whether marital or nonmarital, heterosexual or homosexual—to contribute to the well-being of their members?

Thus, promoting child well-being is one justification for a governmental interest in strong, nurturing families. And marriage is an important form of such families. But due attention to equality among families counsels that government not use marriage as the sole proxy for family forms that secure child well-being.

## Should Government Educate about "Healthy Marriage"?

Government could play a facilitative role in encouraging more thoughtful, informed, reflective decisions to marry and in helping people realize more successful relationships. Doing so would be compatible with the idea of relational autonomy that I discussed in Chapter 1. There, I also distinguished between government using coercive measures, such as the criminal law, and using facilitative or persuasive measures to foster persons' capacities and to promote important public values and virtues. Certainly, the capacity to form and sustain intimate relationships is an important aspect of personal self-government.[67] Is marriage education likely to be truly facilitative?

Because education is a primary means by which parents and schools help children develop their capacities, compulsory relationship education is more readily defensible for children and adolescents than for adults. Such education could be a component of children's healthy development, particularly if it imparts skills useful for a broad range of social and civic relationships.[68] Notably, proponents of relationship training speak of it as a needed "fourth R," joining "*R*eading, w*R*iting, and a*R*ithmetic" as basics of the curriculum.[69]

How does relationship education benefit adults? Suppose such education may help them achieve happier, less conflictual and violent, and more stable intimate relationships. Research suggests that too much conflict and arguing are reasons both men and women frequently give for their decisions to divorce; for women, domestic violence is also a frequent reason.[70] Marital education proponents claim that training in relationships skills, such as how to handle inevitable stress and conflict, can reduce levels of unhappiness as well as domestic violence and divorce.[71] If it is true that many problems in relationships stem from lack of knowledge about how to handle conflict, then government facilitating education in these skills could be helpful.

Marriage education aimed at helping persons make thoughtful, deliberative decisions results in some couples who were planning to marry deciding not to do so.[72] Indeed, as Scott Stanley, a leading expert on marriage education, told Congress, if the goal is encouraging "healthy marriage," then "[m]etaphorically, a goal of marriage education should be to help people in burning houses leave, and to help people considering entry into smoldering buildings to gain the strength and support to flee."[73] Facilitating the relationship decisions of persons considering marriage, and teaching them skills that may contribute to a successful marriage, differs from trying to persuade persons not seeking to marry to do so.

Wade Horn maintains that government is not going to tell anyone to marry or influence their decision to do so; rather, the government will just help those who are considering marriage gain the skills and knowledge important to a "healthy marriage."[74] However, this modest aim seems inadequate to marriage promoters' goal of renewing a "marriage culture," in which children learn about the place of marriage in a good life and in which heterosexual marriage should be the exclusive institution in which persons should express sexuality, reproduce, and parent.[75] This kind of governmental message about marriage would promote a conservative orthodoxy about sexuality and family and fail to respect persons' capacity for responsible self-government as well as reasonable moral pluralism. And Horn's own evidently modest aims of facilitating marriage are at odds with his earlier warnings (prior to his DHHS tenure) that if government promotes women's economic self-sufficiency without promoting marriage, it may enable women to rear children without a father's support.[76] For this reason, welfare scholar Gwendolyn Mink cautions that marriage promotion as a welfare strategy denigrates some women's construction of motherhood as "independent" from marriage.[77]

## The Risks of Marriage Education as an Antipoverty Strategy

The risk that marriage education will not be facilitative—and that promoting "healthy marriage" will slide into promoting marriage as such—intensifies when marriage promotion becomes a welfare policy based on the rationale that marriage is a potent antipoverty strategy. On the one hand, funding marriage education for low-income couples seeking to marry would make available to them a resource that some may want and that is already available to couples who can afford it.[78] The Fragile Families Study found that marriage initiatives might help about one-third of low-income unmarried parents because they face "no serious barriers to marriage," such as unemployment, mental health problems, and domestic violence. On the other hand, the study found that for another one-third, marriage promotion is "unlikely to be effective or desirable" and may even "cause serious harm": this includes unmarried couples with a history of domestic violence as well as unmarried parents who are not romantically involved with one another at the time their child is born. This population, particularly if parents have children from previous relationships, would benefit more from a focus on parenting skills and general relationship skills.[79]

Similarly, creating a "pro-marriage" welfare office, on the premise that marriage leads to "independence," sends a message that government believes that those who apply for public assistance should work *and/or* marry. Will this message carefully convey the idea that government supports only "healthy marriage," and not that any marriage is good if it helps to alleviate poverty? If the latter, then it could be

harmful, given the high percentage of welfare recipients who have
experienced physical violence and nonviolent abuse within marriage
or intimate relationships, especially at the point when they try to move
from welfare to work.[80] As one women who left her physically abusive
husband put it:

> I can't imagine what I would have done if, at the time I left my
> husband, the welfare office had been full of messages praising
> marriage. There is so much emotional trauma involved in being
> abused and then leaving. You need to be supported and lifted up
> for making a good, safe choice for yourself and your children and
> for having the courage to not just stay with somebody, just to
> have a man or a marriage. A welfare system that holds up mar-
> riage as "the right thing to do" just reinforces the shame you feel
> and, if you are dealing with abuse, it weakens your resolve to
> leave.[81]

"Healthy marriage" education programs should help such women,
as Scott Stanley puts it, leave "burning houses" and gain the "strength
and support" to flee dangerous relationships. But will they? Horn, for
example, claims that they will, but H.R. 240, based on the Bush Administration's welfare plan, gives far less attention to domestic violence
than the proposed Senate bill, S. 667.[82] Moreover, some marriage promoters minimize the problem of domestic violence within marriage.
They attribute this feminist concern to "habitual radical feminist hostility to marriage itself," and contend that marriage is far safer for
women than, for example, cohabitation or dating.[83]

Marriage promoters may underestimate the magnitude of the
problem of domestic violence within marriage and its impact on low-
income couples and on women across the socioeconomic spectrum.
When Oklahoma, using TANF funds, undertook an extensive study
of its citizens' experiences with marriage and divorce, researchers
found that 47 percent of low-income Oklahomans, contrasted with 17
percent of other Oklahomans, identified domestic violence as a factor
leading to their divorce.[84] Women generally gave domestic violence as
a factor for divorce at a statistically significant higher rate (44 percent)
than did men (8 percent). A Utah survey modeled on the Oklahoma
study reported similar findings.[85] These troubling findings are consis-

tent with scholarship on the prevalence of women on welfare experiencing domestic violence.[86] They counsel that, as Stanley cautions, marriage education about "healthy marriage" should include "personal safety" as a "foundational" element.[87]

Furthermore, most existing marriage education programs were not designed for, and have not been tested with, the low-income unmarried population targeted by welfare reform. As research commissioned by DHHS indicates, such programs do not address the serious barriers to maintaining healthy relationships and stable family life faced by many economically disadvantaged persons.[88] Even when unmarried low-income couples seek to marry, for government to assume a truly facilitative role would require an investment in human capital that goes beyond marriage education. The Fragile Families Study concluded that about one-third of the couples it followed might be helped by marriage education *if* these programs expanded to address such problems as unemployment, lack of education, and other obstacles to stable family life.[89] Other studies urge going beyond the "policies of persuasion" about the value of marriage to develop "various ways to expand opportunities for people to act on their (responsible) intentions," through a variety of educational, employment, family planning, and parenthood and counseling programs.[90]

A significant obstacle to stable family life is gender conflict, or gender distrust. This issue reveals a close connection between relationship quality and sex equality. For example, Kathryn Edin and Maria Kefalas's ethnographic study of white, black, and Latina low-income mothers found that they valued marriage as an ideal but did not marry owing to concerns over securing sex equality, economic independence, and power within marriage, and over men's infidelity and domestic abuse. Surely it should be relevant to policymakers that such mothers believe "that marriage will probably make their lives more difficult than they are currently."[91] As Edin testified before Congress, they want self-government, or an equal partnership, rather than subservience.[92] The Fragile Families Study found significant gender distrust among low-income unmarried mothers and fathers, and concluded that although "positive attitudes encourage marriage," "women's gender distrust discourages both cohabitation and marriage." If programs seek to encourage women's positive attitudes and reduce their distrust, this "may well require men to change the behavior that leads to distrust or negative attitudes." Relationship quality (for example, "supportiveness"), the study concluded, strongly affects union formation and stability, and thus initiatives should seek to encourage "supportive behaviors" and reduce conflict and violence.[93]

My argument is that governmental initiatives to support marriage should be guided by concerns for the public value of sex equality, and should attend to the relationship between marriage quality and equality.

## Marriage Quality and Marriage Equality

One goal of marriage promoters is to persuade the public that marriage benefits both men and women. They claim that the old social science assumption that men benefit from marriage, but women do not, is outdated; the new social science evidence supports the case for marriage for women as well as men.[94] A prime example of that older social science is sociologist Jessica Bernard's *The Future of Marriage*, which found that there were two forms of marriage: "his" and "hers." Men, she found, benefited more from marriage than women. Thus, it was urgent that marriage be "upgraded" for women through "more sharing of roles by both partners."[95]

Is the problem simply one of teaching people to discard outdated notions? Research indicates that men still benefit more than women from marriage in nearly every respect, and whether women benefit is more directly related to the *quality* of marriage than it is for men.[96] Revisiting Bernard's thesis, one study of marriage in the 1980s and 1990s found that marriages continue to be unequal in ways that are especially costly to women, and that " 'his' marriage continues to be better than 'hers.' "[97] Even some marriage promoters acknowledge this gender differential, particularly with respect to the health benefits of marriage.[98] For example, in *The Marriage Problem*, James Q. Wilson attributes this gender difference to men's greater propensity—without wives' good influence—to engage in risky behavior (like "going to saloons" and associating with "rowdy gangs"; "left alone, a lot of men eat hamburgers and steaks, go out with their buddies to the bar, smoke cigars, and play poker through half the night")![99] Studies find that, after divorce, men have greater declines in physical health and emotional well-being than women,[100] perhaps because they no longer have the benefit of what Linda Waite and Maggie Gallagher call "the virtue of nagging"—the solicitude of wives for husband's health and well-being.[101]

Why do men benefit more from simply being married, whereas women's benefit depends on the quality of the relationship? In *Marriage and Men's Lives*, sociologist Steven Nock stresses marriage's role in conferring masculinity. Marriage is a central site in which men define and display their masculinity. Indeed, for men and women, the family is " 'the gender factory.' " Being married affords a man important social recognition and respect because he has successfully achieved masculinity, a precarious task in all societies.[102]

Is marriage more central to the successful establishment of men's gender identity than to women's? Historically, marriage was *a* central, if not *the* central, defining activity in a woman's life. As discussed in Chapters 2 and 3, marriage expanded a husband's capacity for citizenship even as it limited a wife's. The gradual repudiation of coverture and the legal disabilities attending marriage, and the advent of formal legal equality in various aspects of marriage, have reduced the significance of marriage as a limiting force on how women may form and express their identity and participate as citizens. At the same time, most women still marry, and the institution of marriage continues to exert a normative pull in shaping female identity and gender performance.[103] Thus, it is not obvious that marriage is any less a "gender factory" for women than for men.

## Civilizing Men through Marriage

Marriage promoters echo Nock's claims about the difficult task of establishing masculinity. Although they contend that marriage benefits women as well as men, marriage plays an added role of civilizing men: men need marriage to be responsible fathers and citizens, in a way that women do not need it to be responsible mothers and citizens.[104] Appealing to the natural, biological roles and inclinations of the sexes, they claim that society needs marriage to yoke men—who are otherwise naturally irresponsible, unfaithful, and even dangerous—to mothers and children. In this view, women are gatekeepers who should predicate men's access to sex on marital commitment.

The marriage movement speaks of a "male problematic" that pro-

moting marriage is thought to address: men's inclination toward procreating without taking responsibility for children. The contrasting
"female problematic" is women's inclination toward procreating and
rearing children, even in the absence of adequate resources and commitment by fathers and at the expense of self.[105] Some marriage promoters contend that certain social conditions, such as the decreased
stigma attached to nonmarital childbearing as well as a shortage of
"marriageable" men, intensify this biological inclination, so that more
women are willing to become mothers outside of marriage.[106]

Marriage promoters characteristically argue that the mother-child
bond is less fragile and less dependent on marriage than the father-
child bond. Wilson contends that society creates marriage to ensure
what "biological drives cannot": that men, who would otherwise have
a tendency to depart from a relationship with a mother and child,
provide the resources necessary for the survival of the mother and
child. He draws on evolutionary biology's portraits of men's capability
to sow their seed widely and of women's more limited reproductive
capability and more intensive investment in their young.[107] Similarly,
"The Marriage Movement: A Statement of Principles" observes: "as a
matter of mere biology, men can sire a virtually unlimited number of
children, but a man can provide daily care, protection, love, and financial support to only a few children." Marriage "closes this gap
between a man's sexual and fathering capacities."[108]

The gender role assumptions about the danger posed by unsocial-
ized men and the domesticating role of women are striking. They also
invite the question: if men need marriage more than women do, what
cost will a marriage promotion program have for women's equality
and self-government?

## What's Wrong with Using Marriage to Tame Men?

Viewing marriage as a means of domesticating men has a history
closely intertwined with sex inequality (as explained in Chapter 2).
The contemporary version of the domestication argument, as a justification for governmental promotion of marriage, has several flaws.
First, if men need not only marriage itself but also such hallmarks of
traditional marriage as being head of the household, then promoting
this form of marriage directly conflicts with respecting women's

equality. Constitutional norms of sex equality forbid government from using the law to reinforce a model of family responsibilities that installs men as leaders and providers and women as followers and dependents, or to advance similar schemes of unequal responsibility. Second, skepticism about appeals to "nature" or to sex differences as a justification for policy is in order, given the long history of such appeals to justify sex-based restrictions on women's citizenship and gender hierarchy in families and civil society.[109] Third, this portrait of men insults their capacity to be morally responsible agents. It reinforces women's familiar role as gatekeepers—morally responsible for themselves and for men in the areas of sexuality and family.[110] Fourth, evidence of some men's practices of responsible fathering outside of marriage cast doubt on the claim that only marriage can secure such commitment.

Do men need traditional marriage to establish masculinity? Nock argues that Americans "generally agree" that one component of marriage is that "[t]he husband is the head, and principal earner, in a marriage."[111] Men, in this view, are the principal breadwinners and society still expects men, and not women (at least to the same extent), to provide for their families. In and of itself, Nock argues, the term *head of household* does not imply a power relationship.[112] However, as found in Philip Blumstein and Pepper Schwartz's well-known study, *American Couples*, decision-making authority usually correlates with income earning, and thus the term *head of household* connotes leadership and authority within the household.[113] Indeed, in more recent work, Schwartz concludes: "The linchpin of marital inequality is . . . the provider complex, a combination of roles that give the man the responsibility for financially supporting the family's life-style and the woman all the auxiliary duties that allow the man to devote himself to his work." The provider role brings with it a sense of entitlement to appreciation, in terms of "emotional returns" and "provision of services."[114] Thus, even though, as a legal matter, marriage no longer entails a status relationship in which husbands have a duty to provide and may expect from wives services and obedience, the "provider complex" continues to carry with it such expectations.

Some contemporary research about gender roles within marriage bears out the thesis that men's role continues to be viewed as that of provider. Even with the dramatic increase in wives' and mothers' participation in the paid labor force in recent decades, and an emerging norm of shared responsibility for home work, "the vast majority of women and men continue to endorse the importance of husband as provider and wife as nurturer."[115] Let us grant that, as one recent report to DHHS observed: "Gender role expectations—whether traditional or egalitarian—are believed to exert a powerful influence on prospects for, and experiences in, relationships." How should these expectations shape public policy? As the report frames the question: "do the effects of gender role expectations suggest benefits to altering or working within these attitudes?"[116] I contend that a commitment to sex equality—and not simply concerns of utility or doing what works—should shape the answer to this question.

## Gender Role Expectations and "Marriageable" Men

Marriage promotion, as a tool of welfare policy, aims particularly at low-income men and women. Within this population, the traditional gender role expectation that men should be primary breadwinners may "raise a difficult hurdle for marriage, given the poor earning prospects of men with low skills and disadvantaged backgrounds." Men's economic status is positively related to their likelihood of getting and staying married, and men's lack of employment appears to play a greater role in nonmarriage then women's.[117]

Concerns about men not being "marriageable" surface especially with respect to low-income African Americans, who are disproportionately poor and unmarried. Indeed, DHHS's efforts include an African American Healthy Marriage Initiative.[118] In recent decades, an influential thesis has been that low-income black men's inability to live up to the provider role plays a part in their not marrying and in fathers' absence from their children's lives. William Julius Wilson linked low marriage rates and the rise in black female-headed families to a reduced number of "marriageable" black men owing to increased joblessness.[119] Elijah Anderson's ethnographic studies of inner-city African American men's values suggest that the inability to fulfill the provider role explains why young men do not marry and why they separate fathering children from marrying.[120]

How should governmental efforts to strengthen families take into account gender role expectations and persons' inability to live up to them? Congress proposes to promote "responsible fatherhood" and marriage among low-income men by helping make such men more "marriageable," by having them become better providers for their families—a traditional hallmark of masculinity and fatherhood. Left unexamined is whether this can be done without (consciously or unwittingly) shoring up male dominance and control within the household.

Research on the attitudes of low-income men about fatherhood supports more than one answer to this question. In *Code of the Street*, Anderson reported that the inner-city African American young men he studied aspired to an ideal of the "decent daddy," who provides for and protects his family in exchange for being "the undisputed head of the household" and making "the major decisions concerning the family." In this quid pro quo, "[t]he woman must know her place, which is taking care of the house and preparing food to his satisfaction." Anderson observes: "Many decent women negotiate an arrangement like this in order to obtain a worthy partner, a hardworking man, and a good provider and protector."[121]

Because of the economic transformation from manufacturing to service jobs, Anderson contends, far fewer African American men with limited education and skills than previously can fill the role of the "decent daddy," who can extract this bargain. Yet this ideal of being head of household and being in control continues to exert a hold, leading to troubling consequences. When young men view this ideal as being out of reach, they treat sex and reproduction as a game to "get over" on young females and they father children without having responsibility for them. When men marry and are unable "to establish domestic control, physical abuse sometimes follows."[122]

In contrast, other research on the views of low-income men and women on responsible fatherhood suggests that the provider role is no longer the defining trait of what makes a "good father." Similarly, inability to be a patriarch in the home need not lead to abdication of paternal responsibility. As Maureen Waller describes in her book, *My Baby's Father: Unmarried Parents and Paternal Responsibility*, the low-income parents she interviewed believed that making an effort to provide material support was a basic responsibility of fatherhood, but they ranked material provision after emotional involvement and moral guidance. This finding, which echoes findings from the Fragile Families Study, was consistent between mothers and fathers, and among African American and white parents.[123]

Although discussions of increasing men's "marriageability" stress economics, another important strategy would be to foster (as one report to DHHS put it) "greater acceptance of non-traditional family roles for men, especially those with lower earning capacity." Noting the beneficial effect on marital stability of paternal involvement with children, the report asked: "Can increasing men's commitment to active fathering be a mechanism for improving union quality and stability?"[124] Research on fathering suggests so, and also finds that, cross-culturally, "nurturant fatherhood was the most consistent predictor of gender equity."[125]

Encouraging active, nurturant fathering, or "social fathering"—whether within or outside of marriage—is consonant with the feminist goal of a nonpatriarchal model of fatherhood.[126] Such a focus would better fit the complexity of many fathers' parenting responsibilities in step, blending, and cohabiting families. As one federally commissioned report concluded: "to the extent that social policy is constructed through the lens of the traditional nuclear family model, new forms of responsible fathering by biological fathers or stepfathers are likely to be constrained."[127]

Governmental efforts to support healthy marriage and responsible fatherhood should not lend support to a quid pro quo premised on men's control and women's deference. Some argue that men will not accept the role of "responsible father" and husband without the perks of head of household. George Gilder, conservative welfare pundit of the 1980s, famously claimed not only that "the provider role accords with the deepest instincts of men" but also that it is hard for men to meet the claims of familial and sexual love "without a sense of masculine dominance."[128] However, models of engaged fathering, as Waller's work and the Fragile Families study suggest, do not rest on a link between fatherhood and household dominance.

I support public policy aimed at fostering economic empowerment of low-income men *and women* on the premise that it might facilitate them marrying. One significant reason people do not marry is a lack of economic resources, either their own or those of their potential partner. Studies of low-income couples' marital decisions find that they value marriage as an ideal, but, like other couples, they do not want to marry until they can do it "right" and begin with a solid economic footing. This may help explain why some unmarried couples separate becoming a parent from becoming a spouse.[129] Thus, initiatives to increase parents' "education and economic capacities" as a way to encourage stable families are compatible with my argument for governmental responsibility to foster capacity.[130] And whether or not such initiatives result in marriage, "strengthening families as they exist" still benefits adults and children.[131]

By contrast, economic empowerment aimed at making men more "marriageable" will not address reasons pertaining to marriage quality and equality that some low-income mothers give for not marrying until they can do it "right," such as the "stalled sex-role revolution at home," gender distrust, and concern about domestic abuse.[132] An approach to promoting strong families that responds to such concerns would avoid reinforcing traditional gender roles and attend to the connection between relationship quality and sex equality. But will marriage promoters heed such concerns? Is equality within marriage antithetical to or, to the contrary, central to renewing a marriage culture? What place should sex equality have in a program of supporting marriage?

## Marriage (E)quality and the "Marriage Crisis"

Strong marriages cannot be maintained on the basis of the same cultural assumptions or the same economic relationships that existed thirty years ago. . . . I don't think that anyone would want to turn the clock back. . . . Let's acknowledge that cultural norms of relationships between men and women have changed and that forms of female subordination to men that were widely accepted thirty years are now totally unacceptable. If you're going to have strong marriages today in the twenty-first century, they are marriages that have to be built on the fact of economic interdependence rather than economic dependence. They also have to be built on the premise of equality between men and women rather than inequality.

—*William Galston*, Marriage: Just a Piece of Paper?, *p. 229*

"Traditional" or "gendered" marriages persist because they are considered fair. . . . Even when embracing gender equality in all other realms of their lives, adults show scant willingness to forego their claims to masculinity and femininity inherent in marriage, parenthood, and the division of household tasks. . . . Most people view any legal attempt to require gender equality in their marriages as illegitimate.

—*Steven Nock, "The Future of Public Laws for Private Marriage,"*
The Good Society *11 (2002): 78*

How does sex equality feature in creating the "marriage crisis" as well as in resolving it? The marriage movement generally posits that women's expectations of sex equality within marriage and their diminished reliance on marriage for economic survival have contributed to the weakening of a marriage culture. For example, in a documentary growing out of the marriage movement, *Marriage: Just a Piece of Paper?*, narrator Cokie Roberts poses the question: "Can men and women be reconciled to each other? Is marriage part of the work of reconciliation?"[133]

The contrasting quoted statements by William Galston and Steven Nock, both signatories to "The Marriage Movement: A Statement of Principles," reflect two different views of the place of sex equality in marriage. One embraces sex equality as a foundation for strong marriages. The other draws a sharp distinction between the public realm of sex equality and the private realm in which gendered marriages are both desired and acceptable. Should gender equality within marriage—along with economic interdependence—be the two pillars of strong marriages, as Galston suggests? Should a principle of "equal access" by mothers and fathers to "the responsibilities and privileges of both the public and domestic realms" be, as marriage movement leader Don Browning argues, a part of a public philosophy of marriage that government may appropriately foster?[134]

Or is pursuing such equality, as Nock argues, contrary to what most Americans expect from marriage, and even an illegitimate goal of government? More bluntly, James Q. Wilson characterizes the ideal of "gender equality" as "nonsense," if it goes beyond ending male dominance to viewing men and women as having the same obligation to pursue a career and care for a child. He states: "Ordinary men and women do not think this way." And, he charges: "Gender equality is a fancy of the upper middle class."[135]

I contend that the gap between women's expectations of gender equality and marriage quality and their actual experience in marriage is a significant factor, across lines of class and race, leading to disenchantment with marriage and ultimately to divorce. The marriage movement acknowledges that sex inequality in marriage and women's greater economic independence have played a role in the supposed decline of marriage. For example, the National Marriage Project reports that compared to men, "young women are more disenchanted with marriage." Why? The Project's co-directors, David Popenoe and Barbara Dafoe Whitehead, identify "two convergent realities": (1) women have "higher expectations for emotional intimacy in marriage" and "more exacting standards" for a husband's participation in childrearing and household work, and (2) "because wives are breadwinners, they expect a more equitable division of household work—not always a fifty-fifty split but fairness in the sharing of the work of the home." When men do not share or meet these expectations, the "mismatch may lead to deep disappointment and dissatisfaction." Because women today depend less on marriage as their source of economic security than in the past, they are less likely to " 'put up' with a bad marriage out of sheer economic necessity" and more likely to leave an unhappy marriage.[136]

This account clearly suggests the link between marriage quality and equality. The idea of a "mismatch" between what women expect within marriage and how men behave also features in political scientist Andrew Hacker's diagnosis of a "growing gulf between women and men." He contends that one significant reason marriages do not last is that, increasingly, women expect "full equality" and "few are willing to sustain the former complementarity that required them to play a subordinate role" to men.[137]

The National Marriage Project's diagnosis of women's disenchantment with inequality within marriage also echoes Edin and Kefalas's findings about why low-income women do not marry. For low-income mothers, they conclude, marriage is about "ensuring a certain level of quality in their relationship"; they "want their marriages to be the same 'partnership of equals' that middle-class women now usually demand." Before Congress, Edin reported one woman's comment that "[a] man gets married to have somebody take care of them 'cause their mommy can't do it any more."[138] Similarly, Popenoe and Whitehead report: " 'I don't need a grown-up baby to take care of,' is a complaint often voiced by working married mothers."[139]

Concerns for equality and economic independence may also be one explanation for why women separate motherhood and marriage. Edin and Kefalas found one reason low-income mothers make this division is that, although they viewed their early twenties as the best time to have children, they did not wish to marry until later in their twenties, when they had established enough economic independence through market work to ensure bargaining power within marriage and to avoid economic dependency. Rather than viewing marriage as a means to achieve economic independence (as Bush's welfare plan does), they viewed some degree of economic independence as a precondition for a successful marriage.[140]

Similarly, the National Marriage Project reports poll data indicating that young women do not look to marriage as a form of economic security, and that most young women and men believe it is "extremely important to be economically 'set' as individuals" before they marry.[141] They try to take measures to secure equality and economic independence within marriage. As Whitehead has observed, today young women from economically advantaged homes choose to invest first in themselves, their education, and career, and they no longer view a successful marriage as the defining achievement of their lives.[142]

One form of inequality within marriage that may lead to instability, including divorce, is women's disproportionate performance of caregiving and household tasks. As explained in previous chapters, although most married people accept the premise of shared responsibility within marriage with respect to domestic labor, actual practice falls short. When wives view this unequal division of labor as unfair—but husbands do not—this can lead to marital instability.[143] The birth of a child often aggravates wives' resentment of and dissatisfaction over an unfair division of labor, particularly if the wife works outside the home and has to assume the main responsibility for the "second shift" of child care and housework.[144] In the growing number of marriages in which spouses are equally dependent on one another's earnings, wives are more willing than husbands to leave the marriage. Thus, greater economic interdependence may lead to more marital instability unless husbands change by doing more housework and child care and recognizing their wives' greater efforts.[145]

An unfair division of labor may not hinder marital stability, some research finds, if husband and wife share the perception that it is unfair. Indeed, Nock and family law scholar Margaret Brinig observe: "stable marriages . . . may not be experienced as fair marriages."[146] But does it follow, as Nock suggests, that calls to promote sex equality as a public value with relevance to family life are misguided? Consider that other research suggests that women feel they are entitled to equality in the home, but also perceive that insisting on this would engender conflict. And for women to act as agents of change conflicts with their role as nurturer and maintainer of relationships.[147] Rather than conclude that governmental efforts to support marriage should not attempt to address inequality, I contend that a program of supporting "healthy marriage" should seek to foster (not mandate) equal roles and responsibilities within the family.

For men and women who share a traditional view of gender roles, marriages modeled on the provider complex may be stable marriages. And yet, evolving notions of equality and changing gender role expectations may lead to marital instability.[148] Wives expect their husbands to be good providers, which requires men to invest in employment, but absorption of cultural ideals of equality leads wives to expect their husbands to contribute more to sustaining family life and to view the provider role as "a drain and competitor for the family and marriage's needs and time."[149]

The cultural ideal of male provider/female caregiver may also create tension and impair marriage quality when it poorly fits the reality of family life. The legacy of slavery and race discrimination rendered this ideal unrealistic for most black couples. Donna Franklin contends that the poor fit between this ideal and black marriages—in which both husband and wife work and wives also shoulder more of the burden of home and family work—is one reason black women and men report less marital happiness than others. She finds that "the issue of male dominance remains one of the primary sources of tension in black marriages, especially when the wife is the principal wage earner."[150]

The problems that Schwartz and Franklin identify surrounding the provider complex suggest the importance of supporting models of marriage that are not premised on male provider/female caregiver and that are attentive to the link between marital quality and equality. Such a model may be emerging among young people, who voice changing

perceptions of gender role expectations and of what marriage is *for.*
One National Marriage Project report finds that "an overwhelming
majority (94%) of never-married singles agree that 'when you marry
you want your spouse to be your soul mate, first and foremost,' " and
over 80 percent of young women agreed that it was more important
to them "to have a husband who can communicate about his deepest
feelings than to have a husband who makes a good living."[151]

Is this increasing focus on the quality of marriage a sign of progress
toward healthy marriages or a cause for worry? To the extent these
attitudes and behaviors suggest a departure from the old common law
arrangement of women trading obedience and service for men's financial support, they would seem to be a positive development. But marriage promoters are more ambivalent. They grant that young women's
concerns about achieving economic independence are grounded in
empirical realities. Yet they worry that young people have reduced
marriage to a matter of personal fulfillment and have unrealistic expectations (such as finding a soulmate).[152]

The heightened attention to the quality of marriage is a positive,
not regrettable, consequence of gains in women's equality in other
spheres of life. Over twenty-five years ago, economists Heather Ross
and Isabel Sawhill predicted that "if traditional attitudes about husband and wife roles lag behind changes in the economic status of
women, there may be a period during which men and women will be
less happy within marriage than in the past due to an increasing dis-
sonance between role performance and ideology."[153] But they predicted that, if attitudes also changed, equilibrium would be restored
and marriage would become much more egalitarian. People would
marry and remain married for reasons of personal satisfaction, not
economics. As Sawhill subsequently observed, the rise in divorce in
the 1970s—which leveled off in the 1980s but remained at a higher
level than before—reflects this period of adjustment to altered gender
roles.[154]

The transformation of marriage to reflect altered gender role expectations is hardly complete, however. Addressing calls in the 1990s
to "save marriage," family law scholar Katharine Bartlett cautioned:
"As women place an increasing value on fairness in their marriages
and their options outside of marriage strengthen, they will be less
willing to remain in unequal marital arrangements. . . . [I]f we are to

'strengthen marriage' and thereby take advantage of its powerful, traditional associations to create stable, loving families, marriage has to be made more attractive to women as well as to men."[155] She urged that those who would save marriage by addressing attitudes that compromise marriage should extend their focus to attitudes that support equality within marriage. This challenge to support equality within marriage is one that the marriage movement as well as legislators seeking to promote marriage should confront.

## What Place Does Sex Equality Have in Promoting "Healthy Marriage"?

I have argued that if government is to support "healthy marriages," sex equality should be an ingredient in the prescription for such marriages. It is not clear that marriage promoters agree. On the one hand, the coinage "equal regard" marriage (as defined below) might suggest that marriage promoters recognize that sex equality is a feature of the contemporary landscape. Indeed, some marriage promoters (including Galston and Browning) do call for sex equality and interpret "equal regard" marriage as requiring "equal access" by mothers and fathers to "the responsibilities and privileges of both the public and domestic realms."[156] On the other hand, other marriage promoters (such as James Q. Wilson) dismiss such a model of equal responsibilities as "nonsense." Notably, Horn, responsible for federal government marriage initiatives, derides as "androgyny" a notion that mothers and fathers should share equally in all childrearing activities.[157]

It is not surprising that a social movement includes many perspectives and does not speak with one voice. Yet when the question is whether and how government should promote marriage, it is important to understand whether sex equality is to be an ingredient in "healthy marriages." If so, how is government to promote it?

One key text, "The Marriage Movement: A Statement of Principles," reassures us that "[s]upport for marriage . . . does not require turning back the clock on desirable social change, promoting male tyranny, or tolerating domestic violence." And it seeks to help "more men and women achieve a caring, collaborative, and committed bond, rooted in equal regard between spouses."[158] But it offers no guidance on the relationship between "equal regard" and sex equality. Nor does it make any concrete proposals for how to understand "healthy marriages" in light of contemporary expectations of sex equality and fairness. In the one passage directly addressing household division of labor, the "Statement" urges:

> Do not discourage marital interdependence by penalizing unpaid work in homes and communities. Couples should be free to divide up labor however they choose without pressure from policies that discriminate against at-home parenting and other activities that serve civil society.[159]

This gender-neutral appeal says nothing about who should perform the unpaid labor. We might understandably suspect that, without any cultural transformation, this division of labor is a coded affirmation of women's role as unpaid caregivers.[160]

Marriage promoter David Popenoe explicitly proposes to resolve the gender crisis, or "confusion over marital roles," by embracing a gendered division of labor. Decrying that roles within marriage are subject to "endless negotiation" and choice, he argues that this is "no way to run a family—or a culture": the whole point of a "cultural script," or a set of social norms, is to supply people with social expectations that will shape their behavior to society's long-term benefit. Popenoe advocates a "modified traditional nuclear family." Both men and women invest in education and career, but once children are born, women are encouraged to leave work for the first few years of a child's life and to work part-time until the child's teen-age years. Sex differences, he contends, justify this model; by contrast, androgyny (for example, if a father must act like a mother) could drive men from marriage.[161]

Such appeals to gender specialization bring to mind economic models of marriage and the idea that men and women bring different capacities and skills to marriage and differentially invest in it.[162] Some marriage promoters argue that role specialization in domestic versus market activities benefits children, parents, and society. But the person who invests in domestic activities, at the expense of investing in market activities, may be vulnerable at divorce. Through reforming divorce laws, for example, marriage promoters would reward investment in domestic activities and shift power to those who are committed to permanence.[163] To revisit the pessimistic young women studied by the National Marriage Project, tougher divorce laws might persuade them that investing more than their husbands do in childrearing and domestic labor is not an overly risky strategy.

Thus, the rhetoric of "equal regard" marriage does not carry with it a clear commitment to sex equality, but is compatible with many models of gender-differentiated roles. What follows for public policy about "healthy marriages"? Should government "take sides" in favor of equality? In favor of a "cultural script" of a tradition, or "modified traditional nuclear family"? Or should government be neutral as between egalitarian and traditional marriages? Should it sidestep the issue by urging that the key to a healthy marriage is acquiring a basic "skill set" applicable to any marriage?[164]

Governmental neutrality is neither realistic nor appropriate. For many marriage promoters, a crucial task is not just teaching skills but changing social norms. Moreover, current legislative proposals to promote marriage include funding the efforts of nongovernmental actors, especially faith-based groups. It seems unlikely that these groups will teach skills in a "neutral" manner devoid of other messages and commitments. Thus, if such groups are to help in promoting marriage, we should ask how important public values, such as sex equality, will feature in this enterprise.

Governmentally sponsored relationship education should not embrace models of marriage premised on gender hierarchy.[165] Such governmental action would offend the constitutional principle of sex equality. Thus, government may not promote Popenoe's gendered division of labor as a model of "healthy marriage," for that is tantamount to using law (as government once did) to enforce a gendered allocation of responsibilities that reinforces stereotypes about men and women.[166] And even if there is a biological or evolutionary basis for what the marriage movement calls the "male problematic"—or men's inclination toward a lack of paternal responsibility—government should address this problem in a way that respects women's equal citizenship and does not assign them special responsibility for taming men. Similarly, appeals to child well-being may not justify government promoting a family form structured by sex inequality.[167]

Government should ensure that a commitment to sex equality is part of its educative efforts about healthy marriage. The minimum content of equality begins by rejecting patriarchal governance in favor of mutual self-governance. Rejecting domestic violence and male entitlement to exclusive decision-making power within the household also comes within this minimum. Thus, it is laudable that some state-sponsored marriage education materials inform persons seeking to marry that domestic violence is a crime, not an incident of marriage, and caution them against entering into potentially violent relationships.[168] In addition, family law holds parents equally responsible for the material support and nurture of their children. In light of women's disproportionate responsibility for caregiving work and domestic labor, and the importance of this work to orderly social reproduction, governmental education about marriage should espouse an ideal of equal responsibility.[169] It should not steer couples to the sort of "natural" gender role specialization urged by some in the marriage movement. Nor should it frame the issues couples should consider in ways that reinforce conventional gender role expectations. For example, posing, as discussion items, such questions as: "How will you and your spouse divide responsibility for paid work and child care?" or "How will you discipline your children?" avoids doing so. By contrast, posing questions such as: "A mother should not work outside the home unless her children are in school: agree, disagree, or undecided?"; and "the father should discipline the children: agree, disagree, or undecided?")—as Texas's handbook does—implicitly treats such gender conventions as the status quo.[170]

Direct governmental funding of groups whose vision of "healthy marriage" entails a model of family governance premised on gender hierarchy and male leadership/female deference would also conflict with constitutional norms of sex equality. If their vision derived from religious teaching, this would trigger First Amendment concerns. For example, it would be inappropriate for government to fund marriage promotion efforts by a group like Promise Keepers, which instructs husbands that they must inform their wives that they are reclaiming their proper role of "leading the family" and that, if wives object, "there can be no compromise here." To wives, the instruction is to give the leadership back: "For the sake of your family and the survival of our culture, let your man be a man if he's willing. . . . God never meant for you to bear the load you're carrying."[171] It would similarly be inappropriate to fund biblically based messages about a wife's duty to be subject to her husband or about a husband's special role as head of his family.[172]

One counterargument is that governmental embrace of sex equality as a component of "healthy marriage" would impose a governmental orthodoxy and thwart pluralism. Why not have government take a more pluralistic approach to funding and facilitate many competing visions of healthy marriages and of how best to promote such marriages?[173] Government itself could be neutral about the division of power and roles within marriage. And, one might argue, given that not all couples seek to embrace an egalitarian model of marriage, this pluralism would allow for persons with different values to find the kind of service provider that best comports with their own values. Such an approach would open the purse to Promise Keepers and Nation of Islam, along with feminist marriage advocates, antidomestic violence activists, and religious groups that reject a patriarchal model of family self-government for one premised on gender equality.

The problem with this pluralistic model is that it would allow government to fund groups that espouse sex inequality as a model of family governance. This conflicts with government's obligation not to use law to perpetuate fixed gender roles and "archaic" stereotypes.[174] To the contrary, sex equality should be a constitutive principle in governmental efforts to support strong families. I advocate that government use its educational and persuasive power to promote sex equality, not that it dictate a particular division of labor within families. As discussed in Chapter 2, respect for intimate association, autonomy, and reasonable moral pluralism counsel some governmental restraint.

## Practical Reasons to Include Sex Equality in "Healthy Marriage"

Promoting sex equality within families is consonant with constitutional and legal norms. It is also a practical and effective way to foster strong families. Given the link between marriage quality and equality, a model of marriage premised on equality, or an equal partnership, is a promising way to avoid the problems of dominance and hierarchy that have impaired women's equal citizenship and contributed to the "marriage crisis." Indeed, it would be a just corrective to a long history of governmental promotion of sex inequality within marriage. It may also be a practical approach to the problem of gender distrust and to some of the tensions facing contemporary families in juggling domestic, market, and other responsibilities. As welfare policy debates over increasing men's "marriageability" indicate, both men and women have a stake in models of marriage that move beyond the provider/head of household role for men. Perhaps the rhetoric should be reconstructing, not restoring, a marriage culture.

Fostering a more egalitarian model of marriage would be a valuable step toward reconstruction. Schwartz argues that "peer marriage," a more egalitarian form of marriage than traditional marriage, is a vanguard for such a model. It could also improve marital stability, since it rests on deep friendship and male engagement with children, and it avoids the sorts of resentments that arise from the provider complex.[175] Hetherington's study of divorce found that marriages embracing "gender equity" had the second lowest divorce rate.[176] And contra Popenoe, research suggests that "although equal relationships require more frequent negotiation and compromise, it may be precisely the need for continued interpersonal contact and involvement that contributes to the high levels of satisfaction found among egalitarian couples."[177]

There is considerable evidence that, even though role differentiation continues in practice, a social norm of equality, or marriage as an equal partnership, is emerging.[178] For example, June Carbone argues that a norm of "collaborative, relatively egalitarian relationships" is already in place for middle-class couples (although it is not always fully realized). She suggests that such norms may conflict with working-class marital models, which put more emphasis on hierarchical and authoritarian gender relationships.[179] Yet Francine Deutsch's book, *Halving It All: How Equally Shared Parenting Works*, finds that some dual-earner blue-collar husbands and wives adopt a model of equal parenting because they view it as the fair thing to do, as well as the most practical arrangement. As other research confirms, feminist ideology is neither a necessary nor a sufficient requirement for reaching such an arrangement. Couples may adopt an equal parenting arrangement out of necessity, concern for child well-being, sense of fairness, or in order to avoid repeating the patterns of their parents' marriage (or of their own prior marriage(s)).[180] Moreover, a powerful motivator leading men to agree to an equal partnership is love for, and a desire to preserve the relationship with, a female partner who insists on equality. As Schwartz concludes, in her study, *Love Between Equals:* "People seek an egalitarian relationship because they want fair treatment, respect, and the right to have equal voice in creating and maintaining a fulfilling marriage."[181]

One recent survey of American attitudes toward marriage, devised by Don Browning, found that 55 percent of persons surveyed thought that a model of marital love as a matter of "equal regard and mutuality between husband and wife" best correlated with a successful marriage; "only 38% hold that love as self-sacrifice is the key." But the survey found striking gender differences: women chose the equal regard and mutuality model more often than men (61 percent to 48 percent); men chose the self-sacrifice model more often than women (44 percent to 33 percent). Moreover, the gender differences in the black community were "stunning": "76 percent of women in contrast to 33 percent of men selected mutuality, whereas only 14 percent of women in contrast to 48 percent of men thought love as self-sacrifice correlates with good marriages." It is not clear whose self-sacrifice the male respondents had in mind, that of women or that of men. From this data, Browning concludes that for Americans "mutuality is in; self-sacrifice is going out," and that mutuality is more important to women, "possibly as a consequence of both feminism and the entry of women into the workplace." One reason why more women than men initiate divorce, he infers, is that women want "equal regard marriages more than men" but may not be getting them.[182]

These gender differences are intriguing, given the historic and cultural equation of women's care with self-sacrifice.[183] Perhaps women are resisting that model in the context of marriage. This again underscores the link between marriage quality and equality. However, the marriage movement identifies higher expectations for marriage and the decreased willingness to sacrifice—for example, to invest in family life at personal cost or to stay together for the children even if parents do not get along—as evidence of the decline of a marriage culture and a cause for more divorce.[184] In the renewed marriage culture that the marriage movement seeks, more people would presumably affirm (as only a small minority do today) that it would be better for children if unhappily married parents stayed together (except in cases of high conflict and abuse).[185] But is discontent with sex equality simply a form of low-level conflict and unhappiness to be borne for the sake of the children? Or would a renewed marriage culture aspire to greater equality?

Similarly, the marriage movement identifies a commitment to permanence as an important value in shoring up marriage. To my call for encouraging more equality and equity in marriage, they might well counter that keeping track of who does what is antithetical to marital stability; in stable marriages, couples assume either that the balance will be righted, or that "any imbalance does not matter."[186] But given the current division of labor in most marriages, is this an argument that "healthy marriages" may require that women be willing to bear inequity for the sake of stability? Tellingly, both the Oklahoma and Utah surveys of attitudes about marriage found that a "lack of commitment" was the most frequent reason given for divorce, yet women, more frequently than men, did not think that they should have worked harder to try to preserve the marriage.[187] Perhaps this is because women continue to bear more responsibility for many elements of "emotion work" important to commitment in a marriage.[188] It would seem a prudent strategy to support a model of "healthy marriage" that does not perpetuate such unequal responsibility.

## Conclusion

In this chapter, I have argued that government may foster capacities for forming and sustaining committed, intimate relationships. Government may support marriage, but it should not use marriage as the sole proxy for family forms that foster adult and child well-being. Such efforts should embrace sex equality within families as a guiding norm. The marriage movement and governmental proposals to promote marriage generally fail to do so. A governmental program of supporting marriage, whether through educational or economic measures, raises questions that remain to be addressed. Should government support same-sex marriage? Do concerns for equality among families argue for the abolition of marriage? Or should respect for equality among families entail supporting not only marriage, but also single-parent and other nonmarital families that can promote orderly social reproduction and allow realization of the goods associated with families? The next two chapters take up these questions.

# 5

## Recognizing Same-Sex Marriage

As a public institution and a right of fundamental importance,
civil marriage is an evolving paradigm.
*ᴏ Goodridge v. Department of Public Health (2003)*

After more than two centuries of American jurisprudence and
millennia of human experience, a few judges and local authorities
are presuming to change the most fundamental institution of
civilization. . . . On a matter of such importance, the voice of the
people must be heard. Activist courts have left the people with
one recourse. If we are to prevent the meaning of marriage from
being changed forever, our nation must enact a constitutional
amendment to protect marriage in America.
*ᴏ President George W. Bush,*
*Remarks on Marriage Amendment, February 25, 2004*

𝓘F MARRIAGE IS SUCH A FUNDAMENTAL institution,
should it be made available to same-sex couples? Are states justified
in prohibiting same-sex couples from marrying? If so, why? Should
"We the People" adopt a "federal marriage amendment" to enshrine
in the United States Constitution a definition of marriage—binding
throughout the nation—as limited to the union of one man and one
woman? Or is barring same-sex couples, who seek public recognition
of their committed relationships, an unjustified denial of their individual liberty and equality as well as an unjust form of *inequality among
families?* And would adopting such a constitutional amendment further
entrench such inequality and deny the power of individual states to
make movements toward greater individual and family liberty and
equality?

Public rhetoric about protecting and promoting marriage reveals an
evident tension: even as the marriage movement and governmental
proposals to promote marriage seek to renew a "marriage culture" and

155

expand marriage's reach, they seek to restrict the reach of marriage by preventing same-sex marriage. I would resolve this tension by arguing for legal recognition of same-sex marriage. Critical reflection on the goods of marriage, the functions of families, the needs of same-sex couples, and the aims of contemporary family law support this recognition. So, too, do the commitments to liberty and equality in state constitutions (and, indeed, the federal Constitution). A fundamental disagreement exists between opponents and proponents of same-sex marriage as to whether the best way to support the institution of marriage is to "protect" traditional marriage from any change (as President Bush argues in the opening epigraph) or to understand marriage as an "evolving paradigm" (as Massachusetts's highest court concluded). I argue for the latter view.

In supporting same-sex marriage, I stress government's formative responsibility to foster capacity, equality, and responsibility. Recognizing same-sex marriage shows equal concern and respect for the moral capacity of lesbians and gay men to form intimate relationships and to pursue goods associated with family life and marriage. A focus on capacity directs attention to the practical reality of how families function: despite their exclusion from the institution of marriage, lesbians and gay men form committed intimate relationships and function as responsible and loving parents. Respect for the reasonable moral pluralism that results from persons exercising their capacities for personal self-government flows from toleration as respect.

Recognizing same-sex marriage would remedy an unjust form of inequality among families: denying gay men and lesbians access to the basic civil right to marry and to public recognition and support of their families. Making marriage more inclusive is an important part of reconstructing it to be more compatible with contemporary norms of equality and fairness. Morever, allowing same-sex marriage blunts the criticism that it is wrong for government to support marriage by linking it to a significant set of benefits, protections, and obligations but at the same time to exclude otherwise qualified persons—gay men and lesbians—from this protective umbrella. Permitting same-sex marriage is also an entailment of affirming gender equality—rather than gender hierarchy and rigid gender roles—as a component of marriage.

Normative and functional arguments of the sort I urge have already played a role in bringing about incremental steps within family law toward the support and recognition of same-sex couples' committed relationships. Indeed, the analyses offered by the Massachusetts Supreme Judicial Court in Goodridge v. Department of Public Health and the Vermont Supreme Court in Baker v. State, which interpreted their state constitutions to invalidate marriage laws limiting the benefits of marriage to opposite-sex couples, closely resonate with my own approach. I will proceed by discussing the successful challenges to Vermont's and Massachusetts's marriage laws, which led, respectively, to the recognition of same-sex civil unions and same-sex marriage. I highlight the role played in each case of drawing analogies between the aspirations and capacities, or capabilities, of same-sex couples and those of opposite-sex couples. I also stress each court's focus on the facilitative role of marriage law and on the imperative to accord equality to diverse families.

The chapter will then respond to two contrasting arguments that gay men and lesbians do not need civil marriage. The first argument is that they should challenge—rather than seek access to—the privileged place of marriage as a basis for the range of benefits, rights, and obligations now tied to it. Other models, this argument insists, would better fit the diversity of intimate relationships and families. I argue that supporting same-sex marriage need not force same-sex couples to fit patterns of traditional marriage in order to receive governmental protection. Nor does support for same-sex marriage preclude a more inclusive approach to regulating and supporting families. The second argument is that gay men and lesbians do not need marriage because they can use measures such as private contracts and domestic partnership laws to protect their relationships. I reject this solution as one of partial, rather than full, equality. Using the examples of the domestic partnership laws adopted in California (on the model of the Vermont civil union), Hawaii, and New Jersey, I argue that, once a state recognizes that some affirmative support of same-sex couples' relationships is appropriate, it is difficult to find a persuasive justification to deny them a broader range of supports.

## *Baker:* Expanding the "Family of State-Sanctioned Human Relations"

The State's interest in extending official recognition and legal protection to the professed commitment of two individuals to a lasting relationship of mutual affection is predicated on the belief that legal support of a couple's commitment provides stability for the individuals, their family, and the broader community. . . . [T]he essential aspect of [plaintiffs'] claim is simply and fundamentally for inclusion in the family of state-sanctioned human relations. . . . The extension of the Common Benefits Clause to acknowledge plaintiffs as Vermonters who seek nothing more, nor less, than legal protection and security for their avowed commitment to an intimate and lasting human relationship is simply, when all is said and done, a recognition of our common humanity.

*—Baker v. State, 744 A.2d 864, 889 (Vt. 1999)*

Three same-sex couples who sought—but were denied—a marriage license challenged Vermont's marriage law under the "common benefits clause" of Vermont's constitution (its analogue to the Equal Protection Clause of the United States Constitution). In the stirring language quoted above, Chief Justice Jeffrey Amestoy articulated plaintiffs' claim as a demand for "inclusion in the family of state-sanctioned human relations," and concluded that such inclusion is "a recognition of our common humanity." The Vermont Supreme Court declared that the state's constitution required that the benefits, protections, and obligations linked to marriage must be made available to same-sex couples, but left to the legislature the fashioning of a proper remedy, namely, whether to provide for same-sex marriage or some other institution.

The Vermont legislature declined to extend marriage, as such, to same-sex couples. It instead created an institution called a "civil union," permitting same-sex couples who entered into such a union to have the same package of benefits, protections, and obligations accorded to married couples.[1] With this enactment, Vermont became the first state in which a same-sex couple could enter into a publicly recognized relationship that had the same legal incidents as marriage.

This pathbreaking outcome stands in contrast to the outcomes of the challenges brought in the 1990s to the marriage laws of Hawaii and Alaska, in which victories in the state courts incited the legislatures to propose constitutional amendments and other measures to prohibit same-sex marriage (or, at least, to leave the definition of marriage to the legislature).[2] Similarly, in 1996, the federal government passed the Defense of Marriage Act (DOMA), expressly defining marriage, for federal purposes, as the union between one man and one woman and purporting to protect states from having to give full faith and credit to any same-sex marriages entered into outside their borders.[3] By 2004, thirty-nine states had also passed DOMAs.[4] And in the 2004 election, in which President Bush campaigned on a promise to defend traditional marriage, voters in eleven of those states approved constitutional amendments defining marriage to exclude same-sex unions and (in several states) barring the creation of any domestic union with legal status substantially equivalent to marriage.[5]

Why did Vermont's highest court and legislature take these remarkable steps toward inclusion and equality among families? Analogies between same-sex and opposite-sex couples played a key role. The state had argued that excluding same-sex couples from marriage advanced its purpose in "furthering the link between procreation and child rearing" and in rejecting "the notion that fathers or mothers . . . are mere surplusage to the functions of procreation and childrearing."[6]

The court rejected these arguments. It agreed that the state "has a legitimate and long-standing interest in promoting a permanent commitment between couples for the security of their children" and has advanced this interest by extending marriage to couples considered capable of having children, that is, men and women. However, restricting marriage to opposite-sex couples, the court found, is both over- and underinclusive. It is overinclusive because not all opposite-sex couples wish to (or are able to) have children. The state, nonetheless, permits them to marry. At the same time, it is underinclusive because, "with or without the marriage sanction, the reality today is that increasing numbers of same-sex couples are employing increasingly efficient assisted-reproductive techniques to conceive and raise children." These couples and opposite-sex couples who desire to have and rear children may be similar in needing to make recourse to reproductive technology. Thus, "to the extent that the state's purpose in licensing civil marriage was, and is, to legitimize children and provide for their security, the statutes plainly exclude many same-sex couples who are no different from opposite-sex couples with respect to these objectives."[7]

The Vermont court could readily rely on this analogical argument because Vermont's legislature had already taken affirmative steps toward greater equality among families. It had removed legal barriers so that same-sex couples could legally adopt children and have access to assisted-reproductive technology. Moreover, the court interpreted these legislative developments as reflecting a public policy "diametrically at odds" with that asserted by the state in opposing same-sex marriage: "promoting child rearing in a setting that provides both male and female role models."[8]

The court considered what was at stake for the same-sex couples in the lawsuit: what was the benefit of civil marriage? Marriage laws, the court observed, "transform a private agreement into a source of significant public benefits and protections."[9] Why should these legal benefits and protections flow from a marriage license? The court explains that governmental recognition and protection of "the professed commitment of two individuals to a lasting relationship of mutual affection" rests on the belief that such legal support "provides stability for the individuals, their family, and the broader community." Thus, government may foster stable families. But if so, why exclude same-sex couples? The same-sex couples challenging Vermont's marriage law, the court concluded, simply seek "inclusion in the family of state-sanctioned human relations," and Vermont's constitution requires that they receive the common benefits available to opposite-sex couples who marry: "legal protection and security for their avowed commitment to an intimate and lasting human relationship."[10]

When the Vermont legislature created the "civil union," it also drew analogies between opposite-sex and same-sex couples and stressed the facilitative role of governmental recognition of intimate relationships. It found that, under Vermont law, "legal recognition of civil marriage by the state is" the primary, and, in a number of instances, "the exclusive source of numerous benefits, responsibilities and protections . . . for married persons and their children." Why should government recognize and support civil marriage? The legislature answered: "to encourage close and caring families, and to protect all family members from the economic and social consequences of abandonment and divorce, focusing on those who have been especially at risk."[11] However, the Act establishing civil unions expands this state protection beyond marriage. It declares: "The state has a strong interest in promoting stable and lasting families, including families based upon a same-sex couple." The Act finds similarity in goods realized by same-sex families and married couples:

> Despite longstanding social and economic discrimination, many gay and lesbian Vermonters have formed lasting, committed, caring, and faithful relationships with persons of their same sex. These couples live together, participate in their communities together, and some raise children and care for family members together, just as do couples who are married under Vermont law.[12]

This similarity justified extending the common benefits of marriage to same-sex couples but not the title of "marriage." To respect longstanding social institutions and religious traditions, the Act limits "marriage" to "a union between a man and a woman." At the same time, it draws on Vermont's tradition of "equal treatment and respect" to justify a functional equivalent to marriage—civil unions—for same-sex couples.[13]

The premise that governmental recognition and support of committed intimate relationships may provide stability for such relationships is borne out by experience. The Vermont Civil Union Review Commission, charged by the legislature to evaluate the impact on Vermont residents of civil unions, found: "All couples testified as to the stability afforded by the relationship, from the ability to form a lasting commitment recognized not only by the state, but by family, coworkers, friends and the community." Children of such couples benefited from public acceptance of their family. Being treated as a spouse also brought rights and benefits with respect to matters such as medical decision making, health insurance, and property ownership.[14]

But do civil unions give same-sex couples all the benefits of marriage? One criticism of the civil union remedy is that it denies to same-sex couples access to marriage as a "unique expressive resource" for affirming publicly that one is in a committed relationship.[15] Moreover, participants in a civil union are not married for federal purposes, excluding them from the benefits and obligations linked to marital status in over 1,000 federal laws. And unlike a marital union, a civil union entered into in one state is unlikely to be afforded recognition in most other states.[16]

Why adopt the dual-track scheme of marriage and civil union? The civil union remedy was, no doubt, a political compromise that attempted to honor the court's directive while reckoning with the tenacious hold of the conviction, often rooted in religious tradition, that marriage has been—and must continue to be—a unique male-female relationship. If, for those holding this conviction, extending marriage to same-sex couples would threaten traditional understandings of marriage, a "civil union" might be less threatening because it seems to leave marriage intact. A civil union seems to reconcile this conviction with an impulse toward recognizing that the relationships and families of gay men and lesbians deserve some protection. Of course, many opponents of same-sex marriage also view civil unions as a threat, as efforts to overturn Vermont's law indicate.[17] Does the conviction that marriage must be the union of one man and one woman offer a persuasive reason for government to continue to define civil marriage to exclude same-sex couples? The successful challenge to Massachusetts's marriage law permits reflection on this question.

## Commitment Is the "Sine Qua Non" of Civil Marriage

Unlike the Vermont Supreme Court, the Massachusetts Supreme Judicial Court insisted that the proper remedy to the unconstitutional exclusion of same-sex couples from marriage must be marriage, not civil unions. The challenge to Massachusetts's marriage laws posed afresh significant questions about the place of marriage in society, whether the traditional definition of marriage should control contemporary understandings of it, and whether government has adequate reasons for denying same-sex couples access to marriage. In addressing these questions, the Massachusetts court built on the framework set up by the Vermont court. In addition, although it based its ruling that same-sex couples should be permitted to marry on the requirements of the Massachusetts constitution, its exposition of how human dignity, respect, liberty, and equality are at stake in marriage drew upon the analysis of the U.S. Supreme Court in Lawrence v. Texas, the case invalidating a law prohibiting same-sex sodomy on the ground that it "demeans the lives" of gay men and lesbians.[18] These resources contributed to a rich, nuanced opinion that illustrates powerfully government's formative role in shaping and supporting families and how this formative process includes both governmental action and restraint.

First, what is marriage and what is government's interest in it? The court speaks of the "paradoxical status" of civil marriage as a "[s]tate-conferred benefit" as well as a "multifaceted personal interest of 'fundamental importance.' " Marriage is both a "vital social institution" and a "civil right."[19] In a passage that incensed some marriage defenders, the court declares: "Simply put, the government creates civil marriage. In Massachusetts, civil marriage is, and since pre-Colonial days has been, precisely what its name implies: a wholly secular institution."[20] The court did not deny the existence of rich religious and cultural traditions about marriage; rather, it invited attention to the civil consequences of marriage and to why *government* has an interest in marriage.

Why did the plaintiffs in *Goodridge* seek to marry? They sought the tangible and intangible benefits, protections, and obligations linked to the status of marriage. Like the Vermont court, the Massachusetts court listed the "enormous" number of tangible benefits "accessible only by way of a marriage license," benefits "touching nearly every aspect of life and death." Civil marriage, the court observes, also has expressive value: it is "at once a deeply personal commitment to another human being and a highly public celebration of the ideals of mutuality, companionship, intimacy, fidelity, and family." In addition to adults, children also are "the recipients of the special legal and economic protections obtained by civil marriage," and "reap a measure of family stability and economic security" that is less readily accessible to nonmarital children.[21]

Why does the state link these tangible and intangible benefits to marriage? The court answers in terms of what marriage does for individuals who marry and for society. Government properly creates and regulates civil marriage because it enhances the "welfare of the community": it "anchors an ordered society by encouraging stable relationships over transient ones," and it ensures sources of care for adults and children. Marriage "fulfills yearnings for security, safe haven, and connection that express our common humanity."[22]

In telling the stories of why gay men and lesbians challenging Massachusetts's law sought to marry, the Massachusetts court implicitly appeals to "our common humanity" to portray them not as strangers or "outliers" to the law, but as our friends and neighbors, similar in aspirations and capacity to other Massachusetts residents.[23] Thus, the

court recounts that Gloria and Linda "had been in a committed relationship for thirty years." The named plaintiffs, Hillary and Julie
Goodridge, "had been in a committed relationship for thirteen years
and lived with their five year old daughter." The court observes that
the plaintiffs hold many different occupations and that many are "active in church, community, and school groups." Why do they seek to
marry?: "to affirm publicly their commitment to each other and to
secure the legal protections and benefits afforded to married couples
and their children."[24]

Precisely because same-sex couples are at the margins of marriage
law,[25] prohibited from marrying, their arguments about why they seek
to marry help to reveal the aspirations people bring to marriage and the
goods associated with it. The plaintiffs contended that they "seek to
marry for the same mix of reasons" that opposite-sex couples do and
that "same-sex and different-sex couples are similarly situated with respect to the mutual love and commitment expected in the marital relationship and in needing the structures and supports provided by civil
marriage." Marriage, the plaintiffs argued, helps to secure the goods of
(1) love ("[t]he desire to marry is grounded in the intangibles of love, an
enduring commitment, and a shared journey through life"); (2) happiness ("The profound mutual love, respect, commitment and intimacy
that define the marital relationship are essential for human dignity and
happiness and are valuable to society as a whole"); (3) interdependence
(marriage "represents the possibility and hopefully the reality of a
'shared interdependent life' "); (4) emotional and financial security, for
example, to provide for each other's old age or for medical care; (5) security for their children ("to situate their family within the social recognition and legal rights that only marriage affords," so that their children can "grow up in a world where their parents' relationship is legally
and communally respected"); and (6) community recognition of commitment (same-sex couples "seek to marry so the world can see them as
they see themselves—a deeply loyal and devoted couple who are each
other's mate in every way").[26]

Both the court's and the plaintiffs' accounts of what marriage is and
what it is for show that government's formative role with respect to
marriage entails both action and restraint. As the court explains: "The
individual liberty and equality safeguards of the Massachusetts Constitution protect both 'freedom from' unwarranted government intru-

sion into protected spheres of life and 'freedom to' partake in benefits created by the State for the common good." In explicating "freedom to," the court detailed those benefits. In elaborating the individual right to "freedom from" government, the court held that the right to marry must include the "right to marry the person of one's choice, subject to appropriate government restrictions in the interests of public health, safety, and welfare." The court invoked Loving v. Virginia, Planned Parenthood v. Casey, *Lawrence*, and other U.S. Supreme Court opinions affirming liberty and equality rights in matters of sexual intimacy, marriage, and family.[27]

Can the state offer persuasive justifications for restricting persons from marrying a person of the same sex, and thus denying them the rights, protections, and obligations of civil marriage? In answering this question in the negative, the Massachusetts court offers an instructive model of critical reflection on appeals to tradition—an element lacking in most prior judicial evaluations of challenges to state marriage laws.[28] The Department of Public Health offered three legislative rationales for prohibiting same-sex couples from marrying: (1) providing a "favorable setting for procreation;" (2) ensuring the optimal setting for child rearing, which the Department defined as "a two-parent family with one parent of each sex"; and (3) preserving scarce state and private financial resources.[29] The court assessed these rationales and concluded that none offered a rational justification for barring same-sex marriage.

## Is Procreation the Essence of Marriage?

A common argument against same-sex marriage emphasizes that same-sex couples lack the capacity to procreate—a fundamental purpose of marriage. Until recently, state courts routinely accepted this argument.[30] Some contemporary opponents of same-sex marriage also define the public purpose of marriage in terms of procreation and child-rearing.[31]

Defining the primary purpose—or essence—of marriage as procreation, the Massachusetts court held, was too narrow. The court concluded: "While it is certainly true that many, perhaps most, married couples have children together (assisted or unassisted), it is the exclusive and permanent commitment of the marriage partners to one another, not the begetting of children, that is the sine qua non of civil marriage." The state does not condition granting marriage licenses upon applicants attesting to "their ability or intention to conceive children." Nor does it insist that procreation and parenting take place only in marriage. To the contrary, the state "affirmatively facilitates bringing children into a family regardless of whether the intended parent is married or unmarried, whether the child is adopted or born into a family, whether assistive technology was used to conceive the child, and whether the parent or her partner is heterosexual, homosexual, or bisexual." This more inclusive approach contrasts with an earlier era of family regulation in which "[p]unitive notions of illegitimacy" and of "homosexual identity" reinforced the understanding of marriage as a heterosexual institution. But if procreation were, today, "a necessary component" of civil marriage, the court concluded, "our statutes would draw a tighter circle around the permissible bounds of nonmarital child bearing and the creation of families by noncoital means," instead of facilitating these ways of forming families.[32] Marriage is not the exclusive pathway to family life.

### Marriage and the "Optimal Setting" for Childrearing

The court's disposition of the "marriage is procreation" argument sets the stage for its rejection of the state's second argument, that marriage between a man and a woman provides the "optimal setting for child rearing." The court agreed that protecting the welfare of children is a "paramount" state policy, but held that restricting marriage to opposite-sex couples does not rationally further that policy. First, Massachusetts has "responded supportively to the changing realities of the American family" and "moved vigorously to strengthen the modern family in its many variations."[33] Here, the court points to laws allowing grandparent visitation, co-parent adoption by same-sex partners, and other measures establishing a nonmarital legal relationship between a child and a parent or adult caretaker.

Second, the court appeals to the equal capacities of gay men and lesbians to be good parents, as well as to the needs of children, in concluding that government would more rationally foster child wellbeing by supporting same-sex parenting. Given the state's goal of providing an optimal setting for childearing in marriage, it is irrational to exclude same-sex couples. Although such couples "have children for the reasons others do—to love them, to care for them, to nurture them"—the "task of child rearing" is made "infinitely harder by their status as outliers to the marriage laws." Precisely because "the State provides a cornucopia of substantial benefits to married parents and their children," on the premise that marriage is "the foremost setting for the education and socialization of children," the children of gay men and lesbians, like all children, "need and should have the fullest opportunity to grow up in a secure, protected family unit."[34] This argues for—rather than against—permitting same-sex couples to marry.

The court also concluded that the ban on same-sex marriage did not rationally advance the state's goal of conserving public and private financial resources. First, opposite-sex couples may marry whether or not they demonstrate financial dependence on each other. Second, the Department merely offered a "conclusory generalization" that same-sex couples are less financially dependent on each other than opposite-sex couples, and thus less in need of the public benefits (such as tax advantages) and private benefits (such as employer-financed health insurance) tied to marital status. Yet, many same-sex couples—including plaintiffs—have children and other dependents, such as aged parents, in their care.[35]

## Marriage as an "Evolving Paradigm"

The Department also argued that it rests with the state legislature, not the court, to define the proper boundaries of marriage. In response, the court defended its role in "carefully scrutinizing the statutory ban on same-sex marriages in light of relevant State constitutional provisions." The court's analysis highlights the vital role of critical reflection on tradition in determining the boundaries of marriage.

In explaining why excluding same-sex couples from marriage violates the liberty and equality provisions of the Massachusetts constitution, the court draws analogies to now-prohibited forms of sex inequality and racial inequality. The court observes:

The history of constitutional law "is the story of the extension of constitutional rights and protections to people once ignored or excluded." . . . This statement is as true in the area of civil marriage as in any other area of civil rights. . . . As a public institution and a right of fundamental importance, civil marriage is an evolving paradigm.[36]

One salient example of evolution, offered by the court, is striking down laws barring interracial marriage. Another is the movement by courts and the legislature away from the common law's "exceptionally harsh" treatment of wives and the abrogation of laws reflecting "antediluvian assumptions" about the role and status of women in marriage in society.[37] What is the relevance of this movement toward sex equality?

First, it cautions against clinging to common law understandings of marriage that embodied forms of discrimination—even if they were not then recognized as such—such as laws "denying women's equal partnership in marriage."[38] Second, it invites critical reflection on whether the definition of marriage as the union of one man and one woman rests in part on this earlier model of hierarchical, gender complementarity. If so, then the continuing appeal to this definition of marriage requires a contemporary justification that does not rest on such a hierarchy. In this regard, the Department of Public Health fell short: it contended that marriage's historical role of properly regulating the sexes through sex-linked duties should constrain the court to define marriage as between one man and one woman.[39]

The court implicitly rejects the Department's gender ordering argument when it concludes that, although extending civil marriage to same-sex couples would depart from inherited definitions of marriage, it would not disturb "the fundamental value of marriage in our society." A dissenting justice argued that allowing same-sex couples to marry would grant them a right to "change the institution of marriage itself" because marriage is "intimately tied to the reproductive systems of the marriage partners and to the 'optimal' mother and father setting for child rearing." The court responded: "[t]hat analysis hews perilously close to the argument . . . that men and women are so innately and fundamentally different that their respective 'proper spheres' can be rigidly and universally delineated. An abundance of legislative enactments and decisions of this court negate any such stereotypical premises."[40]

The relevance of the evolution of marriage toward greater sex equality plays a more explicit role in the concurring opinion by Justice John Greaney. Greaney treats the marriage statutes as creating a classification based on sex: it is "[o]nly their gender" that prevents gay men and lesbians from "marrying their chosen partners."[41] The state's justifications are insufficient to sustain such a classification. In commenting on the definitional argument that marriage is, and has always been, "the legal union of a man and a woman," Greaney calls for critical reflection upon tradition:

> [T]he case requires that we confront ingrained assumptions with respect to historically accepted roles of men and women within the institution of marriage and requires that we reexamine these assumptions in light of the unequivocal language of [the state constitution]. . . . [A]s a matter of constitutional law, neither the mantra of tradition, nor individual conviction, can justify the perpetuation of a hierarchy in which couples of the same sex and their families are deemed less worthy of social and legal recognition than couples of the opposite sex and their families.[42]

Thus, Justice Greaney implies that a reexamination of gender role assumptions should lead to rejecting an unjust hierarchy that favors opposite-sex couples and disfavors same-sex couples.

A number of legal scholars have argued that excluding same-sex couples from marriage constitutes sex discrimination. In rebutting the Department's definitional argument, the plaintiffs in *Goodridge* drew on this scholarship, which elaborates more fully than do the opinions in *Goodridge* how critical reflection on gender roles and sex equality supports same-sex marriage.[43] The crux of the argument is that defining marriage as between a man and a woman reflects a gender ideology about proper male and female roles (as Greaney's concurrence recognizes). Gay and lesbian relationships threaten this gender ideology because they "deny the traditional belief and prescription that stable relations require the hierarchy and reciprocity of male/female polarity."[44] They also deviate from a gender role ideology that male desire should be directed only at females, and vice versa, similarly threatening the naturalness and inevitability of heterosexuality. Such theorists find (as did Hawaii's Supreme Court and Justice Greaney) a powerful analogy to Loving v. Virginia, in which the U.S. Supreme

Court struck down Virginia's antimiscegenation law because it lacked any basis other than furthering a governmental orthodoxy of white supremacy.[45] The analogy is that just as antimiscegenation law barred marriage based solely on the race of one's partner (that is, two persons of the same race could marry, but a white man could not marry a black woman), current marriage law bars same-sex marriage solely on the basis of the sex of one's partner. The argument is that, just as *Loving* rejected the claim that Virginia's law was not discriminatory because it applied equally to ban all interracial marriage, so, too, courts should reject the claim that confining marriage to one man and one woman does not discriminate because it equally bars men and women from marrying someone of the same-sex.[46]

Building on these analyses of sex discrimination, my argument based on the idea of toleration is that prohibiting same-sex marriages rests on an unjust imposition of a governmental orthodoxy about gender roles and sexuality. This argument appeals to respect for persons' moral capacities and freedom to pursue their conception of a good life, as well as to constitutional norms of equality and liberty. When government bans gay men and lesbians from marrying their chosen partners, it denies them equal access to cultural resources important to the development and expression of their moral powers. Using the concept of the "paradox of intolerance," David Richards argues that, throughout American history, society has imposed such an unjust orthodoxy (or what feminist scholars call "compulsory heterosexuality") precisely at the point at which debate about gender roles, sexuality, and such institutions as marriage is most needed. Finding analogies among the abolitionist, feminist, and gay rights causes, Richards uses the image of "moral slavery" to connote the harm flowing from the denial of basic rights to dignity, autonomy, and conscience in matters of intimacy, marriage, and family.[47]

It is precisely same-sex marriage's potential to upset traditional understandings of marriage as a status relationship with clearly defined sex-linked roles that leads to some opposition to it. Because it exposes "the historical construction of gender at the heart of marriage," same-sex marriage holds the potential to point to a new understanding of marriage not rooted in gender-based hierarchy and sex inequality.[48] To invoke John Stuart Mill, such marriages may be valuable "experiments of living."

## The Aftermath of *Goodridge*

In contrast to the Supreme Court of Vermont, which left to the state legislature the question of how to remedy the inequality caused by excluding same-sex couples from the benefits, protections, and obligations of marriage, the Supreme Judicial Court of Massachusetts declared a remedy: to "construe civil marriage to mean the voluntary union of two persons as spouses, to the exclusion of all others."[49] In choosing to redefine the common law meaning of marriage "in light of evolving constitutional standards," it followed the example of its northern neighbor, the Court of Appeal for Ontario, which held that the common law definition of marriage in Canada violated the Canadian Charter of Rights and Freedoms.[50] The Massachusetts court stayed its judgment for six months (until May 17, 2004) to "permit the Legislature to take such action as it may deem appropriate in light of" the opinion.[51]

The legislature soon sought the court's advisory opinion on whether same-sex civil unions, as distinguished from marriage, would be a constitutionally acceptable remedy. The court said no, ruling that a bill "to preserve the traditional historic nature and meaning" of civil marriage for opposite-sex couples and to recognize civil unions for same-sex couples constituted a form of "second-class citizenship."[52] In response, the legislature approved a state constitutional amendment that would, on the one hand, ban same-sex marriage and, on the other, create same-sex civil unions—the Vermont remedy which the Massachusetts court had rejected. Because the constitutional amendment process in Massachusetts requires the legislature to propose the amendment in two successive legislative sessions and then submit it for approval through a public referendum, the earliest such an amendment could take effect would be November 2006.[53] Thus, on May 17, 2004, Massachusetts became the first state in the nation in which same-sex couples could legally marry. Even while news reports focused on the jubilation of hundreds of same-sex couples exercising their right to marry and the joy of their children, the specter of the loss of this right loomed.[54]

In the wake of *Goodridge*, as well as reports across the nation of various public officials issuing marriage licenses to same-sex couples—or refusing to issue licenses to any couples until same-sex couples were permitted to marry—conservative lawmakers redoubled their efforts to pass a "federal marriage amendment" to impose a national definition of marriage as between a man and a woman, thus preventing any state from recognizing same-sex marriage.[55] President Bush declared his support, claiming that such an amendment was the only recourse available to defend and protect marriage from "activist" judges and public officials who would change its meaning. But in suggesting that the amendment would leave state legislatures "free to make their own choices in defining legal arrangements other than marriage," he evidently left open the issue that they—but not courts—were free to recognize same-sex civil unions.[56]

What could account for this stance of not opposing civil unions, which would extend the incidents of marriage by another name to same-sex couples? One answer might be a concern for federalism and not trampling on states' rights in the area of family law. For example, former U.S. representative Bob Barr, sponsor of the federal Defense of Marriage Act (DOMA), testified against the federal marriage amendment on the ground that DOMA left it to the states to decide whether to recognize same-sex marriage, while the proposed amendment removed from states the authority to define marriage for themselves.[57] Many conservatives were more ready to limit states, preferring an amendment that would ban same-sex civil unions along with marriage.

Another reason that some opponents of same-sex marriage would permit same-sex civil unions may be that such a compromise preserves the "one man-one woman" definitional element of marriage. Yet merely appealing to tradition and history does not explain why altering this particular element of marriage would destroy marriage. As a careful analysis of the *Goodridge* opinion reveals, merely invoking history and tradition—as though marriage is a static entity rather than "an evolving paradigm"—does not adequately justify why marriage must remain limited to opposite-sex couples today.

Marriage, Bush claimed, "cannot be severed from its cultural, religious, and natural roots without weakening the good influence of society."[58] The *Goodridge* court, however, argued that such "roots" cannot control the contemporary meaning of *civil* marriage or resolve the question of the public purposes and goods at stake in it. After all, the fact that bans on interracial marriage had religious and cultural roots did not protect them from critical examination in light of constitutional principles of liberty and equality.

Treating civil marriage and civil unions as two wholly distinct forms also runs a risk of perpetuating the association of marriage with sex inequality. One might argue, for example, that, because the term *civil union* does not possess the historical associations of marriage as a status relationship linked to gender hierarchy and sex inequality, it may be liberating and it does not saddle same-sex couples with these vestiges of inequality. This might lead to a persuasive argument for making civil unions also available to opposite-sex couples who wish to avoid these historical associations, or even replacing civil marriage with civil unions. However, as Mary Anne Case observes, when government relegates same-sex couples to civil unions and opposite-sex couples to marriage, it unwittingly sends an implicit message that the institution of marriage cannot shed these associations.[59]

Civil unions do not accord full equality to gay men and lesbians and their families. Nonetheless, given stronger public support for civil unions than for same-sex marriage, they may be an important—even necessary—step in that direction.[60] In 2005, for example, without the spur of a judicial ruling, the Connecticut legislature passed a civil union law. Notably, this law was a substitute bill for a proposed bill to recognize same-sex marriage. Governor M. Jodi Rell, who signed the new law, praised it for making it clear that "marriage in Connecticut is defined as the union of a man and a woman," while also "extend[ing] civil rights to all couples, no matter their gender."[61] However, if and when the U.S. Supreme Court faces the question of whether the federal Constitution protects the right of a person to marry someone of the same sex, the Court should, by drawing on its prior marriage precedents and building on *Lawrence*'s idea of "respect" for same-sex intimate associations, answer this question "yes." And this answer should be "yes" even if, as Cass Sunstein argues, a federal right to marry is best understood not as a right that states must create marriage, but a right—if a state does create the institution of marriage—of equal access to the expressive and material benefits the state links to it.[62] In the meantime, *Goodridge* and *Baker* signal that state constitutions are also an important source for vindicating the equal rights of gay men and lesbians. A federal marriage amendment would foreclose both the U.S. Supreme Court and states (whether courts or legislatures) from extending the right to marry to same-sex couples.

## The "Goods" of Marriage and the Capacities, Needs, and Rights of Same-Sex Couples

My review of the successful challenges to Vermont's and Massachusetts's marriage laws demonstrates the powerful appeal of reasoning by analogy and of making functional arguments about the capacities and needs of gay men and lesbians who form families. Why are analogies so powerful in this context? Both the Vermont and Massachusetts's courts appealed to the "common humanity" of opposite-sex and same-sex persons. They stressed the shared aspiration of same-sex and opposite-sex couples to form committed, caring, responsible relationships, their shared capacity to do so, and their shared capacity to be loving and responsible parents. This rhetorical move attempts to portray gay men and lesbians, not as "strangers" or "outliers" to the laws of marriage, but as straights' friends and neighbors. (There may, for example, be a link between the dramatic growth in the number of people who report having a gay friend or family member—and in the "visibility and acceptance" of gay men and lesbians in the mass media—and growing public support for equal rights for gay men and lesbians.)[63] An eloquent attempt to cast gay men and lesbians as neighbors warranting toleration and respect appears in Justice Greaney's concurrence in *Goodridge:*

> I am hopeful that our decision will be accepted by those thoughtful citizens who believe that same-sex unions should not be approved by the State. I am not referring here to acceptance in the sense of grudging acknowledgment of the court's authority to adjudicate the matter. My hope is more liberating. The plaintiffs are members of our community, our neighbors, our co-workers, our friends. . . . We share a common humanity and participate together in the social contract that is the foundation of our Commonwealth. Simple principles of decency dictate that we extend to the plaintiffs, and to their new status, full acceptance, tolerance, and respect. We should do so because it is the right thing to do.[64]

In effect, this is a rejection of empty toleration and a plea for toleration as respect. It is consonant with Michael Sandel's argument that the best path to respect and appreciation for the lives of gay men and lesbians is precisely to make analogical arguments that appeal to the goods that rights make possible, rather than—as he charges liberals do—appealing to the value of choice itself.[65] But appealing to the importance to persons' dignity of a protected realm of choice does not preclude analogical arguments about the goods that choice protects.[66] Indeed, one strength of *Goodridge* is that it weaves analogical reasoning about such goods into a framework of individual rights to choose rooted in liberty and equality.

Drawing analogies between same-sex families and other families also has persuasive power, in part, because such analogies look at how actual families function and not just at an ideal definition of family. A significant trend in family law is the move to recognize "functional" families or families that are the "functional equivalents" of traditional, marital families.[67] No doubt, the Vermont and the Massachusetts courts could confidently speak of state policies favoring a more inclusive approach to supporting families in light of legislative—as well as judicial—efforts in their states to facilitate parenting by gay men and lesbians. For example, the Massachusetts court cited its earlier decision in Adoption of Tammy, in which it upheld an adoption by a biological parent and her lesbian partner because it was in the "best interest of the child." The family court below found that both parents were "functional parents" and many witnesses testified that "the three form a healthy, happy, and stable family unit."[68]

This functional approach is also compatible with a commitment to toleration for diverse family forms because they reflect the reasonable moral pluralism that follows when persons exercise their moral capacities. Thus, I endorse political liberalism's functional approach, which does not require that the family take a particular form, but focuses on whether it "is arranged to fulfill [its] tasks effectively and doesn't run afoul of other political values."[69] In addition to the task of nurturing and rearing children to become capable members of society and good citizens, which Rawls mentions, I have added that society also has an interest in the intimate, interdependent relationships between adults in families.[70]

To accord respect for the equal basic liberties of citizens, government, when it restricts or regulates those liberties, must satisfy the requirements of reason-giving. As political liberalism explains duties of mutual respect and civility, citizens should not attempt to enforce their comprehensive moral doctrines through politics and to appeal to positions that they cannot reasonably expect to be accepted by others who do not share those doctrines.[71] For example, invoking biblical condemnations of same-sex relationships would not suffice as a political argument against same-sex marriage. Nor would natural law arguments, offered by conservative scholars like John Finnis and Robert George, that same-sex couples are not capable of realizing the central goods of marriage: friendship and procreative sexuality.[72] These arguments do not meet the criteria of public reasonableness because they do not offer a view that other citizens can reasonably be expected to affirm.[73] The *Goodridge* court cogently offered reasons to reject the "marriage is procreation" argument. Furthermore, the Supreme Court's contraception and abortion cases and its opinion in *Lawrence* reject such a narrow understanding of the aims of marriage or of sexuality.

The opinions by Vermont's and Massachusetts's highest courts offer valuable examples of how focus on the functions of families, the goods they help family members to realize, and the requirements of reason-giving lead to greater respect and equality for same-sex couples.[74] In these opinions, evaluation of the state's asserted interests took place not through a no-holds-barred airing of competing comprehensive moral doctrines, biases, and prejudices of citizens concerning gay men and lesbians, but through a focused inquiry into the purposes served by the law of marriage, the aspirations of gay men and lesbians seeking to marry, and the needs and competencies of gay and lesbian parents. To the extent the courts overtly embraced moral values, they were political values such as respect for the diversity of actual families and the value of a committed, nurturing parental relationship. For example, the *Goodridge* court admonished that "[n]o one disputes that the plaintiff couples are families," noted that the Department conceded that gay men and lesbians could be "excellent" parents, and drew on Massachusetts's vigorous efforts to "strengthen the modern family in its many variations."[75]

The appeal to the fundamental similarities of opposite-sex and same-sex persons in their needs and capacities also has persuasive power because it invites attention to the goods society associates with intimacy and family life, and with marriage in particular.[76] It invites attention to the role that facilitative governmental efforts play in supporting families. Analyzing marriage in terms of the array of benefits, protections, and responsibilities linked to it helps focus on what is at stake in expanding or restricting access to marriage. For example, looking at the law of marriage and the central benefits and obligations associated with it, and comparing those to the needs of same-sex couples in long-term relationships, legal scholar David Chambers finds that marriage, "as a whole, fit[s] the needs" of such couples.[77] Marriage law recognizes emotional attachments, sets rules concerning parental rights and responsibilities, and regulates the economic relationship of the married couple to each other and to the state. Thus, marriage law helps people to organize their intimate relationships in satisfying ways. But as legal scholar Jennifer Wriggins points out, excluding lesbian and gay male couples from marriage and "the panoply of legal responsibilities and benefits" it affords denies them this "facilitative" aspect of the law.[78]

This diagnosis of the close fit between the needs of same-sex families and marriage invites two objections. First, some proponents of equal rights for gay men and lesbians object to making marriage a central goal because it may force assimilation and mask distinctive differences between heterosexuals and homosexuals. Second, some opponents of same-sex marriage argue that same-sex couples can find adequate protection of their relationships through alternative measures such as entering into private contracts and registering as domestic partners.

## Do Analogies Mask Difference and Force Assimilation?

The strategy of appealing to analogies between opposite-sex and same-sex couples to argue for a right to same-sex marriage is powerful because it encourages critical reflection on what is at stake in these debates. It is also a sensible legal strategy, given that challenges to unequal treatment, under federal and state constitutional law, require claimants to demonstrate that they are similarly situated to other groups, yet are treated differently without adequate justification. However, some supporters of equal rights for gay men and lesbians contend that this approach masks differences and makes same-sex couples look just like opposite-sex couples. They charge that, rather than seeking to include gay men and lesbians in the privileged status of marriage, reformers should challenge marriage's status as a favored, state-sanctioned intimate relationship and the use of that status as the basis for the range of benefits, rights, and obligations now tied to it. Because marriage confers legitimacy on the intimate lives of those who marry, they contend, the intimate lives of gay men and lesbians who do not marry will be deemed unworthy of respect and will remain vulnerable to governmental regulation and punishment. Instead of marriage, they argue for models of family that better fit the diversity of intimate relationships and families.

In an influential critique of making marriage a central goal of "gay liberation," Paula Ettelbrick reported that the thought of appealing to a similarity between same-sex and opposite-sex couples terrified her. She contended that the quest for same-sex marriage "runs contrary to two of the primary goals of the lesbian and gay movement: the affirmation of gay identity and culture and the validation of many forms of relationships."[79] Stressing similarities between opposite-sex and same-sex couples will blunt the distinctiveness of gay or lesbian identity and culture, and embracing marriage will stigmatize those who do not marry. Similarly, queer theorist Michael Warner challenges the push for same-sex marriage: "Marriage sanctifies some couples at the expense of others. . . . [I]f you don't have it, you and your relations are less worthy."[80]

This set of criticisms offers some useful cautions about supporting same-sex marriage but does not demonstrate that such support is misguided. Sociologists Judith Stacey and Stephen Biblarz, for example, caution that arguments that there are no differences between children reared by same-sex couples and those reared by opposite sex couples may downplay some differences. Contrary to the claims of conservative scholars who oppose same-sex marriage,[81] these differences do not reflect deficits, that is, harm to children or a diminution in child well-being. Rather, if one values family environments that foster sex equality and respect for diversity, some differences may be salutary. Daughters raised by lesbian parents, for example, have "higher aspirations to nontraditional gender occupations" and sons are less traditionally masculine on such measures as aggressiveness. Although children reared by lesbian or gay parents and heterosexual parents show no significant differences in social and psychological measures, children of lesbian or gay parents, because they often face "homophobic teasing and ridicule," seem "to exhibit impressive psychological strength."[82]

Another potentially meritorious difference between opposite-sex and same-sex relationships concerns role division. Studies of same-sex couples find that they less often adopt a breadwinner/homemaker model and often consciously try to create models of equal partnership.[83] Nan Hunter contends that opening marriage up to same-sex couples may transform marriage in a more egalitarian direction because such couples must rethink the roles of "husband" and "wife." It may also inspire critical reflection by opposite-sex couples on whether assumptions about gender and innate capacity justify traditional division of roles and responsibilities for nurturing and earning.[84]

Another factor weighing against the worry about forced assimilation is the repudiation, in contemporary marriage laws, of the rigid prescription of roles based on gender in favor of a gender-neutral scheme of equality and mutual rights and responsibility. This erosion of hierarchical gender ordering permits persons greater freedom to shape marriage into their own image.[85]

Marriage critics correctly point out that one component of the gay rights movement has been a critique of marriage. The grounds have included marriage's patriarchal history as well as its hindrance of sexual liberty. However, as William Eskridge demonstrates, another steady theme has been that securing the right to marry is a crucial component of equal citizenship.[86] I contend that affording the many gay men and lesbians who seek to marry the right to do so is a vital step in respecting their equal moral capacity.[87]

At a minimum, permitting same-sex marriage accepts the fact of diversity and properly gives gay men and lesbians the opportunity to exercise their moral powers. It does not ensure acceptance of difference as a positive good. However, it opens the door to moving from accepting the fact of diversity to respecting and appreciating diversity (as Justice Greaney's eloquent concurrence in *Goodridge* hopes). Recognizing the right to same-sex marriage would prompt discourse and engagement among citizens about the meaning and goods of marriage. This could lead to a critique of dominant orthodoxies about gender, family, and sexuality and to a cultural transformation in society's perceptions of gay men and lesbians.[88] Thus, as citizens and lawmakers in Massachusetts have observed that same-sex marriages in their state have not had negative effects, public opposition to same-sex marriage has steadily eroded.[89] In terms of my vision of the place of families, affording greater equality *among* families might in turn promote greater equality *within* families.

But what of the argument that, when government recognizes marriage, it bestows legitimacy on some relationships and denies respect, dignity, and legitimacy to others? This critique of marriage was surely powerful in the era in which Bowers v. Hardwick[90] upheld states' use of criminal law to punish same-sex sodomy and express moral disapproval of homosexuality. Such criminal law also served as a basis to discriminate against gay men and lesbians in matters such as parental rights.[91] However, does this critique still hold in the era of Romer v. Evans,[92] which puts limits on a state's ability to discriminate on the basis of sexual orientation and, even more, in the era of *Lawrence*,[93] which overturned *Bowers* and held that sodomy laws unconstitutionally denied gay men and lesbians liberty and respect for their intimate lives? In effect, *Lawrence* affirms "freedom from" oppressive governmental regulation of the intimate sexual lives of gay men and lesbians, and its language of "dignity," "respect," and "equality" indicates more than mere grudging toleration of the deviant or the unworthy. *Lawrence* also recognized how criminal sodomy laws harm gay men and lesbians in other areas of their lives.

Marriage critics might well concede that *Lawrence's* protection of a sphere of liberty for gay men and lesbians—or freedom from intrusion—is important. But until government also extends "freedom to," that is, supports and recognizes the full range of forms of intimate affiliation chosen by gay men and lesbians, they still will be denied equal respect and dignity. Same-sex marriage, I have argued, is an appropriate form of this "freedom to" (as *Goodridge* illustrates). One critical response is that, even if expanded to include same-sex couples, marriage inevitably leaves out certain conceptions of the good life—for example, models of intimate relationships that reject exclusive commitment and fidelity or that would move beyond the binary of two persons to several persons. But it is important to separate a few distinct arguments.

One argument is simply that marriage, whatever form it takes, should not be the basis on which society assigns particular benefits and goods. Ruthann Robson, for example, would abolish marriage so that the state "would not relate to its citizens on the basis of their intimate relations."[94] My response is that government properly facilitates marriage and assigns important benefits, obligations, and protections to it because of its role in fostering individual happiness and important social goods. Thus, I reject the view that persons' intimate and sexual lives should never be a matter of public concern, let alone public benefits. But I agree with marriage critics that marriage should not be the exclusive institution through which a society ensures that certain basic needs are met. This point seems especially fair given that a lack of economic resources is often a barrier to marriage, and people who are in need of services like health insurance are unlikely to get them.

A second argument is that governmental support of intimate relationships is appropriate, but marriage, even if made more egalitarian and open to same-sex couples, does not have a good fit with the needs of some gay men and lesbians. This argument raises an important concern about whether the model of marriage adequately reflects the diversity of forms of intimate life that warrant governmental support. For example, the complexity of certain gay men's and lesbian's families, in which more than two people may have a parenting relationship to a child, may require public recognition and support for families other than marital families.[95]

Conservatives warn that same-sex marriage leads society down the "slippery slope" to group marriage: that is, not just to polygamy (traditionally, one husband with multiple wives) but also, to use a new coinage, to polyamory (that is, "many loves," or relationships with more than one intimate partner, regardless of gender).[96] But many proponents of same-sex marriage strongly affirm elements like an exclusive commitment between two persons, and find good reasons for protecting the monogamous sexual dyad.[97] Others distinguish the gender hierarchy associated with traditional polygyny (one man with several wives) from contemporary polyamory, arguing that the latter warrants serious consideration as an ethical alternative to monogamy— given the gap between the marital ideal of monogamy and actual practice.[98] No doubt, there will be ongoing debate about the normative, empirical, and regulatory questions raised by polyamory,[99] but I do not believe that recognizing same-sex marriage compels an evolution to embrace plural marriage. As the *Goodridge* court pointed out, the gay men and lesbians seeking to marry "do not attack the binary nature of marriage," and "are willing to embrace marriage's solemn obligations of exclusivity, mutual support, and commitment to one another."[100]

Ultimately, these critiques of marriage raise important questions about the place of marriage, to which I will return in Chapter 6. But it is possible for government to support and recognize marriage in a way that advances equality among families and does not demean the intimate lives of those who do not marry. Fostering such equality does not require abolishing marriage.

## Why Aren't Private Contracts and Domestic Partnership Laws Enough?

A rather different argument is that instead of extending the status of marriage to same-sex couples, society can afford them adequate protection of their relationships through private contract or domestic partnership schemes. By so doing, society would preserve marriage's distinctive meaning but also give some protection to the committed relationships of same-sex couples. I characterize this argument as supporting partial equality: same-sex couples could secure some—but not all—of the benefits, protections, and obligations of marriage.

The Department of Public Health argued for such partial equality in the *Goodridge* case. It contended that the same-sex couples who sought to marry were not seriously harmed—but merely inconvenienced—by the denial of access to marriage, since they could achieve most of the benefits and obligations of marriage through other means. These couples could draw up legal documents, such as partnership agreements, dissolution agreements, powers of attorney, health-care proxies, living wills, coparenting agreements, emergency guardianships, name changes, and wills and trusts. They could register as domestic partners, and many Massachusetts employers and some municipalities would provide benefits to them. In addition, under federal and state constitutional law concerning parental liberty, gay men and lesbians have some rights concerning their children even without marriage. Thus, the Department concluded, because same-sex couples can obtain many of the benefits and protections linked to marriage without marriage itself, denying a marriage license was not so "coercive" as to trigger a constitutional deprivation of due process.[101]

But if an important function of official recognition of marriage is, as the Vermont Supreme Court observed in *Baker*, to foster the security and stability of committed, intimate relationships, then neither private contract nor the partial equality afforded by extending some obligations and benefits of marriage to same-sex couples is an adequate substitute. A cogent response is that given by the Supreme Judicial Court of Massachusetts in *Goodridge*: denying access to civil marriage is far more than an "inconvenience." It is irrational to bar same-sex families, many of whom include children, from access to the "cornucopia" of benefits linked to marriage when those benefits could help such families by fostering stability and child well-being. Moreover, since many of those benefits are available only through marital status, and could not be approximated by contract, same-sex couples and their children are harmed by denying them access to marriage and the "immeasurable advantages" it brings.[102]

Furthermore, if the arguments made in this chapter about the equal capacities of same-sex and opposite-sex couples are persuasive, there is no good justification for this two-tier system. In this system, same-sex couples must structure their intimate relationships through an array of private contracts giving them some, but not all, of the statutory benefits inked to marriage, while opposite-sex couples may do "one-stop shopping" by entering into marriage. Moreover, private contracts and domestic partnership registration do not give same-sex couples access to the unique expressive resource of marriage, which allows those who marry to make a public statement about their intimate commitment.

The rationales that Massachusetts offered for such a two-tier system were unpersuasive and already had been undermined by measures taken by the court and legislature toward greater equality among families. As the Court of Appeal for Ontario aptly concluded, exclusion from marriage "perpetuates the view that same-sex relationships are less worthy of recognition than opposite-sex relationships," and "offends the dignity of persons in same-sex relationships."[103] The *Goodridge* court similarly concluded: "The marriage ban works a deep and scarring hardship on a very real segment of the community for no rational reason."[104] The Department's failure to offer any such reason led the court to conclude that "persistent prejudices" that Massachusetts's constitution cannot "tolerate" (analogous to racial prejudice) were at the root of the marriage restriction.[105] This denial of the equal basic liberties of gay men and lesbians reflects a stance of empty toleration—merely refraining from coercive action without according equal respect to their intimate lives—rather than toleration as respect.

## Partial Equality in Hawaii and New Jersey

In contrast to Vermont's allowance of civil unions and Massachusetts's opening of marriage law to same-sex couples, some states accord partial public recognition of same-sex relationships by extending to them a subset of the benefits and obligations linked to marriage. The examples of Hawaii's "reciprocal beneficiaries" law and New Jersey's domestic partnership law are instructive. These laws bespeak a purpose of facilitating and supporting the intimate relationships of gay men and lesbians. And they draw analogies between such relationships and marriage to justify such support. Yet they hold back from the full support accorded married opposite-sex couples. Why pursue this strategy of partial equality? Why not, as California's domestic partnership law does, move toward greater equality between opposite-sex and same-sex couples?

The impetus for Hawaii's Reciprocal Beneficiaries Act was the initial legal victory of three same-sex couples who challenged the constitutionality of Hawaii's marriage laws and the prospect of a final ruling by Hawaii's Supreme Court that gay men and lesbians must be allowed to marry. The legislature responded by passing this Act and by proposing a constitutional amendment to reserve to it—rather than the court—the authority to define marriage.[106] The Act's stated purpose is to "extend certain rights and benefits which are presently available only to married couples to couples composed of two individuals who are legally prohibited from marrying under state law." Why make this extension? Why not simply extend the right to marry? The legislative findings state that "the people of Hawaii choose to preserve the tradition of marriage as a unique social institution based upon the committed union of one man and one woman" and that a "multiplicity of rights and benefits" are contingent upon marital status. However, "there are many individuals who have significant personal, emotional, and economic relationships with another individual," but are prohibited by legal restriction from marrying, such as individuals who are relatives ("such as a widowed mother and her unmarried son") and "two individuals who are of the same gender." The Act allows such individuals to register as "reciprocal beneficiaries" and become eligible for a subset of rights and benefits "presently available only to married couples."[107]

This strategy of partial equality may be an answer to the question: How can the legislature preserve the "unique" status of marriage and yet recognize "significant personal, emotional, and economic relationships"? Perhaps there is an unstated functional equivalence argument at work here. That is, "significant" relationships create a status enough like marriage in some respects that they should trigger some of the benefits of the status of marriage. What is not stated explicitly is what goods the "unique" status of marriage fosters—for the couple, for their family, and for society—or what important social functions marriage serves. The unquestioned point of reference is simply that marriage should continue to have the unique status and attendant benefits that it has. Reasoning by analogy from marriage, the legislature finds it appropriate to deem other relationships worthy of some support as well.

New Jersey's recently enacted domestic partnership law offers a richer explanation for adopting a strategy of partial equality, though it, too, resists full equality. The Domestic Partnership Act, unlike Hawaii's law, was not prompted by a successful constitutional challenge to its marriage law. To the contrary, the legislature adopted it in early 2004, after a trial court ruling rejected a constitutional challenge by seven same-sex couples to New Jersey's marriage laws.[108] New Jersey's law, like Hawaii's, recognizes the existence of "important personal, emotional, and economic committed relationships" other than marriage. But the Act explains more fully government's interest in supporting such relationships:

> b. These familial relationships . . . assist the State by their establishment of a private network of support for the financial, physical and emotional health of their participants.

c. Because of the material and other support that these familial relationships provide to their participants, . . . these mutually supportive relationships should be formally recognized by statute, and . . . certain rights and benefits should be made available to individuals participating in them.[109]

These findings bring certain nonmarital relationships within the category of "family" and justify governmental support for such families because they afford members mutual support, accepting responsibility for burdens that otherwise might fall upon government.

But the findings also make a striking appeal to autonomy and dignity in explaining why domestic partners should have certain benefits:

The need for all persons who are in domestic partnerships, regardless of their sex, to have access to [certain] rights and benefits [accorded to married couples] is paramount in view of their essential relationship to any reasonable conception of basic human dignity and autonomy, and the extent to which they will play an integral role in enabling those persons to enjoy their familial relationship as domestic partners and to cope with adversity when a medical emergency arises . . . [as illustrated by the aftermath of the events of September 11].[110]

Here, the state links facilitating relationships, or fostering "freedom to" family life, with respect for dignity and autonomy. This finding is evocative of *Lawrence*'s rhetoric about not "demean[ing]" the "existence" of gay men and lesbians[111] and its reference to September 11 offers a powerful illustration of why families need governmental support. (Notably, President Bush signed a federal law, named in honor of Mychal Judge—a gay fire department chaplain who died carrying out his duties at the World Trade Center—affording death benefits to domestic partners of fire fighters and police officers who died in the line of duty.)[112] Although Hawaii's law includes not only same-sex couples but also other relationships between persons who may not marry, New Jersey's law applies only to two persons of the same sex (with the exception of opposite-sex couples if each is over the age of 62, probably because the latter may be reluctant to marry lest they lose retirement benefits).

Why should some, but not all, of the obligations and benefits linked to marriage be extended to same-sex couples (and some other non-marital couples)? How did the Hawaiia and New Jersey legislatures decide which among the multiplicity of benefits linked to marriage should remain exclusive to marriage and which should be extended to reciprocal beneficiaries or domestic partners? The Hawaii legislature extends to reciprocal beneficiaries a diffuse list of about sixty of the hundreds of rights and responsibilities linked to marriage (some of which were later withdrawn), including health insurance, various employment and pension benefits, medical decision making, death benefits, rights of inheritance, an elective share, being an administrator for a decedent's estate, property protections, and recovery in tort actions.[113] New Jersey's law grants some of these protections and includes others that Hawaii does not, such as protecting domestic partners from discrimination in employment, housing, lending, and other areas.[114]

Hawaii's law offers no express rationale for including some, but not other, incidents of marriage. An inference from the New Jersey Act's findings is that the particular set of benefits it includes would facilitate and support "important personal, emotional and economic relationships." No doubt, benefits such as being able to make medical decisions for a loved one or to take family leave to care for one's partner do foster economic and emotional security. They remedy some of the most serious ways in which same-sex partners have not been legally protected in their efforts to care and provide for each other. And yet both laws leave out important incidents of marital status: notably, should the relationship end, neither a domestic partner nor a reciprocal beneficiary has a right to property division or economic support.[115] And neither law confers any rights in one partner concerning the adoption and custody of the other's children. This strategy of partial equality has obvious limits if the goal is facilitating families.

## California's Domestic Partnership Law

The experience in California suggests that once a state embarks on the path of according some respect and recognition to same-sex relationships, it becomes more difficult to justify salient exclusions from the marriage laws. Indeed, in 1999, California established the first statewide domestic partnership law but has expanded its scope several times.[116] With the 2003 amendments, which took effect on January 1, 2005, domestic partnership in California is most akin to the civil union in Vermont in its marriage-like package of rights and responsibilities.

California traveled along this trajectory toward greater equality through the efforts of state legislators to secure equal recognition of same-sex relationships. This progress is all the more notable given that, in 2000, California voters approved a "defense of marriage" initiative, declaring: "Only marriage between a man and a woman is valid or recognized in California." In light of this law, and because voters support domestic partnerships—but not marriage—for same-sex couples, some legislators have reasoned, a robust domestic partnership law can secure more protection for lesbian and gay men's families, even if it is not marriage.[117]

The legislative findings of the California Domestic Partner Rights and Responsibilities Act of 2003 strikingly explain this incremental move toward equality. They observe that despite discrimination, gay, lesbian, and bisexual Californians have formed "lasting, committed, and caring relationships," that the state has an interest in promoting "stable and lasting" family relationships, and that an expanded domestic partnership law would "help California move closer to fulfilling the promises of inalienable rights, liberty, and equality" contained in its constitution. Thus, "expanding the rights and creating responsibilities of registered domestic partners" would promote family relationships and protect family members during life crises, as well as reduce discrimination on the basis of sexual orientation.[118] The law declares that registered domestic partners "shall have the same rights, protections, and benefits, and shall be subject to the same responsibilities, obligations, and duties under law," as "are granted to and imposed upon spouses." For example, the dissolution of a domestic partnership will be subject to the same rules as a marriage. All domestic partners registered under California's current law were sent letters informing them that, on January 1, 2005, when the new law takes effect, domestic partners "will have a great many new rights and responsibilities" and that, should they not wish to be subject to this expanded set, they should dissolve their partnership prior to this date.[119] Although there were more dissolutions in 2004 than in previous years, most couples did not dissolve their partnerships, and nearly 5,000 new couples, including heterosexual senior citizens, joined the registry.[120]

California's expansion of domestic partnership law, rather than following the path of civil union, to approach the full package of marriage is an intriguing example of how domestic partnership law can be used to create a legal form that is nearly equivalent to marriage. By contrast, the various municipal domestic partnership laws enacted in the last few decades to extend some protection and recognition to committed same-sex couples are quite modest in scope.[121] California's expanded domestic partnership law is more akin to the various registered partnership schemes in European countries.[122] One lesson from the evolution of some of these European laws may be that, as lawmakers learn more about the needs and capacities of same-sex couples, they extend more protection to their relationships, moving them closer to what marriage provides.[123]

## Conclusion

As the challenges to more state marriage laws bring new judicial rulings, more states may enact civil union laws (like Vermont) or expansive domestic partnership laws (like California). Or more states may adopt partial equality schemes, as have Hawaii and New Jersey. States should follow Massachusetts's example and recognize same-sex marriage. This remedy would accord equal respect to the moral capacity of same-sex couples to exercise personal self-government and to form intimate, committed, stable relationships. It would allow such couples to benefit from the facilitative role government plays in supporting marriage. It would also acknowledge the practical reality that same-sex partners can be "functional" parents and can act in the best interests of children.

Unfortunately, the likelihood that many states will follow Massachusetts's example—or even that of Vermont, Connecticut, and California—in the near future seems slim. For any that do, arguments about equal capacities and about the fit between the needs of same-sex couples and the goods of marriage are likely to feature prominently. In any case, incremental steps toward equality among families are likely to continue. As states and municipalities take such steps, lawmakers and participants in the public debate inevitably disaggregate (or "unbundle") marriage into the myriad legal rights and benefits, protections, and obligations linked to it[124] and inquire what part of this bundle should be available to relationships other than marriage.

This process should bring to the fore the question of why society uses marriage as the basis for access to so many public benefits. If government sensibly concludes that official recognition of, and extension of benefits to, persons who marry aids the security and stability of the union, that invites the further question of whether other intimate or "significant" relationships would also benefit from such recognition and support. In the next chapter, I turn to the issue of whether discussions about the place of families and of governmental obligation to support families should move "beyond marriage" to a broader focus on government's interest in intimate affiliation.

# 6

## Beyond Marriage?

> [F]or all relevant and appropriate societal purposes, we do not
> need marriage and we should abolish it as a legal category. . . .
> [W]e should transfer the social and economic subsidies and privilege
> that marriage now receives to a new family core connection—that of
> the caretaker-dependent. . . . [F]amily as a social and legal category
> should not be dependent on having marriage as its core relationship.
> ~ *Martha Albertson Fineman*, The Autonomy Myth, *p. 123*

> [Marriage] is no longer a sufficient model to respond to the variety
> of relationships that exist in Canada today. Whether we look at older
> people living with their adult children, adults with disabilities living
> with their caregivers, or siblings cohabiting in the same residence,
> the marriage model is inadequate. . . . All of these personal adult
> relationships could also benefit from legal frameworks to support
> people's need for certainty and stability.
> ~ *Law Commission of Canada*, Beyond Conjugality:
> Recognizing and Supporting Close Adult Personal
> Relationships, *p. 113*

*A* BASIC ARGUMENT OF THIS BOOK is that there are
good reasons to reconstruct marriage to achieve greater equality
within families and greater equality among families. Thus, if government supports and promotes marriage, it should do so consistent with
norms of sex equality. Extending same-sex couples the right to marry
is a just reconstruction that accords respect for the moral capacities of
gay men and lesbians and secures public affirmation of their intimate
commitment.

In current debates, other difficult questions have arisen about
equality among families, implicating the place of marriage in society
and in family law and policy. These questions center on one basic
question: "Should society move beyond marriage?" Put another way,

"Why marriage?" As the opening quotations to this chapter suggest, these questions could have two distinct meanings: (1) "Why *only* marriage?" and (2) "Why marriage *at all?*" To illustrate the first meaning, the Law Commission of Canada, in its report *Beyond Conjugality: Recognizing and Supporting Close Personal Adult Relationships,*[1] recommended moving "beyond marriage" so that government would offer legal frameworks to support committed personal relationships in addition to marriage. To illustrate the second meaning, some marriage critics, notably Martha Fineman, urge the abolition of marriage. Fineman argues that society does not need marriage as a legal category and could better regulate family around the category of the "caretaker-dependent" relationship.[2]

In the "culture wars" over marriage and the family, those seeking to preserve traditional marriage resist moving beyond marriage in both ways. For example, James C. Dobson, of Focus on the Family, declares that maintaining a "productive and humane culture" requires that society treat the marriage relationship as "legally and morally superior" to other forms of sexual expression and domestic relationship.[3] Obviously, he would strenuously reject abolition of marriage, but he also would resist any other move beyond traditional marriage, whether it be recognizing same-sex marriage or extending some of the legal protections of marriage to nonmarital relationships.

To those who question, "Why *only* marriage?," marriage defenders stress the unique capacity of marriage—defined as the union of one man and one woman—to foster certain social goods. They warn that any movement beyond traditional marriage will undermine its unique status as the proper and exclusive institution within which to order and channel sexuality, procreation, and parenting.[4] Thus, they characterize as virtual body blows to the institution of marriage the Supreme Court's opinion in Lawrence v. Texas—which struck down criminal bans on same-sex sodomy as unconstitutional—and the rulings by Vermont's and Massachusetts's highest courts in Baker v. State and Goodridge v. Department of Public Health—which held that, under their state constitutions, gay men and lesbians could not be excluded from the benefits, obligations, and protections of marriage.[5] Such judicial decisions, in the view of marriage defenders, threaten to destroy marriage: not just because they open the door to same-sex marriage, but also because they could lead society down a "slippery slope" to defining marriage as "every conceivable combination of male and female" (including group marriage). Worse, they could lead to abolishing marriage itself as a distinct legal category in favor of a "system of flexible relationship contracts."[6]

My position is that the best answer to the question—"Should society (and family law and policy) move beyond marriage?"—is "yes and no." First, the "yes" part. One appropriate move beyond traditional marriage, as explained in Chapter 4, is to embrace more firmly the public value of sex equality, and thus equality within families, as a principle relevant to the regulation of family life and to governmental support of marriage. In Chapter 5, I argued that a second valuable move, in the direction of equality among families, is to recognize and support same-sex marriage. In this chapter, I argue for a third move beyond traditional marriage, also in the direction of greater equality among families: extending governmental support and recognition to other forms of family that foster some or all of the values and goods associated with marital families.

Second, the "no" part. I argue that society should not move wholly beyond marriage by abolishing it as a distinct legal category. Focusing family law on the caretaking-dependent relationship, as Fineman proposes, has the considerable merits of directing society's attention to the important task of orderly social reproduction and of fostering governmental support—rather than opprobrium—for single-parent and other nonmarital families. But it has the demerit of removing—and treating primarily as a matter of private contract—another valuable dimension of families: the intimate, committed bonds between adults and the role that such relationships play in fostering goods as well as interdependencies.

I shall argue for a kinship registration system that would offer governmental recognition and support to forms of intimate, committed relationships other than marriage. My endorsement of registration builds on the basic idea that public recognition and support of committed intimate relationships may contribute to their security and stability. I draw on the recent report, *Beyond Conjugality*, as an instructive guide to the rationales for such a scheme and its possible contours.

I then consider the hard question of the place, in a scheme of regulation of families, for *ascription*—that is, government imposing obligations or conferring benefits on persons because they are in a relationship (without regard to whether they have explicitly chosen to assume those obligations or partake of those benefits). The rationale for ascription is that responsibility may arise from relationships, independently of whether persons have sought public recognition of their relationships, through marriage or a registered partnership, or whether they have made a private agreement. For example, when an intimate relationship ends, is the state justified in imposing—by analogy to the laws governing divorce—economic obligations and equitable property distribution because of the interdependencies and vulnerabilities that arise in such relationships? I draw on the recent American Law Institute's *Principles of the Law of Family Dissolution*, which supports ascription as a means of remedying economic loss and vulnerability arising in intimate relationships.[7] I conclude by explaining why I adopt the hybrid approach of moving partly, but not wholly, beyond marriage and why I do not support abolishing marriage.

## Avoiding Stark Dichotomies and Sharp Choices

At the outset, three cautions are in order about resorting to overly stark dichotomies or sharp either/or choices concerning family regulation. First, anyone addressing the debate over moving beyond marriage does not write on a clean slate. Indeed, significant developments in family law and constitutional law as well as changing social practices have already brought about a move "beyond marriage." To what extent has this occurred? The current picture of regulation of families in the United States reveals a hybrid system of public and private ordering.[8] Along with civil marriage, a status defined by governmental regulation, there are civil unions (in Connecticut and Vermont) and registration (in those several states and various municipalities that allow persons to register as domestic partners or reciprocal beneficiaries). Persons in both marital and nonmarital relationships use private contracts to define such relationships. Ascription, in addition, imposes child support obligations on parents whether or not they are married and financial obligations on unmarried cohabitants when their relationship ends.

These changes in family law have eroded certain forms of inequality within and among families. They have deinstitutionalized marriage by diminishing its role as the exclusive source of family rights and responsibilities. In rejecting the argument that the essence of marriage is procreation, Massachusetts's highest court, in *Goodridge*, observed that the state "affirmatively facilitates bringing children into a family," whether that family will be marital or nonmarital, two-parent or single-parent, or whether the parents or their partners are heterosexual, homosexual, or bisexual.[9] Visitation laws establish rights of grandparents, and other third parties important in children's lives, to continue relationships with children.[10] Thus, it is simply not accurate to say of marriage, as marriage defender Maggie Gallagher does, that "we have laws only about this one kind of personal relationship as opposed to all other intimate relationships worthy of respect."[11]

Clarity about the extent to which family law already has moved beyond marriage would help to reduce the dramatic rhetoric about the risks to "the family" resulting from such a move. Significant developments in constitutional law have also moved society somewhat beyond marriage by limiting the state's power to use criminal sanctions to further the "channeling" function of marriage as the exclusive site for sexuality, reproduction, and parenting.[12] Whether or not they are married, people have a protected realm of personal liberty, or self-government, with respect to engaging in intimate sexual relationships and in deciding whether or not to procreate and to become parents. *Lawrence* explicitly protected a right concerning sexual intimacy, thus— to the chagrin of marriage defenders—further limiting states' ability to use criminal law to "protect" marriage and marital (heterosexual) sexuality.[13] This protection of the intimate lives of gay men and lesbians may also spill over to afford greater protection of their parental rights because sodomy laws no longer afford a basis for deeming gay and lesbians parents and their partners outlaws and criminals.[14] For marriage promoters, a quandary posed by these developments is how, "in a culture that has rejected criminal and punitive sanctions as a regulatory instrument for sexuality," the law of marriage can continue to sustain and strengthen marriage as a uniquely valuable social institution.[15] For proponents of greater equality among families, including myself, the quandary is how best to continue to support marriage and at the same time support other valuable forms of intimate association.

A second caution is that discussions about the fate of marriage and its place in family policy often pose overly stark choices: either marriage is a normative social institution, with attendant rights and duties fixed by status, or it is a wholly private relationship, by the couple and for the couple, that means whatever its participants want it to mean. Either society supports marriage as a special, unique status, and thereby encourages committed, permanent relationships, or it encourages an atomistic consumers' market for intimacy.[16] For example, Gallagher mischaracterizes *Baker* as rejecting a model of marriage as a fundamental social institution in favor of a model of marriage as a vehicle for self-expression and access to benefits: in other words, rites—and rights—without responsibility.[17] Other marriage promoters similarly critique proposals for kinship registration, ignoring the relational responsibilities and commitments that such schemes might facilitate. Underlying these stark dichotomies are understandable concerns about how to foster such values as commitment, relational responsibility, and permanence. However, such dichotomies suggest too narrow a range of solutions for addressing these concerns.

A third and final caution is that declarations that a particular reform will "reinstitutionalize" marriage as a status relationship, or "deinstitutionalize" it in the direction of a negotiable contract, often overlook the slippery and easily contested nature of these terms. It may be genuinely difficult to determine whether a particular family law reform signals a move in one or the other direction. For example, if family law imposes marriage-like obligations concerning property distribution and support on unmarried couples when their relationship ends, does this weaken or strengthen marriage as a special status relationship? When courts impose such obligations, they often appeal to the idea of an express or implied contract between the couple. By contrast, the recent ALI *Principles* would impose obligations by appealing to status: people who live together and share a life together should be treated as having a status similar to married people and should be subject to similar relational obligations in the event the relationship ends. They can contract out of such obligations, but concerns for public policy will limit their ability to do so.[18]

Marriage promoters criticize this development as deinstitutionalizing and weakening marriage: unmarried couples need not marry to receive the property rights and obligations divorcing spouses have.[19] But this development may actually expand marriage's reach: couples who did not marry are nonetheless subject to laws governing marriage. Marriage retains its primacy as the relationship to which other relationships are compared and to which analogies are drawn.[20]

## Registration Schemes

If the basic premise of the Vermont Supreme Court in *Baker* is sound—that state recognition and support of marriage may facilitate the security and stability of an intimate, committed relationship—why limit such recognition and support to marriage? Why *only* marriage? Why not move beyond marriage to state support of a more diverse range of family forms? Doing so would not abolish marriage, but instead would expand the focus to how government could support a broader array of intimate relationships. To adapt the language from *Baker*, should there be further expansion in "the family of state-sanctioned human relations"?[21]

Is there a need for public recognition and support of relationships other than marriage? Or are marriage defenders correct that personal relationships other than marriage simply do not foster the important public purposes that marriage does, and thus do not warrant similar public recognition or benefits?[22] The *Goodridge* opinion offers a revealing look at the tensions that arise in trying to accord marriage a special place but also to accord some public support for other relationships. On the one hand, Massachusetts treats marriage as a status that bestows on those who marry (and their children) a "cornucopia of substantial benefits," many of which are not otherwise available. On the other hand, it has "moved vigorously to strengthen the modern family in its many variations," for example, facilitating procreation and parenting outside of marriage.[23] Is the remaining disparity in treatment, between marriage and other forms of affiliation, justifiable? Does this disparate treatment reflect a coherent public policy?

Who might be helped by affirmative governmental support of their relationships? By analogy to my assessment of the case for same-sex marriage, is there a good match between the needs of persons in various relationships and a set of government-sponsored benefits, protections, and obligations? Do these relationships have not only private significance (for their contribution to personal happiness and well-being), but also public significance, rooted in important social goods they realize and functions they serve (such as meeting dependencies, giving care, or fostering civic virtues)?

What relationships "beyond marriage" might benefit from public recognition and support? One candidate is unmarried cohabitants—that is, the estimated 5.5 million unmarried couples who live together.

This group would include opposite-sex as well as same-sex couples. Forty percent of these households include children.[24] A second example would be a complex family form that includes either more than two persons acting in a parenting capacity toward children or more than two persons in a sexual affiliation with each other. For example, Judith Stacey describes "lesbigay" families, in which biological parents (such as a lesbian and a gay man who are close friends and conceive a child together) are not sexual affiliates—and would not marry each other—but one or both has a sexual affiliation with a same-sex partner.[25] Whether or not they share a residence, all of the adults play a parenting role toward the children.

A third type of relationship—the subject of the report, *Beyond Conjugality*—is the "close adult personal relationship" that is not conjugal (that is, sexual). Such relationships could include two siblings, a parent and an adult child, a caretaker and a care recipient, or two close friends. For example, one reported trend is of a "friends-helping-friends" model for aging, in which single, widowed, or divorced women team up to live together and care for each other as they age.[26] Finally, a registration system might facilitate not only adult-adult relationships but also various intergenerational relationships centered around caregiving, such as a grandparent and a child.

## The Case for Registration

> We are thirty-six-year-old twin sisters who have never been married or had children and who live together. . . . Our lives are inextricably linked: . . . we have co-habited continuously for the last seventeen years (since leaving our parental home), rely on each other for emotional support, and are entirely dependent on each other financially—we co-own all of our possessions and share all of our living expenses. A more stable relationship cannot be found. Yet, because we are sisters, rather than husband and wife, and because we are not a couple in a presumably sexual relationship, we are denied tax benefits, "family" health coverage, and a multitude of other advantages constructed upon sexist and heterosexist ideas about what constitutes meaningful relationships.
>
> —Beyond Conjugality, *p. 119*

This story is one of many gathered by the Law Commission of Canada in preparing its report, *Beyond Conjugality*. The genesis of the report was a national conversation about how to handle same-sex marriage, in the face of conflicting judicial opinions over whether Canada's Charter of Rights and Freedoms required the recognition of such marriage. But the report takes a broader look at government's role with respect not just to conjugal relationships (be they opposite-sex or same-sex), but to the wider category of close adult personal relationships. One reason for this focus on nonconjugal relationships was that in Canada, unlike in the United States, a federal law (the Modernization of Benefits and Obligations Act) already has extended, to opposite-sex and same-sex couples who have lived in a conjugal relationship for at least a year, "a wide array of rights and obligations previously available only to married couples."[27]

Because many people seek stability and certainty in their personal relationships, the Commission argues that government should "provide an orderly framework in which people can express their commitment to each other, receive public recognition and support, and voluntarily assume a range of legal rights and obligations." Up to now, the state "has focused on marriage as the vehicle of choice for adults to express their commitment." Marriage is facilitative: adults who are committed to each other's well-being can make a public statement of their intentions toward each other and assume "mutual rights and obligations." The law also provides for "orderly and equitable resolution" if marriages break down. However, the Commission finds that marriage "is no longer a sufficient model to respond to the variety of relationships that exist in Canada today."[28]

Offering the examples of "older people living with their adult children, adults with disabilities living with their caregivers," and "siblings cohabiting in the same residence," the report finds that such close personal adult relationships "are also characterized by emotional and economic interdependence, mutual care and concern and the expectation of some duration," and could benefit from "legal frameworks to support people's need for certainty and stability." Entering into private contracts, such as cohabitation agreements or caregiving arrangements, is not sufficient because such arrangements lack an "official or public aspect" as well as a "sufficient guarantee of certainty."[29] For example, when access to various benefits and obligations hinges on relationship status, a registration system creating an official record of that relationship would be more efficient than private contract.

The Commission recommends adopting a registration scheme, looking to examples found in a number of European countries and in some Canadian provinces. Like marriage, these registration schemes foster "voluntariness, stability, certainty, and publicity." Through them, persons can express commitment, receive public recognition and support, "voluntarily assume a range of legal rights and obligations," and, if their relationships break down, have access to "an orderly and equitable resolution" of their affairs. These schemes, the Commission contends, affirm the basic principles and values that ought to guide the regulation of close personal adult relationships, including autonomy, equality, and respect for diversity.[30]

Who could register, and what should be the contours of a registration scheme? The report offers some general guidelines. It favors broad access to registration, including conjugal and nonconjugal relationships, as well as forms of relationship involving more than two individuals. (In this respect, it goes farther than European registration schemes restricting registration to conjugal couples.)

What set of benefits and obligations would follow upon registration? One model is to have registration, like marriage, come with a predetermined set of rights and responsibilities. As in many European registration schemes, these might be nearly identical to those linked to marriage.[31] Another model is to have different sets of rights and responsibilities tailored to particular kinds of relationships. For example, with a caregiving relationship, registration could involve "determinations for care arrangements, consent to treatment or other aspects of the relationship." The legal consequences of registration could also involve matters of property and support obligations during and after the relationship. The report concludes: "The commitment of entering into a registration would be about . . . clarifying this commitment of mutual responsibility in law, both for the parties themselves and for potentially interested third parties."[32]

Would a registration system eliminate the need for marriage? The Commission explores the possibility of eliminating marriage as a legal category (as distinguished from a religious rite) and providing for all adult relationships within a registration scheme. Such a move, it contends, would have some "principled advantages." For example, a civil registration scheme "open to all persons in committed relationships" could help the state better focus on and achieve the objective "incompletely" achieved by marriage: "recognizing and supporting committed personal adult relationships by facilitating an orderly regulation of their affairs." However, the Commission also finds some disadvantages. Removing civil marriage as a choice would prevent couples from using a "legal mechanism that many regard as fundamental to their commitment." Thus, while the Commission recommends further debate, it proposes a hybrid solution of retaining civil marriage and establishing a registration system.[33]

## Reconsidering the Law's Reliance on Relationships

Establishing a registration system would enable government better to carry out one dimension of its formative responsibilities more efficiently: facilitating persons' directing and organizing their lives by providing a framework for public recognition and support of relationships. However, the Law Commission also proposed a new method for evaluating a second governmental role: the law's reliance on relationship status as a basis for legislating rights and responsibilities. Here, too, the Commission proposes to move somewhat beyond marriage. *Beyond Conjugality* offers some helpful guidance about how family law and policy in the United States might be more facilitative and respectful of equality among families. The Commission contends:

> [I]t is time to fundamentally rethink the way in which governments have relied on relational status in allocating rights and responsibilities. Is it possible to [allocate] rights and responsibilities . . . in a manner that reduces the problems of over- and underinclusion? . . . [C]an we imagine a legislative regime that accomplishes its goals more effectively by relying less on whether people are living in particular kinds of relationships?[34]

The Commission proposes a methodology that would review all laws that currently include personal adult relationships and ask four questions concerning them:

> Question 1: Does the law pursue a legitimate policy objective?
> Question 2: If the law's objectives are sound, do relationships

matter? Are the relationships that are included important or relevant to the law's objective?

Question 3: If relationships do matter, could the law allow individuals to choose which of their own personal relationships they want to be subject to the law?

Question 4: If relationships do matter, and public policy requires that the law delineate the relevant relationships to which it applies, can the law be revised to more accurately capture the relevant range of relationships?[35]

This type of systematic review, by government, might be quite burdensome and time-consuming. However, the basic approach of critical reflection on why relationships matter could help clarify government's interest in intimate affiliation. Is marriage an adequate proxy for the sort of intimate familial relationships worthy of societal support? For example, if government seeks to encourage relationships of emotional and economic interdependency in which persons support and care for each other, should it use marriage as a proxy for all such relationships? Or should government extend benefits and protections likely to foster such interdependency to relationships other than marriage?[36] As discussed in Chapter 5, when states adopt domestic partnership or reciprocal beneficiaries laws, they answer this question, "yes."

Reconsidering the relevance of relationships, as the Commission recommends, we should ask not just whether other intimate relationships deserve some or all of the incidents now linked to marriage. We also should ask why government uses relationship status as a basis for assigning rights and responsibilities and whether it is justified in doing so. I believe that critical reflection would support governmental reliance upon relationship status in many cases because families foster social goods and carry out important functions in which society has an interest. In some cases, relationship classifications should reach beyond the family. For example, laws requiring employers to provide caregiving leaves are an important way to support caregiving relationships, but such laws should expand to include nonkin caregiving relationships.[37]

A methodology like that proposed by the Law Commission may already be implicitly at work in some family law and policy that goes "beyond marriage." Family law scholar Nancy Polikoff offers the example of laws protecting against domestic violence. Although early statutes used marriage as the relevant relationship status and limited orders of protection to spouses who were still living together, later laws significantly expanded the scope of orders of protection "to reflect more of the relationships in which women were likely to encounter violent domination" (for example, unmarried partners living together and same-sex intimate partners). Similarly, in drafting the Violence Against Women Act, Congress did not use marriage as "the dividing line between those who are protected under federal law and those who are not." It included not only spouses, but also, among others, former spouses, persons who share a child in common, and present or former cohabitants.[38]

## Hard Questions about a Registration Scheme

There are persuasive arguments for a registration scheme. It is consonant with my argument that, in regulating families, government should foster capacity, equality, and responsibility. First, as the Commission puts it, registration models "would affirm the capacity of people to establish for themselves the terms of their relationships while providing models for doing so."[39] Second, a registration scheme would foster equality among families by extending affirmative governmental support to relationships that now lack such governmental facilitation. Third, such a scheme would foster responsibility by encouraging persons in relationships to make public declarations of their responsibilities to each other.

What objections would critics likely raise against such a registration scheme? Are such objections persuasive? One likely objection would be that opposite-sex couples do not need access to registration schemes because they can marry. In this view, to give them such access inevitably weakens marriage as an institution by eroding its legal distinctiveness. For example, in many registered partnership schemes in European countries, same-sex couples—but not opposite-sex couples—may register as domestic partners, which brings them most of the obligations, benefits, and rights linked to marriage.[40] These schemes are ameliorative: they aim to include persons excluded from marriage, rather than to provide them with an additional option. By analogy, Vermont's remedy of the civil union affords common benefits, if not equal status, to same-sex couples, but excludes them from the institution of marriage. And opposite-sex couples may not choose a civil union. Similarly, opposite-sex couples (except those over age 62) may not register under California's domestic partnership law.

Given current state laws throughout the United States, not to mention the federal Defense of Marriage Act, gay men and lesbians are a long way from having equal opportunity to marry, let alone access to equal benefits and obligations through registration schemes or civil unions. Thus, adopting registration schemes would be an incremental step toward equality among families. Far more typical than California's expansive domestic partnership law are more modest municipal domestic partnership laws. To be sure, such laws declare legislature purposes or make findings supportive of more inclusive definitions of family and appeal to notions of fair treatment. A common declaration is that the municipality creating the ordinance has an interest in "strengthening and supporting all caring, committed, and responsible family forms" and that a domestic partnership is "a relationship and family unit that is deserving of official recognition." Such ordinances find that "[i]t is appropriate and fair that certain of the societal privileges and benefits now accorded to members of a marriage be extended to those who meet the qualifications of a domestic partnership."[41]

Yet there is a gap between this rhetoric of fairness and desert and the small set of obligations and benefits afforded by such ordinances. Moreover, by requiring that domestic partners live together and assume financial responsibility for each other, these laws may have "more rigid requirements of commitment and mutual dependency than marriage laws," even though, unlike marriage laws, they do not impose post-termination obligations on the parties.[42] As domestic partners acknowledge, such laws offer same-sex couples who cannot marry "some recognition and valuation," but "[t]his isn't gay marriage and this isn't civil unions."[43] A more expansive registration system would better link the rhetoric of inclusiveness and fairness with actual legal consequences.

If the countries that now have registration schemes were to open up marriage to same-sex couples, would the need for registered partnership laws disappear? If same-sex couples in the United States were to gain a right to marry in every state, would the need for such ameliorative registration schemes or civil union laws vanish? Why might people choose these forms over marriage?

One reason persons in an intimate, committed relationship might choose a registered partnership is that, although they seek public affirmation and protection of their relationship, they resist marriage. Reasons for resisting it might be rooted in concerns regarding marriage's historical associations with gender hierarchy, fixed gender roles, and organized religion, among other conscientious reasons.[44] I have argued for a more egalitarian conception of marriage, in keeping with contemporary norms of sex equality. However, for many marriage critics, these connotations linger. A registered partnership similar to marriage in its package of rights, benefits, and obligations would offer such persons an alternative. Of course, maintaining marriage and registered partnerships as parallel schemes might reinforce the historical connection between marriage and inequality and signal that, even today, marriage and equality are antithetical.

In some European countries in which registered partnership is open to both opposite-sex couples and same-sex couples, many opposite-sex couples register.[45] Thus, when the Netherlands became the first European country to open up marriage to same-sex couples, it opted to retain, for a five-year period, its registered partnership law. Why? As the memorandum accompanying the Dutch law explained:

> [T]he relatively high number of different-sex couples that contracted a registered partnership in 1998 . . . make[s] it plausible that there is a need for a marriage-like institution devoid of the symbolism attached to marriage. . . . Therefore the government wants to keep the institution of registered partnership in place, for the time being.[46]

After allowing the parallel development of same-sex marriage and registered partnership for five years (the law took effect in 2001), the legislature stated that it would "be possible to assess whether registered partnership should be abolished."[47]

Within the United States, some voices in the debate over the place of marriage seek, as a matter of fair and equal treatment for all families, registered partnership laws that would apply equally to domestic partners the "privileges, benefits, and responsibilities that impact spouses on the federal, state, and municipal levels." For example, Alternatives to Marriage Project founders Dorian Solot and Marshall Miller argue that "cohabitation and marriage are here to stay—most people say they want both, at different times in their lives. . . . The question . . . is whether laws and social customs in the United States will recognize and support unmarried relationships, or continue to target them with stigma, prejudice, and discrimination." Many unmarried couples and families, they contend, lack adequate legal protections.[48]

In demanding fair and equal treatment of unmarried relationships, Solot and Miller appeal both to a fundamental similarity between marital and unmarried relationships and to a public sentiment that society "should value all types of families." Married people and cohabitors, they argue, usually are the same people: "cohabitation has become a normal stage between dating and marriage," as over 50 percent of cohabiting couples—within five years—marry. Cohabitors say that they plan to marry when the time is right, once they feel certain the relationship will endure (and thus not end in divorce), or if and when they can afford to marry. In the case of same-sex couples, law poses a barrier to marriage. However, nearly 40 percent of cohabitors break up within five years, rather than marry, leaving a small percentage of long-term cohabitors.[49]

Solot and Miller stress similarity between the married and unmarried, but there are also differences in terms of couples' aspirations for their relationship and their desire for governmental support. For example, Solot and Miller find that reasons for not marrying include: not wanting to take on the role of "husband" or "wife," with all of its historical baggage; keeping one's personal relationship private and not involving government; and a conviction that there is no compelling reason to marry. A further reason is that "marriage"—assumed to be "a monogamous, lifelong sexual relationship between a man and a woman who live together and may have children"—"doesn't represent the relationship." These couples do not see a good fit between their relationship and the institution of marriage. Such couples may prefer an open (nonmonogamous) relationship or may be reluctant to promise to be together "forever."[50] One objection to marriage, for example, is that it is antithetical to keeping love "fresh," or alive, by making a daily decision to remain together.

Given that people have diverse reasons for cohabiting and that co-habitation has such a range of meanings (even for two persons in a relationship), is it possible to formulate a coherent account of what would be required to treat all families fairly and equally?[51] If cohabitation, for the majority of couples, is a prelude to marriage, but for others, it is either a short-lived relationship or a substitute for marriage,[52] is it possible to generalize about what personal goods and social functions are furthered by cohabitation? Would a registration system with virtually the same benefits and obligations now linked to marriage be attractive to all, or just some, cohabiting couples? Would some couples want forms of registration with a less extensive set of obligations, benefits, and protections?

One argument for different treatment of married couples and un-married couples is that these types of couples are more different than they are alike. Thus, Milton Regan expresses skepticism that "cohab-itors are married in substance but simply not in form." He points to research indicating that "cohabiting relationships are less stable than marriages and generally reflect less commitment by partners to one another." For example, by marrying, couples have taken on legal obligations to each other and have made public promises of commitment that cohabiting couples have not. In Regan's view, when unmarried couples seek benefits available to married spouses (such as health insurance), one argument for rejecting such claims is that they have not taken on the corresponding obligations to which married partners are subject (such as a mutual obligation of economic support). In effect, cohabitors seek rights without responsibilities. Society is justified, he argues, in privileging marriage as a way to "promote intimate commitment."[53] Thus, to the extent an argument for greater equality among families appeals to similarity, or functional equivalence, Regan and other scholars deny such equivalence.

But if unmarried cohabitants did seek to register their relationships, and thus to take on responsibilities as well as rights, would Regan's objection still hold? A registration system with most or all of the benefits and obligations linked to marriage would allow a public declaration of commitment and would link rights and responsibilities. One reason that cohabitation is less stable than marriage may be that, unlike marriage, cohabitation in the United States lacks a firm institutional framework and does not receive the societal support that marriage does.[54] But if cohabitation, a growing trend, is likely to remain a feature of the family system, it would be prudent to provide such a framework. What is more, since 40 percent of cohabiting households include children, fostering stability for adults could also enhance child well-being.[55]

Would moving in the direction of registered partnerships inevitably lead to couples seeking to tailor, or "calibrate," their level of commitment? Would this have a detrimental effect on marriage as an aspirational model of commitment? Allowing persons in intimate relationships to "calibrate" their commitment, by indicating which benefits and obligations they wish to assume, Regan contends, is antithetical to the sort of holistic commitment to which marriage aspires—the "open-ended pledge" to share life "for better or worse." Institutionalizing a scheme of limited commitment may detract from marriage as a "regulative ideal": "Will marriage continue to serve this function if it is one option among a menu of legally recognized intimate relationships?"[56]

Should government facilitate "calibrated commitment"? Would it weaken the regulative ideal of marriage? Is calibrated commitment inevitably a move away from genuine relational commitment and responsibility? Does any move away from marriage as the exclusive public institution for intimacy entail this consequence? Is marriage the only status likely to be able to secure the goods of commitment and responsibility? Do we really face a choice between commitment and a lack of commitment, or between marriage and shopping for intimacy in a "personal relations market"?[57] Surely not.

Offering persons choices by providing various registration options is not detrimental to intimacy and commitment.[58] It would facilitate persons making clear public statements about the nature of their commitment and the desired public consequences of their relationship.[59] If the choice is between marriage and no publicly supported commitment, then registration options could bring some interdependency, stability, and clarity. (France's Civil Solidarity Pact, for example, extends rights and protections relating to inheritance, social security, tax benefits, and being next of kin.)[60] Two persons in a close relationship (whether sexual or not), David Chambers proposes, might register as "designated friends" in order to have the right to family leave to care for each other, to be each other's beneficiaries under inheritance laws, to make decisions for each other in cases of incapacity, and the like.

But they might not wish to have financial obligations toward each other (or to any third parties on each other's behalf), or to be each other's beneficiaries under governmental programs like social security.[61] Such a relationship would entail fewer legal obligations and protections than marriage, but it would advance personal goods like security and caring for others, as well as social goods like ensuring care in the case of incapacity or providing financially for one's survivors.

Caution about calibrated commitment may be in order, but it should not preclude pursuing a tailored registration scheme. We should bear in mind that, given the different kinds and degrees of commitment that registrants might seek to make, for government to *treat persons as equals* may not require it to afford them *equal treatment*:[62] it may legitimately calibrate the menu of rights to the menu of responsibilities to which partners voluntarily agree. Legitimate concerns for the administrative burdens of registration schemes could also limit the options offered.

The worries over the negative impact of calibrated commitment upon marriage seem less apt with regard to two other sorts of relationships that registration schemes might facilitate: the nonconjugal relationships the Law Commission of Canada considered and the complex families of some gay men and lesbians, in which sexual affiliations and parenting relationships are not perfectly aligned. Marriage is generally not an available or appropriate option in these types of relationships, and thus it is not directly competitive with registered partnerships. These kinds of personal relationships deserve governmental support because they both foster valuable personal goods and further important social functions such as caretaking (of adults as well as children). For example, a registration system might help support the close adult personal relationship (featured in the *New York Times*) formed between two chefs, an eighty-seven-year old African American woman and a forty-year-old white gay man who lives with and takes care of her. The reporter observed that this pair has "forged a genuine family, with a devotion too rarely seen among blood relations."[63]

## Status versus Contract: What Place for Ascription?

If family law adopted the reforms proposed in these chapters, recognizing same-sex marriage and developing a kinship registration system, it would meet the needs of more families for public support and recognition. In addition, in some situations law, regardless of persons' choices, may need to impose relational obligations and bestow benefits on persons simply because they are in a relationship. What role should such imposition, or ascription, play? This is a difficult question. It requires reconciling commitments that may be in conflict: on the one hand, respecting relational autonomy and choice and, on the other, requiring relational responsibility and remedying the vulnerabilities and dependencies that may arise in relationships.

The Law Commission of Canada called ascription a "blunt policy tool" because it "treats all conjugal relationships alike, irrespective of the level of emotional or economic interdependency that they may present."[64] The Commission favored registration over ascription because the former respects persons' autonomy. Rather than attributing to unmarried cohabitants the status of domestic partners—whether or not they have made an express agreement about the nature and consequences of their relationship—a registration scheme would afford them the opportunity publicly to affirm their commitment. In so doing, these persons would consciously and voluntarily bring their relationship within a regulatory scheme of benefits and obligations. However, the Commission concluded that ascription should have a place, as an ameliorative tool, to prevent exploitation in conjugal relationships, but that it was not appropriate in nonconjugal relationships.

The recent ALI *Principles of the Law of Family Dissolution* offer a helpful examination of the place of ascription. Consider this story:

Sam, an engineer, is a widower with two young children. He dated a nurse, Molly, for some time and then proposed that they make a home together. Molly moved into Sam's home and became attached to Sam's children. Molly and Sam were concerned that Sam's children were not doing well in day care. They agreed that Molly would quit her nursing job to stay home to care for the children, which would also save Sam the considerable expense of day care. After two-and-a-half years of cohabitation, their relationship deteriorated and Sam asked Molly to leave his home. Molly wishes to claim a property interest in the assets acquired by Sam during their cohabitation.[65]

Should Molly's claim be successful? In some states, courts will not recognize Molly's claim because Molly and Sam are unmarried and they did not make an express agreement about any financial obligations they assumed toward each other. Other states might find an implied agreement to assume such obligations. Some states would not enforce even an express agreement because cohabitation offends public policy favoring marriage.[66]

The ALI *Principles* would treat Sam and Molly as "domestic partners" and apply laws that govern property distribution at divorce. Why? Because "for a significant period of time," they shared "a primary residence and a life together as a couple." Even though two and a half years might not seem like a long period of time, the ALI deems it "significant" in light of Molly's loss of income and benefits from her regular employment during this period, as well as the savings and advantages Sam realized from her care of the children.[67]

But is this outcome justified, given that Molly and Sam did not marry and never entered into a contract about the terms of their relationship? Some critics object to the ALI proposal to regulate the relationships of "domestic partners"—including both married and unmarried couples, and opposite-sex and same-sex couples—by reference to the laws of marital dissolution. One criticism is that the *Principles* are illiberal: they disregard persons' choices about their intimate relationships and are an unfortunate "ex post designation of family status."[68] Another criticism is that they eliminate the law's ability to make distinctions between married and unmarried persons. Marriage movement leader David Blankenhorn argues that this would harm married persons, who would "see themselves being treated just like any other relationship in the eyes of the law"; it also would harm unmarried persons, who "would find themselves . . . involuntarily drafted into a marriage-like legal regime."[69] The *Principles* also draw praise for recognizing that responsibilities may arise from being in a relationship. Regan, for example, contends that the law should be "most willing to extend legal recognition of or protection for cohabitation when doing so reinforces an ethic of care and commitment in intimate relationships."[70]

Do the *Principles* offer sufficient justification for ascription in the face of concerns over infringing autonomy and weakening marriage? They evince a lively tension between the roles of status and contract in family regulation. They support the trend toward greater allowance of private ordering through agreements by couples. However, their rationale for treating persons like Sam and Molly as domestic partners appeals to status, not contract. In contrast to existing case law, the *Principles* do not require, as a predicate for a domestic partnership, an express or implied agreement between the two parties, or a claim that the party who benefited from the other's labor should pay its value. They instead rely "as do the marriage laws, on a status classification: property claims and support obligations presumptively arise between persons who qualify as domestic partners, as they do between legal spouses, without inquiry into each couples' particular arrangement, except as the presumption is itself overcome by contract."[71]

This approach defies easy characterization. On the one hand, it moves beyond marriage in treating unmarried persons like married persons. On the other, it expands the reach of marriage laws, finding an analogy between married couples and couples who are presumed to be domestic partners because they reside together and share a life together. It appeals to an expectation that intimates intend to deal fairly with each other. Couples can contract out of these rules by making an express agreement—that is, a contract, limiting their obligations to each other. Nonetheless, when a domestic partnership lasts for a significant period of time, or when there is a child born to the partners, the contract may be unenforceable.[72]

Is this ALI proposal a useful step toward greater equality among families? Is the state justified in treating unmarried people more like married people by ascribing marriage-like obligations to them? One reason the *Principles* advocate doing so is that "it has become increasingly implausible to attribute special significance to the parties' failures to marry." Thus, cohabiting, rather than marrying, may not mean that the parties intend to avoid any economic obligations to one another. Moreover, when the parties are unequally situated economically or socially, the stronger party may be able to resist the weaker's preference for marriage.[73] The proposal provides parties a chance to make clear what, if any, economic consequences they intend their relationship to have and, if they fail to do so, to apply default rules ascribing relational responsibility.

One argument in favor of the *Principles* and their use of ascription is that, as other areas of law suggest, obligations do not arise from contract alone. Relationships themselves give rise to obligations, as the parent-child relationship illustrates. The ALI also draws support from the use of ascription in other countries to impose obligations and benefits on unmarried couples. It contends that these countries primarily ask the question: "Does this nonmarital family look like a marital family?" If it does, they apply some or all of their family law to its dissolution.[74]

The conscious parallel the ALI draws between its proposals and developments in other countries is striking. Reasoning by analogy from marriage has played a prominent role in the trend in Canadian family law to impose relational obligations and confer benefits on unmarried cohabitants (both opposite-sex and same-sex). One recent survey found that this move rested on the functional similarity of marital and nonmarital relationships, a concern for interdependencies and vulnerabilities arising in such relationships (especially for women), and the idea that the benefits of cohabitation trigger obligations. Another animating idea is that there must be limits to freedom of contract in the context of intimate relationships.[75]

These are sound rationales for ascription. The *Principles* similarly articulate limits to freedom of contract between "domestic partners"— whether married or unmarried—by leaving room for courts to decline to enforce agreements when concerns over limited capacity and public policy warrant doing so. Why these limits? Making a contract about their relationships could help spouses or domestic partners alter the rules that would otherwise apply, the better to "accommodate their particular needs and circumstances." But persons seeking to marry or become domestic partners are different from business associates making commercial agreements. Intimate partners usually assume "a mutual and deep concern for one another's welfare," and their expectations can "disarm their capacity for self-protective judgment, or their inclination to exercise it." Because they do not enter relationships expecting their family to dissolve, they may not evaluate adequately "the impact that the contract terms will have on them in the future when its enforcement is sought." And public policy concerns arise that persons entering into private agreements might waive "rights and obligations . . . designed to protect the interests of persons who enter into family relationships, and the interests of their children."[76] These concerns are strongest in long marriages (or by analogy, domestic partnerships), in which parties may change their circumstances in reliance upon the relationship, and in relationships producing children.

The *Principles* express these concerns in gender-neutral form. However, its examples make clear that a paradigm case in which an agreement may be unenforceable is when a woman invests more heavily in child care and homemaking than does a man, leading to a disparity in their employment pictures and their economic resources. As such, the *Principles* may be seeking to remedy a form of relational inequality and vulnerability that disproportionately harms women (in opposite-sex relationships) arising from what I called the "gendered economy of care" in Chapter 3. One way to address this problem is, as the *Principles* propose, through compensatory economic distribution when relationships terminate. But by applying these rules to men and women, and to opposite-sex and same-sex couples, the *Principles* express a broader concern for protecting against certain consequences of economic interdependency.[77]

A final caution about the use of ascription concerns the impact that expanding private responsibility may have on accepting public responsibility to foster individual and family well-being. Limiting public responsibility for social welfare provision is a secondary objective of the ALI proposal and the movement in Canadian family law toward ascription. The Comments to the *Principles* explain: "Fairness vis-a-vis society requires that individuals closely implicated in the economic circumstances of persons with whom they lived as domestic partners assume some economic responsibility for those circumstances."[78] And Canadian family law scholars note that this motivation plays a role in Canada's more expansive definitions of family and imposition of family obligations on unmarried partners.[79]

The principle of imposing responsibility on family members beyond the marital family is sound, to the extent that it reflects norms about mutual obligation and interdependency that arise in intimate relationships. However, when reducing public responsibility impels this more expansive approach to family, it plays into a denial or evisceration of an important principle, argued for in this book, of affirmative governmental responsibility to provide the basic resources, or goods, that persons and families need.[80] Taken too far, this impulse leads to welfare policies such as the "man in the house" or "substitute father" rule, which the U.S. Supreme Court has struck down as unconstitutional.

These rules denied welfare payments to children if their mother had "frequent" or "continuing" sexual relations with a man, whether or not they lived together as a family and whether or not he was their father or under any legal obligation to support them.[81] In sum, there is wisdom in the Law Commission of Canada's conclusion that ascription is a "blunt policy tool," but one that is necessary to prevent exploitation in certain circumstances.

## Why Not Abolish Marriage?

Both kinship registration schemes and ascription of responsibilities draw analogies between marriage and other family forms worthy of governmental recognition and support. But what if drawing such analogies actually undermines the pursuit of greater equality among families? To return to my opening alternative formulation, "Why marriage *at all?*"

Martha Fineman argues that "for all relevant and appropriate social purposes, we do not need marriage and we should abolish it as a legal category." She proposes to transfer "the social and economic subsidies and privilege[s] that marriage now receives" to a "new family core connection—that of the caretaker-dependent." What becomes of marriage? The "symbolic dimension of marriage—the coming together of two individuals with vows of love and commitment" would likely continue "as a social, cultural and/or religious construct." Marriage, however, would no longer have a legal status and thus "would no longer be the privileged mechanism whereby the state distributes certain social goods."[82] Adults could use private contracts to negotiate the terms of their intimate relationships.

Why move wholly beyond marriage? Fineman contends that shifting from the marital ("sexual") family to the caretaker-dependent dyad, and from state-sanctioned marriage to private contract, would promote a clearer focus on the most important contemporary function of families: managing dependency by performing society-preserving work of caring for children and other dependents. Fineman characterizes the place of families in terms of meeting "inevitable dependency." She describes the "derivative dependency"—the need for resources—of those who provide such care. Redefining families in terms of these dependencies and the caretaking relationship would facilitate acceptance of public responsibility to support this socially necessary work. And if the sexual family were no longer the normative family, then other forms of family—notably, the single-parent family—would no longer be "deviant" and deemed less worthy of support.[83]

Fineman's rationale for the second move, from marriage to private contract, begins with the trajectory from status to contract. She notes the evolution of marriage away from a hierarchical status relationship with clear sex-linked duties toward an equal partnership in which parties can negotiate terms and roles. I appeal to this history to support the idea that governmental policies concerning marriage should foster sex equality, or equality within families, as well as equality among families. By contrast, responding to feminist critiques of marriage as sanctioning abuse and violence, Fineman contends that a necessary step to sex equality is to dethrone marriage as a legal status and relegate all adult-adult intimate relationships to contract.[84]

Fineman develops an intriguing rationale for dethroning marriage: because of the demise of status-based duties and the rise of contractual freedom, marriage has no fixed personal or societal meaning. Such notions as marital privacy, for example, "create a vacuum . . . of legally mandated meaning—leaving open for negotiation the content of every individual marriage." Into this vacuum, couples pour "various . . . and sometimes conflicting aspirations, expectations, fears and longings."[85] Societal meanings of marriage are also multiple (ranging from using marriage to achieve public health objectives to regulating men's sexuality). Given these various personal and societal meanings, how can the state justify using marriage as the vehicle for the allocation of significant economic benefits, and using the absence of marriage as a justification for not extending similar benefits (for example, to same-sex couples)? She contends that "the historic role of marriage as the exclusive mechanism to provide certain economic benefits and protections" cannot be maintained.[86]

Fineman and I concur on a salient starting point: it is important to examine assumptions about the capabilities and capacities of family forms to realize certain goods and perform certain functions, rather than to assume that marriage is the only form that allows realization of those goods or performance of those functions.[87] But we come to different conclusions. I propose to reconstruct marriage to make it more egalitarian and inclusive and to adopt a kinship registration system. She proposes replacing marriage as a legal status with support for the caretaker-dependent dyad, and shifting adult intimate relationships to private contract.

There are several reasons to resist the move to abolishing marriage. First, Fineman is certainly correct that the meaning of marriage has changed over time, allowing more individual freedom to express what it means to be a spouse. But a diminished role for legally mandated meanings does not entail a vacuum of meaning. For example, duties like that of support remain but are now stated in gender-neutral form. In challenges to state marriage laws, gay men and lesbians, on the margins of marriage law, articulate why they seek to marry, identifying goods such as public expression of commitment, friendship and love, emotional and economic interdependency, and security for partners and their children. The *Goodridge* court defined the core of marriage in terms of an exclusive commitment. If marriage is so defined, and it does not unjustly exclude same-sex couples who seek access to it, how is it imposing a sectarian set of meanings at the expense of many others?

Second, relegating intimate relationships between adults to the realm of private contract denies them the expressive benefit of public recognition of—and validation of—their commitment. Marriage, Regan observes, offers a "public ritual" marking entry into "a social institution intended to embody the value of intimate commitment."[88] As the *Baker* court observed, state support for marriage reflects the idea that recognizing and supporting an intimate commitment between two persons may help to foster security and stability. Removing adult-adult intimate bonds from the "family" of "state-sanctioned relationships" would eliminate this facilitative governmental role. A regime of private contract would not be an adequate substitute.

By removing sexual affiliation as a basis for governmental subsidy and protection, Fineman's proposal would address what marriage critics charge is a "necessary implication" of the institution of marriage: it "sanctifies some couples at the expense of others."[89] However, such a drastic remedy to this problem of "selective legitimacy" is not necessary. Opening up marriage to same-sex couples, and adopting a kinship registration system for persons in a broad range of close adult relationships, would greatly diminish this problem, while retaining the facilitative role of government in supporting intimate affiliation.

Third, Fineman gives insufficient attention to government's interest in supporting emotional and economic interdependency between adults. Her redefinition of family around the caretaker-dependent relationships has the admirable aim of directing society's attention to the well-being of children and to the importance of the task of orderly social reproduction. Children trigger obligations and responsibilities on the part of parents and of society. The dependency of children is a social fact that a good society must address. So, too, is the dependency of other persons who cannot care for themselves. However, an exclusive focus on children or adult dependency obscures the point that society has an interest in committed, caring, supportive relationships between adults, and that these relationships also may involve dependency and interdependency and trigger mutual responsibilities. In addition, as Patricia Cain concludes, "state recognition of adult committed relationships is good public policy" considering that functioning households are important economic and social units.[90]

We need a conception of family that is inclusive enough to recognize and value the commitments of adults to each other and their undertaking mutual responsibility for each other. Moreover, important public values are at stake. As Mary Lyndon Shanley observes, "the public does have an interest in the terms of marriage," such as "promoting equality of husband and wife, both as spouses and as citizens," and in "sustaining marital and other family relationships in the face of poverty and illness."[91] When two adults rear children together, a formal recognition of their adult-adult relationship may help stabilize the family. Again, the stories of the same sex-couples seeking to marry in *Goodridge* are instructive.

Fourth, Fineman's proposal of a regime of private contract to order adult intimate relationships raises concerns like those identified in the ALI *Principles* concerning limits to capacity and important public policies at stake in intimate relationships. She is certainly correct to caution against rejecting a model of contract because of stereotypes that women lack the capacity to contract. But the ALI raises significant caveats about real constraints, in the context of bargaining over intimate relationships, that may "disarm" persons' capacity for self-protective judgment. Fineman does indicate that her approach would have some default rules and ameliorating doctrines to accompany contract.[92] But a better approach would allow private ordering within a system that retains marriage and adopts a kinship registration system.

For these reasons, I reject the proposal to abolish marriage.

## Conclusion

In this chapter, I have argued for an approach to family law and policy that retains a place for marriage but also moves beyond marriage to advance equality among families and support other forms of intimate affiliation. These proposals would help government to carry out its formative responsibilities to support families. In the next two chapters, I turn to pressing concerns about another dimension of government's formative responsibilities: what role should government play in shaping persons' decisions whether or not to form families? Does government have a proper interest in encouraging personal responsibility when individuals exercise their constitutional liberty in matters of sexual expression and reproduction? What model of sex education for children and adolescents would best foster their capacity for responsible decision making concerning such matters?

# III
## Fostering Responsibility

# ᔥ 7

## *Rights, (Ir)responsibility, and Reproduction*

> The ability of women to participate equally in the economic and social life of the Nation has been facilitated by their ability to control their reproductive lives.
> ᔥ *Planned Parenthood v. Casey*, 505 U.S. 833, 856 (1992)

> Unfettered access to abortion on demand has addressed none of women's true needs; nor has it brought dignity to women. It has, in fact, done precisely the opposite. It has encouraged irresponsible or predatory men, who find abortion a convenient justification for their lack of commitment. . . .
> ᔥ *A New American Compact: Caring About Women, Caring for the Unborn*, New York Times, *July 14, 1992, p. A23*

*A* FUNDAMENTAL COMPONENT of fostering responsibility and respecting personal self-government with regard to family life is protecting the freedom to decide whether or not to exercise one's capacity to reproduce. Constitutional protection of the right to decide, free from unwarranted governmental interference, whether to bear or beget a child, and whether to continue or terminate a pregnancy, properly follows from a principle of toleration. Governmental restraint accords proper respect for persons' exercise of their moral capacities by allocating to individuals—rather than government—the responsibility to make decisions about the meaning and place of reproduction in their lives. Pregnancy is a condition unique to women, and its burdens are borne by women, not men. Thus, the equality and liberty of women are at stake in unique ways. Significantly, in the above quotation from Planned Parenthood v. Casey, the U.S. Supreme Court recognized that reproductive rights facilitate women's equal citizenship: being able to control the place of reproduction in their lives

223

fosters women's ability to participate equally with men in society. Moreover, from the fact of women's unique relationship to pregnancy, *Casey* concluded that it is "implicit in the meaning of liberty" that a woman must retain "the ultimate control over her destiny and her body" and that "[t]he destiny of the [pregnant] woman must be shaped to a large extent on her own conception of her spiritual imperatives and her place in society."[1]

Reproductive rights, notwithstanding *Casey's* stirring rhetoric and the growing recognition of women's "right to have control over and decide freely and responsibly on matters related to their . . . reproductive health" as a human right,[2] remain controversial. For some opponents of a legal right to abortion, abortion is a paradigmatic case of irresponsibility. It is said to license irresponsibility and to exalt selfishness at the expense of family. As the "Compact" quoted above reveals, one charge is that abortion is not a right but a wrong, perpetrated both on women and on innocent unborn life. It permits sex without responsibility, that is, without the willingness to accept the reproductive consequences.

Even among the majority of the American public who support a legal right to abortion, there is considerable ambivalence about abortion. On the one hand, in the decades since the landmark case, Roe v. Wade, in which the Supreme Court first recognized a pregnant woman's constitutional right to decide whether or not to terminate her pregnancy, a majority of the American public steadily has supported this right and opposed making abortion illegal. On the other hand, support is equivocal: many people believe it should be harder for women to obtain abortions and support various legal restrictions, such as waiting periods and the denial of public funding.[3] Moreover, there remains a gap between the circumstances in which various majorities approve of abortion and the most common reasons that women seek abortions. A steady and fervent minority believes that abortion should be wholly unavailable. In presidential election cycles, abortion is a contentious issue, with Democrats affirming "a woman's right to choose" and proclaiming that abortion should be "safe, legal, and rare," and Republicans supporting a "human life amendment" and vowing to protect "unborn children" from abortion.[4]

Ambivalence about abortion therefore seems to reflect sharp conflict over liberty versus life, or choice versus children. Yet, just as women's decisions to have abortions and thus *not* to bear children generate charges of irresponsibility, so do their decisions *to* bear children, as the so-called culture wars over family values and calls to reform welfare to end "illegitimacy" illustrate. Underlying opposition to women's decisions both to terminate and to continue pregnancies is a lack of trust in women's capacity for responsible decision making about the place of children and family in their lives—and an eagerness to second-guess women's motivations and circumstances. Ambivalence about, or resistance to, women's self-government in forming and not forming families reflects the continuing hold of an objectionable gender ideology that (1) views pregnancy and motherhood as women's proper destiny and (2) critiques reproductive rights for thwarting women's ability to curb the irresponsibility of men.

In this chapter, I explain why personal self-government in matters of reproduction is a precondition for fostering strong families. In contrast to the argument that abortion is simply a wrong right, and not what women really need, I argue that a right to reproductive liberty facilitates the exercise of responsibility. *Casey* offers a rich account of how women's liberty and equality are at stake in decisions about reproduction. However, in the Supreme Court's abortion jurisprudence, affirmations of women's decisional liberty go hand in hand with approval of a range of state regulations that restrict women's access to abortion. I critique these regulations because they too often hinder, rather than foster, the exercise of moral responsibility in making reproductive decisions. They reflect, at best, "empty" toleration for women's decisions rather than the respect that toleration should entail.

The continuing public ambivalence about abortion rights invites the question of whether the problem lies in framing the issue in terms of rights. Does rights talk inevitably invite the charge that rights license irresponsibility? Would a responsibility-based justification for reproductive liberty combat the association of rights with irresponsibility and secure greater respect for it? I maintain that in light of the vicissitudes of public opinion about abortion, appeals to responsibility will likely fail unless they are grounded in a firm commitment to a principle of personal self-government.

Facilitating reproductive responsibility requires not only governmental restraint (or "freedom from") but also governmental action (or "freedom to"). Genuine reproductive freedom requires a governmental commitment to fostering the social and material preconditions for such freedom. By contrast, the intersection between the abortion and the "illegitimacy" issues reveals that, in both contexts, government disapproves of and seeks to discourage women's reproductive choices. Whether government selectively funds childbirth instead of abortion, or refuses to support the children of poor mothers, a common justification is that government has no obligation to facilitate women's exercise of their reproductive rights. As such, these policies illustrate serious limitations in current constitutional jurisprudence and in understandings of government's formative responsibilities. These limitations point to the need for public policy that better respects and fosters capacity, promotes sex equality, and encourages responsibility.

## Is Abortion a Wrong Right?

Understanding the charge that abortion rights license irresponsibility requires careful attention to the meaning of the word "responsibility." I shall distinguish two ideas of responsibility: responsibility as accountability, or conformity, and responsibility as autonomy. I shall argue that rights foster responsibility in the second sense.

Immediately after *Casey* reaffirmed the central holding of *Roe* and linked abortion to women's responsible self-government, "A New American Compact: Caring About Women, Caring for the Unborn" proclaimed that "America does not need the abortion license," which "has ushered in a new era of irresponsibility toward women and children." Instead, it needs policies that "responsibly protect and advance the interests of mothers and their children, both before and after birth." The Compact supported, ideally, a law prohibiting abortion except in very rare cases in which pregnancy poses a "threat to maternal life or health." The rationale for this prohibition was that *Roe* denied prenatal life "the right to life." The Compact indicted abortion as a choice "faced by isolated women exercising private rights," and shifted the locus of choice to the American people to decide "what kind of a people will we be" and "whose rights will we acknowledge."[5]

In this view, abortion rights are wrong rights: rather than addressing women's "true needs," they license the irresponsibility of men ("who find abortion a convenient justification for their lack of commitment") and of society (which fails to "responsibly protect" the interests of women and children). This argument is similar to Mary Ann Glendon's critique of abortion as a right of privacy: such a right isolates pregnant women from the community.[6] By contrast, Glendon praises more communitarian schemes, found in some Western European countries, that treat the abortion matter as one of mutual responsibility: "what the pregnant woman can be required to sacrifice for the common value is related to what the social welfare state is ready and able to do to help with the burdens of childbirth and parenthood."[7]

Responsibility, on this model, is best understood as accountability, or conformity:[8] pregnant women exercise responsibility when they act in accordance with the obligations and duties that society may reasonably demand of them. And although the European schemes Mary Ann Glendon praises do allow women to choose abortion under various circumstances—and thus retain some personal self-government in the matter—the Compact's model would insist that, except in "very rare" cases of "threat to maternal life or health," pregnant women would not be permitted to make that "private" choice.

One basis for regarding the right to abortion as a wrong right is a conviction that such a right ill-serves women's genuine needs. This vision of women's needs overlooks the role that women and women's organizations played, as active agents, to secure a right to legal abortion and to show—by sharing their own experiences—the place of reproductive liberty in fostering personal and family well-being.[9] To the argument that abortion rights help, rather than harm, women, abortion opponents would likely counter that women's liberty must yield to the imperative of protecting a prenatal right to life. For such opponents reject *Roe*'s explicit and *Casey*'s implicit conclusion that prenatal life is not a legal person entitled to constitutional rights.[10] By contrast, my argument accepts the premise that a fetus is not a constitutional person as both established and justified.[11]

Even if one assumes a fetal right to life, this would not necessarily bar a right to abortion. Judith Jarvis Thomson argued that, even if a fetus is a person, a pregnant woman is not morally required to make the large sacrifices needed to sustain the life of another who has no right to demand them.[12] The analogous legal argument is that if a society does not generally impose Good Samaritanism or nurturing burdens on citizens (for example, compelling parents to donate organs to children), then imposing such burdens only on pregnant women violates principles of equal protection and liberty. We might prefer to live in a more communitarian society in which citizens have a legal obligation to be Good Samaritans to one another. But as long as we do not, singling out pregnant women unfairly compels them into nurturing relationships against their will.[13] And it is not just one isolated act of rescue—in which a person might give aid to a stranger and to whom she would have no further obligation—but the compelled support, from conception until birth, of a fetus wholly dependent on her.[14] Moreover, as a practical matter, such a compelled relationship imposes burdens long after childbirth: a woman may bear the burdens of rearing the child herself, and, even if she puts the child up for adoption, having the child may produce an "inescapable" orientation of relatedness to that child.[15] Compelled sacrifice and nurture deprive a woman of the right and power to determine for herself whether she will bear these burdens and make this sacrifice. To compel this relationship is to deny her personal self-government.

## Taking Rights and Responsibilities Seriously

A better view of the relationship between rights and responsibility is that rights call for the exercise of moral responsibility as autonomy. Rather than being a wrong right, the abortion right affords women the opportunity for moral reflection and for the exercise of personal responsibility. As Ronald Dworkin argues, "people have the moral right—and the moral responsibility—to confront the most fundamental questions about the meaning and value of their own lives for themselves, answering to their own consciences and convictions."[16] Constitutional guarantees of liberty and of freedom of conscience protect this realm of what James E. Fleming has called deliberative autonomy.[17]

Responsibility as autonomy includes accountability to self—the responsibility to live up to one's freedom by exercising rights reflectively. It is incompatible with responsibility as conformity. I concur with Dworkin that government, consistent with respect for constitutional liberty, may encourage the goal of "responsibility" in the sense of reflective decision making, but it may not insist that women conform their decisions to society's view of the best decision whether to continue or terminate their pregnancies.[18] The former approach allocates to individuals the responsibility to decide for themselves; the latter compels a result and precludes the exercise of responsibility.

But do rights allow for irresponsibility? Leaving the ultimate decision to pregnant women does risk that some women may make decisions that others deem irresponsible. But this is a cost of freedom and of protecting rights: a "right" merely to do that which the community thinks is the right thing to do or which serves the community's view of the common good would not be a right.[19] Principles of toleration and decisional liberty reflect the conviction that it is better to run the risk that some people may make incorrect (or irresponsible) decisions than to deny everyone outright the right to make decisions profoundly affecting their destiny.[20] For the development and exercise of personal and moral responsibility require freedom to exercise judgment.[21] The *Casey* joint opinion, as I will highlight, related such freedom to a woman's personhood, autonomy, and bodily integrity, while Justice John Paul Stevens's separate opinion linked the "authority to make . . . traumatic and yet empowering decisions" to "basic human dignity."[22] Moreover, such freedom and decisional authority is appropriate in a morally pluralistic society in which people of good conscience inevitably will reasonably disagree about the responsible choice, or the right thing to do.

## The Place of Abortion in Constitutional Liberty

Why should women be permitted to terminate their pregnancies? In a striking passage, the joint opinion in *Casey* spoke of the liberty at stake in the abortion decision as "unique to the human condition and so unique to the law":

> The mother who carries a child to full term is subject to anxieties, to physical constraints, to pain that only she must bear. That these sacrifices have from the beginning of the human race been endured by women with a pride that ennobles her in the eyes of others and gives to the infant a bond of love cannot alone be grounds for the State to insist she make the sacrifice. Her suffering is too intimate and personal for the State to insist, without

more, upon its own vision of the woman's role, however dominant
that vision has been in the course of our history and our culture.
The destiny of the woman must be shaped to a large extent on
her own conception of her spiritual imperatives and her place in
society.[23]

This important passage from *Casey* situates pregnancy in the context
of a woman's own sense of the place of pregnancy and motherhood in
her life. The joint opinion's argument that the "destiny" of a woman
is at stake and, thus, she, not the state, should decide on the resolution
of her pregnancy is a powerful justification for the right to decide
whether to have an abortion. Moreover, because of the "inescapable
biological fact" that abortion regulations will have a "far greater impact" on the liberty of a woman carrying a fetus than on a father, the
Court has held that, "when the wife and the husband disagree" about
how to resolve her pregnancy, the balance weighs in the pregnant
woman's favor (and thus states may not require either husband consent
or notification).[24] And by referring to a woman's right to resist the
state's vision of her role, the joint opinion acknowledges that abortion
implicates sex equality.

A common criticism is that a right to abortion licenses "irresponsibility," and permits women to terminate pregnancies for reasons of
"convenience." By contrast, *Casey*'s description of the "unique" situation of a pregnant woman suggests the serious physical and existential
dimensions at stake. To characterize women's abortion decisions as an
exercise of relational autonomy—how a pregnant woman exercises
self-government in a particular context—is to highlight that, as studies
of women's abortion decisions indicate, women facing an unplanned
or unwanted pregnancy strive to make the right decision in their circumstances.[25]

What relational concerns are at issue? Pregnant women evaluate
their responsibility to themselves as well as their responsibilities to
other persons. One relational concern is a pregnant woman's perception of the prenatal life within her and whether she is capable of, or
ready to assume the responsibility for, nurturing a fetus and, ultimately, mothering a child. Many young women who face unplanned
pregnancies conclude that abortion is the right decision because, although they want to have a child at some point, they are not yet ready

to take on the responsibility of being a parent. This conclusion may rest on their assessment of their capacity and resources, or of competing imperatives such as pursuing education or employment.

Animating these decisions to terminate a pregnancy is often a vision of the right, or optimal, conditions under which to have a child and become a mother. Women are acting on their own view of the place of family in their lives. For example, one young woman, Maria, who had an abortion at age 30 and went on to have a wanted child at age 40, chose abortion because she did not want to replicate her own experience of being an unwanted child, resented by her mother:

> [T]he reason I always knew I would not have an out-of-wedlock child is because I have these really high standards of how one should raise a child and it includes having two people, not necessarily married . . . to take care of each other and also the child. . . . When I was trying to get pregnant [later], it took me nine months to get pregnant. . . . But I never thought for one second I should have kept that first pregnancy, because it was so wrong in terms of what I thought should be the right environment for a child. . . . I didn't want to replicate in my child something that I felt had happened to me [being unwanted].[26]

Opponents of legal abortion characterize reasons like those given by Maria as reasons of "convenience." This label misses young women's sense of responsibility to give a child a good start in life. Studies of women's abortion decisions offer firm support for the feminist, pro-choice argument that pregnant women choose abortion out of a responsible desire "to ensure that a new life will be borne only if it will be nurtured and loved."[27] Indeed, rather than being "anti-life," or "anti-family," women often regard their decisions as "pro-family" and "pro-life." In the words of one woman who had two abortions in her early twenties and went on to have children and grandchildren:

> I was not ready to be a mother. I was not ready to bring those children into the world. . . . I thought, number one, I'm not married, number two, this will kill my mother, and number three, I don't have the money to support a child properly. . . . I was raised to support myself and I wasn't prepared to have a family without

a husband. I didn't consider myself selfish. I knew I was doing it for this unborn child.[28]

In using the term "pro-life," pregnant women who terminate their pregnancies often include a concern for their *own* lives. They express a conviction that they have a responsibility to themselves to mature and develop before they become a parent. As the following woman who chose abortion explained:

Anybody who says an abortion is antilife is saying that a woman's life is unimportant. I don't think that people who have abortions are antilife, they're just pro their own life. A woman is putting their own fully developed life first. It's just a choice you have to make. I'm going to have a great family, and it's going to be because I'm mature enough and practically settled enough to make it as easy as possible, because it's hard enough to have a good family under the best circumstances.[29]

Women who already have children represent a sizable group among those who choose abortion. Although married women, like unmarried women, offer socioeconomic reasons for choosing abortion, a prominent reason they give, one worldwide study found, is the desire to postpone or stop childbearing.[30] Mothers have a vision of the optimal conditions under which to bring additional children into the world. The gap between their circumstances and such conditions is a factor leading them to terminate a pregnancy. A mother's concern for her own well-being and self-development may also shape her decision. Often, relational responsibilities to existing children guide such decisions:

I already had three children and it was very clear that this marriage I was in was not working. I knew he loved the kids but that wasn't enough. . . . There had to be more of a sense of family, more of a sense that this person is going to help me raise these kids, that I wasn't going to be raising them all by myself. He was abusive and was getting more abusive. . . . I had these kids to think about and try to take care of. . . . [I]f I go and leave him, I'm going to have another kid to take care of. And I can't even take care of these that I have. . . . Do I want this baby? Can I take care of it? What about the kids that I already have? What about myself?

Another mother explained her reasoning:

[M]y children were the reason that I had the abortion, because when I had my last child, I had problems. The delivery was hard. I had complications. . . . And I thought, if I have to go into the hospital for some other complications of pregnancy there wouldn't be anybody there for my children. . . . I was sick a lot and always tired, and I was single, and I said, I'm not going through that again.[31]

Women's accounts of their abortion decisions, whether they already have children or are choosing to delay having them, substantiate the insight behind the feminist argument that abortion decisions are decisions about mothering and motherhood. A woman's assessment of her responsibilities and circumstances may lead her to conclude that she cannot be a responsible mother.[32] Moral psychologist Carol Gilligan found, in her study of women's abortion decisions, that women asked themselves whether it was responsible or irresponsible, moral or immoral, to sustain and deepen an attachment under circumstances in which they could not be responsible and exercise care. Gilligan's subjects engaged in a process of moral reasoning that examined their responsibility to themselves, to the prenatal life within them, and to others in their lives, and sought to make the best, or right, decision based on their specific circumstances.[33] One recent comparative study found that in their "everyday deliberations," women "interweave the self-other relationship in their moral calculations all the time, rooting their individual identity in family and community."[34] As one mother explained her reasoning:

At the time, my older daughter was 15 and the younger was 13. Having two children already that I had pretty much at the time raised as a single parent, I realized for sure that I didn't want any more children. I wanted to be able to take good care of them. . . . Not allowing for abortion and not allowing women to choose how many children they have, whether one, or two, or no children, . . . is antifamily. Saying that you must have that child if you happen to get impregnated, saying that you must carry that child to term, and then raise that child . . . is antifamily. [It] doesn't value the women as a unique individual, and it does not value the child.[35]

For some women, terminating a pregnancy is the best choice in their circumstances because having children and being a mother are not part of their vision of their own life or their "destiny."[36] For example:

[The unwanted pregnancy] made me realize I really didn't want children. . . . I can't relate to little children at all. I don't want something demanded of me 24 hours a day. . . . I think women often have children for totally the wrong reason[:] . . . Because their parents expect it, their friends expect it, their husband expects it. . . . [O]kay, abortion does destroy life . . . but an unwanted pregnancy and unwanted children destroy more than one life. Unwanted children do fail to thrive. So I don't think it's a selfish decision at all, to have an abortion.[37]

These women, in particular, might seem to invite the charge that abortion decisions are "selfish" or for a woman's "convenience." However, they conscientiously assess their own capacity for or willingness to take on the enormous responsibility of nurturing a child. They are making decisions about how best to develop their capacities and to foster their own well-being. Instead of rearing children, they may decide to contribute to and participate in society in other ways. They also are alert to—and willing to resist—the cultural pressures on women to become mothers. Whether women should have a right not to be mothers—even if they become pregnant—raises the sex equality dimension of the abortion issue.

## Abortion and Conscription

As the *Casey* joint opinion observed, women have the constitutional liberty to decide for themselves what place motherhood will have in their lives and whether they will make the physical and psychic commitment entailed by pregnancy. Respect for women's equality fortifies the argument for such liberty. Only women become pregnant and bear the burdens of pregnancy and, thus, the consequences of restrictive abortion laws. As Sylvia Law explains, it is not nature, but governmental regulation, that "exaggerate[s] the cost of these burdens" and turns women's reproductive capacity into a source of disadvantage when the state prohibits or restricts abortion.[38] To compel all women who face an unplanned pregnancy to continue their pregnancies, regardless of whether they want to bear a child, and regardless of whether they made efforts to avoid pregnancy, is to treat pregnancy and motherhood as women's natural, or inevitable destiny. This conscription reflects less on women's "nature" than on ideology about women's nature and proper gender role.

*Casey* implicitly rejects such conscription when it bars government from imposing "its own vision of the woman's role" on pregnant women, "however dominant that vision has been in the course of our history and our culture."[39] Drawing on feminist and liberal scholarship, Justice Blackmun's separate opinion in *Casey* explicitly articulates the anticonscription argument:

> A State's restrictions on a woman's right to terminate her pregnancy also implicate constitutional guarantees of gender equality. . . . By restricting the right to terminate pregnancies, the State conscripts women's bodies into its service, forcing women to continue their pregnancies, suffer the pains of childbirth, and in most instances, provide years of maternal care. . . . Th[e] assumption— that women can simply be forced to accept the "natural" status and incidents of motherhood—appears to rest upon a conception of women's role that has triggered the protection of the Equal Protection Clause.[40]

Both appeals to liberty and to gender equality invoke an anticompulsion rationale to support women's right to terminate a pregnancy. A jurisdictional (or personal sovereignty) argument is also at work: respect for women's moral capacity and for their equal citizenship requires allocating to women, rather than to government (or to majorities), the right and responsibility to decide how to resolve their pregnancies.[41] Moreover, a vital normative argument supports an anti-compulsion rationale for allocating this decision to women: compelling women to nurture fetuses (and, as a practical matter, take on the responsibilities of motherhood) not only invades their autonomy and harms their lives, it also forfeits the moral worth that comes from their freely choosing a nurturing relationship.[42] Government does not facilitate the sort of caring, nurturing relationships that promote child well-being when it compels pregnant women to continue unwanted pregnancies and overrides such women's own convictions about the morally responsible decision to make, given their circumstances.

But surely, one might counter, government does compel parents to take care of their children and it imposes duties on mothers and fathers, whether or not becoming a parent was freely chosen. Why not compel similar duties toward prenatal life? Answering this question requires attention to what governmental interests are at stake in the "unique" context of pregnancy.

## What Is Society's Stake in Women's Abortion Decisions?

The *Casey* joint opinion situates the "unique" liberty at stake in women's abortion decisions in terms of a broader range of "intimate and personal choices" that are "central to personal dignity and autonomy." It affirms a "right to define one's own concept of existence, of meaning, of the universe, and of the mystery of human life" and declares: "Beliefs about these matters could not define the attributes of personhood were they formed under compulsion of the State." However, the joint opinion also characterizes abortion as "more than a philosophic exercise." It is "an act fraught with consequences," not only for the pregnant woman herself, but also "for others"—"the persons who perform and assist in the procedure; . . . the spouse, family, and society which must confront the knowledge that these procedures exist . . . ; and, depending on one's beliefs . . . the life or potential life that is aborted."[43]

What follows from recognizing these consequences? *Casey* rejects any idea that a pregnant woman has an entitlement to an inviolate sphere of decision making prior to viability:

> What is at stake is the woman's right to make the ultimate decision, not a right to be insulated from all others in doing so.

Regulations which do no more than create a structural mechanism by which the State, or the parent or guardian of a minor,
may express profound respect for the life of the unborn are permitted, if they are not a substantial obstacle to the woman's exercise of the right to choose. . . . [A] state measure designed to
persuade her to choose childbirth over abortion will be upheld if
reasonably related to that goal.[44]

*Casey*'s reference to "insulation" brings to mind the Court's statement in *Roe* that "[t]he pregnant woman cannot be isolated in her
privacy. She carries an embryo, and, later, a fetus."[45] Neither *Roe* nor
*Casey* concluded that an embryo, and later, a fetus was a "person"
within the meaning of the Fourteenth Amendment of the Constitution. However, in both opinions, the Supreme Court recognized a
state's interest in potential life and framed the abortion issue as "how
best to accommodate the State's interest in potential human life with
the constitutional liberties of pregnant women."[46]

In *Roe*, the Court concluded that the state had a compelling interest
in protecting fetal life after viability, the time when the fetus "presumably has the capacity of meaningful life outside the mother's womb."
States could "go so far as to proscribe abortion during that period,
except when it is necessary to preserve the life or health of the
mother."[47] Prior to that time, especially during the first trimester,
when abortion was safer for women than childbirth, government's authority to regulate abortion to protect prenatal life was limited. During
the second trimester, government's interest in protecting maternal
health became compelling.

*Casey* retained viability as the appropriate point up to which women
should be free to make the "ultimate" decision whether to terminate
their pregnancies. Arguably, at the point of viability, government's interest in restricting abortions reflects a public value rooted in human-
itarian concerns about respect for life, rather than a theological or
sectarian value.[48] However, *Casey* departed from *Roe* in declaring that
the state had a "profound" interest in protecting prenatal life
throughout pregnancy and could regulate to further that interest even
prior to viability as long as it did not impose an "undue burden" on
a pregnant woman's decision. As long as a pregnant woman is free to
make the "ultimate decision" prior to viability, the government may
legitimately facilitate the "wise exercise" of reproductive liberty

through measures designed to persuade her in favor of childbirth over abortion.[49]

*Casey* invokes two interests to justify such governmental persuasion: protecting prenatal life and fostering maternal health. To advance such interests, the state may encourage a pregnant woman "to know that there are philosophic and social arguments of great weight" in favor of continuing her pregnancy.[50] If earlier cases had reflected the judgment that the best way to protect pregnant women's entitlement to decisional privacy was to prohibit government from wedging its "message discouraging abortion" into women's decision-making process,[51] the *Casey* joint opinion significantly retreats from the "privacy" of that process.[52]

What constitutes an "undue" burden on a woman's right to make the ultimate decision? Some of *Casey*'s formulations seem to contemplate that regulations must facilitate women's personal self-government. For example, "the means chosen by the State to further the interest in potential life must be calculated to inform the woman's free choice, not hinder it." However, other formulations suggest that the crucial test is simply *how* burdensome a regulation is: a regulation will pass muster as long as it does not have "the purpose or effect of placing a *substantial* obstacle in the path" of a pregnant woman's decision.[53] The roots of the undue burden test—in prior Supreme Court cases upholding a series of restrictions on a woman's access to public funds, facilities, and even information about abortion—give reason for concern that this test insufficiently protects a woman's right to meaningful self-government. I will illustrate this by critiquing the *Casey* joint opinion's analysis of the informed consent scheme before it and then revisit the public funding and facilities cases in light of *Casey*.

## Abortion as Psychological Peril

The *Casey* joint opinion upholds informed consent measures and waiting periods on the assumption that they inform, rather than hinder, women's "free choice": they promote women's psychological well-being and facilitate the "wise exercise" of their liberty.[54] Governmental persuasion allegedly helps women not simply to choose, but to choose well. If, as I argue, government has a responsibility to facilitate persons' exercise of their moral capacities, would this sort of governmental persuasion be a helpful way to do so? Moreover, if abortion decisions implicate, as Dworkin argues, an important shared value—the sanctity of life—may government attempt to encourage responsibility when people make decisions implicating that value? If government may—and should—do more to foster self-government than simply to leave people alone, does *Casey* offer an attractive vision of how it might do so?

For the *Casey* joint opinion, "informed" choice means, in effect, that the woman is informed that the state prefers childbirth and has "profound" respect for the fetus. The Pennsylvania statute required that a pregnant woman who requests an abortion be informed of the availability of materials describing "the unborn child," of the existence of agencies that would support a decision for childbirth over abortion, and of the fact that financial assistance from the father of the potential child may be available. She then must wait twenty-four hours before implementing a decision to have an abortion.[55] Notwithstanding the Court's elevated reference to encouraging pregnant women to know of "philosophic and social arguments" in favor of childbirth, nothing in the statute remotely resembles or conveys such arguments, without considerable drawing of inferences (for example, from anatomical descriptions of the fetus or the names of social service agencies).

A serious limitation of the joint opinion's vision of how government might foster "wise exercise" of women's reproductive liberty is its evident vision of abortion as fraught with psychological peril. It implies that women are at risk for serious psychological consequences from abortion choices because they are ignorant about what abortion is. Informed consent regulations, *Casey* opines, seek to ensure that women considering an abortion understand the "impact on the fetus," which "most women" would deem "relevant, if not dispositive to the decision." This averts the risk that they may later regret their decisions as ill-informed and suffer "devastating psychological consequences."[56]

This vision of abortion as trauma or psychological peril for women lacks a solid foundation, despite considerable expenditure of governmental resources to find empirical support for it. For example, former Surgeon General Everett Koop (who personally opposed legal abortion) concluded that the psychological effects resulting from abortion are "minuscule from a public health perspective."[57] To the contrary, most studies suggest that the majority of women mainly feel "relief" after an abortion and view it as a positive decision. Although they often experience such feelings as loss, ambivalence, and regret at the time (for example, if the circumstances were different, some might have chosen childbirth), few would reverse their decision.[58] Some women do report negative psychological consequences after an abortion, but they are likely to have had great ambivalence about their decision at the time, or to have suffered emotional and other problems prior to the abortion.[59]

In principle, designing informed consent regulations to encourage thoughtful and informed decisions could flow from government's affirmative responsibility to foster self-government. However, one-sided counseling schemes that fail to accord respect to women's decision-making capacity do not advance this end. The fact that government employs persuasion to steer the exercise of women's deliberative autonomy concerning reproduction, when it does not generally campaign to convince citizens that "the exercise of a right is a wrong," strengthens the argument that an impermissible gender ideology is at work.[60] Particularly if governmental persuasion rests on an underlying vision of abortion as psychological peril, it may, as Justice Stevens argued in his separate opinion in *Casey*, deny women "equal respect" and "equal dignity." Requiring a woman who, "in the privacy of her thoughts and conscience," has chosen abortion to reconsider—"simply because the State believes she has come to the wrong conclusion"— reflects either "outmoded and unacceptable assumptions about the decisionmaking capacity of women" or the "illegitimate premise" that "the decision to terminate a pregnancy is presumptively wrong." As Stevens puts it: "[d]ecisional autonomy must limit the State's power to inject into a woman's most personal deliberations its own views of what is best."[61]

Even though *Casey* describes one-sided informed consent schemes as facilitating women's "free choice," these and many other abortion regulations are the product of an effort by opponents of legal abortion to chip away at abortion rights so that, in one opponent's vivid phrase, abortion will "die a death of a thousand cuts."[62] Often, these regulations are not facilitative. Opponents of legal abortion commonly paint a picture of abortion providers as running "abortion mills" and withholding from women accurate information about prenatal life. This portrait is unfair. Studies of abortion counselors and providers highlight their commitment to helping women to have options, to take control of their lives, and to have the information necessary to make an informed decision about continuing or terminating a pregnancy. For example, one important guideline is that women reach certainty about their decision: if women experience ambivalence about getting an abortion, counselors encourage them to take more time to decide so that they can embrace their decision, whether it be abortion or childbirth.[63]

A legitimate aim of an informed consent scheme would be to afford women adequate information and counseling to enable them to reflect on the best decision given their circumstances. If the goal is facilitating "wise exercise" of reproductive liberty, why not replace persuasion against abortion with counseling that offers a more balanced account of the complex ethical and social issues involved in deciding whether or not to bear a child?[64] If one rationale for such schemes is fostering "maternal health," why not include information on studies of the potentially traumatic or perilous effects on women's well-being and the life of their future children when they continue unwanted pregnancies and raise unwanted children?[65]

One-sided persuasion against abortion also creates the misleading impression that public policy is uniformly pronatalist and will support childbirth. Yet public opinion and public policy offer contradictory messages about when reproduction is responsible or irresponsible and deserves public support. Many young women who choose abortion report that they do so because they are too young, they are unmarried, and they lack financial resources. In one view, these women's assessment of the responsible decision for them tracks public opinion that childbirth under such circumstances would not be responsible and should not garner public resources. However, sizable majorities disapprove of abortion for precisely these reasons.[66] Thus, pregnant women face the dilemma that whichever decision they make will be judged irresponsible.

Finally, the specific scheme approved in *Casey*—an informed consent requirement with a 24-hour waiting period—is likely to impede, rather than facilitate, the "free choice" of some women. The lower federal court found (and Justices Blackmun and Stevens agreed) that the law would impose severe burdens on certain women, including poor women, rural women who traveled long distances, and women who would have difficulty explaining their whereabouts (if they had to travel twice to a clinic). (Bear in mind that eighteen states now have such laws and 87 percent of U.S. counties have no abortion provider.)[67] It would be coercive because it would have the practical effect of delaying or preventing abortion.[68] The joint opinion referred to the district court's "troubling" findings about the burden of these measures on some women, but found that the waiting period did not constitute an undue burden. It left the door open for future challenges on such grounds as applied to particular circumstances. Generally, however, such informed consent procedures have been upheld under the undue burden standard.[69]

Under what circumstances is governmental persuasion likely to be facilitative rather than coercive? What are the earmarks of a facilitative scheme that would, as Dworkin puts it, encourage responsibility rather than coerce conformity with what the state believes to be the responsible decision? Dworkin offers helpful guidelines: the measures "could reasonably be expected to make a woman's deliberation about abortion more reflective and responsible"; they will not prevent some women who have decided responsibly to have an abortion from acting on that decision; and less restrictive means are not available.[70]

A more balanced approach to encouraging women to reflect on their abortion decision would better meet these criteria than one-sided persuasion against abortion. Such governmental efforts to encourage responsibility, in the sense of reflective decision making, are consistent with respect for a principle of deliberative autonomy. One might retort that women who seek abortions do not need persuasion in favor of abortion; to the extent they have not considered the other side, persuasion in favor of childbirth may enhance their decision-making process. But if the goal is reflective decision making, and if abortion may be a morally justifiable and responsible choice, a more balanced presentation of the parameters of responsible reproductive choice would better further it.

## The Abortion Funding Cases

Respect for women's decisional liberty, *Casey* states, requires leaving pregnant women free from governmental compulsion, but not free from regulation aimed at persuading them to choose childbirth over abortion. *Casey*'s endorsement of an undue burden test is troubling, given the Court's prior use of a similar test to uphold restrictions on abortion. For example, Maher v. Roe upheld a state law funding Medicaid recipients' childbirth expenses, but not elective (that is, not "medically necessary") abortions, noting that the state need not be neutral but may "make a value judgment favoring childbirth over abortion" (reflecting its legitimate interest in "protecting potential life"). Moreover, the state may "implement that judgment by the allocation of public funds." The *Maher* Court characterized the right recognized in *Roe* as an interest in making a decision about pregnancy free from "unduly burdensome interference" (for example, severe criminal sanctions), not a right to be free from all governmental regulation. The Court distinguished compulsion from encouragement or persuasion: "Constitutional concerns are greatest when the State attempts to impose its will by force of law; the State's power to encourage actions deemed to be in the public interest is necessarily far broader."[71]

In Harris v. McRae, the Court drew upon *Maher*'s distinction between compulsion and persuasion to uphold the Hyde Amendment. This federal law forbade the use of federal funds to pay for abortions of poor women otherwise eligible for medical treatment under Medicaid (except where continuing pregnancy threatened the "life of the mother"). The Court reasoned: the Amendment "places no governmental obstacle in the path of a woman who chooses to terminate her pregnancy," but uses "unequal subsidization of abortion and other medical services" (childbirth) to establish "incentives" that "encourag[e] childbirth except in the most urgent circumstances."[72] In funding only childbirth, the Amendment does not reduce the range of choices a woman would have had if Congress had subsidized *no* health-care costs; to the extent "financial constraints" restrict her ability fully to exercise her freedom of choice, these constraints result from her poverty, not from the Amendment.[73]

Abortion rights, in this view, entail a "freedom from," not a "freedom to": a woman's right to choose to terminate a pregnancy carries with it no constitutional entitlement to the financial resources necessary to avail herself of the choice. And even "freedom from" government is qualified: it is freedom to decide without "unduly burdensome interference." Government has no obligation to "commit any resources to facilitating abortions,"[74] and may use its resources to facilitate childbirth—but not abortion—because it judges childbirth to be in the public interest. Thus, the Court has upheld such "noncoercive" means as using Medicaid to fund childbirth but not abortion for indigent women who are dependent upon government for their health care, providing public hospitals and medical personnel for childbirth but not abortion, and forbidding medical personnel in family planning clinics receiving federal funding from engaging in counseling about abortion or even making referrals concerning abortion services.[75]

By drawing on this line of cases in approving the undue burden test, *Casey* may seem to embrace a model of empty toleration that conflicts jarringly with its poignant articulation of the "unique" liberty at stake for pregnant women in deciding whether to continue or terminate a pregnancy. By empty toleration, I refer both to the low level of respect afforded to women's decision making about abortion and to the latitude accorded to governmental steering against it. This juxtaposition of lofty rhetoric about individual liberty beside approval of governmental regulations seriously restricting women's capacity to exercise their constitutional rights in a meaningful manner highlights the fragility of the abortion right.[76]

Not surprisingly, the Court's reductive notion of women's uncoerced choice and its narrow conception of governmental responsibility have fueled extensive feminist criticism of the selective funding cases as illustrating the limits of the right of privacy.[77] I concur that the Court's abortion jurisprudence illustrates the limits of a model of reproductive liberty that focuses only on governmental restraint (or freedom from) and does not acknowledge the need for affirmative governmental support of reproductive health and choice (or freedom to).[78] But the disrespect for poor women's autonomy and equality reflected in such cases—and in the regulations they uphold—falls short of the requirements of privacy and toleration. At best, they reflect empty toleration of abortion; and because some regulations may have the effect of coercing women's decisions, they may amount to intolerance of it.

If *Casey*'s stirring language about reproductive liberty and furthering women's "informed choice" were to be given its full effect, we should repudiate these cases. For if the rationale for governmental persuasion is that it promotes the "wise exercise" of reproductive liberty, selective funding surely lacks the earmarks of such persuasion. Such funding purports to pursue the goal of protecting prenatal life and promoting childbirth, but it does so at the expense of protecting (and respecting) women's self-government and well-being.

The *Casey* joint opinion's statement that a state regulation is unconstitutional if it "has the purpose or effect of placing a substantial obstacle in the path" of a pregnant woman's decision should open the door to critical scrutiny of governmental purposes and effects of the sort required by a notion of toleration as respect.[79] The substantial obstacle or undue burden test is not protective enough of women's liberty, for it may entail that little short of outright governmental coercion would be unconstitutional. The public funding cases state the relevant distinction as that between compulsion and persuasion. Yet, one cogent critique of these cases—made by some dissenting members of the Court and by many scholars—is that selective funding crosses the line between persuasion and compulsion.[80] Unequal subsidies are less an offer or subsidy than a threat or penalty, and thus impose an unconstitutional condition on poor women's abortion rights.[81] In any case, measures short of compulsion can also hinder personal self-government. Thus, I concur with constitutional law scholar Kathleen Sullivan's call to shift away from a narrow focus on coercion to strict review of "any government benefit condition whose primary purpose or effect is to pressure recipients to alter a choice about exercise of a preferred constitutional liberty in a direction favored by government."[82] If, for example, a primary purpose of the Hyde Amendment was to put pressure upon or to frustrate the abortion right, such heightened scrutiny is appropriate.[83]

## The Hyde Amendment

Evaluating the purposes and effects of the Hyde Amendment reveals ample ground for invalidation. After examining the Hyde Amendment and the congressional debates, the lower court in *Harris* concluded that the "dominant purpose inferable was to prevent exercise of the right to decide to terminate pregnancy, to prevent the funds of taxpayers who disapproved of abortion on moral grounds from being used to finance abortions that were abhorrent to them."[84] Its purpose was to be a second-best assault on legal abortion, after the failure of the preferred strategy of amending the Constitution to protect a right to life for the unborn and, thus, to bar legal abortion altogether.[85] In initially enacting and in renewing the Hyde Amendment, those whose preferred stance on abortion is intolerance have sought to save as many lives as possible—by stopping as many abortions as possible— through restricting public funds for them.[86] Prior to the Hyde Amendment, nearly one-third of abortions were paid for by Medicaid funds.[87] When criticized for going after only poor women's access to abortion, Congressman Henry Hyde replied: "I certainly would like to prevent, if I could legally, anybody having an abortion, a rich woman, a middle-class woman, or a poor woman. Unfortunately, the only vehicle available is the . . . medicaid bill."[88]

This legislative history strongly indicates that selective funding fails *Casey*'s gloss upon the undue burden test: "the means chosen by the State to further the interest in potential life must be calculated to inform the woman's free choice, not hinder it"[89] Facilitating women's autonomous, reflective decision making is not the point of laws allocating public funds and facilities for childbirth but not abortion; discouraging abortions is. Government promotes childbirth as its preferred choice regardless of a woman's own assessment of her situation and of the impact of childbirth versus abortion on her life. This lack of facilitation of informed choice is most vivid in federal regulations, upheld by the Court in Rust v. Sullivan, barring medical personnel in any federally funded facility from counseling about or providing any information concerning abortion.[90]

Selective funding also fails under *Casey*'s inquiry into the "effects" of governmental regulation of abortion. The Court's formalistic and narrow view of free versus coerced choice in the funding cases contrasts with its solicitude in other contexts for even "subtle and indirect" coercion, particularly when persons' "autonomy and well-being are already compromised by poverty [and] lack of access to good medical care" (as the Court characterized persons who might be pressured to consent to physician-assisted suicide).[91] In *Harris*, the Court upheld steering toward childbirth in the face of lower court findings that pregnancy and childbirth in many cases would pose serious risks to poor women's physical and mental health and conflict with their own conscientious religious beliefs about responsible reproductive choice.[92] Dissenting justices objected that, in the many cases in which women continuing pregnancies would suffer "grievous" harm or in which fetuses would be born with significant abnormalities, government was hardly promoting "normal" childbirth.[93] Studies of the impact of such restrictions reveal that withholding funding for poor women's abortions hinders, rather than fosters, their self-government. The effects include compulsory childbearing, personal and family hardship undergone to obtain an abortion, and increased health risks due to the delay in doing so.[94]

The Hyde Amendment and similar selective funding laws also violate the requirements of toleration because they impermissibly seek to advance a governmental orthodoxy about reproduction. There is considerable conscientious disagreement among citizens about the status and moral claims of prenatal life. When government selectively funds childbirth and not abortion on the ground that such abortions are not "in the public interest," Dworkin argues, this is tantamount "to establishing one interpretation of the sanctity of life as the official creed of the community."[95] In dissent in *Harris*, Justice William Brennan argued that selective funding violated poor women's privacy rights because it allowed the state to "foist" upon them, a politically powerless group, a "state-mandated morality."[96] Persons have an entitlement to a realm of personal self-government, or individual autonomy, free from governmental intrusion. When government uses selective funding to promote its preferred view, it encroaches upon this realm of autonomy.[97] Requirements of respect for women's deliberative autonomy should constrain government's promotion of such an orthodoxy.[98]

To the extent this orthodoxy entails the view that carrying a pregnancy to term and becoming a mother is the "natural" destiny of women, governmental promotion of it through selective funding may implicate the same "constitutional guarantees of gender equality" that Justice Blackmun raised in his separate opinion in *Casey*. If government may not enforce this gender orthodoxy and conscription of women into pregnancy through criminal sanctions, doing so through measures such as selective funding may also raise constitutional problems.[99] By contrast, the public value of respect for life supports governmental restriction of abortion after viability.

A final argument against selective funding is that it disproportionately burdens poor women and thus violates norms of equality and fairness. Government singles out poor women for moralizing against abortion because it can: their dependency on governmental aid affords government greater leverage over them than over other women. Selective funding creates hierarchies among classes of rights holders, which may exacerbate background inequalities of wealth and resources.[100] Notwithstanding public ambivalence about abortion, unequal subsidization of poor women's medical care, which threatens to make abortion rights available to nonindigent or wealthy women only, is not an acceptable means of compromise on the divisive abortion issue.[101] It bears noting—as Justice Thurgood Marshall observed in dissent in *Harris*—that, because women of color are disproportionately poor and dependent upon need-based governmental subsidies, the burden of such unequal subsidization falls heavily upon them.[102] The history of governmental and societal denigration of and disrespect for the reproductive autonomy of women of color, as Dorothy Roberts argues, substantiates the unfairness of this compromise.[103] Principles of equality and fairness impose on government a moral, if not also a constitutional, responsibility to make reproductive rights equally accessible to and meaningful for all women, rich or poor.[104]

## Abortion, Responsibility, and Public Opinion

The right to abortion is necessary to secure responsibility as autonomy. Despite stirring rhetoric about women's reproductive liberty, reliance on a lax undue burden test hinders a facilitative approach to reproductive choice by readily permitting regulations restricting access to abortion. Public ambivalence about abortion exacerbates this problem. Is there a way to give a more solid grounding to women's reproductive liberty?

Would a more explicit focus on responsibility—rather than rights—secure greater respect for women's reproductive liberty? Some thoughtful feminist scholars argue that it would, focusing both on changing the rhetoric and restricting the scope of abortion rights. Showing that calls for responsibility talk rather than rights talk are not the exclusive province of conservative opponents of the right to abortion, for example, progressive feminist scholar Robin West argues that responsibility-based justification for abortion rights would meet the charge that "the demand for abortion reflects the irresponsible worst of us and worst within us." In her view, reproductive freedom should rest on the "moral quality" of the abortion decision and on the "demonstrated capacity of pregnant women to decide whether to carry a fetus to term or to abort responsibly."[105] A focus on responsibility, she contends, would also invite attention to public responsibility to address the social conditions that make pregnancies unwanted.

This feminist appeal to responsibility talk as distinguished from rights talk overstates the dichotomy between rights and responsibility. Responsibility, as West further describes it—"freedom to pursue [women's] authentically chosen and desired life goals"[106]—*is* autonomy, not an alternative to it. I am skeptical that inviting the public to focus on the "moral quality" of women's decisions about abortion would ground reproductive freedom more securely than would a firm embrace of a principle of decisional autonomy or sovereignty: allocating authority to decide a matter so fundamental to women's "destiny" to them rather than to the majority. Although it is tempting to believe that narratives about women's abortion decisions can persuade others that women manifest responsibility in those decisions, I believe that those narratives must be linked to a strong jurisdictional argument that women are the proper locus of decision making. For example, pro-choice organizations linked this argument to the actual stories of women who have had abortions in friend of the court briefs filed in key abortion cases.[107]

Reproductive freedom would be particularly vulnerable if women had to persuade majorities of the "moral quality" and responsibility of their decisions. Resting reproductive freedom on persuading others that women will exercise their freedom responsibly underestimates the controversial nature of the abortion issue and how peoples' convictions about family, religion, and the proper role of women shape their stance on abortion. For this reason, I am also skeptical about Laurie Shrage's recent proposal, in *Abortion and Social Responsibility*, of compromise regulation ending women's right to seek elective abortion far earlier in pregnancy than viability, in order to better fit public sentiment about the morality of abortion. The degree to which this compromise might reduce opposition to legal abortion is a difficult empirical question, but I doubt that it would, as Shrage claims, engender a greater sense of social responsibility (for example, support for public funding of abortion).[108]

A consistent feature of public opinion about abortion is a gap between the reasons for which majorities approve of abortion and the reasons women most commonly give for having abortions.[109] Some people support legal abortion whatever the reason, even if they have personal moral misgivings. But some would restrict legal abortion for reasons they find morally unacceptable. For example, as the narratives used earlier in this chapter indicate, one common reason that women give for getting abortions is that they cannot afford a child.[110] Public opinion polls reveal that small, but steady, majorities disapprove of legal abortion for this reason: in a 2003 poll, 55 percent of those surveyed believed that abortion should not be legally available "if the family has a very low income and cannot afford any more children."[111] Another typical reason women give for abortion is that they are unmarried and/or do not want to marry the father. But a small majority believes that women should not be able to obtain a legal abortion in such circumstances.[112]

Women give various reasons for having abortions, such as "being too young, too poor, without a job; needing to finish school; wanting 'to have a life for herself.' "[113] Some say that they simply do not want a child at this time. However, majorities morally disapprove of abortion for all of these reasons; small majorities also believe that abortion should not be legally available for such reasons. And while the public is more supportive of legal abortion during the first trimester of pregnancy than later in pregnancy, recent polls find that some 40 percent of the public opposes the Supreme Court's ruling that women have a legal right to abortion during that time. Public opinion more strongly (but no means unanimously) supports making abortion available when pregnancy is the result of rape, when it endangers a woman's physical or mental health, or in cases of physical impairment of the fetus.[114]

What accounts for this gap between women's (ostensibly responsible) reasons and publicly approved reasons for abortion? Clearly, women's own assessment of the responsible decision, given their circumstances, does not map well with many persons' ideas of the responsible thing to do. At work may be vestiges of the view of women as properly maternal and self-sacrificing. In this view, abortion allows women to act like men, that is, have sex without consequences—thus undermining their "gatekeeping" role and aiding and abetting male irresponsibility—and is contrary to feminine values of nurture and responsibility.[115] Also at work may be a strong conviction that a fetus is a person (although majorities' willingness to protect abortion at least in some circumstances seems to undercut the reported view that abortion is murder).[116] For example, although over 90 percent of abortions occur during the first trimester of pregnancy (suggesting, Rosalind Petchesky proposes, that women having abortions follow an implicit moral code that is sensitive to stages of fetal development), late-term abortion and near-term fetuses pervade anti-abortion rhetoric.[117] When women's own assessment of their situation comes up against these convictions about women's maternal role and fetal life, women's reasons are more likely to be dismissed as reasons of "convenience" rather than respected for their responsible moral quality. Notably, opponents of legal abortion who use the "convenience" label appeal to the same studies of women's decision making that pro-choice advocates invoke to highlight women's moral responsibility.[118]

Another explanation may be related to what studies of women's abortion decisions call a situational morality, in which a pregnant woman disapproves of legal abortion in the abstract but adopts a different stance when confronting an unplanned or unwanted pregnancy in her own life.[119] By "situational morality," I do not mean the derogatory idea that people abandon their moral convictions to serve their own interests in particular situations. Rather, I mean that people refine and sharpen their moral convictions in the crucible of concrete situations requiring judgment. For example, expectant couples who learn of fetal abnormalities that may result in serious disabilities or a shortened life not uncommonly choose abortion, even though doing so contradicts their previously stated abstract beliefs. Often, their parents or other close relatives who disapprove of abortion support such decisions.[120]

Dramatic illustrations of such situational morality occurred during the 1992 presidential campaign when former president George H. Bush and his vice president, Dan Quayle, were asked how they would handle an abortion decision by their granddaughter and daughter, respectively. Neither responded in a manner consistent with their Republican Party platform by saying, "If I am successful in reforming the law, she will not be able to make such a choice because I will make abortion illegal except in very limited circumstances." Instead, President Bush pondered, "Well, whose else's—who else's [decision] could it be?"[121] First Lady Barbara Bush broke her silence to opine that abortion was a "personal thing" that has no place in political plat-forms.[122] Asked his response if his daughter were to choose abortion even if he counseled her against it, Vice President Quayle answered: "I'd support my daughter."[123] Subsequently, confronting the contra-diction between his opposition to legal abortion and this response, Quayle and his wife, Marilyn Quayle, publicly stated that if their thirteen-year-old daughter became pregnant, they would insist that she continue the pregnancy to term.[124]

This situational morality confirms the wisdom of allocating the abortion decision to individual women rather than to the state and democratic majorities. There is tremendous power in Justice Robert Jackson's famous argument that constitutional rights remove certain matters from the "vicissitudes" of changing political majorities and ensure that rights to personal self-government and self-determination do not rest on the approval of such majorities.[125] This important idea finds expression in *Casey*'s declaration, in the face of recognizing that "men and women of good conscience" disagree about abortion, that "Our obligation is to define the liberty of all, not to mandate our own moral code."[126]

## The Intersection of the Abortion and the "Irresponsible" Reproduction Issues

All this talk about government regulating abortion in order to protect potential life and promote normal childbirth might give the impres-sion that opposition to abortion in America goes hand in hand with a robust, pro-natalist and pro-children public policy. This is not the case. One recent study found "no evidence" that "pro-life states have adopted a comprehensive range of policies designed to protect and assist the weakest and most vulnerable in our society." To the contrary, "pro-life states make it difficult for women to have abortions, but they do not help these women provide for the children once born."[127]

Contemporary rhetoric about reproduction and responsibility offers contradictory messages about when pregnancy, abortion, and moth-erhood (and fatherhood) are responsible. Might one infer, from the fact that majorities disapprove of abortion for the reasons that women are too young, unmarried, and cannot afford a baby, that there is public support for such women's decisions to continue, rather than terminate, pregnancies? To the contrary, reproduction under such circumstances features in political rhetoric as the paradigm case of "irresponsible" reproduction.[128] In a memorable episode in the "family values" wars of the 1990s, Vice President Quayle proclaimed that "[b]earing babies irresponsibly is, simply, wrong" and condemned television character Murphy Brown for setting a bad example by becoming a mother outside of marriage.[129] Yet, when fans of Murphy Brown pointed out that she, in contrast to the father, took responsibility for the child—and when the producer replied that if Quayle thought nonmarital childbearing were "disgraceful," he should support "safe and legal" abortion—Quayle's office praised Murphy Brown for showing "pro-life" and "strong" family values and called single mothers "true heroes and inspirations."[130]

The example of the "family cap" illustrates contradictions regarding responsibility and reproduction. In the political debates that led to the welfare reform of 1996, the Personal Responsibility and Work Opportunity Reconciliation Act (PRWORA), lawmakers stressed inculcating "personal responsibility" in procreative matters and eliminating perverse incentives that were said to encourage women without adequate resources to bear children. One popular measure, permitted by PRWORA and adopted by twenty-three states, has been the "family cap." In contrast to AFDC's system of linking the amount of cash assistance to family size, the cap provides no increase in public assistance when a mother on welfare gives birth to another child.[131]

What unites funding poor women's childbirth expenses (but not abortion) and withholding public assistance benefits for poor women's children? The common denominator is that government has no affirmative responsibility to facilitate women's exercise of their reproductive rights. Indeed, in rejecting constitutional challenges to the first such family cap, both the federal courts and the New Jersey Supreme Court drew on the U.S. Supreme Court's selective funding cases. In *C.K. v. Shalala*, the federal court cited *Harris* for the proposition that it is a woman's poverty, not government, that poses an obstacle to her "ability to enjoy the full range of constitutionally protected freedom of choice," and that government has no obligation to remove that obstacle.[132] The court held that the cap was rationally related to New Jersey's goals of "promoting individual responsibility and family stability," since a welfare household, like a "working family," would no longer be able to expect outside assistance to help provide for an additional child. As the New Jersey Supreme Court put it, in weighing the economic strain of adding a child to the family, "the decision to bring a child to term or to have an abortion remains wholly with the woman."[133]

Yet it was precisely the potential of family cap provisions to steer women toward abortion and to pressure their reproductive choice that led an unusual coalition of "pro-life" and "pro-choice" groups to protest the cap.[134] After all, if government—by not funding abortion— uses the denial of public resources to steer poor women toward childbirth, but also—through the family cap—denies public resources to discourage childbirth, does it send any coherent message about promoting responsible reproductive decision making or valuing human life? Two messages are clear: a lack of respect for women's own reproductive decision making and a lack of public responsibility to facilitate meaningful procreative autonomy and responsible reproduction.

As with the public funding restrictions on abortion, the family cap is not a measure likely to foster responsible self-government. It rests on the flawed assumption that the availability of welfare benefits is a primary cause of poor women's childbearing so that manipulating financial incentives will change birth rates. This ignores the fact not only that many pregnancies are unintended, but also that broader social and cultural factors underlie the rise of nonmarital births.[135] A subsequent review of research on the cap led a federal governmental agency to find no "conclusive evidence about the effect of the family cap on out-of-wedlock births" or on abortions. However, the review did report one clear impact: about 9 percent of TANF families in states with a cap had less cash assistance because of the cap.[136]

The rhetoric of responsible and irresponsible reproduction diverts attention from public responsibility to safeguard reproductive health and to promote the well-being of children. Why, after all, do women need abortions? A study of twenty-seven countries (including the United States) found that "unintended pregnancy, the fundamental and immediate cause of abortion, is a reality worldwide" and that "women and couples have great difficulty in successfully planning births."[137] In the United States, for example, one-half of all pregnancies are unintended. One relevant cause is the failure to use effective forms of contraception. As the proposed federal Equity in Prescription Insurance and Coverage Act of 2003 found, most women of child-bearing age depend on private insurance for help with their medical expenses, but many insurance companies exclude prescription contraceptives, even though they pay for other prescription drugs. Such lack of coverage "places many effective forms of contraceptives beyond the financial reach of many women."[138] Such exclusion limits, rather than facilitates, women's ability to control their reproductive lives and, as one court has held, constitutes a form of sex discrimination.[139] A further constraint on that ability is the growing instances of refusals by "pro-life" pharmacists to fill prescriptions for oral contraception, and proposed "conscience clause" state laws that would support such refusals.[140]

A focus on reproductive health should build on common ground between supporters and opponents of abortion rights: too many women face unwanted pregnancies.[141] Moreover, society does not adequately value children or facilitate mothers and fathers nurturing and supporting their children.

## Conclusion

In this chapter, I have argued that women's right to continue or terminate a pregnancy is a basic component of personal self-government concerning family life. Ambivalence not only about abortion, and the moral issues it raises, but also about women's right—and responsibility—to make decisions about the place of pregnancy and motherhood in their lives has led to a system of empty toleration and a very fragile right. A better approach to promoting responsible personal self-government requires both freedom from—or governmental respect for a protected realm of decision making—and freedom to—or governmental efforts to facilitate the preconditions for responsible decision making. In the next chapter I take up an important element in a more facilitative approach to government's role in fostering sexual and reproductive responsibility in women and men: sex education for children and adolescents.

# 8

## Teaching Sexual and Reproductive Responsibility

> [B]ecause they generally become physically aroused less easily,
> girls are still in a good position to slow down the young man
> and help him learn balance in a relationship.
> ✧ Sex Respect: The Option of True Sexual Freedom
> *(an "abstinence-only" junior high and high school curriculum)*

> Strong marriage systems of the past have been accompanied by a
> high degree of sexual restriction, especially of women's sexuality. . . .
> It is hard to imagine rebuilding a strong marriage system in today's
> sexual climate. Is it possible to move toward a more culturally
> restrictive sexual system for both men and women and if so, how,
> and how restrictive should it be? . . . . The leadership for this
> probably will have to be taken by women; they are traditionally
> assumed to be the gatekeepers of sexuality.
> ✧ *David Popenoe, Co-Director, National Marriage Project*

$\mathcal{S}$TRUGGLES OVER HOW to teach sexual and reproductive responsibility among youths are a constant feature in public debate over educational and family policy. Is it better for society to prepare young people for responsible self-government through teaching "abstinence-only-until-marriage" (or "abstinence-only")? Or is the better approach "abstinence-plus," or "comprehensive" sex education, which combines a message about abstinence with information about sexuality, contraception, and the importance of protection against pregnancy and sexually transmitted diseases?[1] These struggles seem to pit reinforcing traditional families, family values, and the institution of marriage against supporting gender equality and accepting sexual diversity.[2]

A confusing welter of stories about what is happening with teenagers

256

and sexuality heightens concern over sex education. Even as rates of births to teenaged females declined in the 1990s, concern about a perceived epidemic of teen pregnancy, or "children having children," led to federal welfare reform that approved federal funding for "abstinence-only" sex education in the schools. With abstinence a more prominent part of the political agenda, media reports alternate between cover stories on the "the new virginity"—the phenomenon that more teens are choosing not to have sex—and those on the decline of dating in favor of "hooking up," "friends with benefits," and other forms of casual and detached sexual interactions.[3] Stories of a new teen "culture of restraint" and declining rates of sexual activity and pregnancy among poor urban minority youth vie with alarming reports of "transactional sex" (sex as a tool of barter), high rates of AIDS, and life circumstances in which early parenting seems the best option.[4]

What form of sex education can best respond to this complex portrait and increase sexual and reproductive responsibility? In this chapter, I advocate treating sex education as one component of government's affirmative responsibility to promote responsible self-government and to facilitate the work of families in doing so. This education illustrates how both parents and government have a vested interest in and responsibility for pursuing the healthy development of children. Abstinence-plus, or comprehensive, sex education better serves this goal than does abstinence-only sex education. My liberal feminist approach highlights the salience of issues of capacity, equality, and responsibility in meeting the needs of children and adolescents for an education that will prepare them for responsible self-government.

The abstinence-only model reflects the triumph of a conservative sexual economy: a cluster of ideas about the proper arrangement of sexuality that seeks to revive and fortify traditional moral values and social norms. In this view, young people should be sexually abstinent until marriage. Courtship, rather than dating, is the pathway to marriage. As the quotations beginning this chapter suggest, a critical component is that girls and women are gatekeepers, responsible for the proper regulation of boys' and men's sexuality. In this vision, men and women differ not only in sexual desire, but also in their capacities, needs, and ambitions.

But we need to move beyond abstinence-only and women as gate-keepers as a way of teaching sexual and reproductive responsibility. The governmental embrace of the conservative sexual economy in the 1996 welfare reform law as the expected national standard for all cit-izens conflicts with important public values of sex equality, equal con-cern and respect for all members of society (including gay men and lesbians), and respect for reasonable moral pluralism. Viewing women as gatekeepers is in tension with viewing them as responsible, self-governing persons. This vision of personal responsibility places on women the responsibility for men's behavior and men's sexuality, even as it insults men's moral capacity and relieves them of responsibility.

First, I will explain the ascent of abstinence-only sex education in the context of concern for an epidemic of teen pregnancy. Second, I sketch my approach to fostering sexual and reproductive responsibility. Building on the basic premises of abstinence-plus, or comprehensive, sex education, my approach would support clear messages about ab-staining from sexual activity and deferring pregnancy and childrearing until one is emotionally, socially, and financially prepared. But instead of preaching that any expression of sexual desire other than in mar-riage is contrary to an expected national standard, it would treat an emerging sense of sexuality and sexual desire as part of adolescents' healthy development and help them to develop a sense of themselves as responsible sexual subjects. I take seriously the feminist criticism that sex education stresses danger and typically is "missing [a] dis-course of desire," particularly with respect to articulating female sex-uality.[5] I urge attention to the role of gender role stereotypes and of cultural scripts (such as the sexual double standard) that perpetuate inequality, as well as to the underlying realities of sex inequality in adolescent females' and women's lives. Because teen pregnancy has been a central concern in debates over sex education, I illustrate how my model would address that problem, drawing on the findings of the National Campaign to Prevent Teen Pregnancy.

Third, I critique the conservative sexual economy embedded in abstinence-only sex education and suggest why it is not a sound or defensible policy. I also critique the related courtship movement. Courtship proponents call for instructing children on "love, courtship, and marriage as a shared ideal and social institution."[6] Already, some abstinence-only sex education programs used in schools teach about courtship as a pathway to marriage. I concentrate on two problems: (1) the prominent role assigned to women, as gatekeepers, to bring men to marriage and (2) the ambivalence about sex equality manifested in the concern that society's courtship crisis results, in part, from women's economic and educational gains.

## The Conservative Sexual Economy

### *Teen Pregnancy and the Ascent of "Abstinence-Only"*

In the conservative sexual economy, marriage is the only proper site for the expression of sexuality. Heterosexual sex within marriage is the only normatively acceptable form of sex. Marriage is a necessary institution for channeling sexual drives (especially those of men) into the constructive social forms of monogamy, reproduction, and parenting.

One conspicuous embodiment of the conservative sexual economy is the "Abstinence Education" provisions of the Personal Responsibility and Work Opportunity Reconciliation Act of 1996 (PRWORA).[7] Through this Act Congress approved federal funding for sex education programs with an "exclusive purpose" of teaching abstinence. Among the messages that the programs must teach are the following: "abstinence from sexual activity outside marriage [i]s the expected standard for all school age children"; "a mutually faithful monogamous relationship in the context of marriage is the expected standard of human sexual activity"; "sexual activity outside of the context of marriage is likely to have harmful psychological and physical effects"; and "bearing children out-of-wedlock is likely to have harmful consequences for the child, the child's parents, and society."[8] Every state but California (which supports comprehensive sex education as a more effective strategy) has accepted federal funds allocated by PRWORA for abstinence education.[9] Federal programs also fund community-based organizations that teach abstinence-until-marriage to youth.[10]

The specter of "children having children," or "babies having babies," animated the rhetoric of welfare reform in the 1990s. Pregnant teenagers and teen mothers seemed to exemplify the irresponsibility facilitated by the welfare state. These teens lacked the capacity for responsible self-government—hence the image of *children* having children. Their reproduction imposed costs on taxpayers, who had to support their children. The image of the unmarried black mother on welfare had long driven public resentment against welfare, but in the 1990s conservative critics of welfare warned that the "illegitimacy" crisis had spread to young white women as well.[11] Thus, ending "illegitimacy" was a central goal of PRWORA, and abstinence education was one tool. PRWORA channeled millions of governmental dollars into such programs despite "woefully inadequate" efforts to evaluate their effectiveness.[12]

Federal funding of abstinence education pursuant to PRWORA began during the Clinton Administration, but levels of such funding more than doubled during the Bush Administration.[13] When the "abstinence education" provision of PRWORA came up for reauthorization by Congress, the Bush Administration argued that increased funding for abstinence-only education was a bold approach to addressing increases in nonmarital pregnancy and sexually transmitted diseases.[14] The power of abstinence-only education is, literally, an article of faith in Bush's domestic agenda. During his tenure as governor of Texas, for example, Bush championed such education, but Texas continued to have one of the highest teen pregnancy rates in the nation and ranked last in the decline of birth rates for fifteen- to seventeen-year-old females.[15] Proponents of abstinence-only education champion it even in the absence of conclusive evidence that it is effective at altering either expectations to abstain or actual behavior, and despite strong evidence of the effectiveness of abstinence-plus or comprehensive sex education.[16] A succession of surgeon generals has supported comprehensive sex education.[17] The American Pediatrics Association has characterized abstinence-only education as an "incomplete strategy in reducing adolescent health risks" and has urged Congress to expand PRWORA's abstinence education provision to include funding for comprehensive sex education.[18] A report (prepared at the request of Representative Henry Waxman) on the most popular "abstinence-only" curricula used by grantees of the largest federal abstinence initiative concluded that 80 percent of the curricula "contain false, misleading, or distorted information about reproductive health," leading the American Medical Association to oppose federal funding of any programs not proven to be effective.[19]

Proponents of abstinence-only education seem unmoved by the fact that only a small minority of parents favor such education. The vast majority of parents prefer that schools offer a more comprehensive approach to sex education—either one that combines an abstinence message with practical information about contraception or one that focuses on teaching children how to make responsible decisions about sex.[20] Thus, contrary to the claims of abstinence-only champions, far from trampling upon parents' own vision of what form of sex education is best for their children, comprehensive sex education would better facilitate the vision of most parents of how best to promote sexual and reproductive responsibility. This is one reason that some members of Congress have proposed a law approving funds for states to conduct programs in "responsible sexuality education," or "comprehensive sexuality education."[21]

## Is There, in Fact, a Teen Pregnancy "Epidemic"?

The need to address an alleged "epidemic" of teen pregnancy continues to fuel support for abstinence-only education. However, the image of an epidemic is misleading. Even as the rhetoric in mid-1990s debates over welfare invoked a growing crisis of "children having children," the rate of teen births peaked in 1991 and steadily declined throughout the 1990s.[22] These births declined most sharply (30 percent) among blacks, more so than among non-Hispanic whites (22 percent decline) and Hispanics (12 percent decline).[23] The teen birth rate—including that for births to ten- to fourteen-year-old mothers—continues to hit new record lows.[24] For example, in 2002, the National Campaign to Prevent Teen Pregnancy reported: "Teen pregnancy rates are at their lowest level in 20 years and teen birth rates are at the lowest level ever recorded in this country."[25] One difference between pregnant teens of earlier decades and those of today is that far fewer teen-age mothers today marry than in earlier decades.[26]

A fierce dispute is raging between proponents of abstinence-only and abstinence-plus sex education over whether this steady decline stems more from adolescents abstaining from sex or from their using contraception. Evidence suggests that both abstinence and contraception are relevant causes.[27] Indeed, the National Campaign to Prevent Teen Pregnancy (launched in 1996) has shifted from cautioning that there are "no easy answers" to identifying some "emerging answers" about effective ways to encourage the delay of pregnancy and parenting.[28]

Despite this decline, the Campaign and many other observers argue that teen pregnancy and teen birth rates remain at an unacceptably high level. Four in ten adolescent females become pregnant at least once before age 20 (over 900,000 teen pregnancies annually), and there are nearly half a million teen births each year (40 percent of which are to teens seventeen or younger).[29] It should be noted, however, that the majority of teen births are to females aged 18 or 19, considered legal adults. Thus, the common image of "children having children" paints a misleading picture of most teen mothers. Nonetheless, these teen pregnancy and birth rates (as well as abortion rates for teens) are higher than those in other Western industrialized countries with available data.[30] Furthermore, although national rates of teen births have been declining, rates among certain populations, such as Hispanic teens, remain disproportionately higher than rates for other groups.[31] Moreover, the Campaign's research gives reason for concern about sexual activity and pregnancy among very young teens: one in five adolescents has had sexual intercourse before her or his fifteenth birthday, and one in seven of the sexually experienced fourteen-year-old girls has been pregnant.[32]

There has not been a similar downward trend in nonmarital births to unmarried women. The highest rate of nonmarital births is to women in their twenties. And in the last two decades, there have been dramatic increases in the number of nonmarital births to women in their thirties and forties.[33] For this reason, some marriage promoters publicly criticize pregnancy prevention campaigns for simply stressing avoiding pregnancy during adolescence and for not including a positive message about what young people should wait for: a healthy marriage.[34] By contrast, the abstinence education funded under PRWORA must espouse the idea that "a mutually faithful monogamous relationship in the context of marriage is the expected standard of human sexual activity" and that marriage is the proper place for reproduction.

Would abstinence proponents encourage early marriage as a way to address the large number of years between the time children reach puberty and the time young adults enter into a first marriage? Isabel Sawhill, president of the National Campaign to Prevent Teen Pregnancy, cautions against encouraging young women in their teens and twenties to marry, given the instability of early marriages. Instead, society should encourage young women first to invest in their education and skills and delay childbearing until marriage.[35] Abstinence education may implicitly promote early marriage by embracing expansive definitions of "abstinence" that treat the entire domain of premarital sexual expression as potentially dangerous and destructive.[36]

In sum, although the image of a teen pregnancy "epidemic" is misleading, the high rate of teen pregnancy is a significant problem. But when concern for teen pregnancy dominates the discussion about adolescents and sex education, it diverts attention from a broader focus on sexuality as a part of human development.

## Beyond Abstinence-Only

Two distinct concerns are in play with sex education: how to instruct youths about the place of sexuality in their current lives and how to prepare them for the place of sexuality and reproduction in their adult lives. Problems such as teen pregnancy, the prevalence among teens of sexually transmitted diseases, and pressured as well as coerced sexual activity properly lead to a focus on immediate issues in teens' lives. But a broader view of the aims of sex education would prepare them for eventual responsible self-government—as adults—in their intimate and reproductive lives.[37]

My approach to encouraging sexual and reproductive responsibility focuses on capacity, equality, and responsibility. It is liberal in emphasizing affirmative governmental responsibility to foster children's capacity for eventual self-government and in addressing obstacles to such self-government. It is feminist in highlighting how problems such as sex inequality, domination, and sexual violence, along with cultural constructions of femininity and masculinity, constrain young people's development of a sense of personal autonomy and responsibility with respect to sexuality.

### *Teen Pregnancy: The Importance of Fostering Capacity*

We have to work to instill within every young man and woman a sense of personal responsibility, a sense of self-respect, and a sense of possibility.

—*President Bill Clinton, announcing creation of National Campaign
to Prevent Teen Pregnancy*

The best contraceptive is a real future.

—*Marian Wright Edelman, Children's Defense Fund*

We are culpable as a society when we will allow a 13-year old to feel her only vision is having a child.

—*Dr. Henry W. Foster, Jr., Founder, I Have a Future Program*

These three statements all express an important point about teen pregnancy and childbirth. Often, such behaviors take place in circumstances of economic deprivation in which a young person's life prospects seem to offer no better option. A firm liberal response is that promoting sexual and reproductive responsibility is but one facet of government's affirmative responsibility to foster the capacities of such adolescents. Otherwise, in the words of Dr. Henry Foster, "society is culpable" for not helping teens have any other vision for themselves.

The National Campaign to Prevent Teen Pregnancy illustrates the importance of a focus on fostering capacity. Founded in 1996, with the enthusiastic endorsement of the Clinton Administration, the Campaign adopted the mission of "getting the facts straight" about teen pregnancy and teen births and finding out "what works" to prevent teen pregnancy and other risk-taking behavior. Its report, *Emerging Answers*, states the goal of helping teens to avoid "sexual risk-taking," defined as "unprotected" and "unplanned" (and "involuntary") sexual activity. Its approach is facilitative: youth need to identify the situations in which they are most likely to engage in sexual risk-taking, to learn skills to avoid those situations, and to be knowledgeable about methods of contraception. The report finds that "effective" sex education programs are comprehensive, or "abstinence-plus:" they combine a clear message about abstinence, or postponing sexual activity, and if youth do have sex, about the consistent and correct use of contraception. Contrary to the charge by abstinence-only proponents, educating about contraception (and even providing contraception) do not increase teen sexual activity.[38]

The Campaign also found that, to reduce sexual risk-taking by adolescents, it is effective to focus on the "nonsexual antecedents" of sexual activity. For example, poverty is both a contributing factor toward, and consequence of, teen pregnancy and parenthood.[39] The link between poverty and early pregnancy and parenthood underscores why a formative project of fostering children's capacities for self-government is so important generally, but has special relevance for deterring risky sexual behavior and early parenting. Thus, *Emerging Answers* finds that

> teens who are doing well in school and have educational and career plans for the future are less likely to get pregnant or cause a pregnancy. Increasingly, programs to prevent teen pregnancy concentrate on helping young people develop skills and confidence, focus on education, and take advantage of job opportunities and mentoring relationships with adults—thereby helping them create reasons to make responsible decisions about sex.[40]

The idea of helping young people have "reasons to make responsible decisions about sex" illustrates that fostering human capacity is a way to cultivate sexual responsibility. It is the insight behind the slogan (quoted above), "The best contraceptive is a real future." Youth development programs combine such development of capacities with providing sex education and comprehensive health care. Such programs have had significant results among girls in delaying having sex, increasing the use of contraception, and reducing pregnancy and birth rates.[41] As a founder of the Children's Aid Society-Carrera Program observed: "Youngsters who feel that they have a future rarely become teen parents. . . . Education, employment, and self-esteem are the most powerful contraceptives of all."[42] Other studies of teen pregnancy readily confirm that "poverty and lack of life options" are "two powerful underlying causes of teen pregnancy" and endorse prevention strategies that combine sexuality education and "teen-friendly" reproductive health services with promoting economic opportunity and future life options.[43]

A narrow focus on abstinence-only simply fails to address the constrained circumstances in which disadvantaged young people make decisions about sexuality. A sobering recent study of low-income black urban youth, *This Is My Reality? The Price of Sex*, found that becoming a teen parent seems more realistic to such youth than abstaining from sex, getting married, or having a successful future. It also found a disturbing pattern of "transactional sex," in which teen females have sex with adult males in exchange for consumer goods, like new clothes or shoes.[44] But this study is just the latest confirmation that social inequality and a sense of limited options leave some young people with insufficient motivation to avoid early sexual activity, pregnancy, and parenthood.[45] And conversely, for the substantial number of inner-city girls who do avoid pregnancy, a crucial factor is a motivation to postpone motherhood stemming from "access to opportunities to obtain adulthood status through more traditional pathways."[46]

Most disadvantaged teen females do not set out to become pregnant, but they often do not take measures to prevent it, by abstaining from sex or by using contraception. They may engage in sex out of a desire for companionship that is not found elsewhere, and they may desire a baby because of the example of peers as well as the wish to have a special person who will love them. Moreover, in contrast to other possible life plans, becoming a mother appears to be a goal that is within their grasp, one that will confer a sense of competence, maturity, and success.[47] Thus, for some economically disadvantaged teen females, the message of postponing motherhood until one has achieved educational and career success seems inapposite. Early motherhood may appear to be a "rational reproductive strategy" when such teen females look at their likely future options and opportunity structures and costs.[48]

Some economically disadvantaged adolescents view early parenting as inevitable. As one young woman put it: "What are you waiting for anyway? . . . Nothing's coming."[49] Early motherhood also has positive connotations for some adolescents (particularly, African American females): far from viewing their lives as ruined by early motherhood, they view their teen years as "the perfect time to have a baby," and they see themselves as capable of rearing children without marriage and without a commitment by the child's father.[50] And if a teen does not see her situation improving by waiting until her twenties, she may prefer to have children early, when she is healthy and more likely to get help from family with rearing the child.[51] This perception may have some foundation: some studies find that, even if economically disadvantaged adolescents postponed pregnancy and motherhood until they finished high school, got a job, and got married, many would still not be able to afford to have a baby without some public assistance.

Moreover, given the disadvantaged circumstances of many teens who become pregnant, it is difficult to separate out the additional effects of early childbearing on their lives.[52]

A recent film, *Our Song*, offers a powerful cinematic rendering of the relationship between a sense of life options and being motivated to avoid pregnancy and early motherhood.[53] This coming-of-age story chronicles a summer in the lives of three fifteen-year-old females living in Crown Heights, New York—Joycelen, Lanisha ("Lani"), and Maria. Over the summer, they practice hard with the Jackie Robinson Steppers Marching Band, a renowned musical group and a source of great community pride. They must choose a new school for the fall (owing to asbestos at their former school). Maria, a Latina, learns that she is pregnant from a time she had intercourse with an older teen boy who did not want to use a condom. She confides in Lani, a black Latina, who encourages her to think about abortion. Lani, unbeknownst to Maria and Joycelen, was pregnant a year before but, agreeing with her mother that she was too young to have a baby, had an abortion.

Lani has two loving and attentive, divorced parents. Maria's pregnancy, as well as the prevalence of early motherhood among the friends' peers, causes Lani to reflect on whether she made the right decision to have an abortion. When she confides her doubts to her mother, her mother reiterates that she is still too young to have a baby. With her parents' help, Lani learns about and registers for another high school.

By contrast, with her pregnancy Maria's life begins to unravel. But it may be that the pregnancy simply reinforces other problems in her life. She already has heavy child-care responsibilities at home, while her mother is working, and she has a part-time, low-wage job. Her mother resents the time Maria spends at band practice and warns that she must find a better paying job to help out more with expenses. Maria informs her sexual partner about the pregnancy and asks if he will be around for the baby. At first, he denies it is his and says he doesn't want to get married, but then he adamantly protests that she is not going to abort "his" baby, and says he will be around (but not marry her).

After Maria's interest in band practice lags, she is cut from the band.

When she goes for a prenatal visit at a clinic, a friendly and insightful counselor asks her about her dreams for herself and how she pictures her future life. Maria has little to say, other than that she wants to get a better paying job and save some money before the baby is born. At home, she lies in bed hugging her stuffed animals, an especially jarring image given her impending new role as a mother. By film's end, she still has not told her mother about the pregnancy. Nor has she made any effort to register at a new high school.

Feminist analyses of teen pregnancy struggle to show respect for adolescent females' exercise of agency and autonomy in their reproductive decisions, while also recognizing the ways in which social inequality shapes these decisions. Focusing specifically on young, poor black women who become mothers, Regina Austin aptly argues that "[t]eenage pregnancy is a product of the teens' contradictory pursuit of romance, security, status, freedom, and responsibility within the confines of their immediate surroundings." All too often, however, their decisions do not have good outcomes, and young women need guidance about how to make better choices.[54]

Parents, and not just public education programs, also have an important role to play in offering such guidance: the Campaign reports that, across the economic spectrum, adolescents want parental support and guidance concerning sex and that parents are their preferred source of information. But adolescents also feel that adults often let them down.[55] Indeed, in the film, *Our Song*, Lani's close relationship with both parents facilitates how she handles an unexpected pregnancy and guides her to avoid future pregnancies. Could a closer parental relationship have helped Maria avoid early pregnancy and motherhood?

Taking seriously the idea of a public responsibility to foster capacity would require a public investment in creating the situation that young girls and boys would have less reason to view early parenthood as inevitable or as the best path to adult status. Public policies should aim at helping such girls and boys develop into responsible, self-governing citizens by improving their opportunity structure so as to make other life scripts seem attainable. This may be an important point of common ground, since some abstinence-only programs focus on developing a sense of life goals and options.[56]

*Further Obstacles to Fostering Capacity, Equality, and Responsibility*

> Guys can get too strong sometimes; and you should be the ones
> to control them. They can't think for themselves so we need to
> help them sometimes.

> —*Twelve-year-old girl, quoted in* Voices of a Generation *(1999)*

What further obstacles stand in the way of adolescents developing capacities for responsible self-government, or a sense of personal agency, with respect to intimacy and sexuality? Sex inequality and gender role expectations and stereotypes also shape—and pose obstacles to—developing sexual responsibility. An adequate program on sexuality and sex education should address salient gender issues that shape the environment within which girls and boys act and choose. I shall name a few: (1) cultural scripts about female and male sexuality that encourage girls to repress sexual desire and teach boys that male irresponsibility, aggression, and entitlement are natural and inevitable; (2) the persistence of the sexual double standard; and (3) approaches to sexuality that conflate "sex" with sexual intercourse, thus reinforcing the association of desire with danger and hindering the development of a broader conception of sexuality consonant with developing a sense of responsible sexual agency.

One helpful window into these issues is *Voices of a Generation: Teenage Girls on Sex, School, and Self*, which grew out of a series of "summits" of girls sponsored by the American Association of University Women Educational Foundation.[57] The participating girls report that they experience girlhood as a "bewildering social ideal," and that "the social script of female adolescence" constitutes a "disorienting admixture of adulthood, sexual innocence, and sexual maturity." Most girls "do not see themselves as agents within the society that, by their accounts, shapes gender roles." They report a struggle between their "real" self and the "stylizations of girlhood" put forth by the media and society.[58] Another report, *Goodbye to Girlhood: What's Troubling Girls and What We Can Do about It*,[59] written for the Campaign, warns that "girls are exposed to the toxic influences of the culture at younger ages and with fewer buffers and protections than before." It describes a "hypersexualized media and marketplace culture" bent on "selling sex and sexiness" that targets teenage girls.

Among the major struggles and issues facing teenage girls, the girls in these reports identify sex, sexual violence, sexual risks (principally pregnancy), and relationships with boys. *Voices of a Generation* observes: "Sexual relations, interactions, and identity appear the most baffling and problem-fraught social areas for girls, judging by [their] responses."[60] Girls, for example, feel pressures both to have sex and not to have sex, and they are policed by female and male peers in both directions.

Sexual coercion and pressure, as well as sexual insults and disrespect, are problems that occur across racial and ethnic lines. Girls describe a culture of sexual disrespect, manifest in a "numbing litany of incidents in which peers, primarily boys, call girls 'bitches,' 'sluts,' and 'whores,' and boys make crude requests for sex."[61] Although both boys and girls engage in sexual bullying using derogatory language, the type of language directed at girls frequently reinforces the sexual double standard and manifests a disrespect for them.[62]

Problems of sexual violence and unwanted sexual activity also impede responsible sexual self-government. *Goodbye to Girlhood* reports that 7 percent of teen girls aged 15–19 reported that their first sexual experience was not voluntary; the rate is higher for younger girls. About 50 percent of rape victims are between ten and nineteen years of age, and half of this group is under sixteen.[63] Former Surgeon General Jocyeln Elders highlighted the connection between sexual abuse (not only by partners but also by family members and relatives) of very young teens and pregnancy.[64] Studies of the lives of disadvantaged urban female adolescents, such as the recent book, *Random Family*, paint a harrowing portrait of the occurrence of childhood sexual abuse across several family generations.[65]

The Campaign finds that both adolescent males and females, across lines of income, race, and residence, "feel a lot of pressure to have sex, find that pressure hard to counter, and say that they wish they'd waited longer to become sexually active."[66] For example, nearly one-quarter of girls studied said that, while their first experience was voluntary, "they did not want to have sex when they did."[67] Thus, *Emerging Answers* finds that one characteristic of effective sex education programs is helping adolescents address "social pressures that influence sexual behavior" and "provid[ing] examples of and practice with communication, negotiation, and refusal skills." The report does not expressly relate gender issues to such social pressures. But its observation that what is needed is "how to suggest alternative activities, and how to help build the relationship while refusing unprotected sex or refusing to have sex at all" brings to mind the finding that, in programs focusing on girls and sex education, the skill girls say they most want to learn is how to say no to sexual activity without hurting someone's feelings or losing the relationship.[68]

Gender role expectations also shape adolescents' understandings of sexuality and responsibility. Yet, as Kathryn Abrams observes, feminist analyses of sexuality recognize that, even as women face such constraints as coercion and rigid gender scripts, they nonetheless exercise a capacity for self-direction and resistance.[69] Sex education that helps young people recognize and evaluate such gender issues could help them to develop their capacities for responsible sexual agency. Rigid gender role expectations harm both females and males. Men as well as women may be victims of efforts to police proper gender role behavior.[70]

What are the relevant cultural scripts about male sexuality? The Campaign's report, *Not Just for Girls: The Role of Boys and Men in Teen Pregnancy Prevention*, observes: "unfortunately, teen boys and young men have learned from the media and their peers that being a 'real man' means being aggressive, 'scoring' with as many women as possible, and, for some, getting a woman pregnant." It recommends that programs help boys and young men redefine manhood "to emphasize caring, responsibility, commitment to family, self-control, and greater respect for women."[71] The popular book, *Raising Cain: Protecting the Emotional Life of Boys*, argues that boys seek intimacy and can be loving, but they need "emotional education" to counter a "sexual script" of "male cruelty" that stresses power, dominance, and disrespect.[72]

Recognizing the role of cultural scripts in sanctioning boys' disrespect for girls and reinforcing destructive models of masculinity highlights the urgency of focusing on gender in educational efforts. Indeed, some research finds that adolescent males with the most traditional attitudes about masculinity (for example, "men are always ready for sex") are more at risk of engaging in unprotected sex, whereas less traditional beliefs about masculinity are an influential protective factor.[73] To encourage young men to become more self-aware and responsible in matters of sex, contraception, and fatherhood, one recent study concludes, programs would fruitfully encourage reflection on gender relations and alternative conceptions of masculinity.[74] Thus, instead of reviving the female role as "gatekeeper" to tame boys, as abstinence-only and courtship proponents would do, a better approach would be to challenge these gender scripts.

## Cultural Scripts about Female Sexuality

If boys face pressures to act out a sexual script that stresses sexual aggression, dominance, and disrespect for girls, what cultural scripts shape girls' sexuality? Although society worries about adolescent sexuality generally, anxiety and controversy heighten over adolescent female sexuality.[75] Of continuing relevance is the problem Michelle Fine identified as the "missing discourse of desire": approaches to sex education stress sex as a source of danger and afford little validation to female desire.[76]

Adolescent females experience sexual desire and would like to act on it, but they often do not because they associate it with forms of risk and danger. Urban girls, Deb Tolman concludes, "portray a vigilant caution" about their own sexual desire: out of concern for such risks as pregnancy, disease, and harm to one's reputation, they disconnect from—or diminish their curiosity about—such desire.[77] Studying a broader spectrum of girls, *Voices of a Generation* comments on the virtual absence of a "proactive female sexuality." Sex, as girls speak about it, seems to mean "intercourse" and, as such, is "defined heavily by risks—parts of a jeremiad leading inexorably to pregnancy, sexually transmitted diseases, and emotional turmoil." Consequently, girls do not recognize a "domain short of intercourse where their sexuality could be expressed in less potentially dangerous ways." Some are apparently unable to discern their own sexual orientation (whether heterosexual or homosexual) and are uncertain about "how they might behave sexually at all."[78] Conflating sex with intercourse, other studies conclude, leads some female adolescents (1) to give up any attempt at healthy sexual exploration because "there's no established or easy way to stop a sexual encounter," or (2) to have "sex" they did not really want because they saw no alternative.[79] Abstinence-only education, which treats all nonmarital sex as a form of danger, simply exacerbates the problem of a missing domain of female sexuality.

Another factor causing girls to quell their own sexual desire is the lingering cultural script of female responsibility for arousing and thus either satisfying or controlling male sexual desire.[80] In the words of a twelve-year-old girl: "Guys can get too strong sometimes and you should be the ones to control them. They can't think for themselves so we need to help them sometimes."[81] Some girls accept personal responsibility for inappropriate behavior by boys, reasoning that learning to say "no" more firmly will reduce the problems of sexual pressure, threats, censure, and harassment. The authors of *Voices of a Generation* comment: "It is a profound irony of the 'personal responsibility' discourse of the 1990s that girls should express responsibility for the incivilities or violent actions of their male peers against them. The pattern is consistent, however, with suggestions in these responses that some boys may, indeed, act as if sex is an entitlement from girls."[82]

That girls and female adolescents may feel personally responsible for controlling boys and male adolescents is hardly proof that this is the way it should be, or has to be. This sort of scheme of entitlement and responsibility hurts both sexes. Some girls in *Voices of a Generation* report that they would like male-female relations to be less defined by sexuality and more supportive, based on friendship and camaraderie.[83] Cultivating friendship, mutual respect, and communication skills might also help counter the problems of a lack of trust and communication among adolescents[84]—problems that may later pose obstacles to healthy adult relationships.

A continuing obstacle to developing mutual respect and equality is the persistence of a double standard for males and females. Variations among diverse ethnic and cultural groups may render double standards less a "universal mandate" than local constructions, but a common feature is that women's sexual conduct is judged more harshly than men's.[85] Many school-age youths and college students continue to divide girls and women into categories of "good" versus "easy" or "slut," depending on whether they expressed sexual desire or engaged in sexual activity, but they do not apply comparable categories to males.[86] One researcher offered this characterization of the attitudes of the male students he studied: "Men have the right to experiment sexually for a few years. There are a lot of female sluts out there with whom to so experiment. And once I have gotten this out of my system, I will then look for a good woman for a long-term relationship (or for a wife)."[87] Although some women do reject this double standard, females as well as males often apply it, and judge adolescent or young women more harshly than males.[88]

The double standard hinders adolescent females' and women's development of a sense of responsible sexual agency. Society assigns them the role of gatekeepers, and men the role of expert or teacher, even as popular culture portrays women as objects of sexual desire. Thus, if women feel responsible for satisfying male desire, and feel inhibited from initiating sex when they want it, they may feel more object or victim than willing participant or agent.[89] This dynamic may be one factor behind the high rates among adult women of "female sexual dysfunction," associated with a lack of arousal and sexual desire.[90]

To be sure, the double standard has evolved somewhat: adolescent females may now be able to be sexually active without stigma, at least with a steady boyfriend. But they risk being labeled a "slut" and denied respect if they admit to sexual appetite or change boyfriends too quickly. By contrast, adolescent males do not face similar stigma.[91] Even this modified double standard, however, may hinder sexual responsibility and increase sexual risk-taking. An adolescent female or young woman may not take the initiative to protect herself against disease or pregnancy, lest she risk being deemed "easy": "women are left to choose between risky, unprotected sex or negative judgments about their character."[92] For example, the report, *This Is My Reality*, found that when the social norms are that one only uses condoms for casual sex, this puts females in steady relationships at risk of disease and pregnancy unless they are willing to protect themselves and, thus, arouse suspicion or anger from their partner.[93]

To address such obstacles to responsible sexual self-government, sex education should encourage critical reflection upon gender issues. (Notably, gender roles and related issues, such as body image and sexual orientation, receive attention in California's comprehensive sexuality education law and in proposed federal bills to fund such education.)[94] A further component would be to stop conflating sex with the risks of sexual intercourse and to help young people understand sexuality and sexual pleasure as components of healthy human development.[95] As Tolman argues, conflating sexuality with danger leads girls to pursue safety by denying their own sexual desires and to become "the models of control of their own and boys' sexual feelings."[96] The very breadth of some conceptions of "abstinence" that are at work in abstinence-only curricula (for example, including passionate kissing or any intimate touching) sends a message that any and all forms of intimate sexual expression are risky and "off limits" until marriage.[97] A broader conception of sexuality would help girls and boys to identify and accept their sexual feelings and to reflect on when it is responsible to act on them.

One rubric for a broader conception of sexuality is "outercourse," or forms of sexual intimacy that do not involve sexual intercourse (or, on some definitions, any form of penetration).[98] Proponents of "outercourse" present it as a "healthier, simpler, safer, and more natural method" of avoiding pregnancy and sexually transmitted diseases than attempting to forestall all adolescent sexual activity, given the gap of some ten to twenty years between the onset of puberty and first marriage.[99] This range of sexual intimacy could include anything from holding hands to reading erotic stories to solo or mutual masturbation.

When former surgeon general Jocelyn Elders, who supported an abstinence-plus approach to sex education, advocated teaching adolescents how to masturbate, the response was quick and furious, leading inexorably to her resignation. Any governmental official supporting instruction in "outercourse" would likely draw the same response from proponents of abstinence-only education.[100] However, educating about a more restrictive vision of "outercourse," which would eliminate oral and anal sex, would be an improvement over some teens' current understandings of abstinence. Such teens engage in (often unprotected) oral and anal sex because they think that these activities are not "sex" and thus that they are preserving a female's virginity; they may also erroneously assume that such sexual practices carry no risk of sexually transmitted disease.[101] Developing a concept of "outercourse" would also help in thinking about sexuality as including a continuum of forms of expression, some of which are appropriate at certain ages and in certain relationships, and others of which are more appropriate in other circumstances. This approach seems more likely to develop a positive conception of sexuality and its place in a good, self-governing life than a message that "sex" belongs only in marriage or that, implicitly, same-sex intimate desire deviates from the national standard. It would encourage in teens a gradual development and exercise of the capacity for intimate sexual expression in tandem with a developing sense of personal responsibility and autonomy.

## "Abstinence-Only" Education Is Not a Defensible Policy

The liberal feminist approach to sex education that I have sketched would better serve the goal of promoting sexual and reproductive responsibility than abstinence-only sex education. I now will argue that it is not defensible for government to seek to advance a conservative sexual economy through funding abstinence-only education. I focus particularly on two reasons: (1) its starkly dualistic and medically misleading account of sexuality; (2) its perpetuation of rigid gender roles of female responsibility and male irresponsibility. These two flaws relate to the additional problems that, in funding such education, government embraces religious ideology, rather than sound scientific teaching, and shows insufficient respect for diversity. A brief sampling of abstinence-only curricula will illustrate these problems.

### Dualism and Gender Stereotypes in Abstinence-Only Curricula

A prominent message in the abstinence-only curricula currently used in many public schools is that there is no such thing as "good" or "safe" sex outside of marriage. Indeed, "Safe Sex is a Deadly Game."[102] These programs preach "saved sex," sex postponed for marriage, and the place in which sex properly occurs. The starkly dualistic picture of sex in such curricula portrays sex outside of marriage as dangerous and even fatal but sex within marriage as pleasurable and good. In a video used in one program, *No Second Chances*, when a student raises the possibility that he just does not want to wait until marriage to have sex, the instructor responds: "Well, I guess you'll just have to be prepared to die. And you'll probably take with you your spouse and one or more of your children."[103]

Consider the link made between condoms and death. Many abstinence-only proponents inaccurately claim that condoms have holes large enough for the HIV virus to penetrate. Curricula include frightening and inaccurate statements about the ineffectiveness of contraception.[104] For example, an early version of the *Choosing the Best* program advised young people that, if they had intercourse using a condom, they should use the household cleaner and disinfectant Lysol on their genitals. Upon learning of this, the manufacturer wrote a cease and desist letter to the publisher of the program, warning against using Lysol on human bodies.[105] Another tactic is slide shows and videos with graphic images of genitals infected by sexually transmitted diseases, often with misleading claims about the fatal side effects of certain STDs.[106] It is because of such content that the Sexuality Information and Education Council of the United States (SIECUS) labels many abstinence-only programs "fear-based."[107]

Alongside this view that sex outside of marriage is dangerous or deadly, the conservative sexual economy is notably "pro-sex" within marriage. In 1981, Congress enacted the Adolescent and Family Life Act (AFLA), which funded programs addressing teen pregnancy (including those sponsored by religious organizations), as long as they promoted abstinence and not abortion. Such funding spawned a veritable industry of Christian sex education materials, encouraged even more by PRWORA's funding programs.[108] After a legal challenge to the AFLA, on the ground that it impermissibly allowed government to fund religious messages in service of fighting teen pregnancy, many organizations prepared versions of their materials that ostensibly removed references to religion. However, this "virtual boundary" between religious school and public school versions of these abstinence-only programs did not eliminate the underlying religiously based messages about marriage as the only proper place for sex.[109]

If sex outside of marriage is dangerous, sex within marriage is divinely sanctioned, good, joyous, and pleasurable. Indeed, "the best sex is in marriage."[110] The picture of sexuality in the "how-to" manuals marketed to Christian married couples reinforces the role of husband as head of the family and the sexual initiator, and the wife as submitting to the husband's authority.[111]

Abstinence-only curricula appeal to biological and emotional differences between the sexes to justify assigning girls the responsibility for being the gatekeeper. The popular curriculum, *Sex Respect*, attributes a man's strong "natural desire for sex" to testosterone and female desire to more recent cultural conditioning. Accordingly, "because they generally become physically aroused less easily, girls are still in a good position to slow down the young man and help him learn balance in a relationship."[112] Indeed, the *WAIT Training* curriculum claims:

"While a man needs little or no preparation for sex, a woman often needs hours of emotional and mental preparation."[113] *Sex Respect* advises that girls should not "drive guys' hormones" and distract them by wearing sexy clothes. Like other curricula, it includes the truism that "boys tend to use love to get sex," while "girls tend to use sex to get love."[114]

In these curricula, differences between men and women extend beyond their sexual roles to their different roles in relationships and in society. These complementary roles also teach gender hierarchy. The investigative report prepared for Representative Henry Waxman concluded that several curricula "present stereotypes as scientific fact." For example, *WAIT Training* explains that women need "financial support," whereas men need "domestic support"; a man needs a woman's admiration, and a woman needs a man's devotion. A father gives away the bride to symbolize the transfer of his protective role to her husband. *Choosing the Best* cautions that women who give men more than "occasional suggestions and assistance" may lessen a potential suitor's confidence and "turn him away."[115]

### How the Gatekeeping Role Hinders Responsible Self-Government

These portraits of his and hers sexuality reinforce the idea that women are gatekeepers because men, by nature, find self-control difficult. As one scholar aptly observes: "It is not difficult to imagine that a girl reading [the *Sex Respect* curriculum] would feel the weight of responsibility for abstinence on her shoulders, and yet find no validation for any sexual feelings she does have that do not fit this model."[116] Assigning girls the responsibility for putting on the brakes exemplifies the sort of gender role stereotype, or cultural script, that hinders adolescent females and women from developing a sense of their own sexual agency.[117]

The gatekeeping role also perpetuates, rather than dismantles, the sexual double standard. To be fair, the conservative sexual economy preaches abstinence for males as well as for females, and thus its proponents might protest that it seeks a single standard for sexual activity: abstinence until marriage.[118] However, in treating male sexuality as more natural, more readily awakened, and harder to control than female sexuality, it may lend continuing credence to the idea that pre-

marital sexual experience is more natural and more readily explained—
if not also more excusable—for males than females. It may also perpetuate, rather than dismantle, dividing girls and women into good
girls and bad girls/easy girls/sluts, based on whether or not they have
sex. (For example, Nevada used federal funds for a radio advertise-
ment suggesting that girls will feel "dirty and cheap" when they "lose"
their boyfriends after having sex.)[119] The gatekeeping message in
abstinence-only curricula is likely to intensify the double standard's
negative consequences for adolescent and young adult females.

The reinforcement in abstinence-only curricula of gender stereotypes and rigid sex roles offends contemporary constitutional and statutory commitments to sex equality. This vision may be in accord with
traditional notions of women's and men's roles, but such notions themselves rest on impermissible gender stereotypes.[120] The gender role
messages in these curricula are more likely to hinder than foster responsible sexual self-government among adolescent females and males.

### Further Problems with the Governmental Embrace of the Conservative Sexual Economy

Abstinence-only sex education also raises concerns about the governmental embrace of religious ideology, as opposed to sound scientific
teaching. This embrace seems impermissibly to endorse religious and
sectarian views of sexuality. For example, until a successful legal challenge was launched, the Louisiana Governor's Program on Abstinence
funded groups that used religious messages to teach abstinence (for
example, skits with a character named "Bible Guy" and lessons about
Mary, Joseph, and the "virgin birth" to teach that God desires "sexual
purity as a way of life.")[121]

The mere fact that an argument made in support of a public policy
may have religious roots is not enough to bar such an argument from
the public square. But in a deliberative democracy, persons should
justify their proposals by using public reasons—reasons that they reasonably can expect others to accept, whatever their conceptions of the
good, even if those others do not share the defenders' religious commitments.[122] Such reasons cannot be offered in defense of abstinence-
only sex education.

First, its vision of gender roles conflicts with the public value of sex equality. Second, such education is not a sound way to further public health. For example, the misstatements about condoms and other forms of contraception contradict the prevailing scientific evidence. Many leading medical associations and sex education organizations, as well as some religious leaders, have decried the increased funding of abstinence-only sex education as reflecting "extreme religious ideology" that threatens reproductive health.[123] The Union of Concerned Scientists offers the Bush administration's support of such education— rather than comprehensive sex education—as an example of "distorting scientific knowledge on reproductive health issues."[124] Moreover, lawmakers and others contend that ideology plays a similar role in altering—and compromising—public health information about condoms on governmental web sites.[125]

A similar distortion increasingly seems to shape U.S. foreign policy as well. Thus, in announcing the recent Global AIDs bill, which includes billions of dollars for abstinence education, the White House never mentioned the word "condom," despite the pivotal role condoms play in preventing transmission of HIV. Although Bush Administration officials praised Uganda's "ABC" program to reduce the HIV infection rate for its emphasis on abstinence, it was silent for many months about a vital part of this program: using condoms (indeed, "ABC" stands for: "Abstain, Be Faithful, and Wear a Condom").[126] Even as the conservative sexual economy installs women as gatekeepers, it imposes restrictions on access to reproductive health services, which makes it difficult for women to control their sexual and reproductive lives.

Given the effectiveness of comprehensive sex education, one troubling consequence of the abstinence education provisions of PRWORA is that many public schools no longer offer such programs, and some comprehensive sex education programs, ineligible for funding, are creating abstinence-only versions. Notably, California, which has consistently refused federal governmental funding and continued to use comprehensive sex education, has experienced one of the most significant declines in rates of teen pregnancy, teen births, and sexually transmitted diseases. By contrast, Texas, an abstinence-only state, continues with high rates.[127]

Furthermore, the governmental embrace of a "national" standard that all sexual activity belongs in marriage promotes a narrow vision of appropriate human sexuality in conflict with the recognition of a protected realm of constitutional liberty enjoyed by adults, whether married or unmarried, to engage in sexual activity.[128] Similarly, a national standard that confines reproduction to marriage and teaches that reproduction outside of marriage is harmful conflicts both with constitutional rights to privacy in making decisions about reproduction, whether one is married or not, and with family law's recognition of parental rights and responsibilities independent of a marital relationship (as discussed in Chapter 6). Government pursuit of a conservative national sexual standard also fails to accord respect to diversity and denies persons the "moral space" or "imaginary domain" (as Drucilla Cornell puts it) to develop their sexuality as free and equal persons.[129] It is another troubling example (like the Defense of Marriage Act) of how readily federal legislators and governmental officials discard their professed concerns for respecting federalism—thus allowing different states to pursue different experiments—in favor of imposing national standards when they seek to defend "traditional family values" or traditional morality.

To clarify my objection to abstinence-only sex education: sex education is a legitimate governmental project. There are public reasons for such education, rooted in concerns for promoting the healthy development of children and their eventual responsible self-government. But a critical evaluation of sex education programs indicates that comprehensive sex education, or "abstinence-plus," as augmented by my proposed focus on developing capacity and sex equality, is the sounder approach and the one more likely to facilitate responsible decision making.

I will now explain why government should not embrace "courtship education" (as some states have begun to do).[130] Courtship proponents envision courtship education as working hand in hand with abstinence education to model for adolescents a cultural script about the proper pathway to marriage. It is, therefore, crucial to understand how these calls for courtship reinforce the idea of women as gatekeepers, along with fixed gender roles and sex inequality.

## From Dating to Courtship?

For the first time in human history, mature women by the tens of thousands live the entire decade of their twenties—their most fertile years—neither in the homes of their fathers nor in the homes of their husbands; unprotected, lonely, and out of sync with their inborn nature. . . . Once female modesty became a first casualty of the sexual revolution, even women eager for marriage lost their greatest power to hold and discipline their prospective mates . . . [and] the capacity to discover their own genuine longings and best interests.

*—Leon R. Kass, "The End of Courtship," p. 39*

Socially defined courtship is an important pathway to more successful marriages.

*—Norval Glenn and Elizabeth Marquardt,* Hooking Up, Hanging Out, and Hoping for Mr. Right, *p. 7*

In recent years, some conservatives have warned of the decline of the concept of courtship and have called for reviving cultural scripts about love, courtship, and marriage to help young women and men make the journey to marriage. As one recent article stated the problem: "Courtship charts pathways to marriage. . . . Today, the road to marriage is devoid of clear markers and fraught with more accidents and wrong turns."[131]

Parallel to the marriage movement's call for government to teach the skills and knowledge needed for a happy, long-lasting marriage, courtship proponents urge developing and transmitting "a body of thought, knowledge, and skills on how to choose a mate for marriage."[132] Thus, the report, *Hungry Hearts*, sponsored by the Institute for American Values, charges that current high school marriage and relationship education merely helps students to understand "relationships" and "relationships skills" without adequately highlighting the centrality of marriage in American culture. Instead, schools should teach the great cultural narratives or scripts about love, courtship, and marriage and explain the importance of courtship—as contrasted with dating and casual sex—as the proper way to reach that goal.[133] Courtship proponents also urge universities to offer courses on the importance of courtship and marriage.[134] Parents can help by teaching their children "that a successful marriage is at least as important, and worthy of at least as much preparation, as a good job."[135]

What is courtship? If the term *courtship* refers, generally, to the pathway to marriage, it also has more specific, and problematic, gendered dimensions. First, courtship proponents view the decline of courtship as being of special concern to young women. Their proposals speak of a societal responsibility to provide young women with cultural scripts and social support. Second, some diagnoses of the courtship crisis attribute it to feminism and to gains in women's equality. Third, prominent accounts of courtship assign women a special responsibility for gatekeeping: women, by exercising the feminine virtue of modesty, discipline male sexual appetite by insisting on marriage as the prerequisite for sexual access.

Courtship proposals appeal to sources including biblical teachings, "classic" texts in literature and philosophy about courtship and romance, and "natural" differences between the sexes as conceived by evolutionary biology. I shall focus primarily on the picture of courtship found in several prominent calls to revive it.[136]

## *The Decline of Courtship as a Young Woman's Problem*

Proponents of reviving courtship diagnose a "contemporary crisis in mating and dating."[137] Young people continue to espouse marriage as an ideal, but in the cultural vacuum created by the absence of rituals of courtship, they pursue ill-advised strategies. They no longer treat their college years as a time to find their life mate, and they spend their early adult years in relationships that do not lead to marriage. Thus, the Institute for American Values report, *Hooking Up, Hanging Out, and Hoping for Mr. Right*—a study of college women's attitudes and values concerning sexuality, dating, courtship, and marriage—found a widespread practice of "hooking up," sexual interaction lacking commitment or even affection.[138]

The decline of courtship, the report contends, particularly harms young women: in times past, they could rely on a "culture of courtship" that helped them "think about what they wanted when it came to love, sex, commitment, and marriage." Indeed, the report implies that women of earlier generations were better off than today's women: "the absence of appropriately updated social norms, rituals, and relationship milestones leaves many young women confused, and often disempowered, in their relationships with men."[139] Parallel to the marriage movement, the courtship movement links the dating and mating crisis in significant part to the rise of feminist views about equality and to the expansion of educational and employment opportunities for women. It also targets the "sexual revolution" of the 1960s and "the general erosion of shame and awe regarding sexual matters."[140]

Does sex equality have a proper place in courtship, or is equality's toll on courtship, stable marriages, and family life too great? Is feminism the enemy of love, or may feminism and courtship be reconciled? Courtship proponents divide on these questions. Leon Kass, for example, contends that "better educated women can be, other things being equal, more interesting and engaging partners for better educated men," but women's "careerism" is "no friend to love or marriage." Moreover, "the love-poisoning doctrines of radical feminism," which attack traditional sex roles, urge women to deny "all womanly dependence and . . . vulnerability." Rather than calling forth "the protection of strong and loving men," it leads to the "enfeeblement of men."[141] Kass exemplifies those courtship proponents who blame feminism for courtship's decline, and who fear that current beliefs about equality and a denial of salient sex differences will doom efforts by men and women to find marital happiness.

By contrast, Barbara Dafoe Whitehead does not directly attack gains in women's equality or lament the loss of female modesty. To the contrary, she observes that "[w]e've come a long way from the time when the crowning achievement in a woman's life was her youthful marriage."[142] Women today invest, first, in education and career and only then search for a suitable mate. Parents and society encourage achievement, but fail to support young women's ambitions to find such a mate and to achieve a good marriage. To remedy the problem, society should develop a "contemporary courtship system" that fits "the new timetable" of women's lives.[143] However, even Whitehead's account of courtship puts a premium on female self-restraint as a tool to secure a suitable mate.

## The Centrality of Female Sexual Modesty in Courtship

In courtship, its proponents explain, women play an indispensable role as gatekeepers. Thus, Kass argues, the "most crucial prerequisite" for restoring a courtship system would be "a restoration of sexual self-restraint generally and of female modesty in particular," to counter the "deeply ingrained, natural waywardness and unruliness of the human male."[144] In *Proposing Courtship*, Leon and Amy Kass explain that courtship has an "important sexual asymmetry": initiative belongs to the man, and "the correlative of manly ardor is womanly modesty, her reticence, her sexual self-restraint." They contend: "Classical courtship was, in fact, a manifestation of the true power of women as women, residing in their modesty." Contemporary society denies this sexual asymmetry in favor of a misguided "gender-neutral" approach to "relationships between the sexes." Outside of religious communities, society fails to offer "clearly defined positive mores and manners that teach men how to be men in relation to women and women how to be women in relation to men."[145]

In rejecting gender neutrality, Kass and Kass invite careful study of an ancient text, Erasmus's *Colloquy on Courtship*, in which the female character (Maria) understands her womanhood as requiring that she deliver to her suitor—once she secures the exclusiveness, permanence, and fidelity of marriage—"a virginity whole and unblemished." This text, they contend, identifies the basic principles of courtship:

1) how to transform brutish sexual appetite into human loving; 2) how to make a manly man interested in marriage and attached to his children; 3) how to help a woman negotiate between her erotic desires and her concern for progeny; 4) how to enable men to find and win, how to enable women to select and hold, the right person for lasting marriage; 5) how to locate the relations of men and women in the larger contexts of human life—familial, political, religious.

They contend that "[m]ore up-to-date mores and manners that do not come to terms with these issues will not get the job done." This *Colloquy* also "illustrates what may be the central truth about sexual manners and mores: it is women who control and teach them."[146] (So, too, Popenoe, quoted above, argues that restoring a strong marriage system will depend on women's "leadership," since they are "traditionally assumed to be the gatekeepers of sexuality.")[147]

Kass and Kass invoke the sociobiologists' notion of "reproductive strategy": female chastity is how women "attach the man exclusively and permanently to the woman through erotic love and to make him thereby also love and care for her—their—children."[148] But a practical problem arises: restoring "sensible sexual mores, pointing toward marriage" is possible only if "a majority of women reassert the powerful virtue of self-restraint." This appears to be a collective action problem: unless a critical number of women insist upon and play by the new rules, individual women will not have enough power to do so. Whether women are willing to "exercise their power of reform depends," Kass and Kass conclude, on "whether they think that a fulfilling marriage and motherhood are of primary importance in their life."[149]

How restrictive should the new system be? Kass and Kass extol the example of Maria, with her "unblemished" virginity. This approach fits teaching abstinence until marriage as the expected national standard. Some other courtship proponents envision a system of greater sexual restraint, but view complete abstinence until marriage as unrealistic. For example, Popenoe calls for social norms whereby young adults "seek to lead their premarital sex lives with eventual marriage more strongly in mind." He suggests the wisdom of grandmothers' advice that "dictates a measure of [a woman] playing hard to get," such as "refus[ing] to cohabit except when marriage is clearly planned," and even then, only on the woman's terms.[150]

Playing hard to get also features in Whitehead's model of updated courtship norms. She posits two parallel systems, the marriage system—or how persons travel the pathway to marriage—and the relationship system, which does not have marriage as its direct goal and takes a more "flexible, egalitarian, nonjudgmental approach" to the conduct of intimate life. This latter system, which includes "cohabitation-as-courtship," benefits men, who need not take on the responsibilities of husbands to secure many advantages of marriage, such as sex, nurture, and domestic services. But cohabitation ill-serves marriage-minded young women ("she's thinking 'husband,' he's thinking 'boyfriend' "). Thus, Whitehead commends the successful path to marriage taken by Blair, who chose "courtship without cohabitation," which allowed her to minimize her investment in her boyfriend to determine if he was serious about marriage.[151]

## Should Government Support a Return to Female Modesty and to Courtship?

Should government promote sexual responsibility in young people by reviving courtship? Are the cultural scripts of female modesty and male initiative indeed vital texts that should be used in public education to inspire and instruct young people about the proper pathway to marriage? For several reasons, no.

Courtship, as elaborated by its proponents, involves rigid sex-based roles and stereotypes. It would be inappropriate for government to promote such roles and stereotypes because they conflict with the contemporary public value and constitutional norm of sex equality. In the conservative sexual economy, a woman moves from the "protection" of her father's home to the "protection" of a husband, having used her sexual purity to discipline her suitor's otherwise unruly sexual desire. Many courtship proponents reject an ideal of gender neutrality in favor of cultural scripts premised on salient gender differences. Even the more moderate courtship proposals affirm women's role as gatekeepers and view male sexuality as fundamentally irresponsible.[152] Given the role of religious organizations in providing abstinence-only materials for public schools, the gender asymmetry in conservative models of Christian courtship also raises concern. Appealing to biblical texts and traditions, some models teach that moving a relationship beyond friendship falls to the male, who should get the consent of the female's parents (often, the father is specified) to make his move.[153] (Contemporary courtship services, including those aimed at older adults, assume that men will initiate and women respond.[154])

This gender asymmetry reinforces, rather than challenges, the sexual double standard and hinders instilling norms of mutual responsibility. It runs counter to helping young women develop a sense of themselves as subjects with their own sexual desire. By holding women responsible not just for themselves but for men's sexuality as well, courtship proposals unfairly burden women and fail to respect women's and men's equal moral capacity. Moreover, assigning women the responsibility for controlling men's sexual aggression may implicitly assign the blame for men's sexual violence to women who abandon modesty or act on their sexual desire. And it may denigrate the importance of government's obligation to protect all members of society against assault. Thus, Wendy Shalit makes the troubling argument that the legacy of the "sexual revolution" is men's sexual irresponsibility and violence. By contrast, modesty—that is, when women behave in a way that inspires men to treat them with respect—will do more to protect women than laws against sexual harassment and date rape.[155] Similarly, some Christian proponents of courtship unfavorably contrast the "new feminist system" of reliance on law and government to protect women from the unruliness of male sexuality with the "biblical system" of paternal and fraternal protection.[156]

Government should not lend support to these pernicious and sexist ideas about women's responsibility and men's irresponsibility. Female modesty may be, for many, an important religious or cultural value. But it should not be—and cannot be—the sole guarantor of women's bodily integrity. Historically, an ideal of the virtuous woman and her opposite (the bad girl or whore) has exacted costs for women on both sides of the dichotomy.[157] Moreover, both the exploitative "sexual economy of American slavery" and subsequent racial prejudice have excluded certain black women from respectability and protection.[158]

Diagnosing the "dating and mating crisis" as rooted in falling away from courtship may also divert attention from the roles played by the changing place of marriage in persons' conceptions of the good life and important economic and social changes that pose obstacles to marriage. Whitehead's own account hints that the decline of female modesty is less significant than the ascent of education and employment as a path for young women to get many of the "assets and benefits" they once acquired through marriage, such as "a good income, sex, a nest, and a nest egg of their own."[159] (They can also attain motherhood outside of marriage.)

At the same time, for young women who wish to marry but who cannot find a suitable mate, the decline in female sexual modesty may be less relevant than men's relative economic and educational disadvantage. Recent reports on a "new gender gap" in which girls and women are achieving at higher rates than boys and men in education and employment stress the implications for marriage: young women may have difficulty finding men with comparable achievement.[160] I support government investing in human capital to help people secure the economic preconditions for a stable family life. But critical reflection on traditional gender roles in light of women's growing achievements—for example, challenging the idea that husbands must be the primary provider—might also help to facilitate marriage. Courtship education is unlikely to encourage such reflection.

Finally, by their exclusive focus on heterosexuality, cultural scripts about courtship unduly restrain, rather than promote, the exercise of young peoples' moral powers. Courtship proponents, of course, may freely argue for their conception of the good life. But government should not endorse the cultural scripts of courtship as an official message about an expected national standard. There are better ways to foster sexual and reproductive responsibility.

## Conclusion

The stakes in the battles over sex education seem so high because they involve "negotiation about which sexualities will be recognized and valued."[161] How educators instruct children about intimacy, sexuality, and family may help or hinder them in envisioning diverse possibilities for intimate life. The conservative sexual economy of "abstinence-only," with its cultural scripts about male and female sexual asymmetry, is more likely to undermine than to support children and adolescents growing into adults who are responsible sexual agents. So, too, the cultural scripts of courtship. A liberal feminist approach to sex education, emphasizing capacity, equality, and responsibility, is the better path to developing sexual and reproductive responsibility.

# Epilogue

THE IDEA OF THE "PLACE" OF FAMILIES evokes many images. Family is a potent symbol of relationship, connection, interdependency, and responsibility. For many, it connotes, a private space—a home, a dwelling—in which, ideally, a group of persons live with, love, care for, and interact with each other. It also connotes an emotional space, or social environment, in which personal bonds link self and other, forming and shaping family members' senses of identity, values, and goals. Most vividly, terms such as a child's "formative years" or "formative influences" conjure up the critical place of parents and other adult family members in shaping children and who they will become as adults. But as a place where adults form bonds of intimacy, commitment, and responsibility, and pursue a shared life, families also have a formative role extending far beyond childhood.

The notion of the place of families also evokes images of the designated position of families in society. Political rhetoric about families, I have shown, assigns families a special status. Families, we hear, are first among the "seedbeds of civic virtue," the "cradle of citizenship," a fundamental institution on which a strong and healthy society depends. These claims about the public significance of families and the proper niche occupied by families in the political order resonate with more personal meanings of family in this respect: both recognize that families play a vital role in shaping persons. Society's keen interest in

291

the state of families, this book has explained, flows from the formative role that families play in fostering the capacities of persons to be responsible, self-governing members of society and good citizens.

Much of the passionate debate over families stems from conflicting views over how to support the formative role of families. A significant challenge in fashioning family law and policy is to find ways to strengthen and affirm the importance of families in a manner that respects the diversity of actual families. A repeated theme in proposals to strengthen families is that the condition of the marital family is the best barometer of the health of families and that shoring up families must focus on shoring up marriage. At the same time, the battles waged in state courts and legislatures, as well as in the federal government, over same-sex marriage reveal fierce resistance to expanding the scope of marriage to include the intimate commitment of same-sex couples.

Reducing this resistance will require coming to understand that it is possible to reconcile a commitment to protecting the place of families with respect for diversity and equality among families. Such a reconciliation would clarify, for example, that extending legal protection to the intimate, committed relationships of same-sex couples would not threaten—but would affirm—the goods and purposes that society associates with family. Glimmers of awareness that the bonds of same-sex couples and their children *are* family bonds and deserve support seem to underlie the extension of some legal protection and recognition to such families. A remaining step is to come to understand that the security and support that marriage can provide to such couples and their children can strengthen, rather than undermine, the place of marriage. In contrast to marriage defenders and those who would abolish marriage, I believe that it is possible to retain the place of marriage, but to expand public support and recognition for other close relationships and family bonds.

Already, legal developments such as the creation of civil unions, expanded domestic partnership laws, and, in Massachusetts and nearby Canada, same-sex marriage have altered the landscape of family life. In Europe, the landscape continues to alter: in July 2005, the Spanish Parliament passed a law permitting same-sex marriage in Spain, and a new Civil Partnership Act for same-sex couples will take effect in Britain in December 2005.[1] The evolution of the wedding announcement pages of major newspapers to include, along with the familiar photos of new brides and grooms, announcements by same-sex couples of their marriages, civil unions, registered partnerships, and commitment ceremonies are a testament to this changed landscape. This changing public face of families is also testimony to the continuing symbolic importance of marriage as a public affirmation of commitment and of the hope for a shared life. In coming years, as various states wrestle with whether and how to recognize and support the families formed by same-sex couples, and as such couples pursue legal challenges to state marriage laws, this landscape will continue to change. Will federal opposition to same-sex marriage, as in the Defense of Marriage Act and the proposed federal marriage amendment, remain a feature of this terrain? Is it unrealistic to hope that critical reflection not only on the place of civil marriage and on how the federal government might best "defend" it, but also on constitutional commitments, could alter this stance?

Calls to renew a marriage culture and to restore the primacy of marriage, a staple in public discussions about families, invite a second challenge: is it possible to formulate policies to strengthen families that also respect the equal moral capacity and responsibility of men and women? As the examples of the marriage movement and government-funded "abstinence-only-until-marriage" education suggest, a lingering problem is ambivalence about, if not rejection of, sex equality. Such programs share a conviction that strong families depend on a form of gender ordering that regulates unruly heterosexuality by assigning women—through the institution of marriage—responsibility for taming men and would most likely shore up, rather than challenge, traditional gender roles within the family. Too often, defenses of "traditional" marriage and family values regard gains in women's equality and personal self-government as being in tension with strengthening families.

These struggles over the place of sex equality in fortifying the place of families point to a critical question: on what terms will women and men achieve social cooperation in the spheres of intimacy and family life? If, indeed, as marriage promoters contend, no one wants to "turn back the clock" on gains in women's equality, then the answer is not to return to a system of family self-government in which men, by law and custom, were the heads of households and women their dependents. Nor is the answer the newer versions of gender ordering offered by the marriage movement. Rather, it is vital to find forms of social cooperation premised on equal respect for women's and men's personal self-government. Preparing men and women for such social cooperation requires educating children to respect the equal moral capacities of persons regardless of sex (along other markers such as ethnicity and race). Families and government share responsibility for providing this sort of education.

Of course, families, as well as popular culture, hold diverse views about the place of equality in marriage. Some popular advice books teach that the formula for a happy marriage is to embrace, rather than challenge, a gendered division of labor and for wives to accept their husband's "natural" role as head of the household.[2] By contrast, some studies of contemporary marriage suggest that the hard work of challenging such gender roles may be a fruitful path to social cooperation, not to mention greater happiness.[3] Indeed, the expectation of a "partnership of equals" is one shared by women across lines of class. Whether or not parents do educate their children about sex equality, it is appropriate for government to inculcate in children knowledge of and respect for sex equality, both as a public value and as a constitutional principle relevant to family law.

The question of social cooperation also bears on a vital role society assigns to families: nurturing and rearing children. Will public policies address the continuing problem of women's disproportionate responsibility for this vital work by helping mothers and fathers to act on convictions that caring for children and keeping a home should be a shared responsibility? When women become mothers but not wives, will public policies bolster their efforts to support their children and afford them care, or will they discourage such efforts for fear of weakening marriage and demeaning fathers? Similarly, how will public policies encourage men to be responsible fathers? Images of women as gatekeepers complement images of men as naturally irresponsible, with nearly uncontrollable sexual passions. Far better for the task of fostering responsibility, I have suggested, are policies that treat men as morally responsible subjects who are capable of nurturing their children. Policies that derive from a premise of respect for men's and women's equal moral capacity are more likely to encourage reflective, responsible self-government in matters of sexuality, reproduction, and parenting.

To speak of the place of families inevitably invites attention to the relative location of families in society, with respect not only to government but also to the other institutions of civil society. Families have a place in inculcating personal and civic virtues and in nurturing children to become capable and responsible adults. But they do not—and cannot—do so in isolation. Families need many kinds of resources to carry out their formative responsibilities. In speaking of a formative project of fostering persons' self-government, I have referred to the formative responsibilities of government as well as families. An important question for the direction of family policy is whether rhetoric about a governmental obligation to help strengthen families will lead to providing the economic and social resources and supports that families need. Appropriate public policy could be a helpful catalyst to encourage workplace practices that allow parents and other caregivers, across the economic spectrum, to achieve a better balance between family and work, as well as have time to participate in the life of communities, thus building up civil society. Working toward such a balance could be a constructive point of common ground in efforts to strengthen families.

The institutions of civil society, such as workplaces, religious institutions, and other voluntary associations, also play vital roles in the political order. Participation in such institutions shapes persons' capacities, even as such institutions serve as buffers against governmental power. These institutions can complement the formative work of families. In recent years, politicians have shown increasing interest in enlisting the institutions of civil society to address social problems. Among these problems are those faced by many families, such as economic inequality and unsafe neighborhoods. The turn to public-private partnerships could be a significant way to acknowledge that social responsibility and public responsibility should complement personal and family responsibility. But it is crucial that, when government enlists other branches of civil society to help families, it do so in ways that are consistent with public purposes and political values as they relate to families. Without such a constraint, as this book has illustrated, government may be promoting messages about sexuality, family, and marriage that reflect particular religious ideology, rather than justifiable public reasons and governmental purposes.

Finally, just as families have a place within a broader social and political system, discussions about family law and policy should also acknowledge the global dimension of such questions. As this book illustrates, state and federal courts, legislators, law reform committees, and scholars have looked beyond the United States to other countries—and to international human rights norms—for guidance on matters ranging from the scope of constitutional rights of intimate association to the legal recognition of same-sex relationships to policies addressing work/family conflict. In an era of increasing globalization, sources of law beyond the United States, such as norms about individual and family rights, may be of increasing relevance and will also bring valuable, comparative information to bear on challenging aspects of family law and policy. Families have a place not only at home, in civil society, and our nation, but also in the world.

Notes

Index

# Notes

## Introduction

1. Mary Ann Glendon and David Blankenhorn, eds., *Seedbeds of Virtue: Sources of Competence, Character, and Citizenship in American Society* (Lanham, Md.: Madison Books, 1995).

2. "The Marriage Movement: A Statement of Principles" (Institute for American Values, 2000), *www.marriagemovement.org* (accessed September 1, 2002).

3. White House, "Working toward Independence," *www.whitehouse.gov* (accessed February 10, 2002).

4. *"When You Get Married . . ."* (2002 edition including updates from the 77th Legislature) (prepared by the Attorney General of Texas under Texas Family Code §2.104), *www.oag.state.tx.us* (accessed September 1, 2002).

5. 798 N.E.2d 941, 966–967 (Mass. 2003).

6. "Bush's Remarks on Marriage Amendment," *New York Times*, February 25, 2004, A18.

7. Report of the Platform Committee, *Strong at Home, Strong in the World: The Democratic Platform for America* (2004), p. 27.

8. The Platform Committee, *2004 Republican Party Platform: A Safer World and a More Hopeful America* (2004), p. 87 (quoting remarks by President George W. Bush).

9. David Nather, "Social Conservatives Propel Bush, Republicans to Victory," *CQ Weekly*, November 6, 2004, p. 2586. However, subsequent analyses of initial findings that "moral values" were an animating issue for 22 percent of voters identify flaws with polling questions and caution against overemphasizing the role of "moral values" in Bush's reelection. Jim Rutenberg, "Poll Question Stirs Debate on Meaning of 'Values,' " *New York Times*, November 6, 2004, A13. Eleven states passed constitutional amendments barring same-sex marriage. "State Constitutional Amendments Defining Marriage," *washingtonpost.com* (accessed December 2, 2004).

10. "Law and Civil Rights," *www.pollingreport.com* (accessed January 25, 2005).

11. On these moral powers, see John Rawls, *Political Liberalism* (New York: Columbia University Press, 1993), pp. 19, 20; James E. Fleming, *Securing Constitutional Democracy* (Chicago: University of Chicago Press, forthcoming). My emphasis on capacity also has affinities to Martha Nussbaum's capabilities approach to human development. Martha C. Nussbaum, *Women and Human Development: The Capabilities Approach* (Cambridge: Cambridge University Press, 2000).

12. I adapt this schematic of action and restraint from Joseph Raz, *The Morality of Freedom* (Oxford: Clarendon Press, 1986).

13. Martha Albertson Fineman, *The Autonomy Myth: A Theory of Dependency* (New York: The New Press, 2004); Eva Feder Kittay, *Love's Labor: Essays on Women, Equality, and Dependency* (New York: Routledge, 1999).

14. For this turn of phrase, thanks to: E. J. Graff, *What Is Marriage For?* (Boston: Beacon Press, 1999).

15. An Act Relating to Civil Unions, 2000 Vt. ALS 91 (adopted in the wake of Baker v. State, 744 A.2d 864 (Vt. 1999)); An Act Concerning Civil Unions, Connecticut Legislature Public Act No. 05-10, S.S.B. No. 963 (effective October 1, 2005).

16. The Domestic Partnership Rights and Responsibilities Act of 2003, Cal. Family Code, §297.5 et seq.

17. *Goodridge*, 966–967.

18. Fineman, *The Autonomy Myth*, 123.

19. American Law Institute, *Principles of the Law of Family Dissolution: Analysis and Recommendations* (Newark, N.J.: LexisNexis, 2002), pp. 956–957.

20. Law Commission of Canada, *Beyond Conjugality: Recognizing and Supporting Close Adult Personal Relationships* (2001).

21. Milton C. Regan, Jr., "Calibrated Commitment: The Legal Treatment of Marriage and Cohabitation," 76 *Notre Dame Law Review* 1435 (2001).

22. Lawrence v. Texas, 539 U.S. 558 (2003).

23. Planned Parenthood v. Casey, 505 U.S. 833 (1992).

24. Ronald Dworkin develops these distinctions in *Life's Dominion* (New York: Alfred A. Knopf, 1993), pp. 150–151.

25. Public Law No. 104–193, 101 Stat. 2105.

26. Nancy Cott, *Public Vows: A History of Marriage and the Nation* (Cambridge, Mass.: Harvard University Press, 2000); Hendrik Hartog, *Man and Wife in America: A History* (Cambridge, Mass.: Harvard University Press, 2000).

27. Michael J. Sandel, *Democracy's Discontent* (Cambridge, Mass.: Belknap Press of Harvard University Press, 1996).

28. William A. Galston, *Liberal Purposes* (New York: Cambridge University Press, 1991); Stephen Macedo, *Diversity and Distrust* (Cambridge, Mass.: Harvard University Press, 2000); Raz, *The Morality of Freedom*.

29. Susan Moller Okin, *Justice, Gender, and the Family* (New York: Basic Books, 1989).

30. John Rawls, "The Idea of Public Reason Revisited," 64 *University of Chicago Law Review* 765 (1997).

31. A few examples are: Martha Albertson Fineman, *The Neutered Mother, the Sexual Family and Other Twentieth-Century Tragedies* (New York: Routledge, 1995); Robin West, *Caring for Justice* (New York: New York University Press, 1997);

Catharine A. MacKinnon, *Toward a Feminist Theory of the State* (Cambridge, Mass.: Harvard University Press, 1989).

32. Nancy J. Hirschmann, *The Subject of Liberty: Toward a Feminist Theory of Freedom* (Princeton, N.J.: Princeton University Press, 2002).

## 1. The Place of Families and Government

1. Michael J. Sandel, *Democracy's Discontent* (Cambridge, Mass.: Belknap Press of Harvard University Press, 1996), pp. 3–6.

2. Steven Wall, *Liberalism, Perfectionism and Restraint* (Cambridge: Cambridge University Press, 1998), p. 8.

3. Jeremy Waldron, "Autonomy and Perfectionism in Raz's *Morality of Freedom*," 62 *Southern California Law Review* 1097 (1989).

4. James E. Fleming, *Securing Constitutional Democracy* (Chicago: University of Chicago: Press, forthcoming).

5. John Rawls, *Political Liberalism* (New York: Columbia University Press, 1993), p. 19. Ronald Dworkin's famous argument that government must treat persons with equal concern and respect derives from a conception of persons as having the capability for "suffering and frustration" and the capability to form and act on a conception of "how their lives should be lived." See Ronald Dworkin, *Taking Rights Seriously* (Cambridge, Mass.: Harvard University Press, 1977), p. 272.

6. Amy Gutmann and Dennis Thompson, *Democracy and Disagreement* (Cambridge, Mass.: Belknap Press of Harvard University Press, 1996).

7. Sandel, *Democracy's Discontent*, p. 5.

8. Linda Barclay, "Autonomy and the Social Self," in Catriona Mackenzie and Natalie Stoljar, eds., *Relational Autonomy* (New York: Oxford University Press, 2000), p. 53.

9. Fleming, *Securing Constitutional Democracy*, p. 1.

10. Influential examples include Jennifer Nedelsky, "Reconceiving Autonomy: Sources, Thoughts, and Possibilities," 1 *Yale Journal of Law & Feminism* 7 (1989); Robin West, "Jurisprudence and Gender," 55 *University of Chicago Law Review* 1 (1988).

11. I address this critique in Linda C. McClain, " 'Atomistic Man' Revisited: Liberalism, Connection, and Feminist Jurisprudence," 65 *Southern California Law Review* 1171 (1992).

12. Mackenzie and Stoljar, eds., "Introduction: Autonomy Refigured," in *Relational Autonomy*, p. 4.

13. Martha Minow and Mary Lyndon Shanley, "Relational Rights and Responsibilities," 11 *Hypatia* 4 (1996).

14. Joseph Raz, "Liberty and Trust," in Robert P. George, ed., *Natural Law, Liberalism, and Morality* (New York: Clarendon Press, 1996), p. 113; Joseph Raz, *The Morality of Freedom* (Oxford: Clarendon Press, 1986), p. 418.

15. Lawrence v. Texas, 539 U.S. 558, 565 (2003) (discussing prior cases).

16. Baker v. State, 744 A.2d 864 (Vt. 1999); Goodridge v. Department of Public Health, 798 N.E.2d 941 (Mass. 2003); Carlos A. Ball, *The Morality of Gay Rights* (New York: Routledge, 2003), pp. 12–13.

17. Rawls, *Political Liberalism*, pp. 178, 179–181, 325, 331–334.

18. Eva Feder Kittay, *Love's Labor* (New York: Routledge, 1999), pp. 100–103. Unlike Kittay, I do not posit a third moral power, the power to care.

19. Amartya Sen, *Inequality Reexamined* (New York: Russell Sage Foundation, 1992), pp. 4–5.

20. Martha C. Nussbaum, *Sex and Social Justice* (New York: Oxford University Press, 1999), pp. 41–42; Mary Becker, "Towards a Progressive Politics and a Progressive Constitution," 69 *Fordham Law Review* 2007 (2001) (drawing on the capabilities approach to argue for a primary governmental goal of care).

21. Nussbaum, *Sex and Social Justice*, pp. 78–80.

22. Sen, *Inequality Reexamined*, pp. 122–125; Amartya Sen, *Development as Freedom* (New York: Anchor Books, 1999), pp. 189–203.

23. Martha C. Nussbaum, *Women and Human Development: The Capabilities Approach* (New York: Cambridge University Press, 2000), pp. 1, 243.

24. Pierce v. Society of Sisters, 268 U.S. 510 (1925).

25. Anne C. Dailey, "Constitutional Privacy and the Just Family," 67 *Tulane Law Review* 955, 1022 (1993).

26. Martha Albertson Fineman, *The Neutered Mother, the Sexual Family, and Other Twentieth Century Tragedies* (New York: Routledge, 1995), pp. 161–176.

27. Martha Albertson Fineman, *The Autonomy Myth: A Theory of Dependency* (New York: The New Press, 2004).

28. John Rawls, "The Idea of Public Reason Revisited," 64 *University of Chicago Law Review*, 765, 788 (1997).

29. Rawls, *Political Liberalism*, p. 43.

30. E. J. Graff, *What Is Marriage For?* (Boston: Beacon Press, 1999). Emphasis added.

31. Loving v. Virginia, 388 U.S. 1, 12 (1967).

32. Griswold v. Connecticut, 381 U.S. 479, 486 (1965).

33. Turner v. Safley, 482 U.S. 78, 95–96 (1987).

34. Bruce Hafen, "The Constitutional Status of Marriage, Kinship, and Sexual Privacy: Balancing the Individual and Social Interests," 81 *Michigan Law Review* 463, 469 (1983) (citing Roscoe Pound, "Individual Interests in Domestic Relations," 14 *Michigan Law Review* 177 (1916)).

35. Frances Olsen, "The Myth of State Intervention in the Family," 18 *University of Michigan Journal of Law Reform* 835 (1985); Martha Minow, *Making All the Difference* (Ithaca, N.Y.: Cornell University Press, 1990); Dailey, "Constitutional Privacy and the Just Family."

36. Jill Elaine Hasday, "Federalism and the Family Reconsidered," 45 *UCLA Law Review* 1297 (1998).

37. Rawls, "The Idea of Public Reason Revisited," p. 793.

38. Carl Schneider, "The Channeling Function in Family Law," 20 *Hofstra Law Review* 495 (1992).

39. Weber v. Aetna Casualty & Surety Co., 406 U.S. 164 (1972).

40. June Carbone, *From Partners to Parents: The Second Revolution in Family Law* (New York: Columbia University Press, 2000).

41. Troxel v. Granville, 530 U.S. 57, 63 (2000).

42. Rawls, "The Idea of Public Reason Revisited," 788 n. 60. Calling for a focus on "social functions" is Harry D. Krause, "Marriage for the New Millen-

nium: Heterosexual, Same Sex—Or Not at All?," 34 *Family Law Quarterly* 271 (2000).

43. Brown v. Board of Education, 347 U.S. 483 (1954).

44. A liberal argument for such support appears in Ronald Dworkin, *A Matter of Principle* (Cambridge, Mass.: Harvard University Press, 1985), pp. 221–233, 293–331.

45. Bruce Ackerman and Anne Alstott, *The Stakeholder Society* (New Haven, Conn.: Yale University Press, 1999).

46. Ronald Dworkin, *Sovereign Virtue: The Theory and Practice of Equality* (Cambridge, Mass.: Harvard University Press, 2000). Rawls's famous difference principle specified that forms of inequality within society, to be justifiable, must benefit the worse off. John Rawls, *A Theory of Justice* (Cambridge, Mass.: Belknap Press of Harvard University Press, 1971), pp. 75–78.

47. Sotirios A. Barber, *Welfare and the Constitution* (Princeton, N.J.: Princeton University Press, 2003); Frank I. Michelman, "Foreword: On Protecting the Poor Through the Fourteenth Amendment," 83 *Harvard Law Review* 7 (1969); Frank I. Michelman, "In Pursuit of Constitutional Welfare Rights: One View of Rawls' *Theory of Justice*," 121 *University of Pennsylvania Law Review* 962 (1973); Lawrence G. Sager, *Justice in Plainclothes* (New Haven, Conn.: Yale University Press, 2004).

48. Cynthia Estlund, *Working Together* (New York: Oxford University Press, 2003); Vicki Schultz, "Life's Work," 100 *Columbia Law Review* 1881 (2000); Nancy L. Rosenblum, *Membership and Morals* (Princeton, N.J.: Princeton University Press, 1998); Robert D. Putnam, *Bowling Alone* (New York: Simon & Schuster, 2000).

49. Roberts v. United States Jaycees, 468 U.S. 609 (1984).

50. Susan Moller Okin, *Justice, Gender, and the Family* (New York: Basic Books, 1989).

51. "Intimate Partner Violence: Fact Sheet," National Center for Injury Prevention and Control, *www.cdc.gov* (accessed January 25, 2005).

52. Scott Coltrane, *Family Man* (New York: Oxford University Press, 1996), p. 200; Scott Coltrane, "Research on Household Labor," 62 *Journal of Marriage & Family* 1208 (2000).

53. Catharine A. MacKinnon, "Reflections on Sex Equality under Law," 100 *Yale Law Journal* 1281, 1311 (1991); Catharine A. MacKinnon, *Toward a Feminist Theory of the State* (Cambridge, Mass.: Harvard University Press, 1989), pp. 193–194.

54. Robin West, *Caring for Justice* (New York: New York University Press, 1997), pp. 94–178.

55. Deborah Rhode, "Feminism and the State," 107 *Harvard Law Review* 1181, 1187–1189 (1994); Robin West, *Progressive Constitutionalism* (Durham, N.C.: Duke University Press, 1994), pp. 45–72; Mary E. Becker, "The Politics of Women's Wrongs and the Bill of 'Rights': A Bicentennial Perspective, 59 *University of Chicago Law Review* 453–457 (1992).

56. Catharine A. MacKinnon, "Difference and Dominance: On Sex Discrimination," in *Feminism Unmodified* (Cambridge, Mass.: Harvard University Press, 1987), 32, 44–45.

57. Nancy J. Hirschmann, *The Subject of Liberty: Toward a Feminist Theory of*

*Freedom* (Princeton, N.J.: Princeton University Press, 2003); MacKinnon, *Toward a Feminist Theory of the State*, pp. 106–125; Tracy E. Higgins, "Democracy and Feminism," 110 *Harvard Law Review* 1657, 1694–1701 (1997).

58. Joan Williams, *Unbending Gender* (New York: Oxford University Press, 2000).

59. The influential work of Amartya Sen addresses this problem in the context of developing or poorer countries. See Amartya Sen, *Commodities and Capabilities* (New York: Oxford University Press, 1999).

60. Hirschmann, *The Subject of Liberty*, 204.

61. Barrie Thorne, "Feminism and the Family: Two Decades of Thought," in Barrie Thorne and Marilyn Yalom, eds., *Rethinking the Family: Some Feminist Questions* (Boston: Northeastern University Press, rev. ed., 1992).

62. Marilyn Friedman, *Autonomy, Gender, Politics* (New York: Oxford University Press, 2003), pp. 81–112.

63. Virgina Held, ed., *Justice and Care* (Boulder, Colo.: Westview Press, 1995); Amy R. Baehr, ed., *Varieties of Feminist Liberalism* (Lanham, Md.: Rowman & Littlefield, 2004).

64. Nussbaum, *Women and Human Development*, p. 246.

65. Rawls, "The Idea of Public Reason Revisited," p. 791.

66. Rawls, *Political Liberalism*, p. 41.

67. For an early liberal feminist argument, see John Stuart Mill, *On the Subjection of Women*, in John Stuart Mill and Harriet Taylor Mill, *Essays on Sex Equality*, ed. Alice S. Rossi (Chicago: University of Chicago Press, 1970). For contemporary arguments, see Diana T. Meyers, *Self, Society, and Personal Choice* (New York: Columbia University Press, 1989); and Jean Grimshaw, *Philosophy and Feminist Thinking* (Minneapolis: University of Minnesota Press, 1986). Some feminists nonetheless argue that a liberal framework cannot secure women's substantive equality because it cannot criticize the choices they make. See Kimberly A. Yuracko, *Perfectionism and Contemporary Feminist Values* (Bloomington: Indiana University Press, 2003).

68. West, *Progressive Constitutionalism*, pp. 267–268; *Relational Autonomy*, pp. 3–26; Nedelsky, "Reconceiving Autonomy"; Minow, *Making All the Difference*, p. 383.

69. Seyla Benhabib, *Situating the Self* (New York: Routledge, 1992), p. 214. Some feminists argue for focusing on "agency" rather than autonomy. See Kathryn Abrams, "From Autonomy to Agency," 40 *William and Mary Law Review* 805 (1999).

70. MacKinnon, *Toward a Feminist Theory of the State*; West, *Progressive Constitutionalism*; Ruth Colker, "Anti-Subordination Above All: Sex, Race, and Equal Protection," 61 *New York University Law Review* 1003 (1986).

71. Hirschmann, *The Subject of Liberty*, 201; Tracy E. Higgins, "Reviving the Public/Private Distinction in Feminist Theorizing," 75 *Chicago-Kent Law Review* 847, 853–857 (2000); Martha Albertson Fineman, "What Place for Family Privacy?" 67 *George Washington Law Review* 1207 (1999).

72. Mary Ann Glendon, *Rights Talk* (New York: The Free Press, 1991); Milton Regan, *Family Law and the Pursuit of Intimacy* (New York: New York University Press, 1993).

73. Carl Schneider, "Moral Discourse and the Transformation of American Family Law," 83 *Michigan Law Review* 1803 (1985).

74. Bruce Hafen, "Individualism and Autonomy in Family Law: The Waning of Belonging," 1991 *Brigham Young University Law Review* 1, 6.

75. Glendon, *Rights Talk*, pp. 56–58; Sandel, *Democracy's Discontent*, pp. 94–98; Janet L. Dolgin, "The Family in Transition: From *Griswold* to *Eisenstadt* and Beyond," 82 *Georgetown Law Journal* 1519 (1994) (discussing Griswold v. Connecticut, 381 U.S. 479 (1965), and Eisenstadt v. Baird, 405 U.S. 438 (1972)).

76. Sandel, *Democracy's Discontent*, pp. 91–119.

77. Family law casebooks trace this evolution, for example: D. Kelly Weisberg and Susan Frelich Appleton, *Modern Family Law* (New York: Aspen Law and Business, 2nd ed., 2002), pp. 245–396.

78. Mary Lyndon Shanley, "Unencumbered Individuals and Embedded Selves," in Anita L. Allen and Milton C. Regan, Jr., eds., *Debating Democracy's Discontent* (New York: Oxford University Press, 1998), p. 233.

79. Betsey Stevenson and Justin Wolfers, "Bargaining in the Shadow of the Law: Divorce Laws and Family Distress," NBER Working Paper Series, Working Paper 10175 (December 2003).

80. Anita L. Allen, *Uneasy Access: Privacy for Women in a Free Society* (Totowa, N.J.: Rowman and Littlefield, 1988); Julie Inness, *Privacy, Intimacy, and Isolation* (New York: Oxford University Press, 1992).

81. John Horton, "Toleration as a Virtue," in David Heyd, ed., *Toleration: An Elusive Virtue* (Princeton, N.J.: Princeton University Press, 1996), pp. 28, 28–35; Raz, *The Morality of Freedom*, pp. 401–403.

82. George P. Fletcher, "The Instability of Tolerance," in Heyd, ed., *Toleration: An Elusive Virtue*, p. 158.

83. John Locke, *A Letter Concerning Toleration*, Patrick Romanell, ed. (Indianapolis, Ind.: Bobbs-Merrill, 1955; 1st ed. 1689), p. 18.

84. Ronald Dworkin, "Liberal Community," 77 *California Law Review* 479, 486 (1989).

85. John Stuart Mill, *On Liberty*, David Spitz, ed. (New York: W. W. Norton, 1975; 1st ed. 1859), pp. 12, 14, 56.

86. Rawls, *Political Liberalism*, pp. 18–20, 201–203; H. L. A. Hart, "Introduction," in *Essays in Jurisprudence and Philosophy* (Oxford: Oxford University Press, 1983), pp. 1, 17 (discussing Mill, *On Liberty*).

87. Locke, *A Letter Concerning Toleration*, pp. 17, 58. But Locke did not extend toleration to, for example, atheists and Catholics.

88. Mill, *On Liberty*, pp. 10–11.

89. Locke, *A Letter Concerning Toleration*, p. 57. Some scholars contend that Locke's argument did not rest on the value of diversity. See Susan Mendus, *Toleration and the Limits of Liberalism* (Atlantic Highlands, N.J.: Humanities Press International, 1989), pp. 37–39.

90. Mill, *On Liberty*, pp. 53–69.

91. Rawls, *Political Liberalism*, pp. 36–37.

92. Ibid., p. 154.

93. Ibid., pp. 10–15, 99, 146–147, 206.

94. Ibid., p. 147.

95. Ibid., pp. 36, 144.
96. Ibid., p. 217.
97. Ibid., p. 50.
98. Gutmann and Thompson, *Democracy and Disagreement*, p. 92.
99. Sandel, *Democracy's Discontent*, pp. 318–321.
100. A continuing controversy is government's proper authority to reach or burden religious exercise through laws of general application. Employment Div., Dep't of Human Resources of Oregon v. Smith, 494 U.S. 872 (1990) (upholding, against free exercise of religion claim, denial of unemployment benefits to members of Native American Church fired by private employer for use of peyote for sacramental purposes; ingestion of peyote prohibited under Oregon law). In response to *Smith*, Congress passed the Religious Freedom Restoration Act of 1993 (RFRA), 42 U.S.C. §2000bb (1996), which required—because even laws "neutral" toward religion may interfere with religious exercise—that such laws must satisfy a compelling governmental interest test. The Supreme Court struck down RFRA in City of Boerne v. Flores, 521 U.S.507 (1997).
101. Lee v. Weisman, 505 U.S. 577, 589–592 (1992).
102. West Virginia State Board of Education v. Barnette, 319 U.S. 624, 641–642 (1943).
103. 268 U.S. 510, 535 (1925).
104. Dailey, "Constitutional Privacy and the Just Family."
105. Troxel v. Granville, 530 U.S. 57, 65–69 (2000).
106. Planned Parenthood v. Casey, 505 U.S. 833, 851 (1992).
107. 539 U.S. 558 (2003) (overruling Bowers v. Hardwick, 478 U.S. 186 (1986)).
108. *Bowers*, 190–191.
109. *Lawrence*, 562, 578.
110. *Casey*, 847–853.
111. *Lawrence*, 562.
112. Laurence H. Tribe, "Lawrence v. Texas: The 'Fundamental Right' That Dare Not Speak Its Name," 117 *Harvard Law Review* 1893, 1898 (2004).
113. *Lawrence*, 567.
114. *Casey*, 850.
115. *Lawrence*, 571.
116. Maynard v. Hill, 125 U.S. 190, 205–206 (1888) (stating deep public interest in marriage because it is the foundation of family and society, civilization, and progress). Zablocki v. Redhail, 434 U.S. 374 (1978) (right to marry is fundamental, but it is subject to reasonable regulations).
117. Poe v. Ullman, 367 U.S. 497, 542 (1961) (Harlan, J., dissenting).
118. The famous Hart-Devlin debate on the legal enforcement of morality concerned arguments for intolerance, even when no direct harm to the rights of others is involved, because of society's right of self-protection of its moral code. Patrick Devlin, *The Enforcement of Morals* (New York: Oxford University Press, 1965), pp. 7–25; Hart, "Immorality and Treason," in Mill, *On Liberty*, p. 250.
119. Hart, "Immorality and Treason," pp. 246–247 (quoting Wolfendon Committee on Homosexual Offences and Prostitution Report).
120. For invocations of the right to be let alone as a foundation of the right of privacy: Roe v. Wade, 410 U.S. 113, 152 (1973); Stanley v. Georgia, 394 U.S.

557 (1969); Olmstead v. United States, 277 U.S. 438, 478 (1928) (Brandeis, J., dissenting). On the influence of Mill's *On Liberty* upon the right to privacy, see Glendon, *Rights Talk*, pp. 47–75.

121. *Poe*, 545–552 (Harlan, J., dissenting).

122. *Bowers*, 212–213 (Blackmun, J., dissenting).

123. *Lawrence*, 567, 572.

124. David D. Meyer, "Domesticating *Lawrence*," 2004 *University of Chicago Legal Forum* 445.

125. *Lawrence*, 578.

126. Sandel, *Democracy's Discontent*, p. 107.

127. Larry Cata Backer, "Exposing the Perversions of Toleration," 45 *Florida Law Review* 755, 786–796 (1993).

128. Romer v. Evans, 517 U.S. 620, 636–637 (1996) (Scalia, J., dissenting).

129. John Finnis, "Law, Morality, and 'Sexual Orientation,' " 69 *Notre Dame Law Review* 1049, 1049–1055 (1994).

130. *Casey*, 995 (Scalia, J., concurring in part, dissenting in part) (describing the "natural," though inaccurate, view that "if the Constitution guarantees abortion, how can it be bad?").

131. Gary Bauer, "Takeover, Not Tolerance, Is the Homosexual Agenda, but Marriage Is Not for Sale," PR Newswire, June 24, 1996 (remarks by president of Family Research Council on the Defense of Marriage Act).

132. *Romer*, 631–636.

133. *Lawrence*, 573–576.

134. *Goodridge*, 948–949, 958–959 (discussing *Lawrence*). Constitutional law scholar Cass Sunstein, by contrast, reads *Romer* as "minimalist"; that is, it prohibits sweeping, categorical exclusions against gay men and lesbians and leaves open the question of the constitutionality of more narrowly tailored measures distinguishing gay men and lesbians from other citizens. Cass R. Sunstein, "Foreword: Leaving Things Undecided," 110 *Harvard Law Review* 6, 53–71 (1996) (discussing *Romer*). And *Lawrence*, he argues, rests on desuetude; that is, the criminal law was rarely enforced and lacked a justification in contemporary values. Sunstein, "What Did *Lawrence* Hold?," 2003 *Supreme Court Review* 27.

135. MacKinnon, "Reflections on Sex Equality under Law," p. 1311.

136. West, *Progressive Constitutionalism*, pp. 105–128, 162–164; Higgins, "Democracy and Feminism," pp. 1671–1676.

137. Reva B. Siegel, " 'The Rule of Love': Wife Beating As Prerogative and Privacy," 105 *Yale Law Journal* 2117 (1996).

138. People v. Liberta, 474 N.E.2d 567 (N.Y. 1984); Pennsylvania v. Shoemaker, 518 A.2d 591 (Pa. Super. Ct. 1986); Williams v. State, 494 So. 2nd 819 (Ala. Crim. App. 1986).

139. *Casey*, 896–898.

140. Elizabeth M. Schneider, *Battered Women and Feminist Lawmaking* (New Haven, Conn.: Yale University Press, 2000), p. 228.

141. *Lawrence*, 578.

142. Anita L. Allen, "The Jurispolitics of Privacy," in Mary Lyndon Shanley and Uma Narayan, eds., *Reconstructing Political Theory: Feminist Perspectives* (University Park: Pennsylvania State University Press, 1997), pp. 68, 80–81.

143. Sager, *Justice in Plainclothes*, pp. 110–111.

144. The Violence Against Women Act of 2000, 42 U.S.C. §§13931–14040 (2000) (first enacted in 1994); United States v. Morrison, 529 U.S. 598 (2000).

145. Sally F. Goldfarb, "The Supreme Court, the Violence Against Women Act, and the Use and Abuse of Federalism," 71 *Fordham Law Review* 57 (2002); Judith Resnik, "Categorical Federalism," 111 *Yale Law Journal* 619 (2001).

146. Barbara Bennett Woodhouse, " 'Who Owns the Child?': *Meyer* and *Pierce* and the Child as Property," 33 *William & Mary Law Review* 995 (1992).

147. Dailey, "Constitutional Privacy and the Just Family," pp. 984–985.

148. In re Gault, 387 U.S. 1 (1967) (minors have rights to due process protections in delinquency proceedings); Tinker v. Des Moines Independent Community School District, 393 U.S. 503 (1969) (minors have rights to freedom of speech in schools); Bellotti v. Baird, 443 U.S. 622 (1979) (minor female's right to terminate pregnancy must not be unduly burdened by parental notice and consent laws).

149. *Troxel*, 88–91 (Stevens, J., dissenting).

150. *Lee*, 587–592; Lynch v. Donnelly, 465 U.S. 668, 678 (1984).

151. Steven Shiffrin, "Government Speech," 27 *UCLA Law Review* 565, 605–606 (1980) (rejecting Establishment Clause model for nonreligious speech).

152. 319 U.S. 624, 640–641 (1943). Some commentators argue that, in light of *Lee*, even a voluntary pledge of allegiance led by teachers in public schools is unconstitutional. Abner S. Greene, "The Pledge of Allegiance Problem," 64 *Fordham Law Review* 451 (1995). Dissenting in *Lee*, Justice Scalia argued that *Barnette* "did not even hint that [public school students] could not be compelled to observe respectful silence—indeed, even to stand in respectful silence—when those who wished to recite it did so." *Lee*, 638–639.

153. Michael W. McConnell, "The Selective Funding Problem: Abortions and Religious Schools," 104 *Harvard Law Review* 989, 1034–1036 (1991); Cass R. Sunstein, "Why the Unconstitutional Conditions Doctrine Is an Anachronism (With Particular Reference to Religion, Speech, and Abortion)," 70 *Boston University Law Review* 593, 606–610 (1990).

154. *Eisenstadt*, 453; *Casey*, 874–879. When fundamental constitutional rights are not at issue, for example, when government passes social or economic legislation, it may pursue "legitimate" governmental ends by any means "rationally related" to those ends. Williamson v. Lee Optical Co., 348 U.S. 483, 491 (1955).

155. Loving v. Virginia, 388 U.S. 1, 11 (1967).

156. 434 U.S. 374, 387 (1978).

157. Ibid., 386–387.

158. Carey v. Population Serv. Int'l, 431 U.S. 678, 694–695 (1977).

159. Ibid., 715 (Stevens, J., concurring).

160. Maher v. Roe, 432 U.S. 464 (1977); Harris v. McRae, 448 U.S. 297 (1980).

161. *Casey*, 877–879.

162. Mark G. Yudof, *When Government Speaks* (Berkeley: University of California Press, 1983).

163. Similarly, some scholars argue that a limiting principle for permissible governmental speech is whether it aids self-government, or fosters citizens' capacity for self-direction. Ibid., p. 34.

164. Locke, *A Letter Concerning Toleration*, pp. 16–19; Mill, *On Liberty*, pp. 11, 71; Raz, *The Morality of Freedom*, pp. 407–420; William Galston, *Liberal Purposes* (New York: Cambridge University Press, 1991), p. 222.

165. Ronald Dworkin, *Life's Dominion* (New York: Alfred A. Knopf, 1993), pp. 150–151.

166. Waldron, "Autonomy and Perfectionism in Raz's *Morality of Freedom*," pp. 1140–1143; Stephen Gardbaum, "Liberalism, Autonomy, and Moral Conflict," 48 *Stanford Law Review* 385, 398 (1996).

167. Yudof, *When Government Speaks*, p. 34.

168. Sandel, *Democracy's Discontent*, pp. 4–7.

169. Rawls, *Political Liberalism*, p. 205; Galston, *Liberal Purposes*; Stephen Macedo, *Liberal Virtues* (New York: Clarendon Press, 1990).

170. Rawls, *Political Liberalism*, pp. 194–195. Political liberalism also embraces "neutrality of aim": that society should not design basic institutions to favor any particular comprehensive doctrine. Ibid., pp. 191–194.

171. Raz, *The Morality of Freedom*, pp. 417–418.

172. Waldron, "Autonomy and Perfectionism in Raz's *Morality of Freedom*," p. 1149.

173. Thus, I disagree with the view that, pursuant to liberalism's ideal of political neutrality, the "constitutive ties" formed in marriage (versus marriage as a legal contract) are not "politically or legally relevant." See Charles Larmore, *Patterns of Moral Complexity* (New York: Cambridge University Press, 1987), p. 106.

174. Even some defenses of governmental persuasion about contested conceptions would rule out expressly religious arguments. See Abner S. Greene, "Government of the Good," 53 *Vanderbilt Law Review* 1 (2000).

175. Galston, *Liberal Purposes*, pp. 2–3, 283–287 (offering functional argument for favoring marriage); Iris Marion Young, "Mothers, Citizenship, and Independence: A Critique of Pure Family Values," 105 *Ethics* 535 (1995) (critiquing Galston's emphasis on marriage); Karen Struening, *New Family Values: Liberty, Equality, and Diversity* (Lanham, Md.: Rowman and Littlefield, 2002) (critiquing focus on marriage).

176. Drawing on Rawls to reach a similar conclusion is Drucilla Cornell, *At the Heart of Freedom* (Princeton, N.J.: Princeton University Press, 1998), pp. 11–17, 58–59.

## 2. Families as "Seedbeds of Civic Virtue"?

1. Robert D. Putnam, "Bowling Alone: America's Declining Social Capital," *Journal of Democracy* 65 (January 1995); Robert Putnam, *Bowling Alone* (New York: Simon & Schuster, 2000).

2. The Council on Civil Society, *A Call to Civil Society: Why Democracy Needs Moral Truths* (New York: Institute for American Values and the University of Chicago Divinity School, 1998), pp. 5–6; The National Commission on Civic Renewal, *A Nation of Spectators: How Civic Disengagement Weakens America and What We Can Do about It* (1998), pp. 5–6.

3. *A Call to Civil Society*, pp. 5–6; *A Nation of Spectators*, pp. 5–6.

4. *A Nation of Spectators*, pp. 13, 24; *A Call to Civil Society*, p. 18.

5. Mary Ann Glendon, *Rights Talk* (New York: The Free Press, 1991), pp. 110–120; Mary Ann Glendon, "Introduction: Forgotten Questions," in Mary Ann Glendon and David Blankenhorn, eds., *Seedbeds of Virtue: Sources of Competence, Character, and Citizenship in American Society* (Lanham, Md.: Madison Books,

1995), pp. 1–9; David Popenoe, "The Roots of Declining Social Virtue: Family, Community, and the Need for a 'Natural Communities Policy,' " in Glendon and Blankenhorn, eds., *Seedbeds of Virtue*, pp. 71–73.

6. *A Call to Civil Society*, p. 6.

7. Glendon, "Introduction: Forgotten Questions," p. 2.

8. *The Federalist*, No. 55 (James Madison), Clinton Rossiter, ed. (1961), p. 346 cited in Glendon, "Introduction: Forgotten Questions," p. 1; *A Nation of Spectators*, p. 4, 12; and *A Call to Civil Society*, p. 7.

9. John M. Broder, "For Hillary Clinton at 50, Yet Another Beginning," *New York Times*, October 26, 1997, §1 p. 20.

10. Todd S. Purdum, "Clinton Calls for Volunteers in Communities and Schools," *New York Times*, May 11, 1996, §1, p. 8.

11. White House, "Rallying the Armies of Compassion," January 2001, *www .whitehouse.gov* (accessed January 15, 2003). Both John DiIulio, the first director of the White House Office of Faith-Based and Community Initiatives (OFBCI), and Don Eberly, Deputy Director of OFBCI, were members of the Council on Civil Society and signatories to *A Call to Civil Society*. "Compassionate conservatism" and some civil society-revivalists support such partnerships. See *A Nation of Spectators*, p. 12; *A Call to Civil Society*, p. 21; Senator Rick Santorum, "A Compassionate Conservative Agenda: Addressing Poverty for the Next Millennium," 26 *Journal of Legislation* 93 (2000) (invoking John DiIulio).

12. "Statement by Wade F. Horn, Ph.D., Assistant Secretary for Children and Families, U.S. DHHS, on the International Year of the Family, in the General Assembly, December 6, 2004," USUN Press Release #272(04).

13. Elizabeth Norell, "Civil Society, Studied," *Foundation News & Commentary*, September–October 1997, p. 15.

14. Glendon, "Introduction: Forgotten Questions," p. 3; David Blankenhorn, "Conclusion: The Possibility of Civil Society," in Glendon and Blankenhorn, eds., *Seedbeds of Virtue*, pp. 271, 275; *A Call to Civil Society*, pp. 6–7.

15. *A Call to Civil Society*, p. 7.

16. *A Nation of Spectators*, pp. 12–19; *A Call to Civil Society*, pp. 6, 19–26.

17. *A Nation of Spectators*, p. 13.

18. *A Call to Civil Society*, p. 19.

19. Ibid., pp. 19–20. Glendon has criticized no-fault divorce law as "no responsibility" divorce (Glendon, *Rights Talk*, p. 107), and Galston has proposed "braking mechanisms" such as waiting periods. See William Galston, *Liberal Purposes* (New York: Cambridge University Press, 1991), p. 286.

20. *A Call to Civil Society*, pp. 15, 19.

21. Ibid., p. 24.

22. Glendon, *Rights Talk*, pp. 116–120. The "responsive communitarian" movement, with which Glendon has ties, makes similar claims. "The Responsive Communitarian Platform: Rights and Responsibilities," 2 *Responsive Community*, 4–5 (Winter 1991–1992).

23. Glendon, "Introduction: Forgotten Questions," p. 12.

24. Ibid.

25. *A Call to Civil Society*, p. 16.

26. *A Nation of Spectators*, p. 7.

27. Ibid.

28. Galston, *Liberal Purposes,* p. 269.

29. Ibid., pp. 267–270.

30. James Q. Wilson, "Liberalism, Modernism, and the Good Life," in Glendon and Blankenhorn, eds., *Seedbeds of Virtue,* pp. 17, 29.

31. James Q. Wilson, *The Marriage Problem* (New York: HarperCollins, 2002), pp. 92–105.

32. Nancy Cott, *Public Vows: A History of Marriage and the Nation* (Cambridge, Mass.: Harvard University Press, 2000), pp. 9–23.

33. Hendrik Hartog, *Man and Wife in America: A History* (Cambridge, Mass.: Harvard University Press, 2000), p. 101.

34. Linda Kerber, *Women of the Republic* (New York: W. W. Norton, 1980).

35. Linda Kerber, *No Constitutional Right to Be Ladies* (New York: Hill and Wang, 1998), pp. 8–15.

36. Peggy Cooper Davis, *Neglected Stories* (New York: Hill and Wang, 1997).

37. John Witte, Jr., *From Sacrament to Contract* (Louisville, Ky.: Westminster John Knox Press, 1997), pp. 131, 171–191.

38. Michael Grossberg, *Governing the Hearth* (Chapel Hill: University of North Carolina Press, 1985), pp. 7–8, 23.

39. Sandra F. VanBurkleo, *"Belonging to the World": Women's Rights and American Constitutional Culture* (New York: Oxford University Press, 2001).

40. Kerber, *No Constitutional Right to Be Ladies,* p. 12 (quoting letter, Abigail Adams to John Adams, May 31, 1776).

41. VanBurkleo, *"Belonging to the World,"* p. 110.

42. John Stuart Mill, *The Subjection of Women,* in John Stuart Mill and Harriet Taylor Mill, *Essays on Sex Equality* Alice S. Rossi, ed. (Chicago: University of Chicago Press, 1970), pp. 174–175. But for John Stuart Mill, marriage, shorn of despotism, still assigned to women the responsibilities of domesticity. Ibid., pp. 179–180.

43. David A. J. Richards, *Women, Gays, and the Constitution* (Chicago: University of Chicago Press, 1998); Cott, *Public Vows,* pp. 57–68.

44. Witte, *From Sacrament to Contract,* p. 208.

45. Grossberg, *Governing the Hearth,* pp. 300–304.

46. VanBurkleo, *"Belonging to the World,"* p. 169 (quoting antisuffrage arguments made by Orestes Brownson in 1869 and 1873).

47. Cott, *Public Vows,* pp. 92–93, 122. These conventional gender roles were in tension with the economic conditions of African American life, which made wives' market labor necessary for survival. Peggy Cooper Davis and Carol Gilligan, "Reconstructing Law and Marriage," 11 *The Good Society,* 62–64 (No. 2, 2002).

48. Cott, *Public Vows,* pp. 132–155.

49. Hoyt v. Florida, 368 U.S. 57 (1961).

50. Cott, *Public Vows,* pp. 156–179.

51. For example, the Ohio Revised Code of 1973 stated: "The husband is the head of the family. He may choose any reasonable place or mode of living and the wife must conform thereto." Ohio Revised Code Annotated §3103.02 (Baldwin, 1973).

52. Orr v. Orr, 440 U.S. 268, 279 n.9 (1979).

53. Stanton v. Stanton, 421 U.S. 7, 14–15 (1975).

54. Laurence H. Tribe, *American Constitutional Law* (Mineola, N.Y.: Foundation Press, 2nd ed., 1988), p. 1565 (footnotes omitted).

55. United States v. Virginia, 518 U.S. 515, 524 (1996) (quoting Mississippi University for Women v. Hogan, 458 U.S. 718, 724 (1982)).

56. Kirchberg v. Feenstra, 450 U.S. 455 (1981) (striking down Louisiana community property law treating husband as "head and master" of property jointly owned with wife).

57. Planned Parenthood v. Casey, 505 U.S. 833, 897–898 (1992). Thus, Linda Kerber invokes the repudiation of the patriarchal marriage relation in *Casey* as "the moment when coverture, as a living legal principle, died." See Kerber, *No Constitutional Right to Be Ladies*, p. 307.

58. Center for Civic Education, "The Role of Civic Education: A Report of the Task Force on Civic Education" (1995) (prepared for Second Annual White House Conference on Character Building for a Democratic, Civil Society, May 19–20, 1995), pp. 4, 8; *CIVITAS: A Framework for Civic Education*, Charles F. Bahmueller, gen. ed. (Calabasas, Calif.: Center for Civic Education, 1991), pp. 3–8; Rosemary C. Salomone, *Visions of Schooling* (New Haven, Conn.: Yale University Press, 2000), pp. 228–234; "Symposium: Civics Education and America's Founding Documents," 175 *Journal of Education* 5–129 (1993).

59. *CIVITAS*, pp. 375–376.

60. Ibid., pp. 262–276. For example, Stephen Macedo's otherwise excellent book, *Liberal Virtues* (New York: Oxford University Press, 1990), has little explicit discussion of sex equality. One notable counterexample is Toni Marie Massaro, *Constitutional Literacy* (Durham, NC: Duke University Press, 1993), pp. 116–121, 128–153.

61. Holloway Sparks, "Dissident Citizenship: Democratic Theory, Political Courage, and Activist Women," 12 *Hypatia* 74, 75 (Fall 1997).

62. Reva B. Siegel, "Collective Memory and the Nineteenth Amendment," in Austin Sarat and Thomas R. Kearns, eds., *History, Memory, and the Law* (Ann Arbor: University of Michigan Press, 1999), p. 131.

63. Richards, *Women, Gays, and the Constitution*, pp. 224–233; Jill Elaine Hasday, "Contest and Consent: A Legal History of Marital Rape," 88 *California Law Review* 1373 (2000); Siegel, "Collective Memory and the Nineteenth Amendment," pp. 173–174, 181–182.

64. *A Call to Civil Society*, p. 5.

65. Glendon, *Rights Talk*, p. 174; William A. Galston, "Won't You Be My Neighbor?" *American Prospect*, 17 (May–June 1996). A helpful history appears in Kathryn Kish Sklar, "A Historical Model of Women's Voluntarism," in Robert K. Fullinwider, ed., *Civil Society, Democracy, and Civic Renewal* (Lanham, Md.: Rowman & Littlefield., 1999), p. 185.

66. David Blankenhorn et al., eds., *Rebuilding the Nest: A New Commitment to the American Family* (Milwaukee, Wis.: Family Service America, 1990), p. xii.

67. These issues do not feature in the agendas of two task force reports, *A Call to Civil Society* and *A Nation of Spectators*. Responding to this critique, Galston states: "[d]omestic violence is not a private matter, and it cannot be condoned." William Galston, "Civil Society, Civic Virtue, and Liberal Democracy," 75 *Chicago-Kent Law Review* 607–608 (2000).

68. Michael Schudson, *The Good Citizen* (Cambridge, Mass.: Harvard University Press, 1998), pp. 291, 302.

69. Rogers M. Smith, *Civic Ideals: Conflicting Visions of Citizenship in U.S. History* (New Haven, Conn.: Yale University Press, 1997), p. 2.

70. Loving v. Virginia, 388 U.S. 1 (1967) (striking down as unconstitutional Virginia's miscegenation law).

71. Rachel Moran, *Interracial Intimacy* (Chicago: University of Chicago Press, 2001), p. 30 (discussing restrictions on Chinese immigrants).

72. Dorothy E. Roberts, "The Moral Exclusivity of the New Civil Society," 75 *Chicago-Kent Law Review* 555 (2000).

73. Kerber, *No Constitutional Right to Be Ladies*, pp. 161–185.

74. Richard Dagger, *Civic Virtues* (New York: Oxford University Press, 1997), p. 13.

75. Michael J. Sandel, *Democracy's Discontent* (Cambridge, Mass.: Belknap Press of Harvard University Press, 1996), p. 25; "The Role of Civic Education," p. 10.

76. Stephen Macedo, *Diversity and Distrust* (Cambridge, Mass.: Harvard University Press, 2000), p. 10

77. *CIVITAS*, p. 11.

78. Ibid.

79. John Rawls, *Political Liberalism* (New York: Columbia University Press, 1993), pp. 194–195.

80. *A Call to Civil Society*, pp. 6–7.

81. Ibid., p. 7; Glendon, "Introduction: Forgotten Questions," p. 2 ("first and foremost among these 'seedbeds of virtue' is the family").

82. *A Nation of Spectators*, p. 12.

83. *Webster's Ninth New Collegiate Dictionary* (Springfield, Mass.: Merriam-Webster, 1987), p. 1062 (defining "seedbed" as "a place or source of growth or development").

84. Macedo, *Liberal Virtues*, p. 272.

85. Rawls, *Political Liberalism*, p. 14; John Rawls, "The Idea of Public Reason Revisited," 64 *University of Chicago Law Review* 765, 788 (1997).

86. Nancy Rosenblum refers to Rawls's assumption about the effects of associational life as an example of "liberal expectancy." Nancy L. Rosenblum, *Membership and Morals* (Princeton, N.J.: Princeton University Press, 1998), pp. 51–53.

87. Press Release, "The White House at Work, The Clinton-Gore Administration: Working to Help Families Raise Responsible Teenagers" (May 2, 2000).

88. Council of Economic Advisers, *Teens and Their Parents in the 21st Century: An Examination of Trends in Teen Behavior and the Role of Parental Involvement* (2000), pp. 2, 18–23. For more recent studies, see Laurie Tarkan, "Benefits of the Dinner Table Ritual," *New York Times*, May 3, 2005, p. F9 (summarizing studies).

89. Putnam, *Bowling Alone*, p. 100 (reporting that "[t]he fraction of married Americans who say 'definitely' that 'our whole family usually eats dinner together' has declined by a third over the last twenty years, from about 50 percent to 34 percent").

90. Glendon, *Rights Talk*, p. 174.

91. *Teens and Their Parents*, pp. 18–23.

92. Dennis R. Papini, "Family Interventions," in Sally L. Archer, ed., *Interventions for Adolescent Identity Development* (Thousand Oaks, Calif.: SAGE Publications 1994), pp. 47, 52; Urie Bronfenbrenner, "Discovering What Families Do," in Blankenhorn et al., eds., *Rebuilding the Nest*, pp. 27–38; David Popenoe,

"The Roots of Declining Social Virtue," in Glendon and Blankenhorn, eds., *Seedbeds of Virtue*, pp. 71, 74–79.

93. Jennifer L. Wainright, Stephen T. Russell, and Charlotte J. Patterson, "Psychological Adjustment, School Outcomes, and Romantic Relationships of Adolescents With Same-Sex Parents," 75 *Child Development* 1886, 1897 (2004).

94. Meira Levinson, *The Demands of Liberal Education* (New York: Oxford University Press, 1999), pp. 103–104; Macedo, *Diversity and Distrust*, p. 239; Eamonn Callan, *Creating Citizens* (New York: Oxford University Press, 1997).

95. *A Call to Civil Society*, p. 10.

96. William Damon, *The Moral Child* (New York: The Free Press, 1988), p. 52.

97. Ibid., pp. 65–67.

98. Amy Gutmann, *Democratic Education* (Princeton, N.J.: Princeton University Press, 1987), pp. 50–52.

99. Damon, *The Moral Child*, p. 119.

100. Ibid., p. 116.

101. Ibid., p. 145.

102. "The Role of Civic Education," p. 5.

103. Macedo, *Diversity and Distrust*, p. 239.

104. Steven Gilles, "A Parentalist Manifesto," 63 *University of Chicago Law Review* 937, 949 (1996).

105. Ibid., pp. 976–977.

106. Macedo, *Diversity and Distrust*, p. 233. Two cases, in particular, exemplify this dilemma and have sparked enormous debate. Wisconsin v. Yoder, 406 U.S. 205 (1972) (holding that compulsory high school attendance up to age 16 as applied to Amish children violated the Amish parents' rights to free exercise of religion and parental liberty); Mozert v. Hawkins, 827 F.2d 1058 (6th Cir. 1987) (rejecting fundamentalist parents' challenge to compulsory "character education" program that conflicted with their religious beliefs).

107. Levinson, *The Demands of Liberal Education*; Macedo, *Diversity and Distrust*; Gutmann, *Democratic Education*.

108. Susan Moller Okin and Rob Reich, "Families and Schools as Compensating Agents in Moral Development for a Multicultural Society," 28 *Journal of Moral Education* 283, 286–290 (1999).

109. Galston, *Liberal Purposes*, pp. 255–256.

110. Galston, "Civil Society, Civic Virtue, and Liberal Democracy," pp. 604–605.

111. Gilles, "A Parentalist Manifesto," p. 997.

112. Callan, *Creating Citizens*, p. 9.

113. Gilles, "A Parentalist Manifesto," p. 997.

114. Damon, *The Moral Child*, p. 14.

115. Ibid., pp. 16–17.

116. Levinson, *The Demands of Liberal Education*, pp. 34–35.

117. Mark Mellman, Edward Lazarus, and Allan Rivlin, "Family Time, Family Values," in Blankenhorn et al., eds., *Rebuilding the Nest*, pp. 73, 81–82.

118. Don Browning, "Altruism, Civic Virtue, and Religion," in Glendon and Blankenhorn, eds., *Seedbeds of Virtue*, p. 116.

119. Putnam, *Bowling Alone*, pp. 134–135.

120. Dagger, *Civic Virtues*, p. 197.

121. Susan Moller Okin, "Reason and Feeling in Thinking about Justice," 99 *Ethics* 229, 236–237 (1989) (discussing John Rawls, *A Theory of Justice*, 1971).

122. Ruthellen Josselson, *Finding Herself* (San Francisco, Calif.: Jossey-Bass, 1987), p. 65.

123. Putnam, *Bowling Alone*, pp. 22–23.

124. Robert Coles, *The Story of Ruby Bridges* (New York: Scholastic, 1995); Robin West, *Caring for Justice* (New York: New York University Press, 1997), p. 75 (critiquing this conduct as parental care unconstrained by an ethic of justice).

125. Scott Coltrane, "Research on Household Labor: Modeling and Measuring the Social Embeddedness of Routine Family Work," 62 *Journal of Marriage & the Family* 1208 (2000); Janet C. Gornick and Marcia K. Meyers, *Families That Work* (New York: Russell Sage Foundation, 2003).

126. Janice M. Steil, *Marital Equality* (Thousand Oaks, Calif.: Sage Publications, 1997); Philip Blumstein and Pepper Schwartz, *American Couples* (New York: William Morrow, 1983).

127. Susan Moller Okin, "*Political Liberalism*, Justice, and Gender," 105 *Ethics* 23, 38 (1994).

128. Okin and Reich, "Families and Schools as Compensating Agents," pp. 286–290.

129. Damon, *The Moral Child*, p. 68.

130. Susan Moller Okin, *Justice, Gender, and the Family* (New York: Basic Books, 1989), p. 183.

131. Susan Moller Okin, "Thinking Like a Woman," in Deborah L. Rhode, ed., *Theoretical Perspectives on Sexual Difference* (New Haven, Conn.: Yale University Press, 1990), p. 146.

132. *A Nation of Spectators*, p. 41.

133. Nancy L. Rosenblum, "Democratic Families," 32 *Hofstra Law Review* 145, 151 (2003).

134. *A Nation of Spectators*, p. 41.

135. Rosenblum, "Democratic Families," pp. 154–155.

136. William Galston, "Liberal Virtues and the Formation of Civic Character," in Glendon and Blankenhorn, eds., *Seedbeds of Virtue*, pp. 56–57.

137. *CIVITAS*, pp. 258–277. The discussion of "Gender Issues" is part of a section on "Politics and Government." The sections on "Equality" as a fundamental value include political, social, legal, and economic equality, but do not refer to gender, race, or any similar category. Ibid., pp. 375–376.

138. Ibid., pp. 273, 276.

139. Salomone, *Visions of Schooling*, pp. 235–237.

140. Mary Anne Case, "Reflections on Constitutionalizing Women's Equality," 90 *California Law Review* 765, 786 (2002).

141. Kathleen Sullivan, "Constitutionalizing Women's Equality," 90 *California Law Review* 735, 755 (2002).

142. Martha C. Nussbaum, *Women and Human Development: The Capabilities Approach* (New York: Cambridge University Press, 2000), pp. 279–280.

143. Griswold v. Connecticut, 381 U.S. 479, 485–486 (1965).

144. Okin, *Justice, Gender, and the Family*, pp. 172–181.

145. For example, New York City has carried out prominent public awareness

campaigns along these lines (for example, with dramatic subway advertisements) and enacted the first municipal civil rights law in the nation protecting against gender-motivated violence. See Nina Bernstein, "Council Readies Unique Sex Bias Measure," *New York Times*, December 1, 2000, p. B3.

146. Nussbaum, *Women and Human Development*, pp. 280–283 (emphasis added).

147. Roberta S. Sigel, *Ambition and Accommodation* (Chicago: University of Chicago Press, 1996), p. 191.

148. Gornick and Meyers, *Families That Work*, pp. 119–120; Joanna L. Grossman, "Job Security Without Equality: The Family Medical Leave Act of 1993," 15 *Washington University Journal of Law & Policy* 17 (2004).

149. Edward J. McCaffery, *Taxing Women* (Chicago: University of Chicago Press, 1997); Mary E. Becker, "Obscuring the Struggle," 89 *Columbia Law Review* 264 (1989) (social security law).

150. Rawls, "The Idea of Public Reason Revisited," pp. 791–793.

151. Okin, *Justice, Gender, and the Family*, pp. 181–182. One ameliorative—and controversial—proposal she made is for mandatory wage-splitting in "two-parent families who do not believe in or wish to practice shared parental roles." Ibid. For a critique, see Ian Shapiro, *Democratic Justice* (New Haven, Conn.: Yale University Press, 1999), pp. 117–122.

152. Nussbaum, *Women and Human Development*, p. 275.

153. Robert H. Mnookin and D. Kelly Weisberg, *Child, Family, and State: Problems and Materials on Children and the Law* (New York: Aspen Law and Business, 4th ed., 2000), pp. 310–329 (discussing provision of education as part of parental support obligation).

154. Prince v. Massachusetts, 321 U.S. 158 (1944) (upholding against constitutional challenge application of state law prohibiting child labor to child distributing religious pamphlets).

155. Okin, "*Political Liberalism*, Justice, and Gender," pp. 30–31; see Rawls, *Political Liberalism*, p. xxix ("The same equality of the Declaration of Independence which Lincoln invoked to condemn slavery can be invoked to condemn the inequality and oppression of women."). Nonetheless, Okin and Nussbaum find Rawls's account of toleration too permissive toward sex inequality in civil society. Okin, "*Political Liberalism*, Justice, and Gender"; Nussbaum, *Women and Human Development*, pp. 270–283.

156. Clifford Krauss, "When the Koran Speaks, Will Canadian Law Bend?" *New York Times*, August 4, 2004, p. A4; Joshua Cohen et al., eds., *Is Multiculturalism Bad for Women?* (Princeton, N.J.: Princeton University Press, 1999).

157. Okin and Reich, "Families and Schools as Compensating Agents."

158. Stephen Holmes, *Passions and Constraints* (Chicago: University of Chicago Press, 1995), p. 262.

159. Rosenblum, "Democratic Families," p. 153.

160. Pierce v. Society of Sisters, 268 U.S. 510 (1925).

161. *A Nation of Spectators*, p. 14.

162. Rosenblum, "Democratic Families," p. 155.

163. Levinson, *The Demands of Liberal Education*, pp. 57–63.

164. One way to reconcile parental autonomy (in choosing private schools) with government's interest might be to allow private schools discretion concerning curriculum but have students take an examination evaluating their civic literacy.

Richard W. Garnett, "Regulatory Strings and Religious Freedom," in Patrick J. Wolf and Stephen Macedo, eds., *Educating Citizens* (Washington, D.C.: Brookings Institution Press, 2004), p. 332 (discussing system in Alberta, Canada).

165. Amy Gutmann and Dennis Thompson, *Democracy and Disagreement* (Cambridge, Mass.: Belknap Press of Harvard University Press, 1996), pp. 63–67.

166. Gilles, "A Parentalist Manifesto," p. 987.

167. Massaro, *Constitutional Literacy*, pp. 140–141.

168. Abner S. Greene, "Civil Society and Multiple Repositories of Power," 75 *Chicago-Kent Law Review* 477 (2000).

169. Martha Albertson Fineman, *The Neutered Mother, the Sexual Family and Other Twentieth Century Tragedies* (New York: Routledge, 1995), pp. 177–193 (discussing lack of privacy accorded families headed by single mothers).

170. Jane Mansbridge, "Using Power/Fighting Power: The Polity," in Seyla Benhabib, ed., *Democracy and Difference* (Princeton, N.J.: Princeton University Press, 1996), pp. 46, 55.

171. Patricia Hill Collins, "Shifting the Center: Race, Class, and Feminist Theorizing about Motherhood," in Evelyn Nakano Glenn et al., eds., *Mothering: Ideology, Experience, and Agency* (New York: Routledge, 1994); Fredrick C. Harris, "Will the Circle Be Unbroken? The Erosion and Transformation of African-American Civic Life," in Fullenwider, ed., *Civil Society, Democracy, and Civic Renewal*, 317, 323–324 (describing "oppositional civic culture" characteristic of African Americans' civic life).

172. Kath Weston, *Families We Choose: Lesbians, Gays, Kinship* (New York: Columbia University Pres, 1991); Suzanne Slater, *The Lesbian Family Life Cycle* (New York: The Free Press, 1995).

173. But Rosenblum, who did not study families, concludes that participation in associations encourages a "democracy of everyday life," including the virtue of reciprocity. Rosenblum, *Membership and Morals*, pp. 8–10, 15–17, 349–363.

174. Rosenblum, "Democratic Families," pp. 146, 156.

175. Andrew Cherlin, "Going to Extremes: Family Structure, Children's Well-Being, and Social Science," 36 *Demography* 421 (1999).

176. Barbara Risman, *Gender Vertigo* (New Haven, Conn.: Yale University Press, 1998).

177. Levinson, *The Demands of Liberal Education*, 57.

178. S. A. Lloyd, "Situating a Feminist Criticism of John Rawls's *Political Liberalism*," 28 *Loyola of Los Angeles Law Review* 1319 (1995).

179. Nussbaum, *Women and Human Development*, p. 121; Uma Narayan, *Dislocating Cultures* (New York: Routledge, 1997), p. 11.

180. Rosenblum, "Democratic Families," p. 157.

## 3. Care, Families, and Self-Government

1. Report of the Platform Committee, *Strong at Home, Respected in the World: The Democratic Platform for America*, July 10, 2004, p. 27.

2. White House, "Working Toward Independence" (2002), *www.whitehouse.gov* (accessed August 10, 2004).

3. Jerry A. Jacobs and Kathleen Gerson, *The Time Divide: Work, Family, and Gender Inequality* (Cambridge, Mass.: Harvard University Press, 2004), p. 166.

4. Mona Harrington, *Care and Equality* (New York: Routledge, 1999), p. 39.

5. United Nations Development Programme, "The Invisible Heart—Care and the Global Economy," in *Human Development Report 1999* (1999): 77, 79; *Care and Equality*, p. 49; Berenice Fisher and Joan Tronto, "Toward a Feminist Theory of Caring," in Emily K. Abel and Margaret K. Nelson, eds., *Circles of Care* (New York: State University of New York Press, 1990), pp. 35, 40 ("On the most general level, . . . *caring [is] a species activity that includes everything that we do to maintain, continue, and repair our 'world' so that we can live in it as well as possible.*").

6. Harrington, *Care and Equality*, p. 48; Mary Becker, "Towards a Progressive Politics and A Progressive Constitution," 69 *Fordham Law Review* 2007, 2040–2041 (2001) (invoking Harrington and arguing for a "politics of care").

7. Deborah Stone, "Why We Need a Care Movement," *Nation* (March 13, 2000), pp. 13, 15.

8. Fisher and Tronto, "Toward a Feminist Theory of Caring," pp. 40–46.

9. John Rawls, "The Idea of Public Reason Revisited," 64 *University of Chicago Law Review* 765, 788 (1997).

10. Martha Fineman, *The Neutered Mother, the Sexual Family, and Other Twentieth-Century Tragedies* (New York: Routledge, 1995), pp. 161–163; Eva Feder Kittay, *Love's Labor* (New York: Routledge, 1999), pp. 29–42 (positing "inescapable" and "derived" dependency).

11. Paula England and Nancy Folbre, "Who Should Pay for the Kids?" 563 *Annals of the American Academy of Political and Social Science* 194 (1999).

12. Marcy Whitebook, "The Silent Crisis in U.S. Child Care: Child Care Workers: High Demand, Low Wages," 563 *Annals of the American Academy of Political and Social Science* 146, 159 (May 1999).

13. Martha Albertson Fineman, *The Autonomy Myth: A Theory of Dependency* (New York: The New Press, 2004), pp. 50, 284–287.

14. For a recent affirmation of this constitutional liberty, see Troxel v. Granville, 530 U.S. 57, 64–66 (2000) (also citing earlier precedents).

15. John Rawls, *Political Liberalism* (New York: Columbia University Press, 1993), pp. 187–190; John Rawls, *A Theory of Justice* (Cambridge, Mass.: Harvard University Press, 1971), pp. 90–95; Marsha Garrison, "Toward a Contractarian Account of Family Governance," 1998 *Utah Law Review* 241, 257–261 (making a Rawlsian argument for "governance principles that will ensure each child a fair opportunity of attaining a fruitful, self-selected adulthood").

16. Kittay, *Love's Labor*, pp. 102–113; Amy R. Baehr, "Feminist Politics and Feminist Pluralism: Can We Do Feminist Political Theory Without Theories of Gender?" 12 *Journal of Political Philosophy* 411–436 (2004); Susan Moller Okin, *Justice, Gender, and the Family* (New York: Basic Books, 1989), pp. 106–109.

17. Harrington, *Care and Equality*, pp. 177–187.

18. Martha A. Fineman, "What Place for Family Privacy?" 67 *George Washington Law Review* 1207, 1207–1209 (1999).

19. Fineman, *The Autonomy Myth*, p. 7.

20. Michael J. Sandel, *Democracy's Discontent* (Cambridge, Mass.: Belknap Press of Harvard University Press, 1996), p. 25.

21. William E. Forbath, "Caste, Class, and Equal Citizenship," 98 *Michigan Law Review* 1 (1999). Many contemporary discussions of "social citizenship" invoke T. H. Marshall's description of citizenship as entailing civil rights, political rights, and social rights, or "the right to share to the full in the social heritage

and to live the life of a civilized being according to the standards prevailing in the society." See T. H. Marshall, *Citizenship and Social Class* (Cambridge: Cambridge University Press, 1950), pp. 10–11. President Franklin Delano Roosevelt spoke of a "second bill of rights" that included social rights, such as freedom from want. See Cass R. Sunstein, *The Second Bill of Rights* (New York: Basic Books, 2004).

22. Sandel, *Democracy's Discontent*, pp. 123–316. For example, Sandel quotes Louis Brandeis on industrial policy: "It is the development of manhood to which any industrial and social system should be directed." Ibid., p. 213.

23. Linda K. Kerber, *Women of the Republic: Intellect and Ideology in Revolutionary America* (Chapel Hill: University of North Carolina Press, 1980); Nancy F. Cott, *The Bonds of Womanhood: "Women's Sphere" in New England, 1780–1835* (New Haven, Conn.: Yale University Press, 1977).

24. Forbath, "Caste, Class, and Equal Citizenship," p. 8. Forbath continues: "Nor did the servant's or hireling's labor equip him for citizenship in the eyes of Jefferson, Madison, or most other eighteenth-century political thinkers." Ibid.

25. Kerber, *Women of the Republic*, pp. 11–12.

26. Nancy Fraser and Linda Gordon, "A Genealogy of Dependency: Tracing a Keyword of the U.S. Welfare State," 19 *Signs* 309 (1994).

27. Forbath, "Caste, Class, and Equal Citizenship," p. 1. Vicki Schultz argues for a right to participate meaningfully in life-sustaining work because of the importance of work to citizenship, community, and personal identity. Vicki Schultz, "Life's Work," 100 *Columbia Law Review* 1881 (2000).

28. Sandel, *Democracy's Discontent*, pp. 205–208, 233–234; Forbath, "Caste, Class, and Citizenship," pp. 3–4.

29. Joel Handler, "Low-Wage Work 'as We Know It': What's Wrong/What Can Be Done," in Joel F. Handler and Lucie White, eds., *Hard Labor: Women and Work in the Post-Welfare Era* (New York: M. E. Sharpe, 1999), pp. 3, 5–6 (defining a "good job" as paying "at least $8 an hour for at least 35 hours of work a week"); Shawn Fremstad, "Recent Welfare Reform Research Findings" (Center on Budget and Policy Priorities, January 30, 2004), p. 3 (reporting definition of "good jobs" as full-time jobs paying at least $7 per hour with health insurance or, without insurance, at least $8.50 per hour).

30. Department of Workforce Development, *An Evaluation: Wisconsin Works (W-2) Program* (April 2005), pp. 62, 104.

31. On the struggles of the working poor: Barbara Ehrenreich, *Nickel and Dimed: On (Not) Getting By in America* (New York: Metropolitan Books, 2001); David Shipler, *The Working Poor* (New York: Alfred A. Knopf, 2004).

32. Sharon Hays, *Flat Broke with Children* (New York: Oxford University Press, 2003), p. 61; Karen Syma Czapanskiy, "Parents, Children, and Work-First Welfare Reform: Where Is the C in TANF?" 61 *University of Maryland* 308 (2002).

33. Forbath, "Caste, Class, and Citizenship," pp. 23–62; Kenneth L. Karst, "The Coming Crisis of Work in Constitutional Perspective," 82 *Cornell Law Review* 523, 552–559, 570–571 (1997); Schultz, "Life's Work," p. 1883.

34. "The Democratic Platform for America," p. 19.

35. Fineman, *The Autonomy Myth*, p. 280.

36. Janet Gornick and Marcia Meyers, *Families That Work* (New York: Russell Sage Foundation, 2003), p. 88; Alice Kessler-Harris, *In Pursuit of Equity: Women,*

*Men, and the Quest for Economic Citizenship in 20th Century America* (New York: Oxford University Press, 2002).

37. Gornick and Meyers, *Families That Work*, pp. 89–111; Fineman, *The Autonomy Myth*, p. 280.

38. Amara Bachu and Martin O'Connell, U.S. Census Bureau, "Fertility of American Women: Population Characteristics: June 1998" (September 2000), p. 9; Bureau of Labor Statistics, "Employment Characteristics of Families in 2002," *News: U.S. Department of Labor* (July 9, 2003), pp. 1–2, www.bls.gov (accessed November 15, 2004).

39. Harrington, *Care and Equality*, p. 17.

40. Jacobs and Gerson, *The Time Divide*, pp. 161–168; Ann Crittenden, *The Price of Motherhood* (New York: Henry Holt and Co., 2001).

41. Annie E. Casey Foundation, *Kids Count Data Book* (1998), p. 5; Bachu and O'Connell, "Fertility of American Women," p. 8 (reporting 1998 Census Bureau data); Ellen E. Kisker and Christine M. Ross, "Arranging Child Care," 7 *The Future of Children* 99, 103–104 (1997); Joan Lombardi, *Time to Care: Redesigning Child Care* (Philadelphia, Penn.: Temple University Press, 2003), pp. 2–14; Melissa Ludtke, *On Our Own: Unmarried Motherhood in America* (New York: Random House, 1997), pp. 175–177.

42. Marcy Whitebook et al., *Worthy Work, Unlivable Wages: The National Child Care Staffing Study, 1988–1997* (Center for the Child Care Workforce, 1998), p. 7 (finding that only 16 percent of child-care centers that employ TANF recipients offer college-credit-bearing training, the best avenue to better-paying child-care jobs); Marcy Whitebook and Deborah Phillips, "Child Care Employment: Implications for Women's Self-Sufficiency and for Child Development" (Foundation for Child Development, Working Paper Series, January 1999); Whitebook, "The Silent Crisis in U.S. Child Care," pp. 154–155; Annie E. Casey Foundation, *Kids Count Data Book*, pp. 10–11; Lucie White, "Quality Care for Low-Income Families: Despair, Impasse, Improvisation," in Handler and White, eds., *Hard Labor*, pp. 116, 124–125.

43. U.S. General Accounting Office, *Welfare Reform: Implications of Increased Work Participation for Child Care* (GAO/HEHS-97-75, May 1997), pp. 3, 8–16; U.S. General Accounting Office, *Welfare Reform: States' Efforts to Expand Child Care Programs* (GAO/HEHS-98-27, January 1998), p. 4; S. Jody Heymann, "Work and Parenting: The Widening Gap," *CLASP Update* (Center for Law & Social Policy, April 2001), pp. 1, 3 (reporting on eight years of research on low-income families); Karen DeBord et al., "Understanding a Work-Family Fit for Single Parents Moving from Welfare to Work," 45 *Social Work* 313 (2000), available at 2000 WL 10784697; Margy Waller, "Welfare, Working Families, and Reauthorization: Mayors' Views" (The Brookings Institution, Survey Series, May 2003), p. 5; Annie E. Casey Foundation, *Kids Count Data Book*, p. 10 ("Nationwide, businesses lose $3 billion each year because of child care-related absenteeism, turnover, and lost productivity.").

44. Lisa Dodson, Tiffany Manuel, and Ellen Bravo, *Keeping Jobs and Raising Families in Low-Income America: It Just Doesn't Work* (2002), p. 3. An earlier study similarly described child care as a "perpetual emergency" for low-income working families. See Annie E. Casey Foundation, *Kids Count Data Book*, p. 6.

45. Dodson, Manuel, and Bravo, *It Just Doesn't Work*, p. 1.

46. Lisa A. Gennetian et al., *How Welfare and Work Policies for Parents Affect Adolescents: A Synthesis of Research* (Manpower Demonstration Research Cooperative, May 2002), pp. 12–15; Katherine Boo, "After Welfare," *The New Yorker* (April 9, 2001), p. 93.

47. Annie E. Casey Foundation, *Kids Count Data Book*, pp. 10–11; White, "Quality Child Care for Low-Income Families," pp. 124–125.

48. Boo, "After Welfare," p. 100 (reporting on District of Columbia neighborhood called "the Shrimp Boat").

49. Toby L. Parcel and Elizabeth G. Menaghan, "Effects of Low-Wage Employment on Family Well-Being," 7 *The Future of Children* 116, 116–117 (1997); Martha J. Zaslow and Carol A. Emig, "When Low-Income Mothers Go to Work: Implications for Children," 7 *The Future of Children* 110, 110–115 (1997).

50. Gennetian, *How Welfare and Work Policies for Parents Affect Adolescents*, p. iii.

51. Sharon Vandivere et al., "Left Unsupervised: A Look at the Most Vulnerable Children" (ChildTrends Research Brief, 2003) (children under age 13 in "self-care").

52. David T. Ellwood, "Anti-Poverty Policy for Families in the Next Century: From Welfare to Work—and Worries," 14 *Journal of Economic Perspectives* 187 (Winter 2000); "Testimony by Tommy G. Thompson, Secretary, Department of Health and Human Services, before Senate Finance Committee Hearing on Welfare" (March 12, 2003), *www.dhhs.gov* (accessed August 11, 2003); "Testimony of Ron Haskins, Senior Fellow, Brookings Institution, in Hearing on House Budget Committee" (August 1, 2001).

53. Will Marshall and Anne Kim, "Finishing the Welfare Revolution" (Progressive Policy Institute Policy Brief, January 2002), p. 2; *The Democratic Platform for America*, p. 24.

54. White House, "Working Toward Independence," p. 14.

55. "Testimony by Tommy G. Thompson."

56. The 2004 Democratic Platform mentions—in the context not of welfare reform but of helping families cope with rising child-care costs—expanding family and medical leave to help parents balance work and family responsibilities. See *The Democratic Platform for America*, p. 23.

57. White House, "Working Toward Independence," 15–16.

58. William Blackstone, *Commentaries on the Law of England*, 1: *430–445 (1765).

59. Kerber, *Women of the Republic*, pp. xx–xxiv, pp. 11–15; Theda Skocpol, *Protecting Soldiers and Mothers* (Cambridge, Mass.: Belknap Press of Harvard University Press, 1992), pp. 322–343; Barbara Welter, "The Cult of True Womanhood: 1820–1860," in Michael Gordon, ed., *The American Family in Social-Historical Perspective* (New York: St. Martin's Press, 1973), p. 255.

60. Hoyt v. Florida, 368 U.S. 57, 61–62 (1961); Deborah L. Rhode, *Justice and Gender* (Cambridge, Mass.: Harvard University Press, 1989).

61. Nevada Department of Human Resources v. Hibbs, 538 U.S. 721, 729 (2003).

62. Reva B. Siegel, "Home as Work: The First Woman's Rights Claims Concerning Wives' Household Labor, 1850–1880," 103 *Yale Law Journal* 1073 (1994).

63. Katharine Silbaugh, "Turning Labor into Love: Housework and the Law,"

91 *Northwestern University Law Review* 1 (1996); Edward J. McCaffery, *Taxing Women* (Chicago: University of Chicago Press, 1997); Nancy C. Staudt, "Taxing Housework," 84 *Georgetown Law Journal* 1571 (1996).

64. Martha Minow, " 'Forming Underneath Everything That Grows': Toward a History of Family Law," 1985 *Wisconsin Law Review* 819; Kerber, *Women of the Republic*, pp. 124–220; Sylvia A. Law, "The Founders on Families," 39 *University of Florida Law Review* 583 (1987).

65. Skocpol, *Protecting Soldiers and Mothers*, pp. 321–372; Linda Gordon, *Pitied but Not Entitled* (New York: The Free Press, 1994), pp. 37–64, 165–167.

66. Paula Giddings, *When and Where I Enter: The Impact of Black Women on Race and Sex in America* (New York: William Morrow, 1984), pp. 17–56; Dorothy Roberts, *Killing the Black Body* (New York: Pantheon Books, 1997), pp. 22–56; Patricia Hill Collins, *Black Feminist Thought* (New York: Routledge, 1991), pp. 43–78; Tera W. Hunter, *To 'Joy My Freedom: Southern Black Women's Lives and Labors after the Civil War* (Cambridge, Mass.: Harvard University Press, 1997), pp. viii–ix.

67. Dorothy E. Roberts, "Spiritual and Menial Housework," 9 *Yale Journal of Law and Feminism* 51, 70–75 (1997).

68. Giddings, *When and Where I Enter*, pp. 119–134; Gordon, *Pitied but Not Entitled*, pp. 111–143. On kinship patterns; see Collins, *Black Feminist Thought*, pp. 49, 55–58; Carol B. Stack, *All Our Kin* (New York: Harper & Row, 1971), pp. 62–89.

69. Gordon, *Pitied but Not Entitled*, p. 126.

70. Ibid., pp. 37–66.

71. Skocpol, *Protecting Soldiers and Mothers*, p. 337 (quoting Roosevelt's address to the First International Congress in America for the Welfare of the Child, organized by the Congress of Mothers in 1908).

72. Gordon, *Pitied but Not Entitled*, pp. 44–49, 165–167, 298–299; Skocpol, *Protecting Soldiers and Mothers*, pp. 535–539; Gwendolyn Mink, "The Lady and the Tramp: Gender, Race, and the Origins of the American Welfare State," in Linda Gordon, ed., *Women, the State, and Welfare* (Madison: University of Wisconsin Press, 1990), pp. 92–114.

73. Gordon, *Pitied but Not Entitled*, p. 107.

74. Ibid., pp. 107, 287–293.

75. Mimi Abramovitz, *Regulating the Lives of Women* (Boston: South End Press, 1988), pp. 181–206; Joel F. Handler, " 'Constructing the Political Spectacle': The Interpretation of Entitlements, Legalization, and Obligations in Social Welfare History," 56 *Brooklyn Law Review* 899, 912–941 (1990); Roberts, *Killing the Black Body*, pp. 202–208; Rickie Solinger, *Wake Up, Little Susie: Single Pregnancy and Race before Roe v. Wade* (New York: Routledge, 1992), pp. 41–85.

76. Abramovitz, *Regulating the Lives of Women*, pp. 349–381. For example, in 1988, Congress passed the Family Support Act, which included an employment program (JOBS).

77. Ed Gillespie and Bob Schellhaus, eds., *Contract with America: The Bold Plan by Rep. Newt Gingrich, Rep. Dick Armey and the House Republicans to Change the Nation* (New York: Times Books, 1994), pp. 65–77.

78. Clinton and Gore, *Putting People First*, pp. 164–168.

79. "Working toward Independence," p. 4.

80. Charles Murray, "The Coming White Underclass," *Wall Street Journal*, October 29, 1993, pp. A14; "Written Welfare Testimony of William J. Bennett: Delivered Before the House of Representatives Ways and Means Subcommittee on Human Resources" (January 20, 1995).

81. Fineman, *The Neutered Mother*, p. 106; Jill Quadagno, *The Color of Welfare* (New York: Oxford University Press, 1994), pp. 117–134; Roberts, *Killing the Black Body*, pp. 208–245.

82. Fineman, *The Neutered Mother*, pp. 101–125.

83. Kathryn Edin and Laura Lein, *Making Ends Meet* (New York: Russell Sage Foundation, 1997); Alan M. Hershey and LaDonna A. Pavetti, "Turning Job Finders into Job Keepers," 7 *The Future of Children* 74, 75–80 (1997).

84. General Accounting Office, *Welfare to Work: Child Care Assistance Limited; Welfare Reform May Expand Needs* (September 1995), pp. 3–4 (discussing JOBS program in Family Support Act of 1988); Abramovitz, *Regulating the Lives of Women*, p. 341 (discussing WIN program).

85. Robert Pear, "Defying Bush, Senate Increases Child Care Funds for the Poor," *New York Times*, March 31, 2004, p. A1; Robert Pear, "Senate, Torn by Minimum Wage, Shelves Major Welfare Bill," *New York Times*, April 2, 2004, p. A15.

86. "Senator Grassley Comments on House Views on Welfare Bill, General Mischaracterizations," *US Fed News*, April 8, 2005 (available on LexisNexis) (discussing child care funding in the proposed bipartisan Personal Responsibility and Individual Development for Everyone [PRIDE] Act of 2005, S. 667). By contrast, the proposed Personal Responsibility, Work, and Family Promotion Act of 2005, H.R. 240, has lower levels of child-care funding.

87. For example, the proposed Personal Responsibility and Individual Development Act of 2005, S. 667, and the Personal Responsibility, Work, and Family Promotion Act of 2005, H.R. 240, include initiatives on responsible fatherhood.

88. David Blankenhorn, *Fatherless America: Confronting Our Most Urgent Social Problem* (New York: Basic Books, 1995); Anna Gavanas, "The Fatherhood Responsibility Movement: The Centrality of Marriage, Work, and Male Sexuality in Reconstructions of Masculinity and Fatherhood," in Barbara Hobson, ed., *Making Men into Fathers* (Cambridge: Cambridge University Press, 2002), pp. 213, 227. Some of the organizations associated with this movement are the National Fatherhood Initiative, the Institute for Responsible Fatherhood and Family Revitalization, and Promise Keepers.

89. *Fathering: The Man and the Family, the Department of Health and Human Services' Response to President Clinton's June 16, 1995 Memorandum to Strengthen the Role of Fathers in Families* (October 16, 1995), *fatherhood.hhs.gov* (accessed December 1, 2004); Federal Interagency Forum on Child and Family Statistics, *Nurturing Fatherhood: Improving Data and Research on Male Fertility, Family, Formation, and Fatherhood* (June 1998), *fatherhood.hhs.gov* (accessed December 1, 2004).

90. Since 1999, legislators in the House and Senate have introduced various bills to promote responsible fatherhood (for example, the Fathers Count Act of 1999, H.R. 3073 [106th Congress], the Responsible Fatherhood Act of 2001, S. 653 [107th Congress), and the Strengthening Families Act of 2003, S. 657 (108th

Congress]). On state initiatives: Theodore Ooms et al., *Beyond Marriage Licenses: Efforts in States to Strengthen Marriage and Two-Parent Families* (Center for Law and Social Policy, April 2004).

91. Office of the Press Secretary, "Father's Day, 2000," *M2 Presswire* (June 19, 2000), 2000 Westlaw 22277024.

92. William J. Clinton, "Statement on Welfare Reform," *Weekly Compilation of Presidential Documents* (August 28, 2000), available on Westlaw at 2000 WL 13131444; "Vice President Gore Calls for "Father-Friendly" Workplaces," *U.S. Newswire* (May 3, 1996), available at LEXIS, News Library, U.S. Newswire File.

93. "Governor Bush Addresses National Summit on Fatherhood" (June 2, 2000), *www.prnewswire.com* (accessed January 12, 2005).

94. Scott Coltrane, "Research on Household Labor," 62 *Journal of Marriage & the Family* 1208 (2000); Ira Mark Ellman, "Divorce Rates, Marriage Rates, and the Problematic Persistence of Traditional Marital Roles," 34 *Family Law Quarterly* 1, 17–31 (2000); Joan Williams, *Unbending Gender* (New York: Oxford University Press, 2000), p. 1; "Time-Use Survey—First Results Announced by BLS" (September 14, 2004), pp. 2–3, *www.bls.gov* (accessed October 1, 2004); Janice Steil, *Marital Equality* (Thousand Oaks, Calif.: Sage Publications, 1997), pp. 24–36, 85–89 (on "emotion work").

95. Coltrane, "Research on Household Labor," pp. 1209–1210.

96. Nancy Chodorow, *The Reproduction of Mothering* (Berkeley: University of California Press, 1978).

97. Coltrane, "Research on Household Labor," p. 1212 (citations omitted).

98. Jacobs and Gerson, *The Time Divide*, pp. 159–168; Williams, *Unbending Gender*, pp. 59–60.

99. Steil, *Marital Equality*, pp. 104–105.

100. Scott Coltrane, *Family Man: Fatherhood, Housework, and Gender Equity* (New York: Oxford University Press, 1996), p. 78.

101. Williams, *Unbending Gender*, p. 1.

102. For a few recent examples: Claudia Wallis, "The Case for Staying Home," *Time* (March 22, 2004), p. 50; Lisa Belkin, "The Opt-Out Revolution," *New York Times Magazine*, October 26, 2003, p. 42.

103. Michael Selmi and Naomi Cahn, "Caretaking and the Contradictions of Contemporary Policy," 55 *Maine Law Review* 289 (2003).

104. Carol Gilligan, *In a Different Voice* (Cambridge, Mass.: Harvard University Press, 1982); Robin West, *Caring for Justice* (New York: New York University Press, 1997).

105. Judith A. Baer, *Our Lives before the Law* (Princeton, NJ: Princeton University Press, 1999), p. 195.

106. Catharine A. MacKinnon, "Difference and Dominance: On Sex Discrimination," in *Feminism Unmodified* (Cambridge, Mass.: Harvard University Press, 1987), pp. 32, 45.

107. Gilligan, *In a Different Voice*, p. 74; Carol Gilligan, "Prologue: Adolescent Development Reconsidered," in Carol Gilligan et al., eds., *Mapping the Moral Domain*, pp. vii, xxx–xxxi (Cambridge, Mass.: Harvard University Press, 1988).

108. West, *Caring for Justice*, pp. 9, 79–84, 98–99; Virginia Held, ed., *Justice*

*and Care: Essential Readings in Feminist Ethics* (Boulder, Colo.: Westview Press, 1995).

109. Whitebook and Phillips, "Child Care Employment."

110. Taunya Lovell Banks, "Toward a Global Critical Feminist Vision: Domestic Work and the Nanny Tax Debate," 3 *Journal of Gender, Race and Justice* 1 (1999); Coltrane, "Research on Household Labor," p. 1221; Jennifer Nedelsky, "Dilemmas of Passion, Privilege, and Isolation: Reflections on Mothering in a White, Middle-Class Nuclear Family," in Julia E. Hanigsberg and Sara Ruddick, eds., *Mother Troubles* (Boston: Beacon Press, 1999), p. 304; Joan C. Tronto, *Moral Boundaries: A Political Argument for an Ethic of Care* (New York: Routledge, 1993), pp. 112–114.

111. Jacobs and Gerson, *The Time Divide*, p. 196.

112. Arlie Russell Hochschild, "The Nanny Chain," *American Prospect* (January 3, 2000), p. 32. Immigrant mothers working as nannies and housekeepers may transform the meaning of motherhood to accommodate their separation from their children. Pierrette Hondagneu-Sotelo and Ernestine Avila, " 'I'm Here, but I'm There': The Meanings of Latina Transnational Motherhood," 11 *Gender & Society* 548 (1997).

113. Audrey Macklin, "On the Outside Looking In: Foreign Domestic Workers in Canada," in Wenona Giles and Sedef Arat-Koc, eds., *Maid in the Market* (Halifax, Nova Scotia: Fernwood Publications, 1994).

114. Caitlin Flanagan, "How Serfdom Saved the Women's Movement," *The Atlantic Monthly* (March 2004), p. 109.

115. Jacobs and Gerson, *The Time Divide*, p. 195; Donna E. Young, "Working across Borders: Global Restructuring and Women's Work," 2001 *Utah Law Review* 1.

116. Joan C. Tronto, "The 'Nanny' Question in Feminism," 17 *Hypatia* 34, 40 (2002); Susan Moller Okin, *Justice, Gender, and the Family* (New York: Basic Books, 1989).

117. Mary Romero, "Nanny Diaries and Other Stories," 52 *DePaul Law Review* 809, 831 (2003).

118. Dodson, *Don't Call Us Out of Name: The Untold Lives of Women and Girls in Poor America* (Boston: Beacon, 1998), pp. 14–49; Michelle Fine and Nancie Zane, "Bein' Wrapped Too Tight: When Low-Income Women Drop Out of High School," 19 *Women's Studies Quarterly* 77 (1991).

119. Gennetian, *How Welfare and Work Policies for Parents Affect Adolescents,* pp. iii, 46–47.

120. Anthropologist and primatologist Sarah Blaffer Hrdy stresses that all mothers, animal and human, juggle domestic and other work, and rely upon "allomothers," that is, others who assist the mother in caring for her children. Sarah Blaffer Hrdy, *Mother Nature: A History of Mothers, Infants, and Natural Selection* (New York: Pantheon Books, 1999), pp. 498–499.

121. Dodson, *Don't Call Us Out of Name*, p. 220; Harrington, *Care and Equality*, pp. 176–187; Julie Anne White, *Democracy, Justice, and the Welfare State: Reconstructing Public Care* (University Park: Pennsylania State University Press, 2000), pp. 164–173; Fineman, *The Autonomy Myth*, pp. 93–94; White, "Quality Child Care for Low-Income Families."

122. White, "Quality Child Care for Low-Income Families," p. 138.

123. A few useful models include Williams, *Unbending Gender*, pp. 4–6 (deconstructing "ideal worker"); Nancy Fraser, "After the Family Wage: A Postindustrial Thought Experiment," in *Justice Interruptus* (New York: Routledge, 1997), p. 41 (shift from "Universal Breadwinner" to "Universal Caregiver"); Gornick and Meyers, *Families That Work*, p. 84 ("dual-earner-dual-carer" model).

124. Gornick and Meyers, *Families That Work*, pp. 4–6, 84–94.

125. Dodson, Manuel, and Bravo, *It Just Doesn't Work*, p. 19.

126. Gornick and Meyers, *Families That Work*, p. 117.

127. Ibid., pp. 112–146; Fineman, *The Autonomy Myth*, pp. 285–286. Anne Alstott focuses on children's need for continuity of care in arguing that a fair society should expect parents to care for their children, but should address the costs of such care to parents' autonomy and economic opportunity. Anne L. Alstott, *No Exit: What Parents Owe Their Children—And What Society Owes Parents* (New York: Oxford University Press, 2004).

128. *Kids Count 2003* (Minnesota and Montana programs); NGA Center for Best Practices, "Child and Youth Well-Being under Welfare Reform: State Policy Options," *Issue Brief* (January 2004), p. 6.

129. Pamela A. Morris et al., Manpower Demonstration Research Corp., *How Welfare and Work Policies Affect Children: A Synthesis of Research* (March 2001), pp. 61, 63 (study of eleven welfare and employment programs).

130. Gornick and Meyers, *Families That Work*, p. 147.

131. Jacobs and Gerson, *The Time Divide*, p. 186.

132. Fineman, *The Autonomy Myth*, pp. 288–289.

133. Deborah L. Rhode, "Balanced Lives," 102 *Columbia Law Review* p. 834 (2002).

134. Elinor Burkett, *The Baby Boon: How Family Friendly America Cheats the Childless* (New York: The Free Press, 2000); Mary Anne Case, "How High the Apple Pie? A Few Troubling Questions about Where, Why, and How the Burden of Care for Children Should Be Shifted," 76 *Chicago-Kent Law Review* 1753, 1766 (2001).

135. Gornick and Meyers, *Families That Work*, p. 185; Dodson, Manuel, and Bravo, *It Just Doesn't Work*, pp. 2, 19; Lombardi, *Time to Care*, pp. 178–180.

136. Lombardi, *Time to Care*, pp. 18–22.

137. White, "Quality Child Care for Low-Income Families," pp. 122–123, 125–126.

## 4. Marriage Promotion

1. "The Marriage Movement: A Statement of Principles," found at *www. marriagemovement.org* (accessed August 1, 2004), was adopted in 2000; its sponsors are the Institute for American Values, the University of Chicago's Religion, Culture, and Family Project, and the Coalition for Marriage, Family and Couples Education.

2. Ibid., p. 3; *Marriage: Just a Piece of Paper?*, Katherine Anderson, Don Browning, and Brian Boyer, eds. (Grand Rapids, Mich.: William B. Eerdmans, 2002), p. 333. (Wade Horn comments, "We can help men understand the skills necessary to form and sustain healthy, equal regard marriages.") *Turning the Corner*

*on Father Absence in Black America* (Morehouse Research Institute and Institute for American Values, 1999), p. 5 (affirming "the vital importance of fathers as equal partners with mothers in the raising of children").

3. At an Institute for American Values symposium, "American Values and the Future of the Marriage Movement," which I attended on February 12, 2002, Maggie Gallagher, a prominent figure in the marriage movement, responded to a question about same-sex marriage by saying that "it is hard to have a marriage movement" or a strong and healthy "marriage culture" if the idea is that children do just as well whether they have a mother or father; "something will collide."

4. The marriage movement includes a number of organizations that have issued "calls" or "reports" to the nation, urging that reinvigorating marriage be put on the public agenda. For example, in addition to "The Marriage Movement: A Statement of Principles," the Religion, Culture and Family Project produced a television documentary, *Marriage: Just a Piece of Paper?*, and the accompanying book, *Marriage: Just a Piece of Paper?* The Institute for American values (IAV), the Center of the American Experiment, and the Coalition for Marriage, Family and Couples Education produced the booklet, A Report from Family Scholars, *Why Marriage Matters* (2002). IAV also supported the Council on Families in America's book, *Promises to Keep*, David Popenoe et al., eds. (Lanham, Md.: Rowman & Littlefield, 1996), pp. 293–318. Barbara Dafoe Whitehead and David Popenoe, co-directors of the National Marriage Project, release annual reports on "The State of Our Unions," available at *marriage.rutgers.edu.* Since the 1990s, IAV has also participated in a related social movement to promote "responsible fatherhood."

5. Wade F. Horn, "Marriage and Welfare Reform," 19 *Brookings Review* 39, 40 (Summer 2001); Linda J. Waite and Maggie Gallagher, *The Case for Marriage: Why Married People Are Happier, Healthier, and Better-Off Financially* (New York: Broadway Books, 2000).

6. "The Marriage Movement," p. 8.

7. Ibid.

8. Statement by Wade F. Horn, Ph.D., Assistant Secretary for Children and Families, Department of Health and Human Services, Before the Committee on Finance, United States Senate (May 16, 2002), *www.acf.dhhs.gov* (accessed August 12, 2004).

9. "The Marriage Movement," pp. 8–10.

10. "Testimony of David Popenoe," National Marriage Project, in Hearing on Welfare and Marriage, House Ways and Means Committee (May 22, 2001).

11. Ibid. Other texts also contrast (natural) motherhood and (problematic) fatherhood: see *Turning the Corner on Father Absence in Black America*, pp. 10, 15; James Q. Wilson, *The Marriage Problem* (New York: HarperCollins, 2002), pp. 24–32.

12. "The Marriage Movement," p. 8.

13. Horn, "Marriage and Welfare Reform," p. 42.

14. "The Marriage Movement," p. 20.

15. David Popenoe and Barbara Dafoe Whitehead, "The State of Our Unions: The Social Health of Marriage in America, 2000," pp. 3, 4, *marriage. rutgers.edu* (accessed August 1, 2004).

16. "The Marriage Movement," p. 22.

17. David Popenoe, "A Marriage Research Agenda for the Twenty-First Century: Ten Critical Questions," in Alan J. Hawkins et al., eds., *Revitalizing the Institution of Marriage for the Twenty-First Century* (Westport, Conn.: Praeger 2002), p. 200; "Marriage in America: A Report to the Nation," in Popenoe et al., eds., *Promises to Keep* pp. 293, 294 ("What brings us together is our concern for children").

18. Theodora Ooms et al., *Beyond Marriage Licenses: Efforts in States to Strengthen Marriage and Two-Parent Families* (Washington D.C.: Center for Law and Social Policy, April 2004), p. 10.

19. Ibid., pp. 8–10. Information on ACF's "Healthy Marriage Initiative" appears in Administration for Children and Families, U.S. Department of Health and Human Services, "Healthy Marriage Initiative Activities and Accomplishments 2002–2004" (2005) and on DHHS's web site: *www.acf.hhs.gov* (accessed August 12, 2004).

20. "Testimony of Wade F. Horn, Ph.D., Assistant Secretary, Children and Families, Department of Health and Human Services, Before the Committee on Health, Education, Labor and Pensions, Subcommittee on Children and Families" (April 28, 2004), *www.acf.dhhs.gov* (accessed August 12, 2004).

21. "Statement by Wade F. Horn."

22. I heard Dr. Horn make this statement in his remarks at the Institute for American Values and Center of the American Experiment symposium, "American Values and the Future of the Marriage Movement," held on February 12, 2002.

23. Neal Conan, *Talk of the Nation* (NPR, January 22, 2004) (remarks by Horn).

24. Personal Responsibility and Work Opportunity Reconciliation Act of 1996, Pub. L. No. 104–193, 110 Stat. 2105.

25. "Opening Statement of Rep. Wally Herger," Hearing on Welfare and Marriage before House Subcommittee on Human Resources (May 22, 2001), web.lexis-nexis.com; Robert Rector and Kirk A. Johnson, "The Effects of Marriage and Maternal Education in Reducing Child Poverty" (Heritage Foundation, August 2, 2002).

26. Statement of Ron Haskins, Senior Fellow, Brooking Institution, before Social Security and Family Policy Subcommittee, Senate Finance Committee (May 5, 2004).

27. "Testimony of David Popenoe."

28. The Fragile Families and Child Well Being Study, conducted by researchers at Princeton University and Columbia University, is described at crcw.princeton.edu (accessed September 15, 2003).

29. For example, the proposed bill, H.R. 3113, TANF Reauthorization Bill of 2001, named after the late representative Patsy Mink.

30. "Statement by Chairman Max Baucus," Senate Committee on Finance, Hearing on TANF Reauthorization: Building Stronger Families (May 16, 2002), *finance.senate.gov* (accessed May 15, 2003) (Montanans don't think marriage, a "personal and private choice," is government's business.)

31. The Senate Finance Committee (chaired by Baucus) approved a bill, the Work, Opportunity, and Responsibility for Kids (WORK) Act of 2002, which contained marriage promotion and responsible fatherhood provisions similar to the House version.

32. White House, "Working Toward Independence," pp. 2, 19, available at *www.whitehouse.gov*. (accessed February 10, 2002).

33. The Personal Responsibility, Work, and Family Promotion Act of 2002, H.R. 4737; the Personal Responsibility, Work, and Family Promotion Act of 2003, H.R. 4. On February 14, 2003, several Republican senators introduced the Compassion and Personal Responsibility Act, S. 5, with marriage and fatherhood promotion provisions identical to H.R. 4. For the extension, see H.R. 2350, Welfare Reform Extension Act of 2003.

34. Joseph Curl, "Bush Names Leavitt Health Secretary," *Washington Times*, December 14, 2004.

35. "Statement of U.S. Senator Max Baucus on Welfare Reform Reauthorization Markup," March 9, 2005, *http://finance.senate.gov* (accessed March 30, 2005) (discussing the PRIDE Act, S. 667). *See* S. 667, §103 (C) (voluntary participation); 103 (E)–(I) (domestic violence).

36. H.R. 240, §101 ("Purposes"); Statement by Tommy G. Thompson, Secretary, DHHS, "Welfare Reform: Building on Success," before the Senate Committee on Finance (March 12, 2003), *www.dhhs.gov* (accessed September 15, 2003). (The Bush plan would "clarify and underscore" TANF's family formation goal.)

37. H.R. 240, §103 ("Promotion of Family Formation and Healthy Marriage"); §119 ("Fatherhood Program"). It also allows DHHS to offer "technical assistance" to public and private entities in implementing local fatherhood promotion programs. The focus on parental education, economic empowerment of low-income men, and marriage promotion are also features of the responsible fatherhood provisions in S. 667, Section 118.

38. Ooms, *Beyond Marriage Licenses*, pp. 7, 10–11.

39. *Marriage: Just a Piece of Paper?*, pp. 335–336.

40. U.S. Department of Health and Human Services, *State Policies to Promote Marriage: Preliminary Report* (2002); Ooms, *Beyond Marriage Licenses*, pp. 10–11.

41. Chapter 98–403; Ooms, *Beyond Marriage Licenses*, p. 12 (describing Maryland, Minnesota, Oklahoma, and Tennessee laws).

42. DHHS, *State Policies to Promote Marriage*, pp. 11–12.

43. Ooms, *Beyond Marriage Licenses*, pp. 24–25, 36.

44. Chapter 98–403, included in handbook prepared by Florida Bar Association for marrying couples.

45. The statement about government's duty appears on the jacket of *The Marriage News You Can Use* video provided by the Governor's Commission on Marriage and the Utah Department of Workforce Services.

46. *"When You Get Married . . . "* (2002 Edition including updates from the 77th Legislature) (prepared by the Attorney General of Texas under Texas Family Code §2.104), *www.oag.state.tx.us* (accessed September 1, 2003).

47. "Testimony of Howard H. Hendrick, Oklahoma Cabinet Secretary of Health and Human Services, before Senate Finance Committee in Hearing on Issues in TANF Reauthorization: Building Stronger Families" (May 16, 2002).

48. *The Marriage News You Can Use* (text on jacket of video).

49. The PEW Research Center, "Americans Struggle With Religion's Role at Home and Abroad," *people-press.org* (reporting that 79 percent of Americans believe "government should not develop programs to encourage people to get and stay married").

50. Anita Bernstein, "For and Against Marriage: A Revision," 102 *Michigan Law Review* 129 (2003).

51. *Why Marriage Matters*, pp. 4–9 (summarizing social science).

52. Andrew Cherlin, "Going to Extremes: Family Structure, Children's Well-Being, and Social Science," 36 *Demography* 421 (1999); Paul Amato and Alan Booth, "The Legacy of Parents' Marital Discord," 81 *Journal of Personality and Social Psychology* 627 (2001).

53. Philip A. Cowan and Carolyn Pape Cowan, "Strengthening Couples to Improve Children's Well-Being: What We Know Now," 6 *Poverty Research News* 18 (May–June 2002); Stephanie Coontz and Nancy Folbre, "Marriage, Poverty, and Public Policy," *The American Prospect* (March 19, 2002), *www.prospect.org* (accessed August 12, 2004).

54. Andrew J. Cherlin and Paula Fomby, "A Closer Look at Changes in Children's Living Arrangements in Low-Income Families" (Working Paper 02–01, February 20, 2002).

55. Sara McLanahan and Gary Sandefur, *Growing Up with a Single Parent* (Cambridge, Mass.: Harvard University Press, 1994), p. 134.

56. Henry N. Ricciuti, "Single Parenthood, Achievement, and Problem Behavior in White, Black, and Hispanic Children," 97 *Journal of Educational Research* 196, 197, 203–205 (March/April 2004).

57. Margaret F. Brinig and Steven L. Nock, "What Does Covenant Mean for Relationships?," 18 *Notre Dame Journal of Law, Ethics & Public Policy* 137, 166 (2004) (attributing finding that, for African American children, "kinship care cannot be statistically distinguished from living with a birth family or being adopted" to "long tradition of reliance on extended families in times of crisis").

58. Velma McBride Murry, Emilie Phillips Smith, and Nancy E. Hill, "Race, Ethnicity, and Culture in Studies of Families in Context," 63 *Journal of Marriage and Family* 911 (2001); Paul R. Amato, "The Consequences of Divorce for Adults and Children," 62 *Journal of Marriage and Family* 1269, 1282 (2000).

59. Judith Stacey, *In the Name of the Family* (Boston, Mass.: Beacon Press, 1996), pp. 83–104.

60. E. Mavis Hetherington and John Kelly, *For Better or for Worse: Divorce Reconsidered* (New York: W. W. Norton, 2002), p. 5.

61. Cherlin, "Going to Extremes," critiquing Judith S. Wallerstein and Sandra Blakeslee, *Second Chances: Men, Women, and Children a Decade after Divorce* (New York: Ticknor & Fields, 1989); Mary Duenwald, "Two Portraits of Children of Divorce: Rosy and Dark," *New York Times*, March 26, 2002, p. F6 (featuring Hetherington and Wallerstein as two sides of the debate).

62. Karen S. Peterson, "Kids, Parents Can Make Best of Divorce," *USA Today*, January 14, 2002 pp. 1A, 2A (reporting that Hetherington's book "will incense those who see divorce as undermining American society"; quoting David Blankenhorn on risk of "backlash" and reporting criticism of book by Linda Waite and Judith Wallerstein and praise of Hetherington by Andrew Cherlin and Stephanie Coontz).

63. Elisabeth Bumiller, "Bush Urges Nation to Follow His Lead and Get Fit," *New York Times*, June 21, 2002, p. A13; Ron Winslow and Peter Landers, "Obesity: A World-Wide Woe," *Wall Street Journal*, July 1, 2002, p. B1.

64. Amato, "The Consequences of Divorce for Adults and Children," p. 1278.

65. Tara Parker-Pope, "When Your Spouse Makes You Sick: Research Probes Toll of Marital Stress," *Wall Street Journal*, May 4, 2004, p. D1.

66. "ACF Healthy Marriage Mission," *www.acf.hhs.gov* (accessed August 1, 2004); "Statement by Wade F. Horn."

67. Martha C. Nussbaum, *Sex and Social Justice* (New York: Oxford University Press, 1999), p. 41.

68. Claiming such broader applicability are Florida Act, Chapter 98–403; Don S. Browning and Gloria C. Rodriguez, *Reweaving the Social Tapestry* (New York: W. W. Norton, & Co., 2002), pp. 137–138.

69. So states a pamphlet by the widely used PEERS program (Practical Exercises Enriching Relationships Skills), *It's Time to Fully Prepare Our Youth for Life!*

70. Christine Johnson et al., *Marriage in Oklahoma: 2001 Baseline Statewide Survey on Marriage and Divorce* (Oklahoma State University Bureau for Social Research, 2002), pp. 15–16.

71. Ibid., pp. 15, 28–30 (reporting that the majority of Oklahomans surveyed would be interested in relationship training; 42 percent gave little or no helpful premarital preparation as a reason for their divorce).

72. Scott M. Stanley, "Making a Case for Premarital Education," 50 *Family Relations* 272 (2001).

73. "Testimony by Scott M. Stanley," Co-Director, Center for Marital and Family Studies, before Senate Finance Committee, Social Security and Family Policy Subcommittee (May 5, 2004).

74. "Statement by Wade F. Horn."

75. Dana Mack, *Hungry Hearts: Evaluating the New Curricula for Teens on Marriage and Relationships* (Institute for American Values, 2000); Maggie Gallagher, "Rites, Rights, and Social Institutions: Why and How Should the Law Support Marriage?," 18 *Notre Dame Journal of Law, Ethics & Public Policy* 225 (2004).

76. Wade F. Horn and Andrew Bush, "Fathers, Marriage, and Welfare Reform," *Hudson Institute Executive Briefing* (1997).

77. Gwendolyn Mink, "From Welfare to Wedlock: Marriage Promotion and Poor Mothers' Inequality," 11 *The Good Society* 68 (No. 3, 2002).

78. Neal Conan, *Talk of the Nation* (NPR, January 22, 2004) (remarks by Horn).

79. Fragile Families Research Brief, "Barriers to Marriage among Fragile Families" (May 2003). For similar findings, see M. Robin Dion et al., *Helping Unwed Parents Build Strong and Healthy Marriages: A Conceptual Framework for Interventions* (Washington, D.C.: Mathematica Policy Research, January 15, 2003), pp. 28, 46.

80. Martha R. Burt et al., "The Urban Institute: Strategies for Addressing the Needs of Domestic Violence Victims Within the TANF Program" (2000), *www.urban.org* (accessed July 3, 2004).

81. *Welfare Reform as WE Know It* (Applied Research Center, 2001) (story of "Mary").

82. "Testimony of Wade F. Horn." Compare references to domestic violence in H.R. 290, Section 103 with S.667, Section 103.

83. Patrick F. Fagan et al., "Why Congress Should Ignore Radical Feminist Opposition to Marriage," *Heritage Foundation Backgrounder* (June 16, 2003).

84. Johnson, *Marriage in Oklahoma*, pp. 15–16, 34.

85. *Marriage in Utah: 2003 Baseline Statewide Survey on Marriage and Divorce* (Governor's Commission on Marriage, October 2003), pp. 13, 26 (37 percent of women and 6 percent of men gave domestic violence as factor contributing to divorce; 52 percent of low-income respondents and 21 percent of general sample did so).

86. Lisa D. Brush, "Poverty, Battering, Race, and Welfare Reform: Black-

White Differences in Women's Welfare-to-Work Transitions," 5 *Journal of Poverty* 67 (2001) (47 percent of women in a job readiness program answered "yes" on at least one violence-related item of questionnaire). In the recent *Frontline* documentary, *Let's Get Married*, two of the three low-income mothers profiled by journalist Alex Kotlowitz had experienced domestic violence (script available at *www.pbs.org*) (accessed February 1, 2003).

87. "Testimony by Scott M. Stanley."

88. Dion, *Helping Unwed Parents Build Strong and Healthy Marriages*, pp. xviii, 42–43.

89. "Barriers to Marriage among Fragile Families."

90. Research Brief: Welfare Reform and Family Formation Project, "What Do They Think? Welfare Recipients' Attitudes Toward Marriage and Childbearing" (Abt Associates, November 2002).

91. Kathryn Edin, "What Do Low-Income Single Mothers Say about Marriage?," 47 *Social Problems* 112 (2000); see Kathryn Edin and Maria Kefalas, *Promises I Can Keep: Why Poor Women Put Motherhood Before Marriage* (Berkeley: University of California Press, 2005).

92. "Testimony of Kathryn Edin before House Ways and Means Committee Hearing on Welfare and Marriage," May 22, 2001, 2001 Westlaw 553936 (F.D.C.H).

93. Marcia Carlson, Sara McLanahan, and Paula England, "Union Formation in Fragile Families," 41 *Demography* 237, 255–257 (May 2004).

94. *Why Marriage Matters*, pp. 13–17; Waite and Gallagher, *The Case for Marriage*, pp. 162–173.

95. Jessica Bernard, *The Future of Marriage* (New Haven, Conn.: Yale University Press, 2nd ed., 1982), pp. 247, 289.

96. Steven Nock, *Marriage in Men's Lives* (New York: Oxford University Press, 1998), p. 3.

97. Janice M. Steil, *Marital Equality* (Thousand Oaks, Calif.: SAGE Publications, 1997), p. xix.

98. *Marriage: Just a Piece of Paper?*, pp. 166–167 (Linda Waite discussing effects of marriage and divorce). One study found that, for men, the positive effect of marriage on longevity was stronger than high income, and also exactly offset the largely negative effect of smoking. Jonathan Gardner and Andrew Oswald, "Is It Money or Marriage that Keeps People Alive?" (August 2002), *repec.org* (accessed January 24, 2005).

99. Wilson, *The Marriage Problem*, pp. 16–17.

100. Hetherington and Kelly, *For Better or for Worse*, pp. 8–9; *Marriage: Just a Piece of Paper?*, pp. 166–167 (Waite discussing gender differential).

101. Wilson, *The Marriage Problem*, pp. 16–17 (discussing Waite and Gallagher, *The Case for Marriage*).

102. Nock, *Marriage and Men's Lives*, pp. 58–59, citing Sarah Fenstermaker Burk, *The Gender Factory* (New York: Plenum Press, 1985).

103. Barrie Thorne and Marilyn Yalom, eds., *Rethinking the Family* (New York: Longman, 1992).

104. "Marriage in America: A Report to the Nation," p. 303. Some proponents of same-sex marriage make a similar argument about marriage's civilizing effects on gay men. William Eskridge, *The Case for Same-Sex Marriage* (New York: The Free Press, 1996), pp. 8–9.

105. Don S. Browning et al., *From Culture Wars to Common Ground* (Louisville, Ky.: Westminster John Knox Press, 2nd ed., 2000), pp. 22, 68–69 (discussing these ideas and their historical and theological roots).

106. Wilson, *The Marriage Problem*, pp. 62–63.

107. Ibid., pp. 28–31.

108. "The Marriage Movement," p. 7.

109. Deborah L. Rhode, *Justice and Gender: Sex Discrimination and the Law* (Cambridge, Mass.: Harvard University Press, 1989).

110. Drucilla Cornell, *At the Heart of Freedom* (Princeton, N.J.: Princeton University Press, 1998), pp. 131–140 (critiquing the fatherhood movement's use of rigid gender roles within family to "conscript" men into marriage); Lynne Henderson, "Rape and Responsibility," 11 *Law & Philosophy* 127 (1992).

111. Nock, *Marriage and Men's Lives*, p. 6. The other elements are as follows: "Marriage is a free personal choice, based on love"; "Marriage is a heterosexual relationship"; "Marriage typically involves children"; "Sexual fidelity and monogamy are expectations for marriage"; and "Maturity is a presumed requirement for marriage." Ibid.

112. This is a point expressed in an e-mail from Nock to the author.

113. Philip Blumstein and Pepper Schwartz, *American Couples* (New York: William Morrow, 1983).

114. Pepper Schwartz, *Love Between Equals: How Peer Marriage Really Works* (New York: The Free Press, 1994), pp. 111–113.

115. Steil, *Marital Equality*, pp. 50, 111.

116. David J. Fein et al., *The Determinants of Marriage and Cohabitation among Disadvantaged Americans: Research Findings and Needs* (Cambridge, Mass.: Abt Associates, March 2003), p. 35.

117. Ibid., pp. 35–36.

118. Information appears at *www.acf.hhs.gov* (accessed August 1, 2004).

119. William Julius Wilson, *The Truly Disadvantaged* (Chicago: University of Chicago Press, 1987); William Julius Wilson, *When Work Disappears* (New York: Vintage Books, 1996).

120. Elijah Anderson, *Code of the Street* (New York: W. W. Norton & Co., 1999).

121. Ibid., p. 183.

122. Ibid., p. 189. bell hooks contrasts the generation of hardworking, patriarchal black men of her father's time with more misogynist, destructive contemporary images of masculinity. bell hooks, *Salvation: Black People and Love* (New York: HarperCollins, 2001).

123. Maureen R. Waller, *My Baby's Father: Unmarried Parents and Paternal Responsibility* (Ithaca, N.Y.: Cornell University Press, 2002), pp. 48–69; Nancy E. Dowd, *Redefining Fatherhood* (New York: New York University Press, 2000), pp. 70–74, 157–180 (noting black fathers' difficulty in fulfilling provider role and proposing to redefine fathering around nurture of children).

124. Fein, *The Determinants of Marriage and Cohabitation among Disadvantaged Americans*, p. 37.

125. Scott Coltrane, *Family Man: Fatherhood, Housework, and Gender Equality* (New York: Oxford University Press, 1996), pp. 78–79, 190–191.

126. Dowd, *Redefining Fatherhood*, pp. 157–180.

127. Federal Interagency Forum on Child and Family Statistics, *Nurturing Fa-*

*therhood: Improving Data and Research on Male Fertility, Family Formation, and Father-hood* (June 1998), Chapter 4, p. 22, *fatherhood.hhs.gov* (accessed October 1, 2004).

128. George Gilder, *Wealth and Poverty* (New York: Basic Books, 1981), p. 136.

129. Waller, *My Baby's Father*, pp. 18–37; *Let's Get Married* (interviews with Ronald Mincy and Kathyrn Edin on their research findings).

130. Carlson, McLanahan, and England, "Union Formation in Fragile Families," p. 257.

131. Ronald B. Mincy, "What about Black Fathers?" *The American Prospect* (April 7, 2002), pp. 36–38.

132. Edin, "What Do Low-Income Single Mothers Say about Marriage?" p. 130. One feminist criticism of William Julius Wilson's thesis is that it fails to take into account the range of reasons—other than economics—that black women may decide not to marry. See Maxine Baca Zinn, "Family, Race, and Poverty in the Eighties," 14 *Signs* 857 (1989).

133. *Marriage: Just a Piece of Paper?* (television documentary shown on many PBS stations, February 14, 2002).

134. Don S. Browning, "The Language of Health versus the Language of Religion: Competing Models of Marriage for the Twenty-First Century," in Hawkins, ed., *Revitalizing the Institution of Marriage for the Twenty-First Century*, pp. 29, 36.

135. Wilson, *The Marriage Problem*, pp. 189–190.

136. Whitehead and Popenoe, "The State of Our Unions, 1999," p. 6.

137. Andrew Hacker, *Mismatch: The Growing Gulf between Women and Men* (New York: Scribner, 2003).

138. Edin and Kefalas, *Promises I Can Keep*, 203; "Testimony of Kathryn Edin." For a similar account, see Kathryn Edin, "A Few Good Men: Why Poor Mothers Don't Marry or Remarry," *American Prospect* (January 3, 2000), p. 28.

139. Whitehead and Popenoe, "The State of Our Unions, 1999," p. 6.

140. Edin and Kefalas, *Promises I Can Keep*, pp. 104–118. These low-income mothers did consider economics: they did not wish to marry men who were unemployed or could not contribute to the household. Given the negative consequences they linked to marriage, they would marry only if doing so would improve their economic situations.

141. Barbara Dafoe Whitehead and David Popenoe, "Who Wants to Marry a Soulmate? New Survey Findings on Young Adults' Attitudes about Love and Marriage" (National Marriage Project, 2001), p. 5, *marriage.rutgers.edu* (access October 15, 2003).

142. Barbara Dafoe Whitehead, *Why There Are No Good Men Left* (New York: Broadway Books, 2003).

143. Steven L. Nock, "The Marriage of Equally Dependent Spouses," 22 *Journal of Family Issues* 755, 773 (2001).

144. Hetherington and Kelly, *For Better or for Worse*, p. 34. Coining this term is Arlie Hochschild, *The Second Shift: Working Parents and the Revolution at Home* (New York: Viking, 1989).

145. Nock, "The Marriage of Equally Dependent Spouses."

146. Steven L. Nock and Margaret F. Brinig, "Weak Men and Disorderly Women: Divorce and the Division of Labor," in Antony W. Dnes and Robert Rowthorn, eds., *The Law and Economics of Marriage and Divorce* (New York: Cambridge University Press, 2002), pp. 171, 188.

147. Roberta Sigel, *Ambition and Accommodation* (Chicago: University of Chicago Press, 1996), p. 191; Steil, *Marital Equality*, pp. 106–107. For an argument stressing the role played by unequal bargaining power within marriage, see Amy L. Wax, "Bargaining in the Shadow of the Market: Is There a Future for Egalitarian Marriage?" 84 *Virginia Law Review* 509 (1998).

148. Hetherington and Kelly, *For Better or for Worse*, pp. 30–31.

149. Schwartz, *Love Between Equals*, p. 125.

150. Donna L. Franklin, *What's Love Got to Do with It? Understanding and Healing the Rift between Black Men and Women* (New York: Simon & Schuster, 2000), p. 210; Orlando Patterson, *Rituals of Blood: Consequences of Slavery in Two American Centuries* (Washington, D.C.: Civitas, 1998) (analyzing data suggesting that black women's attitudes on gender issues are more egalitarian and feminist and black men's are more patriarchal).

151. Whitehead and Popenoe, "Who Wants to Marry a Soul Mate?" p. 1.

152. Ibid., pp. 5–6.

153. Heather Ross and Isabel Sawhill, *Time of Transition: The Growth of Families Headed by Women* (Washington, D.C.: Urban Institute, 1975), pp. 62–63.

154. Isabel V. Sawhill, "Reversing Teen Pregnancy and Single Parenthood," *American Experiment Quarterly* (Summer 2001): 77.

155. Katharine T. Bartlett, "Saving the Family from the Reformers," 31 *University of California-Davis Law Review* 809, 842–843 (1998).

156. Browning, *From Culture Wars to Common Ground*, p. 328.

157. Robert Pear, "Human Services Nominee's Focus on Married Fatherhood Draws Both Praise and Fire," *New York Times*, June 7, 2001, p. A24 (quoting Horn on androgyny: " 'The idea,' he says sarcastically, 'is that moms and dads should each be doing precisely 50 percent of the diapers, 50 percent of the burping and 50 percent of the bathing. Special allowance is made for the fact that men cannot be expected to do 50 percent of the breast-feeding—although I'm sure some androgyny advocate somewhere is working to overcome even that little biological obstacle.' "); see David Blankenhorn, *Fatherless America*, pp. 117–123 (critiquing "androgyny" as an ideal because it denies sexual complementarity). For a rebuttal, see Dowd, *Redefining Fatherhood*, pp. 44–47 (when fathers spend as much time nurturing as mothers, there are no significant differences in what they do, but generally, fathers do far less nurturing than mothers).

158. "The Marriage Movement," p. 3.

159. Ibid., p. 18.

160. By contrast, Browning and his associates, like others in the marriage movement, advocate achieving workfamily balance through a combined 60-hour work week (in a two-parent family), but they make clear that equality should be a guiding principle. See Browning, *From Culture Wars to Common Ground*, p. 328.

161. David Popenoe, "Modern Marriage: Revising the Cultural Script," in Popenoe et al., eds., *Promises to Keep*, pp. 247–261.

162. Allan Carlson, "Building Family-Centered Communities," 4 *American Experiment Quarterly* 36, 40 (2001) (family wage system of an earlier era was not perfect, since it "intentionally embraced gender discrimination in employment," but it "encouraged a gendered specialization of tasks that reinforced fertility and one vision of the home economy"). For a feminist treatment of economic models of the family (including Gary Becker's idea of the family firm), see Margaret F.

Brinig, *From Contract to Covenant: Beyond the Law and Economics of the Family* (Cambridge, Mass.: Harvard University Press, 2000).

163. Allen M. Parkman, "Good Incentives Lead to Good Marriages," in Hawkins, ed., *Revitalizing the Institution of Marriage for the Twenty-First Century*, pp. 69, 72–77. Maggie Gallagher, "Re-creating Marriage," in Popenoe et al., eds., *Promises to Keep*, pp. 233–245.

164. *Marriage: Just a Piece of Paper?*, pp. 372, 380–381 (remarks by Diane Sollee, Coalition for Marriage, Family, and Couples Education, about "basic tool kit").

165. In agreement is Herma Hill Kay, " 'Making Marriage and Divorce Safe for Women' Revisited," 32 *Hofstra Law Review* 71, 72 (2003).

166. Orr v. Orr, 440 U.S. 268 (1979); Mary Anne Case, "Reflections on Con-stitutionalizing Women's Equality," 90 *California Law Review* 765 (2002).

167. Compare Palmore v. Sidoti, 466 U.S. 429 (1984), in which the U.S. Su-preme Court held that an argument that a white child would be better off in a white neighborhood than in a black neighborhood did not justify awarding cus-tody to the child's father, rather than the mother, who lived with a black partner.

168. Florida Handbook, 7 (discussing domestic violence).

169. For example, Utah's video, *Marriage News You Can Use*, features a clinical social worker expressing the view that, although mothers carry the baby, after birth, parenting should be an equal responsibility for mothers and fathers.

170. *When You Get Married*, p. 9.

171. Browning, *From Culture Wars to Common Ground*, pp. 233–234 (quoting from Tony Evans, "A Man and His Integrity," in Bill Bright et al., eds., *Seven Promises of a Promise Keeper* Nashville, Tenn.: W. Publishing Group, 1994), p. 74.

172. The Southern Baptist convention drew national attention (and triggered President Jimmy Carter's defection) when it embraced a wife's biblical duty to be subject to her husband.

173. This argument is made for giving faith-based groups an equal chance to compete for governmental contracts. The White House, "Unlevel Playing Field: Barriers to Participation by Faith-Based and Community Organizations in Social Service Provision" (August 2001), *www.whitehouse.gov* (accessed August 1, 2004).

174. Orr v. Orr, 440 U.S. 268 (1979).

175. Schwartz, *Love Between Equals*, pp. 10–11, 181–185; Pepper Schwartz, "Peer Marriage," *Responsive Community* (Summer 1998): 48.

176. Hetherington and Kelly, *For Better or for Worse*, pp. 30–31.

177. Steil, *Marital Equality*, p. 106.

178. June Carbone, "Has the Gender Divide Become Unbridgeable? The Im-plications for Social Equality," 5 *Journal of Gender, Race, and Justice* 31 (2001); Elizabeth Scott, "Social Norms and the Legal Regulation of Marriage," 86 *Vir-ginia Law Review* 1901 (2000).

179. Carbone, "Has the Gender Divide Become Unbridgeable?"

180. Francine M. Deutsch, *Halving It All: How Equally Shared Parenting Works* (Cambridge, Mass.: Harvard University Press, 1999); Coltrane, *Family Man*, pp. 116–150.

181. Schwartz, *Love Between Equals*, p. 125.

182. Don S. Browning, "What Kind of Love? The Equal-Regard Marriage and Children," 4 *American Experiment Quarterly* 47, 49–51 (Summer 2001).

183. Carol Gilligan, *In a Different Voice* (1982); Peggy Cooper Davis and Carol Gilligan, "Reconstructing Law and Marriage," 11 *The Good Society* 57 (No. 3, 2002).

184. Whitehead and Popenoe, "Who Wants to Marry a Soul Mate?," p. 6; Norval D. Glenn, "Values, Attitudes, and American Marriage," in Popenoe et al., eds., *Promises to Keep*, p. 24.

185. Gallagher, "Re-creating Marriage," pp. 236–237.

186. Nock and Brinig, "What Does Covenant Mean for Relationships?," p. 145.

187. "Marriage in Utah," p. 14; "Marriage in Oklahoma," p. 17.

188. Steil, *Marital Equality*, pp. 74, 85–86.

## 5. Recognizing Same-Sex Marriage

1. An Act Relating to Civil Unions, 2000 Vt. ALS 91.

2. In Baehr v. Lewin, 852 P.2d 44 (Haw. 1993), a state court for the first time accepted a constitutional challenge by gay men and lesbians to a state marriage law that precluded them from marrying. On remand, the trial court concluded that the state had not demonstrated a compelling interest to preclude such marriages. Baehr v. Miike, 1996 WL 694235 (Hawaii Cir. Ct. 1996). Pending final resolution, the Hawaii legislature proposed—and the public approved—a constitutional amendment that did not prohibit same-sex marriage, but declared: "The legislature shall have the power to reserve marriage to opposite-sex couples." Hawaii Constitution, art I., §23.

3. P.L. No. 104–199, 110 Stat. 2419 (1996), codified as amended at 28 U.S.C. §1738C.

4. American Bar Association Section of Family Law, *A White Paper: An Analysis of the Law Regarding Same-Sex Marriage, Civil Unions, and Domestic Partnerships* (2004), pp. 30–33 (thirty-eight states as of March 2004); Kavan Peterson, "50-State Rundown on Gay Marriage Laws," *Stateline.org* (accessed December 2, 2004) (thirty-nine states as of November 2004).

5. "State Constitutional Amendments Defining Marriage," *washingtonpost.com* (accessed December 2, 2004).

6. *Baker*, 881.

7. Ibid., 881–882.

8. Ibid., 882–885.

9. Ibid., 883–884. Among the rights listed by the court are: rights relating to inheritance, worker's compensation, testimonial privilege, health insurance, homestead rights, property rights, hospital visitation, and rights to support and property division in the event of divorce.

10. Ibid., 888–889.

11. An Act Relating to Civil Unions, §1.

12. Ibid., §1.A(9).

13. Ibid., §1.A(1) and A(2). The Vermont law also creates a category of "reciprocal beneficiaries," for two blood-relatives or persons related by adoption. Choosing this status permits persons to receive benefits and protections and to be subject to responsibilities that pertain to hospital visitation and patients' rights, medical decision making, and granting power of attorney. Ibid., §2(B). To date,

Vermont residents have shown little interest in this status. Report of the Vermont Civil Union Review Commission (January 2002), *www.leg.state.vt.us* (accessed August 15, 2003).

14. Report of the Vermont Civil Union Review Commission.

15. David B. Cruz, " 'Just Don't Call It Marriage': The First Amendment and Marriage as an Expressive Resource," 74 *Southern California Law Review* 925, 933–939 (2001) (drawing on Kenneth L. Karst, "The Freedom of Intimate Association," 89 *Yale Law Journal* 624 (1980)).

16. Evan Wolfson, *Why Marriage Matters: America, Equality, and Gay People's Right to Marry* (New York: Simon and Schuster, 2004), pp. 126–144. New York, by contrast, apparently will recognize these out-of-state marriages because they do not offend public policy. Advisory Letter from New York Attorney General (March 3, 2004).

17. Yuval Merin, *Equality for Same-Sex Couples* (Chicago: University of Chicago Press, 2002), pp. 210–211.

18. 539 U.S. 558, 575, 578 (2003).

19. *Goodridge*, 948, 957.

20. Ibid., 954. James C. Dobson, "Marriage Is the Foundation of the Family," 18 *Notre Dame Journal of Law, Ethics & Public Policy* 1 (2004) (citing *Goodridge* as evidence that "the courts have moved from being one of marriage's historical primary caretakers, to being its molder and master and . . . destroyer").

21. *Goodridge*, 954–958.

22. Ibid., 954–955.

23. Ibid., 955, 963.

24. Ibid., 949.

25. This helpful idea of marriage at the margins came up in the remarks by Ariela Dubler, Michael Grossberg, and Rachel Moran on the history panel at the Conference on Marriage, Democracy, and Families, held at Hofstra University School of Law, March 14–15, 2003.

26. Brief of Plaintiffs-Appellants in Goodridge v. Department of Public Health, No. SJC-08860.

27. *Goodridge*, 958–959.

28. An important turning point toward such critical reflection was the Supreme Court of Hawaii's opinion in Baehr v. Lewin and the subsequent Circuit Court opinion in Baehr v. Miike.

29. *Goodridge*, 961.

30. Another argument accepted by the courts in prior challenges to state marriage laws is the definitional one: marriage has always been defined as the union between a man and a woman. Baker v. Nelson, 191 N.W.2d 185 (Minn., 1971); Singer v. Hara, 522 P.2d 1187 (Wash., 1974) (using definitional and incapacity arguments). Under a strict scrutiny test, Baehr v. Lewin correctly rejected such arguments as "circular and unpersuasive" and instead found that a bar on same-sex marriage constituted sex discrimination. Baehr v. Lewin, 61.

31. Maggie Gallagher, "Rites, Rights, and Social Institutions," 18 *Notre Dame Journal of Law, Ethics & Public Policy* 225, 241 (2004); Matthew Spalding, "A Defining Moment: Marriage, the Courts, and the Constitution," *Heritage Foundation Reports* (May 17, 2004).

32. *Goodridge*, 961–962.

33. Ibid., 961–963.

34. Ibid., 963–964.

35. Ibid., 964.

36. Ibid., 966–967.

37. Ibid.

38. Ibid., 968.

39. Brief of Defendants-Appellees in Goodridge v. Department of Public Health, No. SJC-08860, 13–18. The Department acknowledged movement toward a more companionate model of marriage, yet argued that "that model 'did not imply sexual equality or a blurring of gender boundaries.' " Ibid., 18.

40. *Goodridge*, 965.

41. Ibid., 970–971 (drawing on the sex discrimination arguments made in: Baehr v. Lewin, 852 P.2d 33 (Haw., 1993) and Baker v. State, 744 A.2d 864, 904–912 (Vt., 1999) (Johnson, J., concurring in part, dissenting in part)). The Hawaii Supreme Court concluded that Hawaii impermissibly denied same-sex couples the right to marry merely because of the sex of one member of the couple; that is, if a woman had sought to marry a man, instead of a woman, she would have been permitted to do so. Baehr v. Lewin, 59–67.

42. *Goodridge*, 972–973.

43. Andrew Koppelman, *Antidiscrimination Law and Social Equality* (New Haven, Conn.: Yale University Press, 1996); Sylvia Law, "Homosexuality and the Social Meaning of Gender," 1988 *Wisconsin Law Review* 187 (1988); William Eskridge, *The Case for Same-Sex Marriage* (New York: The Free Press, 1996), pp. 162–172; Brief of Plaintiffs-Appellants, 60 n.35 (citing Koppelman and Law).

44. Law, "Homosexuality and the Social Meaning of Gender," p. 218.

45. Baehr v. Lewin, 61–63 (discussing Loving v. Virginia, 388 U.S. 1 (1967)); Koppelman, *Antidiscrimination Law and Social Equality*, pp. 53–58 (analogizing antimiscegenation laws to laws barring same-sex marriage).

46. *Goodridge*, 971–972; Eskridge, *The Case for Same-Sex Marriage*, pp. 162–163.

47. David Richards, *Women, Gays, and the Constitution* (Chicago: University of Chicago Press, 1998), pp. 448–452, 459–466; Peggy Cooper Davis, *Neglected Stories: The Constitution and Family Values* (New York: Hill & Wang, 1997) (invoking the Fourteenth Amendment's antislavery history to support same-sex marriage). On compulsory heterosexuality, see Adrienne Rich, "Compulsory Heterosexuality and Lesbian Existence," in Ann Snitow, Christine Stansell, and Sharon Thompson, eds., *Powers of Desire* (New York: Monthly Review Press, 1983), p. 177.

48. Nan D. Hunter, "Marriage, Law, and Gender: A Feminist Inquiry," 1 *Law & Sexuality* 9, 17–18 (1991).

49. *Goodridge*, 969.

50. Ibid. (citing Halpern v. Toronto (City), 172 O.A.C. 276 (2003)). The Court of Appeal for Ontario reformulated the common law definition of marriage to be: "the voluntary union for life of two persons to the exclusion of all others." 172 O.A.C. 276, para. 155.

51. *Goodridge*, 969–970.

52. Opinions of the Justices to the Senate, SJC-09163 (February 3, 2004).

53. Pam Belluck, "Setback Is Dealt to Gay Marriage," *New York Times*, March 30, 2004, p. A1.

54. Pam Belluck, "Hundreds of Same-Sex Couples Wed in Massachusetts,"

*New York Times*, May 18, 2004, p. A1; Yvonne Abraham and Michael Paulsen, "Wedding Day: First Gays Marry, Many Seek Licenses," *Boston Globe*, May 18, 2004, p. A1. If the amendment passes, same-sex marriages will then become civil unions.

55. Kate Zernike, "Gay? No Marriage License Here. Straight? Ditto," *New York Times*, March 27, 2004, p. A8 (county commissioner of Willamette Valley declines to issue any marriage licenses); Roberto D. McFadden, "With Polite Refusal, Same-Sex Marriage Issue Reaches City Hall," *New York Times*, March 5, 2004, p. B1 (mayor of New Paltz solemnized same-sex marriage).

56. "Bush's Remarks on Marriage Amendment."

57. "Statement of the Honorable Bob Barr," Hearing on the Defense of Marriage Act Before the Subcommittee on the Constitution of the Committee on the Judiciary, House of Representatives (March 30, 2004), *commdocs.house.gov* (accessed August 1, 2004).

58. "Bush's Remarks on Marriage Amendment."

59. Mary Anne Case, "Why Straight Women Have a Stake in Civil Unions" (unpublished paper).

60. On public opinion: National Gay and Lesbian Task Force, "Recent State Polls on Same-Sex Marriage and Civil Unions," *www.thetaskforce.org* (accessed December 2, 2004).

61. An Act Concerning Civil Unions, Connecticut Legislature Public Act No. 05–10, S.S.B. No. 963 (effective October 1, 2005); "Statement of Governor M. Jodi Rell on House Approval of Amendment to SSB 963" (April 13, 2005), *www.ct.gov* (accessed June 24, 2005).

62. Cass R. Sunstein, "The Right to Marry" (Chicago Public Law and Legal Theory Working Paper No. 76), *www.law.uchicago.edu* (accessed December 1, 2004).

63. George Chauncey, *Why Marriage?* (New York: Basic Books, 2004), pp. 51–55.

64. *Goodridge*, 973.

65. Michael J. Sandel, *Democracy's Discontent* (Cambridge, Mass.: Belknap Press of Harvard University Press, 1996) pp. 103–108.

66. I have elaborated this response to Sandel elsewhere: Linda C. McClain and James E. Fleming, "In Search of a Substantive Republic," 76 *Texas Law Review* 509 (1997).

67. Harry D. Krause, "Marriage for the New Millennium: Heterosexual, Same Sex—Or Not at All?" 34 *Family Law Quarterly* 271 (2000); Nancy D. Polikoff, "This Child Does Have Two Mothers," 78 *Georgetown Law Journal* 459 (1990).

68. In re Adoption of Tammy, 619 N.E.2d 315, 316–317, 320 (Mass., 1993). The Massachusetts legislature had already sanctioned adoption into "nonstandard" families by permitting unmarried persons to adopt.

69. John Rawls, "The Idea of Public Reason Revisited," 64 *University of Chicago Law Review* 765, 788 n. 60 (1997).

70. This addition may address criticism that Rawls's focus on social reproduction is too thin to capture the goods of same-sex marriage. See Carlos Ball, *The Morality of Gay Rights* (New York: Routledge, 2003), pp. 22–30.

71. Rawls, "The Idea of Public Reason Revisited," p. 771.

72. John Finnis, "Law, Morality, and 'Sexual Orientation,' " 69 *Notre Dame Law Review* 1049 (1994); Robert P. George, "Public Reason and Political Conflict," 106 *Yale Law Journal* 2475, 2477–2487 (1997).

73. Stephen Macedo, "Homosexuality and the Conservative Mind," 84 *Georgetown Law Journal* 261 (1995).

74. Even though subsequent legislative developments in Hawaii blunted its impact, an excellent example is Baehr v. Miike. There, the Hawaii Circuit Court— following the Hawaii Supreme Court's decision in Baehr v. Lewin—concluded that the state of Hawaii had failed to demonstrate that a compelling state interest in the optimal development of children justified excluding same-sex couples from marriage. The state's own experts testified that gay and lesbian parents can be "as fit and loving parents as non-gay people and different-sex couples." The state also presented "meager" evidence that same-sex marriage would harm the institution of marriage.

75. *Goodridge*, 963–964. The Hawaii Circuit Court noted that there is a "diversity in the structure and configuration of families" providing a nurturing relationship for children. Baehr v. Miike, 17.

76. Ball, *The Morality of Gay Rights*.

77. David L. Chambers, "What If? The Legal Consequences of Marriage and the Legal Needs of Lesbian and Gay Male Couples," 95 *Michigan Law Review* 447 (1996).

78. Jennifer Wriggins, "Marriage Law and Family Law: Autonomy, Interdependence, and Couples of the Same Gender," 41 *Boston College Law Review* 265, 301–302 (2000) (discussing the idea of the "facilitative" function of family law identified in Carl Schneider, "The Channeling Function of Family Law," 20 *Hofstra Law Review* 495 (1992)).

79. Paula L. Ettelbrick, "Since When Is Marriage a Path to Liberation?" in Suzanne Sherman, ed., *Lesbian and Gay Marriage* (Philadelphia: Temple University Press, 1992), pp. 20, 21. Offering the other side of the debate is Thomas B. Stoddard, "Why Gay People Should Seek the Right to Marry," in Sherman, ed., *Lesbian and Gay Marriage*, p. 13.

80. Michael Warner, *The Trouble with Normal* (Cambridge, Mass.: Harvard University Press, 1999), p. 82.

81. Lynn D. Wardle, "The Potential Impact of Homosexual Parenting on Children," 1997 *University of Illinois Law Review* 833. For rebuttal, see Carlos A. Ball and Janice Fareell Pea, "Warring with Wardle: Morality, Social Science, and Gay and Lesbian Parents," 1998 *University of Illinois Law Review* 253.

82. Judith Stacey and Timothy J. Biblarz, "(How) Does the Sexual Orientation of Parents Matter?" 66 *American Sociological Review* 159, 161–163, 167–179 (2001).

83. Philip Blumstein and Pepper Schwartz, *American Couples* (New York: William Morrow, 1983); Suzanne Slater, *The Lesbian Family Life Cycle* (New York: The Free Press, 1995).

84. Hunter, "Marriage, Law, and Gender," pp. 17–18; Robin West, "Integrity and Universality," 65 *Fordham Law Review* 1313, 1329–1334 (1997). For a skeptical response to Hunter, see Nancy D. Polikoff, "We Will Get What We Ask For: Why Legalizing Gay and Lesbian Marriage Will Not 'Dismantle the Legal Structure of Gender in Every Marriage,' " 79 *Virginia Law Review* 1535 (1993).

85. Evan Wolfson, "Crossing the Threshold: Equal Marriage Rights for Les-

bians and Gay Men and the Intra-Community Critique," 21 *New York University Review of Law & Social Change* 567 (1994–1995).

86. Eskridge, *The Case for Same-Sex Marriage*, pp. 52–63.

87. Ibid., pp. 78–79 (reporting poll data); Wolfson, "Crossing the Threshold," pp. 585–587.

88. Richards, *Women, Gays, and the Constitution*, pp. 346–354; Jane Schacter, "Skepticism, Culture and the Gay Civil Rights Debate in a Post-Civil-Rights Era," 110 *Harvard Law Review* 684 (1997).

89. Raphael Lewis, "Passage of Marriage Amendment in Doubt," *Boston Globe*, May 16, 2005, *www.boston.com* (accessed June 13, 2005).

90. 478 U.S. 186 (1986).

91. Ruthann Robson, *Sappho Goes to Law School* (New York: Columbia University Press, 1998), p. 132.

92. 517 U.S. 620 (1996).

93. 539 U.S. 558 (2003).

94. Robson, *Sappho Goes to Law School*, p. 150.

95. Judith Stacey, "Toward Equal Regard for Marriages and Other Imperfect Intimate Affiliations," 32 *Hofstra Law Review* 331 (2003).

96. Stanley Kurtz, "Beyond Gay Marriage," *Weekly Standard*, August 11, 2003; "Loving More, about Polyamory," *www.lovemore.com* (accessed September 10, 2004).

97. Maura L. Strassberg, "Distinctions of Form or Substance: Monogamy, Polygamy and Same-Sex Marriage," 75 *North Carolina Law Review* 1501 (1997); Maura L. Strassberg, "The Challenge of Post-Modern Polygamy: Considering Polyamory," 31 *Capital University Law Review* 493 (2003).

98. Elizabeth F. Emens, "Monogamy's Law: Compulsory Monogamy and Polyamorous Existence," 29 *New York University Review of Law & Social Change* 277 (2004); see also David Chambers, "Polygamy and Same-Sex Marriage," 26 *Hofstra Law Review* 53, 80–81 (1997).

99. Martha M. Ertman, "Marriage as a Trade: Bridging the Private/Private Distinction," 36 *Harvard Civil Rights-Civil Liberties Law Review* 79 (2001).

100. *Goodridge*, 965.

101. Brief of Defendant-Appellees, at 71–72.

102. *Goodridge*, 963–964.

103. Halpern v. Toronto, para. 107.

104. *Goodridge*, 968.

105. Ibid.

106. Note, "Hawaii's Reciprocal Beneficiaries Act: An Effective Step in Resolving the Controversy Surrounding Same-Sex Marriage," 37 *Brandeis Law Journal* 81 (1998/1999).

107. Reciprocal Beneficiaries, Michie's Hawaii Revised Statutes Annotated, §572C-1 & C-2 (2003).

108. Lewis v. Harris, 2003 Westlaw 23191114 (N.J. Super. L., November 5, 2003) (unpublished opinion), *affirmed*, New Jersey Appellate Division (Docket No. A-2244-03T5, June 14, 2005).

109. Domestic Partnership Act, New Jersey Statutes, §26:8A-2 (2004).

110. Ibid.

111. *Lawrence*, 578.

112. Mychal Judge Police & Fire Chaplains Public Safety Officers' Benefit Act of 2002, Public Law No. 107–196, 116 Stat. 719.

113. Reciprocal Beneficiaries, §572 (detailing legal benefits); Partners Task Force for Gay & Lesbian Couples, "Reciprocal Beneficiaries: The Hawaiian Approach" (June 2002), *www.buddybuddy.com* (noting Hawaii's web site specifies "50–60" rights are included) (accessed July 15, 2004).

114. Domestic Partnership Act, §26.8A-2.

115. A reciprocal beneficiary relationship can be terminated unilaterally by giving notice. The New Jersey statute requires a judicial dissolution. Joanna Grossman, "The New Jersey Domestic Partnership Law," *FindLaw's Writ* (January 13, 2004), *writ.news.findlaw.com* (accessed August 1, 2004).

116. A helpful evaluation of California's evolving domestic partnership law appears in Grace Ganz Blumberg, "Legal Recognition of Same-Sex Conjugal Relationships: The 2003 California Domestic Partner Rights and Responsibilities Act in Comparative Civil Rights and Family Law Perspective," 51 *UCLA Law Review* 1555 (2004).

117. California Defense of Marriage Act, California Family Code, §308.5 (2004); Knight v. Superior Court of Sacramento County, 26 Cal. Rptr. 3d 687 (Cal. Ct. App., Third Dist., 2005) (holding that California's domestic partnership law does not conflict with its defense of marriage law); Matthew Yi and Robert Salladay, "Governor Signs Trio of Gay Rights Bills," *San Francisco Examiner*, October 3, 1999, p. A1 (quoting Assemblywoman Carole Midgen on 1999 domestic partnership law as a "landmark step" toward equal recognition); Nancy Vogel, "Bill Giving Gay Partners More Legal Rights Sent to Governor," *Los Angeles Times*, September 4, 2003, p. B6 (discussing poll data); Lee Romney, "Though They Can't Wed, Gays May Now Divorce," *Los Angeles Times*, January 1, 2005, p. A1 (quoting Assemblywoman Jackie Goldberg on protecting families).

118. California Family Code, §299.3.

119. Ibid., §297.5, 299.3.

120. Jim Sanders, "Law Expands Gay Couples' Rights," *Modesto Bee*, January 4, 2005, p. A1.

121. William C. Duncan, "Domestic Partnership Laws in the United States: A Review and Critique," 2001 *Brigham Young University Law Review* 961 (2001); Craig A. Bowman and Blake M. Cornish, "Note: A More Perfect Union: A Legal and Social Analysis of Domestic Partnership Ordinances," 92 *Columbia Law Review* 1164 (1992). Ordinances include such items as employment benefits for municipal employees and, for all partners, benefits concerning hospital visitation and power of attorney.

122. Merin, *Equality for Same-Sex Couples.*

123. Initially, legislators in the Nordic countries sharply distinguished between the needs of married couples and those of same-sex couples, separating out issues concerning children. They came to realize that same-sex couples often were rearing children and were more similar to married couples than they had thought. Merin, *Equality for Same-Sex Couples*, pp. 61–110.

124. James Herbie DiFonzo, "Unbundling Marriage," 32 *Hofstra Law Review* 31 (2003).

## 6. Beyond Marriage?

1. Law Commission of Canada, *Beyond Conjugality: Recognizing and Supporting Close Personal Adult Relationships* (2001), pp. 113–114.

2. Martha Albertson Fineman, *The Autonomy Myth: A Theory of Dependency* (New York: The New Press, 2004), p. 123.

3. James C. Dobson, "Marriage is the Foundation of the Family," 18 *Notre Dame Journal of Law Ethics & Public Policy* 2 (2004).

4. Council on Family Law, "The Future of Family Law: Law and the Marriage Crisis in North America" (New York: Institute for American Values, 2005).

5. Lawrence v. Texas, 539 U.S. 558 (2003); Baker v. State, 744 A.2d 864 (Vt. 1999); Goodridge v. Department of Public Health, 798 N.E.2d 941 (Mass. 2003).

6. Stanley Kurtz, "Beyond Gay Marriage: The Road to Polyamory," *Weekly Standard*, August 4, 2003, p. 26.

7. American Law Institute, *Principles of the Law of Family Dissolution: Analysis and Recommendations* (Newark, N.J.: LexisNexis, 2002).

8. Brian H. Bix, "The Public and Private Ordering of Marriage," 2004 *University of Chicago Legal Forum* 295.

9. *Goodridge*, 962.

10. Troxel v. Granville, 530 U.S. 57 (2000); John DeWitt Gregory, "Blood Ties: A Rationale for Child Visitation by Legal Strangers," 35 *Washington & Lee Law Review* 351 (1998) (evaluating this trend).

11. Maggie Gallagher, "Rites, Rights, and Social Institutions: Why and How Should the Law Support Marriage?" 18 *Notre Dame Journal of Law, Ethics & Public Policy* 225, 241 (2004).

12. Carl Schneider, "The Channeling Function in Family Law," 20 *Hofstra Law Review* 495 (1992).

13. Dobson, "Marriage Is the Foundation of the Family," p. 2.

14. For a critique of Bowers v. Hardwick, 478 U.S. 186 (1986), along these lines, see Ruthann Robson, *Sappho Goes to Law School* (New York: Columbia University Press, 1998), pp. 132–133. Lower courts have disagreed as to whether *Lawrence* invalidates state law restrictions on the rights of gay men and lesbians to be adoptive and foster parents. This issue may eventually reach the Supreme Court. See Linda Greenhouse, "Justices Refuse to Consider Law Banning Gay Adoption," *New York Times*, January 11, 2005, p. A14 (discussing contrasting rulings in Arkansas and Florida).

15. Gallagher, "Rites, Rights, and Social Institutions," pp. 235, 238.

16. Milton C. Regan, Jr., *Family Law and the Pursuit of Intimacy* (New York: New York University Press, 1993).

17. Gallagher, "Rites, Rights, and Social Institutions," pp. 226–229.

18. ALI, *Principles*, 31–39.

19. Neal Conan, "New Principles for Family Law," *Talk of the Nation* (NPR, January 15, 2003) (remarks by David Blankenhorn, Institute for American Values).

20. An instructive historical example is the debate over recognizing common law marriage. Ariela R. Dubler, "Note: Governing through Contract: Common Law Marriage in the Nineteenth Century," 107 *Yale Law Journal* 1885 (1998).

21. *Baker*, 889.

22. Richard Stith, "Keep Friendship Unregulated," 18 *Notre Dame Journal of Law, Ethics & Public Policy* 263 (2004).

23. *Goodridge*, 962–964.

24. Christopher Marquis, "Total of Unmarried Couples Surged in 2000 U.S. Census," *New York Times*, March 13, 2003, p. A22.

25. Judith Stacey, "Toward Equal Regard for Marriages and Other Imperfect Intimate Affiliations," 32 *Hofstra Law Review* 331 (2003).

26. Jane Gross, "Older Women Team Up to Face Future Together," *New York Times*, February 27, 2004, p. A1.

27. *Beyond Conjugality*, p. 116 (discussing Modernization of Benefits and Obligations Act, S.C. 2000, Chapter 12).

28. Ibid., p. 113.

29. Ibid., pp. 113–114.

30. Ibid., p. 117.

31. Yuval Merin, *Equality for Same-Sex Couples* (Chicago: University of Chicago Press, 2002).

32. *Beyond Conjugality*, p. 121.

33. Ibid., pp. 123–124.

34. Ibid., p. 29.

35. Ibid., p. 30.

36. Standing Committee on Justice and Human Rights, 37th Parliament, 2nd Session, "Evidence" (January 30, 2003) (remarks by Nathalie Des Rosiers, President, Law Commission of Canada on *Beyond Conjugality*).

37. *Beyond Conjugality*, pp. 41–43.

38. Nancy Polikoff, "Ending Marriage as We Know It," 32 *Hofstra Law Review* 201, 213–215 (2003) (quoting Violence Against Women Act, 18 U.S.C. §2266(7)(B)).

39. *Beyond Conjugality*, p. 116.

40. Merin, *Equality for Same-Sex Couples*, pp. 238–239 (for example, Denmark, Norway, Sweden, Iceland, Germany, and Finland).

41. William C. Duncan, "Domestic Partnership Law in the United States: A Review and Critique," 2001 *Brigham Young University Law Review* 961, 965–966 (quoting from Ithaca ordinance).

42. Sanford Katz, "Emerging Models for Alternatives to Marriage," 33 *Family Law Quarterly* 663, 672 (1999).

43. Alfonso A. Castillo, "Domestic Partner Registry Kicks Off," *Newsday*, June 15, 2004, p. A18.

44. Dorian Solot and Marshall Miller, *Unmarried to Each Other* (New York: Marlowe & Co., 2002), pp. 41–43, 52–53.

45. Sarah Lyall, "In Europe, Lovers Now Propose: Marry Me, a Little," *New York Times*, February 15, 2004, §1:3.

46. Merin, *Equality for Same-Sex Couples*, pp. 128–129 (quoting Bill of Opening Up of Marriage).

47. Ibid., p. 129.

48. Solot and Miller, *Unmarried to Each Other*, pp. 251, 258.

49. Ibid., pp. 38–41, 58–60, 250, 254.

50. Ibid., pp. 38–62.

51. Katz, "Emerging Models for Alternatives to Marriage."

52. Pamela J. Smock, "Cohabitation in the United States: An Appraisal of Research Themes, Findings, and Implications," 26 *Annual Review of Sociology* 1 (2000).

53. Milton C. Regan, Jr., "Calibrated Commitment: The Legal Treatment of Marriage and Cohabitation," 76 *Notre Dame Law Review* 1435, 1438, 1450–51 (2001).

54. Katz, "Emerging Models for Alternatives to Marriage," p. 665.

55. Smock, "Cohabitation in the United States," pp. 1–4, 10–12.

56. Regan, "Calibrated Commitment," p. 1463.

57. Regan, *Family Law and the Pursuit of Intimacy*, pp. 62–66.

58. Polikoff, "Ending Marriage as We Know It," p. 223 (supporting multiple options).

59. Barbara Stark uses similar logic to argue for offering multiple legal models of marriage itself. Barbara Stark, "Marriage Proposals: From One-Size-Fits-All to Postmodern Marriage Law," 89 *California Law Review* 1479 (2001).

60. Lyall, "In Europe, Lovers Now Propose: Marry Me, a Little."

61. David L. Chambers, "Unmarried Partners and the Legacy of Marvin v. Marvin," 76 *Notre Dame Law Review* 1347 (2001).

62. Here I borrow Ronald Dworkin's famous distinction. See Dworkin, *Taking Rights Seriously* (Cambridge, Mass.: Harvard University Press, 1977), p. 227.

63. Alex Witchel, "Savoring the Chemistry of Southern Cooking," *New York Times*, May 7, 2003, p. F1.

64. *Beyond Conjugality*, pp. 116–117.

65. ALI, *Principles*, p. 924 (§6.03, Illustration 10).

66. Ibid., pp. 918–919, 928–935 (discussing case law).

67. Ibid., 924.

68. Elizabeth S. Scott, "Marriage, Cohabitation, and Collective Responsibility for Dependency," 2004 *University of Chicago Legal Forum* 225, 250.

69. Conan, "New Principles for Family Law" (remarks by Blankenhorn).

70. Regan, "Calibrated Commitment," p. 1450.

71. ALI, *Principles*, p. 919 (§6.03).

72. Ibid., pp. 960–961 (§7.04).

73. Ibid., p. 33.

74. Ibid., p. 34.

75. Nicholas Bala and Rebecca Jaremko Bromwich, "Context and Inclusivity in Canada's Evolving Definition of the Family," 16 *International Journal of Law, Policy and the Family* 145 (2002).

76. ALI, *Principles*, pp. 954–957 (§7.02).

77. The tensions between viewing economic vulnerability as a special hazard for wives and seeing it as a more general concern in any interdependent relationship appear in M. v. H., [1999] 2 S.C.R. 3 (Supreme Court of Canada, 1999) (extending spousal support rights to same-sex cohabitant).

78. ALI, *Principles*, p. 915 (§6.02).

79. Mary Jane Mossman, "Conversations about Families in Canadian Courts and Legislatures," 32 *Hofstra Law Review* 171 (2003); Bala and Bromwich, "Context and Inclusivity in Canada's Evolving Definition of the Family," p. 147. For example, the Canadian Supreme Court found, in M. v. H., that a secondary leg-

islative purpose of the Family Law Act was "to alleviate the burden on the public purse by shifting the obligation to provide support for needy persons to those parents and spouses who have the capacity to provide support to those individuals." M. v. H., 69.

80. On this risk of more "expansive, functional definitions of family," see Martha Minow, "Redefining Families: Who's in and Who's Out?" 62 *University of Colorado Law Review* 269, 283 (1991); Mossman, "Conversations about Families in Canadian Courts and Legislatures," pp. 171–175.

81. King v. Smith, 392 U.S. 309 (1968). In *King,* some officials testified that having sexual relations once every three or six months would be sufficient to count as "frequent."

82. Fineman, *The Autonomy Myth,* p. 123; See also Michael Kinsley, "Abolish Marriage," *Washington Post,* July 3, 2003, p. A23.

83. Martha Albertson Fineman, *The Neutered Mother, the Sexual Family, and Other Twentieth Century Tragedies* (New York: Routledge, 1995), pp. 143–200.

84. Fineman, *The Autonomy Myth,* pp. 134–136.

85. Ibid., p. 99.

86. Ibid., pp. 106–107.

87. Ibid., pp. 107–108.

88. Milton C. Regan, Jr., "Law, Marriage, and Intimate Commitment," 9 *Virginia Journal of Policy & Law* 116, 146 (2001).

89. Michael Warner, *The Trouble With Normal* (Cambridge, Mass.: Harvard University Press, 1999), p. 82.

90. Patricia A. Cain, "Imagine There's No Marriage," 16 *Quinnipiac Law Review* 27, 53–59 (1996).

91. Mary Lyndon Shanley, "Just Marriage: On the Public Importance of Private Unions," in Mary Lyndon Shanley, ed., *Just Marriage* (New York: Oxford University Press, 2004), p. 16.

92. Fineman, *The Autonomy Myth,* pp. 134–135.

## 7. Rights, (Ir)responsibility, and Reproduction

1. *Casey,* 852, 869.

2. United Nations, Fourth World Conference on Women, Beijing, *Declaration and Platform for Action* (1995), paragraph 96.

3. Roe v. Wade, 411 U.S. 113 (1973). Carey Goldberg and Janet Elder, "Public Still Backs Abortion, But Wants Limits, Poll Says," *New York Times,* January 16, 1998, p. A1 (reporting shift in public opinion from general acceptance of abortion to a "permit but discourage model"); Greg M. Shaw, "The Polls— Trends: Abortion," 67 *Public Opinion Quarterly* 407 (2003); "Abortion," www.pollingreport.com (accessed August 12, 2004).

4. Report of the Platform Committee, *Strong at Home, Strong in the World: The Democratic Platform for America* (2004), p. 36; The Platform Committee, *2004 Republican Party Platform: A Safer World and a More Hopeful America* (2004), p. 92.

5. "A New American Compact," *New York Times,* July 14, 1992, p. A23. Its signatories included legal scholars Mary Ann Glendon and Michael McConnell, as well as many organizations and public figures prominent in opposition to legal abortion.

6. Mary Ann Glendon, *Rights Talk* (New York: The Free Press, 1991), pp. 47–75.

7. Mary Ann Glendon, *Abortion and Divorce in Western Law* (Cambridge, Mass.: Harvard University Press, 1987), p. 39.

8. Ronald Dworkin, *Life's Dominion* (New York: Alfred A. Knopf, 1993), pp. 150–151.

9. Rosalind Petchesky, *Abortion and Woman's Choice* (Boston: Northeastern University Press, 1990 revised ed.), pp. 125–132.

10. *Roe*, 159.

11. For arguments supporting this premise, see *Casey*, 911–919 (Stevens, J., concurring and dissenting); Dworkin, *Life's Dominion*, pp. 109–116.

12. Judith Jarvis Thomson, "A Defense of Abortion," 1 *Philosophy and Public Affairs* 47 (1971).

13. Sylvia A. Law, "Rethinking Sex and the Constitution," 132 *University of Pennsylvania Law Review* 955, 1016 (1984); Donald Regan, "Rewriting Roe v. Wade," 77 *Michigan Law Review* 1569 (1979). One variant on this argument is that of the "Captive Samaritan": a woman has a right to refuse consent to a fetus's taking of her body because government has an obligation to protect persons from private aggression. Eileen McDonagh, *Breaking the Abortion Deadlock: From Choice to Consent* (New York: Oxford University Press, 1996).

14. Law, "Rethinking Sex and the Constitution," p. 1016.

15. Frances Kamm, *Creation and Abortion* (New York: Oxford University Press, 1992).

16. Dworkin, *Life's Dominion*, p. 166.

17. James E. Fleming, *Securing Constitutional Democracy* (Chicago: University of Chicago Press, forthcoming).

18. Ibid., pp. 150–151.

19. Ronald Dworkin, *Taking Rights Seriously* (Cambridge, Mass.: Harvard University Press, 1977), p. 204; Stephen Holmes, *The Anatomy of Antiliberalism* (Cambridge, Mass.: Harvard University Press, 1993), p. 4.

20. Thornburgh v. American College of Obstetricians and Gynecologists, 476 U.S. 747, 781–782 (1986) (Stevens, J., concurring).

21. Katherine T. Bartlett, "Re-expressing Parenthood," 98 *Yale Law Journal* 293, 300 (1998).

22. *Casey*, 911, 916 (Stevens, J., concurring and dissenting).

23. Ibid., 852. In *Roe*, the Court observed: "maternity, or additional offspring, may force upon the woman a distressful life and future." *Roe*, 153.

24. *Casey*, 896 (citing with approval Planned Parenthood of Central Missouri v. Danforth, 428 U.S. 52, 71 (1976)).

25. My account in the paragraphs that follow draws upon Patricia Lunneborg, *Abortion: A Positive Decision* (New York: Bergin & Garvey, 1992); Akinrinola Bankole, Susheela Singh, and Taylor Hass, "Reasons Why Women Have Induced Abortions: Evidence from 27 Countries," 24 *International Family Planning Perspectives* 117 (1998); Carol Gilligan, *In a Different Voice* (Cambridge, Mass.: Harvard University Press, 1982), pp. 106–127.

26. Lunneborg, *Abortion*, pp. 141–144.

27. Robin West, "Foreword: Taking Freedom Seriously," 104 *Harvard Law Review* 43, 83 (1990); Faye D. Ginsburg, *Contested Lives* (Berkeley: University of California Press, 1989), pp. 146–171.

28. Lunneborg, *Abortion*, p. 129.

29. Ibid., pp. 100–101.

30. Bankole, Singh, and Hass, "Reasons Why Women Have Induced Abortions."

31. Lunneborg, *Abortion*, pp. 130, 131.

32. Julia E. Hanigsberg, "Homologizing Pregnancy and Motherhood," 94 *Michigan Law Review* 371, 373 (1995); Catherine A. MacKinnon, "Reflections on Sex Equality Under Law," 100 *Yale Law Journal* 1281, 1318 (1991).

33. Gilligan, *In a Different Voice*, pp. 70–105.

34. Rosalind P. Petchesky and Karen Judd, eds., *Negotiating Reproductive Rights* (London: Zed Books, 1998), p. 15.

35. Lunnenborg, *Abortion*, p. 18.

36. Ibid., pp. 132–138.

37. Ibid., pp. 137–138.

38. Law, "Rethinking Sex and the Constitution," p. 1016. Justice Ginsburg has also offered a sex equality justification for abortion rights: Ruth Bader Ginsburg, "Some Thoughts on Autonomy and Equality in Relation to Roe v. Wade," 63 *North Carolina Law Review* 375 (1985).

39. *Casey*, 852.

40. Ibid., 928–929 (Blackmun, J., concurring and dissenting) (citing: Laurence H. Tribe, *American Constitutional Law* §15–10 (2nd ed. 1988); Reva Siegel, "Reasoning from the Body: A Historical Perspective on Abortion Regulation and Questions of Equal Protection," 44 *Stanford Law Review* 261 (1992); Cass Sunstein, "Neutrality in Constitutional Law," 92 *Columbia Law Review* 1 (1992); MacKinnon, "Reflections on Sex Equality under Law"; and, using a privacy analysis to make an analogous point, Jed Rubenfeld, "The Right of Privacy," 102 *Harvard Law Review* 737 (1989)).

41. Law, "Rethinking Sex and the Constitution," p. 1017; Kenneth L. Karst, "Foreword: Equal Citizenship under the Fourteenth Amendment," 91 *Harvard Law Review* 1, 58 (1977).

42. Robin West, *Caring for Justice* (New York: New York University Press, 1997), pp. 105–107.

43. *Casey*, 852.

44. Ibid., 877–878.

45. *Roe*, 159.

46. *Casey*, 932 (Blackmun, J., concurring and dissenting).

47. *Roe*, 163–164.

48. Ibid., 164; *Casey*, 932 (Blackmun, J., concurring and dissenting).

49. *Casey*, 877–878, 887.

50. Ibid., 872.

51. Ibid., 882–883 (overruling in part Thornburgh v. American College of Obstetricians and Gynecologists, 476 U.S. 747 (1986), and City of Akron v. Akron Ctr. for Reprod. Health, 462 U.S. 416 (1983)).

52. Linda C. McClain, "The Poverty of Privacy?" 3 *Columbia Journal of Gender and Law* 119 (1992); Jean L. Cohen, *Regulating Intimacy* (Princeton, N.J.: Princeton University Press, 2002), 57–64.

53. *Casey*, 877–878.

54. Ibid., 877, 887.

55. Ibid., 902–911.

56. *Casey,* 882–883.

57. President Reagan directed Koop to report on such effects. Koop concluded that he could not file a report claiming such effects "that could withstand scientific and statistical scrutiny." Koop asserted that he personally had counseled women with "severe psychological problems after an abortion," but that studies were flawed and inconclusive and would not support a scientific report. In Congress, Koop was closely questioned about his characterization of over 270 studies on the health effects of abortion as "flawed." *Medical and Psychological Impact of Abortion, Hearing Before the Human Resources and Intergovernmental Subcomm.,* 101st Cong., 1st Sess., March 16, 1989 (including Report and testimony of Koop).

58. Brief for Amicus Curiae American Psychological Association in Support of Petitioners, Planned Parenthood v. Casey, 505 U.S. 833 (1992), at 21 (citing studies); Gilligan, *In a Different Voice,* 70, 105; Lunneborg, *Abortion,* pp. 89–93; Kathleen McDonnell, *Not an Easy Choice* (Boston: South End Press, 1984), p. 35; Petchesky, *Abortion and Woman's Choice,* pp. 371–379.

59. Jane E. Brody, "Study Disputes Abortion Trauma," *New York Times,* February 2, 1997, p. C8 (describing highly religious Catholic women who get abortions). In the dramatic collection of narratives by members of Women Exploited by Abortion, it is clear that many of these women's lives were already very troubled before they made the abortion decision. David C. Reardon, *Aborted Women: Silent No More* (Chicago: Loyola University Press, 1987).

60. Jane Maslow Cohen, "A Jurisprudence of Doubt," 3 *Columbia Journal of Gender & Law* 175, 222–231, 234–235 (1992).

61. *Casey,* 916–919 (Stevens, J., concurring and dissenting).

62. John Cochran, "Religious Right Lays Claim to Big Role in GOP Agenda," *CQ Weekly* (November 13, 2004), pp. 2684, 2685–2686 (quoting Richard Land, Southern Baptist Convention); Karen Tumulty and Viveca Novak, "Under the Radar; Thirty Years After Roe v. Wade, The White House Is Pressing Its Case Against Abortion Delicately," *Time* (January 27, 2003), p. 38.

63. Lunnenborg, *Abortion,* pp. 29–47, 69–85.

64. Ruth Colker, "Feminism, Theology, and Abortion," 77 *California Law Review* 1011, 1066–1067 (1989).

65. For example, the Surgeon General's Report noted the existence of "well-conducted studies" documenting that children born of an unwanted pregnancy "are more likely to experience detrimental psychosocial development, emotional adjustment problems, and a poorer quality of life than are children born to women who desired or otherwise accepted their pregnancies." See *Medical and Psychological Impact of Abortion,* p. 221.

66. Shaw, "The Polls—Trends: Abortion."

67. NARAL, " 'Informed' Consent/Waiting Periods," *www.naral.org* (accessed August 1, 2004); L. B. Finer and S. K. Henshaw, "Abortion Incidence and Services in the United States in 2000," 35 *Perspectives on Sexual and Reproductive Health* 6 (2003).

68. *Casey,* 920–921 (Stevens, J.); ibid., 937–938 (Blackmun, J.); Cohen, "A Jurisprudence of Doubt," pp. 236–243.

69. *Casey,* 885–887. For example, the Supreme Court declined to review an unsuccessful challenge to Mississippi's informed consent law. Barnes v. Moore, 970 F.2d 12 (5th Cir. 1992), cert. denied, 506 U.S. 1021 (1992). Relying on *Casey,*

the Mississippi Supreme Court upheld a twenty-four-hour waiting period over three dissenting justices' argument that it created an undue burden on low-income women by increasing the time and financial burden of obtaining an abortion. Pro-Choice Mississippi v. Fordice, 716 So. 2d 645 (Miss. 1998).

70. Dworkin, *Life's Dominion*, pp. 172–174.

71. Maher v. Roe, 432 U.S. 464, 473–474, 476 (1977).

72. Harris v. McRae, 448 U.S. 297, 314–315, 325 (1980). The original Hyde Amendment did not include exceptions for rape and incest, but Congress included such exceptions in later versions.

73. *Harris,* 316. Echoing this argument are: Richard A. Epstein, "Foreword: Unconstitutional Conditions, State Power, and the Limits of Consent," 102 *Harvard Law Review* 4, 89–90 (1988); McConnell, "The Selective Funding Problem: Abortions and Religious Schools," 104 *Harvard Law Review* 989, 1018–1019 (1991).

74. Webster v. Reproductive Health Services, 492 U.S. 490, 511 (1989); Rust v. Sullivan, 500 U.S. 173, 201 (1991); *Harris,* 316.

75. *Rust* (upholding federal regulation barring recipients of Title X funds from engaging in abortion counseling and referral services); *Webster,* 490 (upholding state refusal to allow public employees to perform abortions in public hospitals); *Harris,* 297 (upholding federal Hyde Amendment barring Medicaid reimbursement of most abortions); Beal v. Doe, 432 U.S. 438 (1977) (upholding state regulations barring funding of abortions not certified as medically necessary); *Maher,* 464 (upholding state regulation limiting Medicaid benefits to first trimester abortions that are "medically necessary"); Poelker v. Doe, 432 U.S. 519 (1977) (upholding bar on use of publicly financed hospital services for abortions).

76. When the executive branch (for example, Presidents Reagan and both Bushes) uses its power to place further restrictions on abortion (such as barring female military personnel from obtaining abortions in military hospitals and barring foreign aid to any organization that includes abortion services), women's abortion rights become even more precarious.

77. Catharine A. MacKinnon, "Privacy v. Equality: Beyond Roe v. Wade," in *Feminism Unmodified* (Cambridge, Mass.: Harvard University Press, 1987), pp. 93–102.

78. Dorothy Roberts, *Killing the Black Body: Race, Reproduction, and the Meaning of Liberty* (New York: Vintage Books, 1997), pp. 308–310.

79. It is often said that the Court will not inquire into legislative motive in deciding whether a law is unconstitutional. United States v. O'Brien, 391 U.S. 367, 382–386 (1968). But scrutinizing the purposes or ends of legislation is an unavoidable part of judicial review, and, at least in some contexts, it is appropriate that the Court show heightened concern for flushing out illicit purposes. See John Hart Ely, *Democracy and Distrust* (Cambridge, Mass.: Harvard University Press, 1980), pp. 136–148. For Ely's critique of *Maher,* see ibid., 162*, 246 n.38, 248–249 n.52.

80. *Harris,* 330–334 (Brennan, J., dissenting) ("government literally makes an offer that the indigent woman cannot afford to refuse"); Amy Gutmann and Dennis Thompson, *Democracy and Disagreement* (Cambridge, Mass.: Belknap Press at Harvard University Press, 1996), p. 88 (selective funding "creates an almost irresistible pressure on indigent women to carry a child to term"); Susan Bandes,

"The Negative Constitution: A Critique," 88 *Michigan Law Review* 2271, 2297–2308 (1990) (critiquing subsidy/penalty distinction); Seth F. Kreimer, "Allocational Sanctions: The Problem of Negative Rights in a Positive State," 132 *University of Pennsylvania Law Review* 1293, 1359–1376 (1984) (the Hyde Amendment reduced women's choices).

81. The literature on unconstitutional conditions addresses the question of when governmental imposition of burdens upon, or attachment of conditions to, the exercise of constitutional rights is unconstitutional. One common approach to distinguishing permissible from impermissible governmental action is to distinguish between subsidy and penalty, or offer and threat. See Kreimer, "Allocational Sanctions," pp. 1300–1301, 1359–1376.

82. Kathleen M. Sullivan, "Unconstitutional Conditions," 102 *Harvard Law Review* 1413, 1499 1500 (1989). For a similar proposal, see Cass Sunstein, "Why the Unconstitutional Conditions Doctrine is an Anachronism (With Particular Reference to Religion, Speech, and Abortion)," 70 *Boston University Law Review* 593 (1990).

83. Michael Dorf, "Incidental Burdens on Fundamental Rights," 109 *Harvard Law Review* 1175, 1235 (1996).

84. McRae v. Califano, 491 F. Supp. 630, 739 (E.D.N.Y. 1980). The Supreme Court reversed this decision in *Harris*.

85. The legislative history is summarized in: Annex to the District Court's opinion in *McRae*, 742–844; Laurence H. Tribe, *Abortion: The Clash of Absolutes* (New York: W. W. Norton, 1990), pp. 144–159.

86. *McRae*, 752–753, 766 (reporting views of Rep. Hyde); 139 Cong. Rec. S12574, *S12576 (daily ed. September 28, 1993) (statement of Senator Smith supporting renewal).

87. *McRae*, 639; Tribe, *The Clash of Absolutes*, p. 151.

88. *McRae*, 773 (quoting Representative Hyde).

89. *Casey*, 877.

90. Dorothy E. Roberts, "Rust v. Sullivan and the Control of Knowledge," 61 *George Washington Law Review* 587 (1993).

91. Lee v. Weisman, 505 U.S. 577, 593 (1992) ("subtle and indirect" pressure from prayer at graduation ceremony "can be as real as any overt compulsion"); Washington v. Glucksberg, 521 U.S. 702, 732 (1997) (recognizing state interest in protecting vulnerable groups from being pressured into physician-assisted suicide; rejecting constitutional right to physician-assisted suicide). Chief Justice William Rehnquist, who wrote *Glucksberg*, has consistently voted to uphold selective funding and facilities regulations.

92. *McRae*, 668–690.

93. *Harris*, 353–354 (Stevens, J., dissenting); 345 (Marshall, J., dissenting).

94. James Trussell et al., "The Impact of Restricting Medicaid Financing for Abortion," 12 *Family Planning Perspectives* 120, 130 (1980) ("one-fifth of Medicaid-eligible women who needed abortions were, in their view, forced to undergo compulsory childbearing"); Stanley K. Henshaw and Lynn S. Wallish, "The Medicaid Cutoff and Abortion Services for the Poor," 16 *Family Planning Perspectives* 170, 179 (1984) (reporting "relatively serious" consequences in 58 percent of Medicaid-eligible women and their families, including financial sacrifice and delays in obtaining abortions for some women due to time needed to get financing). For a different assessment, see Deborah Haas-Wilson, "Women's Reproductive

Choices: The Impact of Medicaid Funding Restrictions," 29 *Family Planning Perspectives* 228, 231 (1997) ("[r]estrictions on Medicaid funding have little, if any, effect, on women's reproductive decisions," but "the use of aggregate abortion rates may hide the effects" of policies targeting poor women).

95. Dworkin, *Life's Dominion*, pp. 175–176. Dworkin suggests that the funding cases may warrant reconsideration because unequal funding comes close to compulsion.

96. *Harris*, 332 (Brennan, J., dissenting).

97. Sullivan, "Unconstitutional Conditions," pp. 1491–1493.

98. Rubenfeld, "The Right of Privacy," pp. 788–790; Fleming, *Securing Constitutional Democracy.*

99. Sullivan, "Unconstitutional Conditions," 1506; Sunstein, "Why the Unconstitutional Conditions Doctrine Is an Anachronism," pp. 614–620 (arguing for funding abortions in cases of rape and incest).

100. Sullivan, "Unconstitutional Conditions," pp. 1496–1498.

101. Gutmann and Thompson, *Democracy and Disagreement*, pp. 88–89; Tribe, *Abortion*, p. 206; *Harris*, pp. 349–354 (Stevens, J., dissenting) (restricting funding of abortions medically necessary for women's health violates Equal Protection requirement of governmental impartiality in the distribution of governmental benefits and inflicts severe punishment on pregnant women).

102. *Harris*, 337, 343–344 (Marshall, J., dissenting).

103. Roberts, *Killing the Black Body*, pp. 8–21, 304–312.

104. Opposition to the Hyde Amendment sounds this theme. *McRae*, 751–844; 139 Cong. Rec. H4323 (daily ed. June 30, 1993) (statement of Representative Lowey); 139 Cong. Rec. S12583 (daily ed. September 28, 1993) (statement of Senator Metzenbaum).

105. West, "Foreword: Taking Freedom Seriously," pp. 82–83.

106. Ibid., p. 83.

107. Brief for the Amici Curiae Women Who Have Had Abortions and Friends of Amici Curiae in Support of Appellees, filed by NOW Legal Defense and Education Fund and NARAL, Webster v. Reproductive Health Services, 492 U.S. 490 (1989), 1989 Westlaw 1115239; Brief for the National Abortion Rights Action League (and other organizations) as Amici Curiae in Support of Appellees, Thornburgh v. American College of Obstetricians & Gynecologists, 476 U.S. 747 (1986), 1985 Westlaw 669630.

108. Laurie Shrage, *Abortion and Social Responsibility: Depolarizing the Debate* (New York: Oxford University Press, 2003), pp. 28–40, 71–75.

109. Shaw, "The Polls—Trends: Abortion;" "Abortion."

110. Bankole, Singh, and Hass, "Reasons Why Women Have Induced Abortion"; Aida Torres and Jacqueline D. Forrest, "Why Do Women Have Abortions?," 20 *Family Planning Perspectives* 169 (1988).

111. Shaw, "The Polls—Trends: Abortion," p. 422.

112. Ibid.

113. Petchesky, *Abortion and Woman's Choice*, p. 369.

114. Shaw, "The Polls—Trends: Abortion," pp. 420–422; "Abortion," pp. 1–7; Petchesky, *Abortion and Women's Choice*, pp. 351–352.

115. Ginsburg, *Contested Lives*, pp. 172–197; Kristin Luker, *Abortion and the Politics of Motherhood* (Berkeley: University of California Press, 1984), pp. 192–215.

116. Dworkin, *Life's Dominion*.

117. Petchesky, *Abortion and Women's Choice*, pp. 350–351.

118. For example, Brief of the American Association of Prolife Obstetricians and Gynecologists and the American Association of Prolife Pediatricians as Amici Curiae in Support of Respondents, Planned Parenthood v. Casey, 505 U.S. 833 (1992) (citing Torres and Forrest, "Why Do Women Get Abortions?").

119. Petchesky, *Abortion and Woman's Choice*, pp. 369–379.

120. Amy Harmon, "In New Tests for Fetal Defects, Agonizing Choices for Parents," *New York Times*, June 20, 2004, p. A1.

121. "Excerpts from an Interview with President Bush," *New York Times*, August 12, 1992, p. A15.

122. Alessandra Stanley, "First Lady on Abortion," *New York Times*, August 14, 1992, p. A1.

123. "Vice President Confronted with Abortion Question in Interview," *New York Times*, July 23, 1992, p. A20 (reporting remarks Quayle made on *Larry King Live*, July 22, 1992).

124. Kevin Sack, "Quayle Insists Abortion Remarks Don't Signal Change in His View," *New York Times*, July 24, 1992, p. A1.

125. West Virginia Board of Education v. Barnette, 319 U.S. 624, 638 (1943).

126. *Casey*, 850.

127. Jean Reith Schroedel, *Is the Fetus a Person? A Comparison of Policies Across the Fifty States* (Ithaca, N.Y.: Cornell University Press, 2000), p. 157.

128. Linda C. McClain, " 'Irresponsible' Reproduction," 47 *Hastings Law Journal* 339 (1996).

129. Andrew Rosenthal, "Quayle Says Riots Sprang from Lack of Family Values," *New York Times*, May 20, 1992, p. A20.

130. John E. Yang and Ann Devroy, "Quayle: 'Hollywood Doesn't Get It': Administration Struggles to Explain Attack on TV's Murphy Brown," *Washington Post*, May 21, 1992, p. A1.

131. General Accounting Office, *Welfare Reform: More Research Needed on TANF Family Caps and Other Policies for Reducing Out-of-Wedlock Births* (September 2001), p. 2.

132. C.K. v. Shalala, 883 F. Supp. 991, 1015 (D. N. J. 1995) (citing *Harris*, 316), *aff'd*, 92 F.3d 171 (3d Cir. 1996).

133. Sojourner A. v. New Jersey Department of Human Services, 828 A.2d 306, 314–316 (N.J. 2003).

134. Arthur Jones, "Foes Join to Fight Welfare Cuts," *National Catholic Reporter* (February 10, 1995), p. 5.

135. Written Testimony of Rebecca M. Blank, offered in Illegitimacy and Welfare: Hearings on H.R. 4 before the Subcommittee on Human Resources, 104th Cong., 1st Sess. (January 20, 1995).

136. GAO, *Welfare Reform*, pp. 2–3, 20, 23.

137. Bankole, Singh, and Hass, "Reasons Why Women Have Induced Abortions," pp. 5, 19.

138. Equity in Prescription Insurance and Contraceptive Coverage Act of 2003, S. 1396 (introduced July 11, 2003, 108th Cong.).

139. Erickson v. Bartell Drug Company, 141 F. Supp. 1266 (W.D. Wash. 2001) (construing Title VII's Pregnancy Discrimination Act and citing Sylvia A. Law, "Sex Discrimination and Insurance for Contraception," 73 *Washington Law Review* 363 (1998)).

140. Gretchen Cook, "The Battle over Birth Control," April 27, 2005, *www. Salon.com* (accessed May 1, 2005).

141. Andrea Walsh, "The Common Ground Network for Life and Choice Promotes Non-adversarial Dialogue on Abortion," *www.cpn.org* (accessed January 27, 2005).

## 8. *Teaching Sexual and Reproductive Responsibility*

1. For these definitions, see Douglas Kirby, *Emerging Answers* (National Campaign to Prevent Teen Pregnancy, 2001).

2. Janice M. Irvine, *Talk about Sex: The Battles over Sex Education in the United States* (Berkeley: University of California Press, 2002), pp. 6–7.

3. Lorraine Ali and Julie Scelfo, "Choosing Virginity," *Newsweek* (December 9, 2002), p. 61; Benoit Denizet-Lewis, "Friends, Friends with Benefits and the Benefits of the Local Mall," *The New York Times Magazine*, May 30, 2004, §6, p. 30.

4. Nina Bernstein, "Behind Fall in Pregnancy, A New Teenage Culture of Restraint," *New York Times*, March 7, 2004, §1, p. 1; Susan Reimer, "Some Teens in Inner City Barter With Sex," *The Baltimore Sun*, January 25, 2004, p. 1N.

5. Michelle Fine, "Sexuality, Schooling and American Females: The Missing Discourse of Desire," 58 *Harvard Education Review* 29 (1988).

6. "Press Release by Institute for American Values," September 20, 2000 (announcing publication of Institute for American Values report on marriage education, Dana Mack, *Hungry Hearts: Evaluating the New Curricula for Teens on Marriage and Relationships* (Institute for American Values, 2001)).

7. 42 U.S.C. §701 et seq.

8. Section 510, Title V. On state implementation, see Anna Marie Smith, "The Sexual Regulation Dimension of Contemporary Welfare Law: A Fifty State Overview," 8 *Michigan Journal of Gender & Law* 121 (2002).

9. SIECUS Public Policy Office, *State Profiles (2004): A Portrait of Sexuality Education and Abstinence-Only-Until-Marriage Programs in the States* (Sexuality Information and Education Council of the United States, 2005), *www.siecus.org* (accessed April 4, 2005).

10. U.S. House of Representatives Committee on Government Reform—Minority Staff Special Investigations Division, "The Content of Federally Funded Abstinence-Only Education Programs" (December 2004), *www.democrats.reform. house.gov* (accessed December 20, 2004) (Waxman Report).

11. Rickie Solinger, *Wake Up Little Susie: Single Pregnancy and Race before Roe v. Wade* (New York: Routledge, 1992); Charles Murray, "The Coming White Underclass," *Wall Street Journal*, October 29, 1993, p. A14.

12. The National Campaign to Prevent Teen Pregnancy, *Evaluating Abstinence-Only Interventions* (August 1998), p. 1.

13. Waxman Report, p. 1.

14. White House, "Working Toward Independence" (2002), pp. 22–23, *www.whitehouse/gov* (accessed February 10, 2002).

15. Union of Concerned Scientists, *Scientific Integrity in Policymaking: An Investigation into the Bush Administration's Misuse of Science* (March 2004), p. 11.

16. Kirby, *Emerging Answers*, pp. 88–96 (reviewing evidence about abstinence-only and other sex education programs); Minnesota Department of Health, *Min-*

*nesota Education Now and Babies Later, Evaluation Report 1998–2002* (2003) (effects of abstinence-only curriculum inconclusive); Rebecca A. Maynard et al., *First Year Impacts of Four Title V, Section 510 Abstinence Education Programs* (Princeton, N.J.: Mathematica Policy Research, June 2005), p. 74. Some conservatives counter that abstinence-only is effective: Robert Rector, "The Effectiveness of Abstinence Education Programs in Reducing Sexual Activity Among Youth," *Heritage Foundation Report* (April 8, 2002).

17. "Advocates for Youth Commend New Surgeon General's Support for Comprehensive Sex Education," *U.S. Newswire* (May 14, 2003) (noting support of Surgeon Generals Richard Carmona, C. Everett Koop, Jocelyn Elders, and David Satcher for comprehensive sex education).

18. "Essential Health Services for Children Needed in Welfare Reform Legislation," *PR Newswire* (June 23, 2003).

19. Waxman Report, p. i; Cheryl Wetzstein, "AMA Revised Sex-Ed Policy," *Washington Times*, December 11, 2004, p. A3.

20. Neal Conan, "Sex Education Programs in Schools," *Talk of the Nation* (National Public Radio, January 29, 2004) (Marcus Rosenbaum, NPR Senior Editor, reporting survey results). On this program, Sarah Brown, director of the National Campaign to Prevent Teen Pregnancy, reported a national "consensus" of sorts: "parents really prefer that young people delay sex," and thus prefer a "strong delay message," but "Americans are also a very practical group and they understand that a number of young people are sexually active and must have information."

21. See the proposed Family Life Education Act, H.R. 768 and the parallel Responsible Education About Life Act, S. 368 (109th Cong., 2005).

22. Stephanie J. Ventura et al., "Trends in Pregnancy Rates for the United States, 1976–97: An Update," 49 (No. 4) *National Vital Statistics Reports* (June 6, 2001).

23. Kirby, *Emerging Answers*, p. 18.

24. Fay Menacker, "Births to 10–14 Year Old Mothers, 1990–2002: Trends and Health Outcomes," 53 (No. 7) *National Vital Statistics Reports* (November 15, 2004).

25. The National Campaign to Prevent Teen Pregnancy, *Not Just Another Single Issue: Teen Pregnancy Prevention's Link to Other Critical Social Issues* (February 2002); Cheryl Wetzstein, "Birthrate Figures for Nation, Teens Hit Record Lows," *Washington Times*, June 26, 2003, p. A1 (National Center for Health Statistics reports "record low" for 2003).

26. Melissa Ludtke, *On Our Own: Unmarried Motherhood in America* (New York: Random House, 1997), p. 48; Susan E. Harari and Maris A. Vinowskis, "Adolescent Sexuality, Pregnancy, and Childbearing in the Past," in Annette Lawson and Deborah Rhode, eds., *The Politics of Pregnancy* (New Haven, Conn.: Yale University Press, 1993), pp. 23–45.

27. C. Flanigan, *What's Behind the Good News: The Decline in Teen Pregnancy Rates During the 1990s* (National Campaign to Prevent Teen Pregnancy, 2001) (attributing decline to abstinence and to contraception). Illustrating this dispute are: Melissa G. Pardue, "Increased Abstinence Causes a Large Drop in Teen Pregnancy," *Heritage Foundation Reports* (May 2, 2003) (attributing 67 percent of decline to abstinence); Cynthia Dailard, "Understanding 'Abstinence': Implica-

tions for Individuals, Programs and Policies," 6 *The Guttmacher Report* (No. 5, December 2003) (crediting 75 percent of decline to contraceptive use; 25 percent to abstinence).

28. Douglas Kirby, *No Easy Answers* (National Campaign to Prevent Teen Pregnancy, 1997); Kirby, *Emerging Answers*, pp. v–vi.

29. *Not Just Another Single Issue.*

30. Kirby, *Emerging Answers*, pp. 16–19.

31. Cornerstone Consulting Group, Inc., *Three Policy Strategies Central To Preventing Teen Pregnancy* (Center for Health Improvement, March 2003); Norman A. Constantine and Carmen R. Nevarez, *No Time for Complacency: Teen Births in California* (Public Health Institute, March 2003), pp. 7–10.

32. The National Campaign to Prevent Teen Pregnancy, *14 and Younger: The Sexual Behavior of Young Adolescents* (2003).

33. Ludtke, *On Our Own*, p. 117 (reporting a 104 percent increase in the birth rate for unmarried white women ages 30–34 from 1984 to 1994; for unmarried black women, 31 percent; for all unmarried women ages 35–39, an increase of 82 percent; for women ages 40–49, 88 percent).

34. Wade Horn, Assistant Secretary, Department of Health and Human Services, voiced this criticism at a symposium, "American Values and the Future of the Marriage Movement," co-sponsored by the Institute for American Values and the Center of the American Experiment, held on February 12, 2002, in Washington, D.C.

35. Isabel V. Sawhill, "Is Lack of Marriage the Real Problem?" *The American Prospect* (April 8, 2002).

36. SIECUS's curricula reviews give many examples at *www.siecus.org* (accessed January 20, 2005).

37. Roger J. R. Levesque, "Sexuality Education: What Adolescents' Rights Require," 6 *Psychology Public Policy & Law* 953 (2000).

38. Kirby, *Emerging Answers*, I, pp. 3–7, 88–92.

39. Ibid., pp. 3–4, 28.

40. Ibid., p. 8.

41. Ibid., pp. 9–10, 112–113.

42. "The Best Contraceptive: How to Teach Kids to Postpone Parenthood? Show Them a Positive Future," *People* (October 24, 1994), p. 56 (quoting Michael Carrera). The program did not have similar positive effects on the boys in the program. See Kirby, *Emerging Answers*, p. 113.

43. *Three Policy Strategies Central to Preventing Teen Pregnancy*, p. 2.

44. *This Is My Reality: The Price of Sex* (Motivational Educational Entertainment, 2004).

45. Ludtke, *On Our Own*, pp. 44–47.

46. Velma McBride Murry, "Inner-City Girls of Color: Unmarried, Sexually Active Nonmothers," in Bonnie J. Ross Leadbeater and Niobe Way, eds. *Urban Girls: Resisting Stereotypes, Creating Identities* (New York: New York University Press, 1996), pp. 272, 287.

47. Ludtke, *On Our Own*, pp. 34–86; Judith S. Musick, *Young, Poor, and Pregnant* (New Haven, Conn.: Yale University Press, 1993); Constance Willard Williams, *Black Teenage Mothers: Pregnancy and Child Rearing From Their Perspective* (Lexington, Mass.: Lexington Books, 1991).

48. Ludtke, *On Our Own,* p. 82 (quoting from Arline Geronimus); Kristin Luker, *Dubious Conceptions: The Politics of Teenage Pregnancy* (Cambridge, Mass.: Harvard University Press, 1996), p. 170.

49. Lisa Dodson, *Don't Call Us Out of Name: The Untold Lives of Women and Girls in Poor America* (Boston: Beacon Press, 1998), p. 83.

50. Ludtke, *On Our Own,* pp. 77–79.

51. Ibid., pp. 83–84 (discussing Arline Geronimus's findings that poor, black teen females' desire to have their children early, out of a concern to live to be a grandmother, had some basis in fact: poor black women's health deteriorates as they age at a faster rate than other women's).

52. Christopher Jencks and Kathryn Edin, "Do Poor Women Have a Right to Have Children?" *American Prospect* (Winter 1995): 43; Luker, *Dubious Conceptions,* pp. 113–132.

53. *Our Song* (MGM/UA Video, 2000).

54. Regina Austin, "Sapphire Bound!" 1989 *Wisconsin Law Review* 539, 555, 561–564.

55. National Campaign to Prevent Teen Pregnancy, "New Report Details Sexual Trends Among Low-Income Black Urban Youth," *Campaign Update* (Spring 2004), pp. 8–9 (quoting Sarah Brown).

56. Patricia Goodson et al., "Defining Abstinence: Views of Directors, Instructors, and Participants in Abstinence-until-Marriage Programs in Texas," 73 *Journal of School Health* 91 (2003) (finding "positive" dimension in definitions of abstinence that focused on investment and life options).

57. Pamela Haag, *Voices of a Generation: Teenage Girls on Sex, School, and Self* (AAUW Educational Foundation, 1999), pp. 3–6.

58. Ibid., 9–12.

59. Barbara Dafoe Whitehead and Theodora Ooms, *Goodbye to Girlhood: What's Troubling Girls and What We Can Do about It* (National Campaign to Prevent Teen Pregnancy, 1999).

60. Haag, *Voices of a Generation,* p. 17. The report continues: "Sexual violence, sexual risks—principally, pregnancy—and 'sex' or relations to boys are cited 875 times by 723 respondents as 'major struggles and issues for teenage girls.' " Ibid.

61. Ibid., pp. 22, 25.

62. Neil Duncan, *Sexual Bullying: Gender Conflict and Pupil Culture in Secondary Schools* (London: Routledge, 1999), pp. 53, 60; *This Is My Reality,* p. 6 (reporting that "males, and even some females, regularly use derogatory sexual terms" to describe women and girls).

63. Whitehead and Ooms, *Goodbye to Girlhood,* p. 3.

64. M. Jocelyn Elders et al., "Adolescent Pregnancy: Does the Nation Really Care?" 5 *Berkeley Women's Law Journal* 170, 171 (1989/1990) ("a poor teenager with a baby is captive to a slavery the 13th Amendment did not anticipate.")

65. Adrian Nicole LeBlanc, *Random Family* (New York: Scribner, 2003).

66. "New Report Details Sexual Trends among Low-Income Black Urban Youth," pp. 8–9.

67. National Campaign to Prevent Teen Pregnancy, *Not Just for Girls: The Roles of Boys and Men in Teen Pregnancy Prevention* (November 1997).

68. Kirby, *Emerging Answers,* pp. 6, 93; Marion Howard and Judith Blamey McCabe, "Helping Teenagers Postpone Sexual Involvement," 22 *Family Planning*

*Perspectives* 21, 22 (January/February 1990) (reporting results of study of 1,000 sexually active girls age 16 and younger).

69. Kathryn Abrams, "Sex Wars Redux: Agency and Coercion in Feminist Legal Theory," 95 *Columbia Law Review* 304 (1995).

70. Katherine M. Franke, "What's Wrong With Sexual Harassment?," 49 *Stanford Law Review* 691 (1997).

71. *Not Just for Girls*, p. 20.

72. Dan Kindlon and Michael Thompson, *Raising Cain: Protecting the Emotional Life of Boys* (New York: Ballantine Books, 2000), pp. 193–217.

73. Joseph H. Pleck et al., "Individual, Family, and Community Factors Modifying Male Adolescents' Risk Behavior 'Trajectory,' " Research Paper, Publication no. 406604 (Urban Institute, May 1996).

74. William Marsiglio and Sally Hutchinson, *Sex, Men, and Babies: Stories of Awareness and Responsibility* (New York: New York University Press, 2002), pp. 220–240.

75. Deborah L. Tolman, "Adolescent Girls' Sexuality: Debunking the Myth of the Urban Girl," in Leadbeater and Ross, eds., *Urban Girls*, pp. 255–271.

76. Fine, "Sexuality, Schooling, and American Females."

77. Tolman, "Adolescent Girls' Sexuality," p. 265. Feminist analyses of female sexuality have used the rubric "pleasure and danger" to express this problem. See Carole S. Vance, ed., *Pleasure and Danger: Exploring Female Sexuality* (London: Pandora Press, 1989).

78. Haag, *Voices of a Generation*, p. 27.

79. Mary Pipher, *Reviving Ophelia: Saving the Selves of Adolescent Girls* (New York: Ballantine Books, 1994), p. 208.

80. Tracy E. Higgins and Deborah L. Tolman, "Law, Cultural Media[tion] and Desire in the Lives of Adolescent Girls," in Martha A. Fineman and Martha T. McCluskey, eds., *Feminism, Media, and the Law* (New York: Oxford University Press, 1997); Michelle Oberman, "Turning Girls Into Women: Re-evaluating Modern Statutory Rape Law," 85 *Journal of Criminal Law & Criminology* 15, 53–68 (1994).

81. Haag, *Voices of a Generation*, p. 29.

82. Ibid., p. 28.

83. Ibid., p. 31.

84. *This Is My Reality*, pp. 33–36.

85. Mary Crawford and Danielle Popp, "Sexual Double Standards: A Review and Methodological Critique of Two Decades of Research," 40 *Journal of Sex Research* 13 (2003). For example, studies of Hispanic/Latin culture suggest that "[p]articularly among the upper social classes, women's virginity before marriage is a cultural imperative"; married women are to be completely monogamous, but are to accept husbands' extramarital affairs. Ibid. Studies of teen females find considerable variation in how they construct teenage romance, depending on local and individual differences. See Sharon Thompson, *Going all the Way* (New York: Hill & Wang, 1995), pp. 13–14.

86. Crawford and Popp, "Sexual Double Standards"; Lynn Ponton, *The Sex Lives of Teenagers* (New York: Plume, 2000), pp. 9–26 (describing teen culture of "studs and sluts").

87. Crawford and Popp, "Sexual Double Standards" (citation omitted).

88. One study of Canadian university women found that although young women believe that the double standard persists, they personally reject it by, for example, asserting that sex is important to them, and being more willing to view negatively sexually active men who are "players" or "predators." See Robin R. Milhausen and Edward S. Herold, "Does the Sexual Double Standard Still Exist? Perceptions of University Women," 36 *Journal of Sex Research* 361 (1999).

89. Crawford and Popp, "Sexual Double Standards."

90. "Female Sexual Dysfunction," Medline Plus, *www.nlm.nih.gov* (accessed January 28, 2005).

91. Barbara Risman and Pepper Schwartz, "After the Sexual Revolution: Gender Politics in Teen Dating," *Contexts* (Spring 2002), pp. 16, 20.

92. Crawford and Popp, "Sexual Double Standards." Similar strategic calculations featured in Kristin Luker's study of why women might not use contraception despite the risk of pregnancy. Kristin Luker, *Taking Chances: Abortion and the Decision Not to Contracept* (Berkeley: University of California Press, 1975).

93. *This Is My Reality*, p. 23.

94. California Comprehensive Sexual Health and HIV/AIDS Prevention Education Act, Cal. Educ. Code § 51930 (2004); Responsible Education About Life Act, Section 3 (c)(4).

95. Ponton, *The Sex Lives of Teenagers*, pp. 1–4.

96. Tolman, "Adolescent Girls' Sexuality," p. 268.

97. Goodson et al., "Defining Abstinence."

98. "Facts about Birth Control," *www.plannedparenthood.org* (accessed July 15, 2003); "Contraceptive Choices: Outercourse," *www.advocatesforyouth.org* (accessed July 15, 2003).

99. Letter to editor by John C. Cobb, "Outercourse as a Safe and Sensible Alternative to Contraceptives," 87 *American Journal of Public Health* 1380–1381 (1997) (repeating proposal first made in 1973 Presidential Address to American Association of Planned Parenthood Physicians).

100. Jennifer Garrett, "Why Congress Should Reject the Failed Sex Education Agenda in the Baucus Bill," *Heritage Foundation Reports (Backgrounder No. 1576)* (August 23, 2003).

101. Lisa Remez, "Oral Sex among Adolescents: Is It Sex or Is It Abstinence?," 32 *Family Planning Perspectives* 298 (2000); Tamar Lewin, "Survey Shows Sex Practices of Boys," *New York Times*, December 19, 2000, p. A22.

102. Abstinence Clearinghouse website, *www.abstinence.net* (accessed August 1, 2004).

103. Irvine, *Talk about Sex*, 117.

104. Ibid., pp. 116–11; Waxman Report, pp. 8–12.

105. Irvine, *Talk about Sex*, p. 120.

106. Debra Rosenberg, "The Battle over Abstinence," *Newsweek* (December 9, 2000), p. 67.

107. SIECUS uses this label to describe programs that, among other things, use scare tactics, omit information about contraception, include misinformation about STDs, and emphasize only negative consequences of sexual behavior. Reviews appear at *www.siecus.org* (accessed May 15, 2003).

108. Irvine, *Talk about Sex*, 81–106.

109. Ibid., pp. 98–106. One abstinence educator explains: "In the public schools

never am I changing the message. I'm changing the way I deliver it. . . . Instead of saying [like] in the Catholic schools, I'll say, 'Sexual intercourse belongs in marriage, where God intended it to be.' In a public school I'll say, 'Place sexuality in marriage where it belongs.' " Ibid., pp. 100–101.

110. Hank Stuever, "Viva Las Virgins!," *The Washington Post,* June 29, 2003, p. D1 (quoting Leslie Unruh, of the Abstinence Clearinghouse: "We love sex, don't we?! And the best sex is in marriage.")

111. Irvine, *Talk about Sex,* pp. 82–88.

112. SIECUS Curriculum Review, *www.siecus.org* (accessed January 15, 2005).

113. Waxman Report, p. 18.

114. SIECUS Curriculum Reviews, quoting from *Sex Respect* and *FACTS (Family Accountability Communicating Teen Sexuality).*

115. Waxman Report, pp. 16–18. SIECUS gives many examples of "sexism and gender bias" in its curriculum reviews, found at *www.siecus.org.*

116. Naomi K. Seiler, "Abstinence-Only Education and Privacy," 24 *Women's Rights Law Reporter* 27, 38–39 (2002)(describing Sex Respect curricula and Student Workbook).

117. Lynne Henderson, "Rape and Responsibility," 11 *Law and Philosophy* 127 (1992).

118. There are some nineteenth-century parallels in the social purity movements that sought a single standard for male and female sexual behavior.

119. "The Five Most Egregious Uses of Welfare's Title V Abstinence-Only-Until-Marriage Funds," *www.siecus.org* (accessed January 5, 2005).

120. But see Michael M. v. Superior Court of Sonoma County, 450 U.S. 464 (1981) (justifying statutory rape laws protecting females, not males, because of sex differences, including that males, rather than females, can cause pregnancies).

121. Order on preliminary injunction motion, ACLU v. Foster, No. 02–1440 (E.D. La. July 24, 2002). The settlement of this suit required the GPA to cease funding groups conveying religious messages and to exercise better oversight over program materials. Settlement Order (July 24, 2002).

122. John Rawls, *Political Liberalism* (New York: Columbia University Press, 1993), pp. 216–217.

123. "Religious Leaders Express Alarm at Extreme Ideology in Women's Health Policy," *U.S. Newswire,* October 22, 2002 (reporting alarm expressed by the Religious Coalition for Reproductive Choice)); James Wagoner, "Advocates for Youth," *U.S. Newswire,* May 1, 2003 ("triumph of ideology over public health").

124. Union of Concerned Scientists, *Scientific Integrity in Policymaking,* pp. 10–11.

125. Jennifer Burek Pierce, "What Ails Access to Government Health Information?" 34 *American Libraries* 59 (2003).

126. National Public Radio, *Morning Edition,* January 21, 2003 (interviewing Claude Allen, DHHS, and Shepherd Smith, Institute for Youth Development, on the Uganda program); David E. Sanger and Donald G. McNeil, Jr., "Bush Backs Condom Use to Prevent Spread of AIDS," *New York Times* June 24, 2004, p. A20 (reporting Bush's first mention of role of condoms in Uganda's ABC program).

127. Constantine and Nevarez, *No Time for Complacency,* pp. 8–9.

128. Griswold v. Connecticut, 381 U.S. 479 (1965); Eisenstadt v. Baird, 405 U.S. 438 (1972); Lawrence v. Texas, 539 U.S. 558 (2003).

129. Drucilla Cornell, *At the Heart of Freedom* (Princeton, N.J.: Princeton University Press, 1998), p. 14.

130. Louisiana's "Abstinence Education Program for Seventh Graders" includes a lesson on courtship, in which students are to understand "the purpose of courtship as a prerequisite to marriage."

131. Daniel Cere, "Courtship Today: The View from Academia," *The Public Interest* (March 22, 2001), p. 53.

132. Barbara Dafoe Whitehead, *Why There Are No Good Men Left: The Romantic Plight of the New Single Woman* (New York: Broadway Books, 2003), p. 194. Persons affiliated with both movements include, for example, Whitehead, David Blankenhorn, Norval Glenn, and Amy and Leon Kass.

133. Mack, *Hungry Hearts;* Dana Mack, "Educating for Marriage, Sort of; High School Courses on Marriage," *First Things* (March 1, 2001), p. 18.

134. Leon R. Kass, "The End of Courtship," *The Public Interest* (January 1997).

135. Mack, *Hungry Hearts,* p. 48.

136. These include Amy A. Kass and Leon R. Kass, "Proposing Courtship," *First Things* 96 (October 1999), 32; *www.firstthings.com* (accessed July 15, 2003); Kass, "The End of Courtship"; Norval Glenn and Elizabeth Marquardt, *Hooking Up, Hanging Out, and Hoping for Mr. Right: College Women on Dating and Mating Today* (An Institute for American Values Report to the Independent Women's Forum, 2001), p. 7; Wendy Shalit, *A Return to Modesty* (New York: Free Press, 1999); and Whitehead, *Why There Are No Good Men Left.*

137. Whitehead, *Why There Are No Good Men Left,* p. 1.

138. Glenn and Marquardt, *Hooking Up,* pp. 13–29. The report derived from an eighteen-month study, including in-depth interviews with sixty-two college women on eleven campuses and telephone interviews with a nationally representative sample of 1,000 college women. Ibid., pp. 4, 65.

139. Ibid., pp. 7, 39–41. Barbara Dafoe Whitehead claims that the decline of courtship leaves many single women today in "bewilderment," left "roaming around on their own" to select mates. Whitehead, *Why There Are No Good Men Left,* pp. 5, 7.

140. Kass, "The End of Courtship."

141. Ibid.

142. Whitehead, *Why There Are No Good Men Left,* p. 126.

143. Ibid., pp. 1–14, 186–195. Barbara Dafoe Whitehead, "Forget Sex in the City, Women Want Romance in Their Lives," *Washington Post,* February 9, 2003, p. B2.

144. Kass, "The End of Courtship."

145. Kass and Kass, "Proposing Courtship." They also have co-edited an anthology: Amy A. Kass and Leon R. Kass, eds., *Wing to Wing, Oar to Oar: Readings on Courting and Marrying* (Notre Dame, Ind.: University of Notre Dame Press, 2000).

146. Kass and Kass, "Proposing Courtship," pp. 2–14.

147. David Popenoe, "A Marriage Research Agenda for the Twenty-First Century: Ten Critical Questions," in Alan J. Hawkins et al., eds., *Revitalizing the*

*Institution of Marriage for the Twenty-First Century* (Westport, Conn.: Praeger, 2002), pp. 197–98. Similarly, Shalit argues that a return to modesty—the "positive content of womanhood"—is critical because female modesty civilizes men; indeed, female behavior not only "regulates relations between the sexes," but also influences behavior for the entire society. See Shalit, *A Return to Modesty*, pp. 95–98, 137.

148. Kass and Kass, "Proposing Courtship," p. 16.

149. Ibid., p. 17. Popenoe notes that a more sexually restrictive system "would likely have to be reestablished by a large majority of women." Popenoe, "A Marriage Research Agenda for the Twenty-First Century," pp. 197–198.

150. Popenoe, "A Marriage Research Agenda for the Twenty-First Agenda," pp. 197–198.

151. Whitehead, *Why There Are No Good Men Left*, pp. 123–124, 144–150.

152. Glenn and Marquardt, *Hooking Up*, p. 68 (recommending "a need for greater male initiative" in mating and dating).

153. Laurie Goodstein, "New Christian Take on Old Dating Ritual," *New York Times*, September 9, 2001, p. 1. At Patrick Henry College, in Purcellville, Virginia, which fills its classes with home-schooled Christians, Christian courtship replaces casual dating; proponents cite biblical teachings for the rule that it falls to male initiative to move relationships beyond friendship, a step that requires parental approval. Helen Mondloch, "Homegrown Virtue on Campus," *World and I* (November 1, 2001), p. 111.

154. Valerie Richardson, "Courtship Idea Appeals to Ranks of Older Singles," *Washington Times*, May 25, 2000, p. A2 (describing rules of True Love Ministries in Reston, Virginia).

155. Shalit, *A Return to Modesty*, pp. 102–105, 157–158; Kass, "The End of Courtship."

156. Michael Miller, "Father Knows Best: Is It Demeaning?" *Peoria Journal Star* (February 8, 2003) (quoting Reverend Douglas Wilson).

157. Historically, "social purity campaigns" (supported by some feminists) invoked ideals of female innocence and virtue, and male vice and sexual aggression, in order to protect women, with both beneficial and harmful regulatory consequences for women. Judith Walkowitz, "Male Vice and Female Virtue: Feminism and the Politics of Prostitution in Nineteenth-Century Britain," in Ann Snitow et al., eds., *The Powers of Desire* (New York, Monthly Review Press, 1983), p. 419; Ellen Carol DuBois and Linda Gordon, "Seeking Ecstasy on the Battlefield: Danger and Pleasure in Nineteenth-Century Feminist Sexual Thought," in *Pleasure and Danger*, p. 31.

158. Adrienne Davis, " 'Don't Let Nobody Bother Yo' Principle': The Sexual Economy of American Slavery," in Sharon Harley and the Black Women and Work Collective, eds., *Sister Circle: Black Women and Work* (New Brunswick, N.J.: Rutgers University Press, 2002), p. 103; Patricia Hill Collins, *Black Feminist Thought* (New York: Routledge, 1990), pp. 67–78, 163–180.

159. Whitehead, *Why There Are No Good Men Left*, p. 77.

160. Michelle Conlin, "The New Gender Gap," *Business Week Online* (May 26, 2003).

161. Irvine, *Talk about Sex*, pp. 14–15.

*Epilogue*

1. Civil Partnership Act 2004, 2004 Chapter 33, *www.legislation.hmso.gov.uk* (accessed May 2, 2005); Renwick McClean, "First Gay Couples Apply For Marriage Under New Spanish Law," *New York Times*, July 5, 2005, p. A3.

2. Dr. Laura C. Schlessinger, *The Proper Care and Feeding of Husbands* (New York: HarperCollins, 2004); Laura Doyle, *The Surrendered Wife* (New York: Simon & Schuster, 2001).

3. Pepper Schwartz, *Love Between Equals: How Peer Marriage Really Works* (New York: The Free Press, 1994).

# Index

365